8

COTOJI

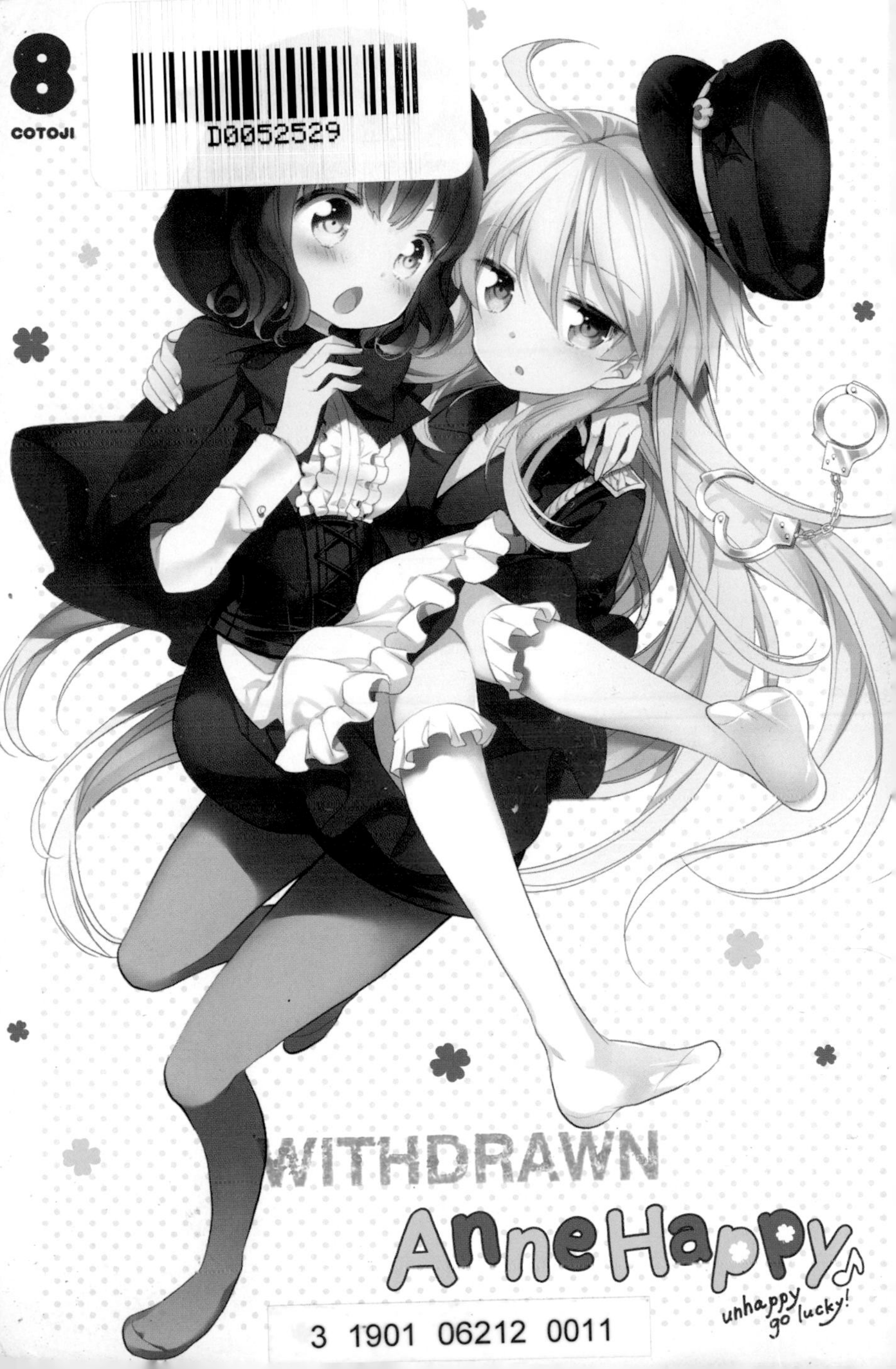

Anne Happy♪

unhappy go lucky!

CONTENTS
ANNE HAPPY
VOLUME EIGHT
COTOJI

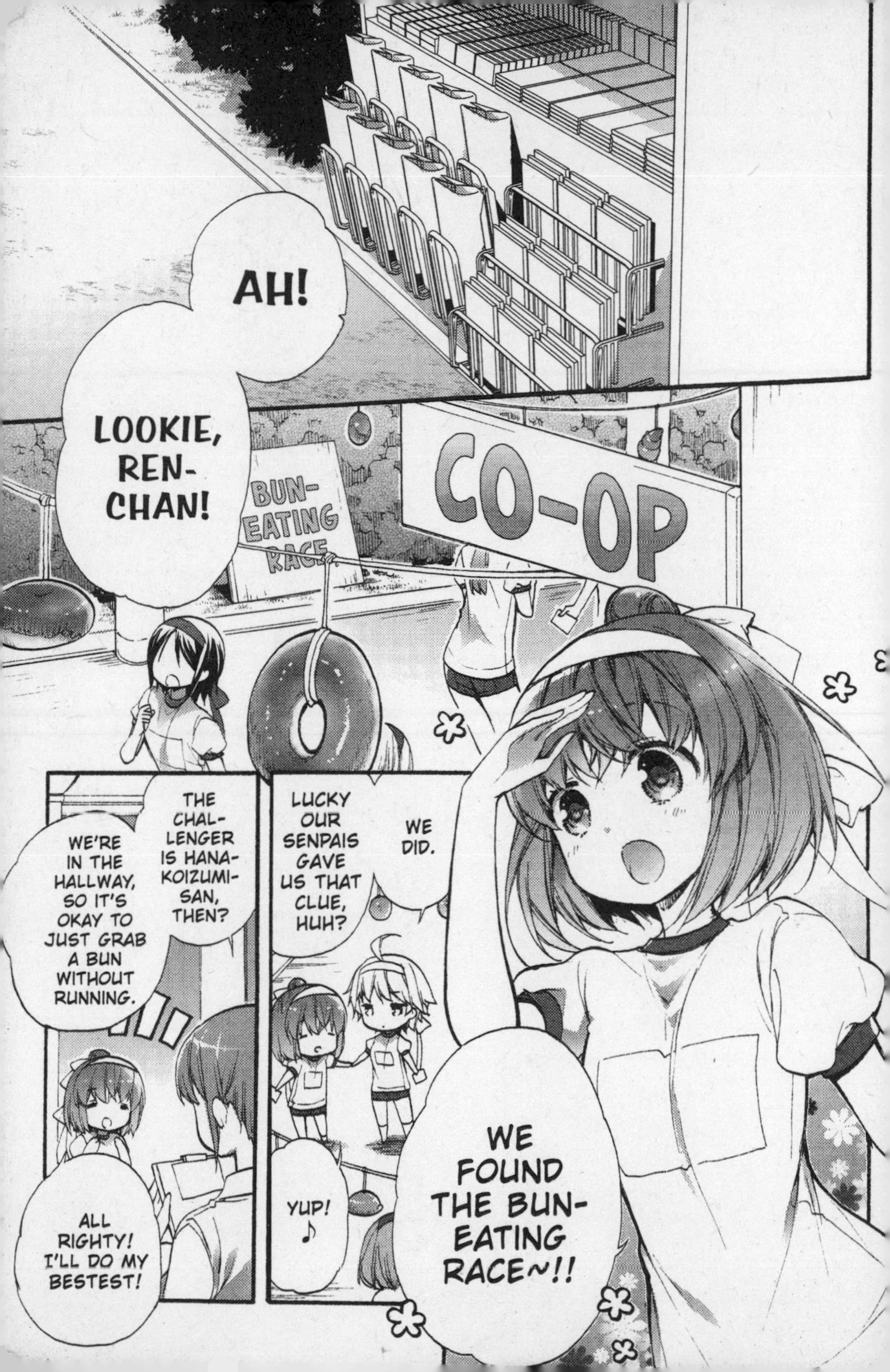

AH!
LOOKIE, REN-CHAN!
CO-OP
BUN-EATING RACE
WE FOUND THE BUN-EATING RACE~!!
LUCKY OUR SENPAIS GAVE US THAT CLUE, HUH?
WE DID.
YUP! ♪
THE CHALLENGER IS HANAKOIZUMI-SAN, THEN?
WE'RE IN THE HALLWAY, SO IT'S OKAY TO JUST GRAB A BUN WITHOUT RUNNING.
ALL RIGHTY! I'LL DO MY BESTEST!

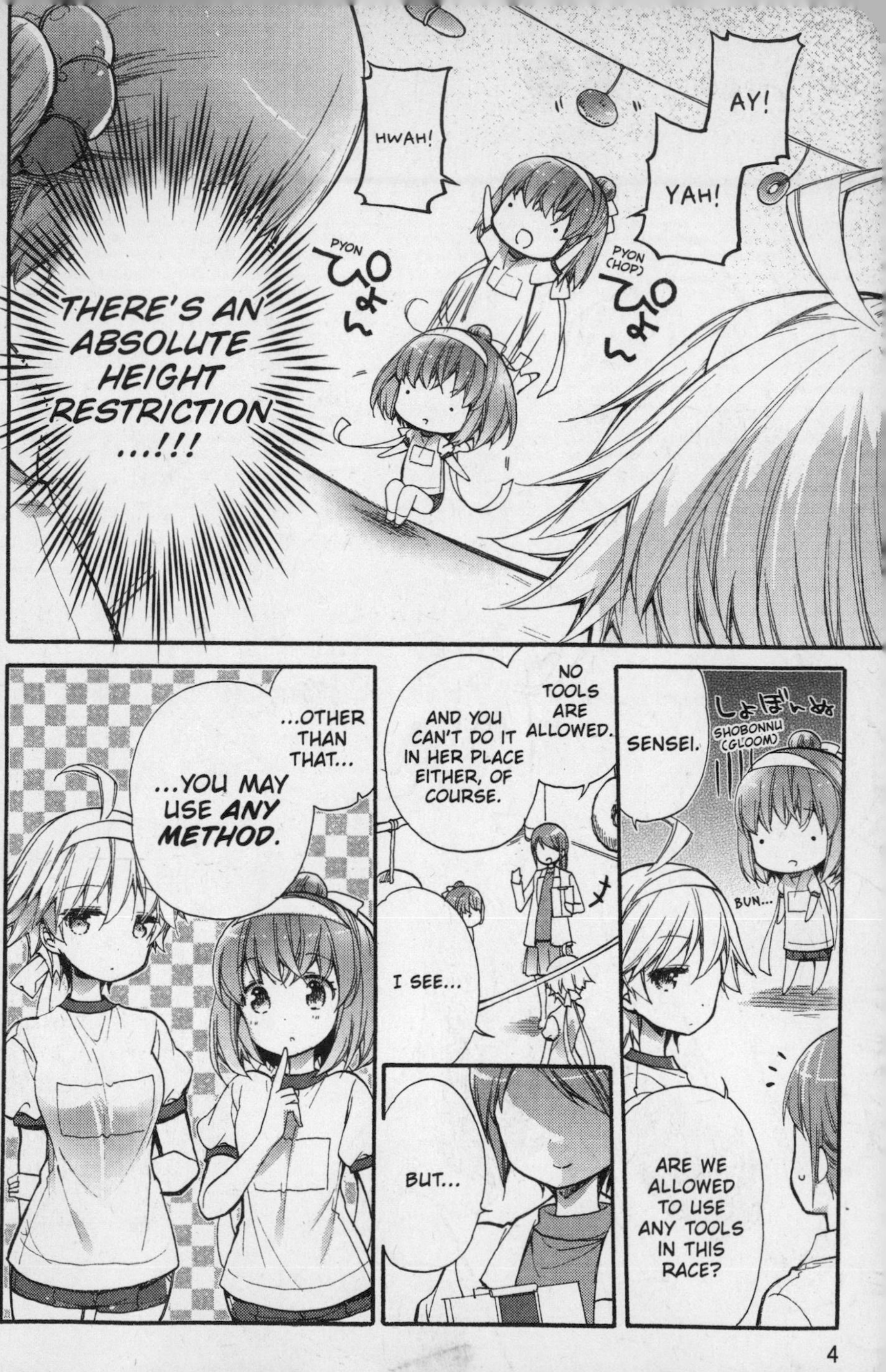
AY!
YAH!
PYON (HOP)
ぴょん
HWAH!
PYON
ぴょん
THERE'S AN ABSOLUTE HEIGHT RESTRICTION ...!!!
SENSEI.
しょぼんぬ
SHOBONNU (GLOOM)
BUN...
ARE WE ALLOWED TO USE ANY TOOLS IN THIS RACE?
NO TOOLS ARE ALLOWED.
AND YOU CAN'T DO IT IN HER PLACE EITHER, OF COURSE.
I SEE...
BUT...
...OTHER THAN THAT...
...YOU MAY USE ANY METHOD.

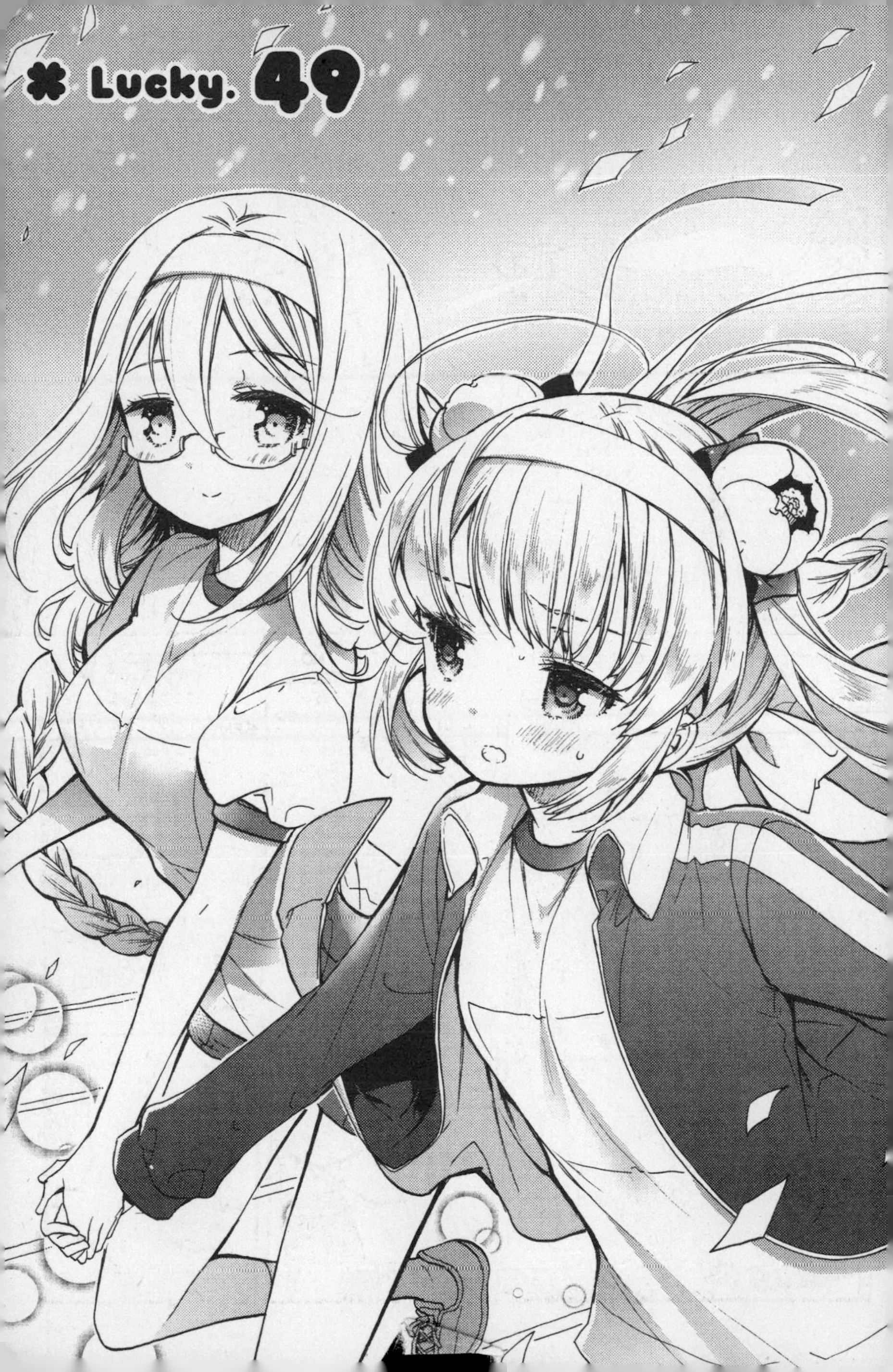
Lucky. 49

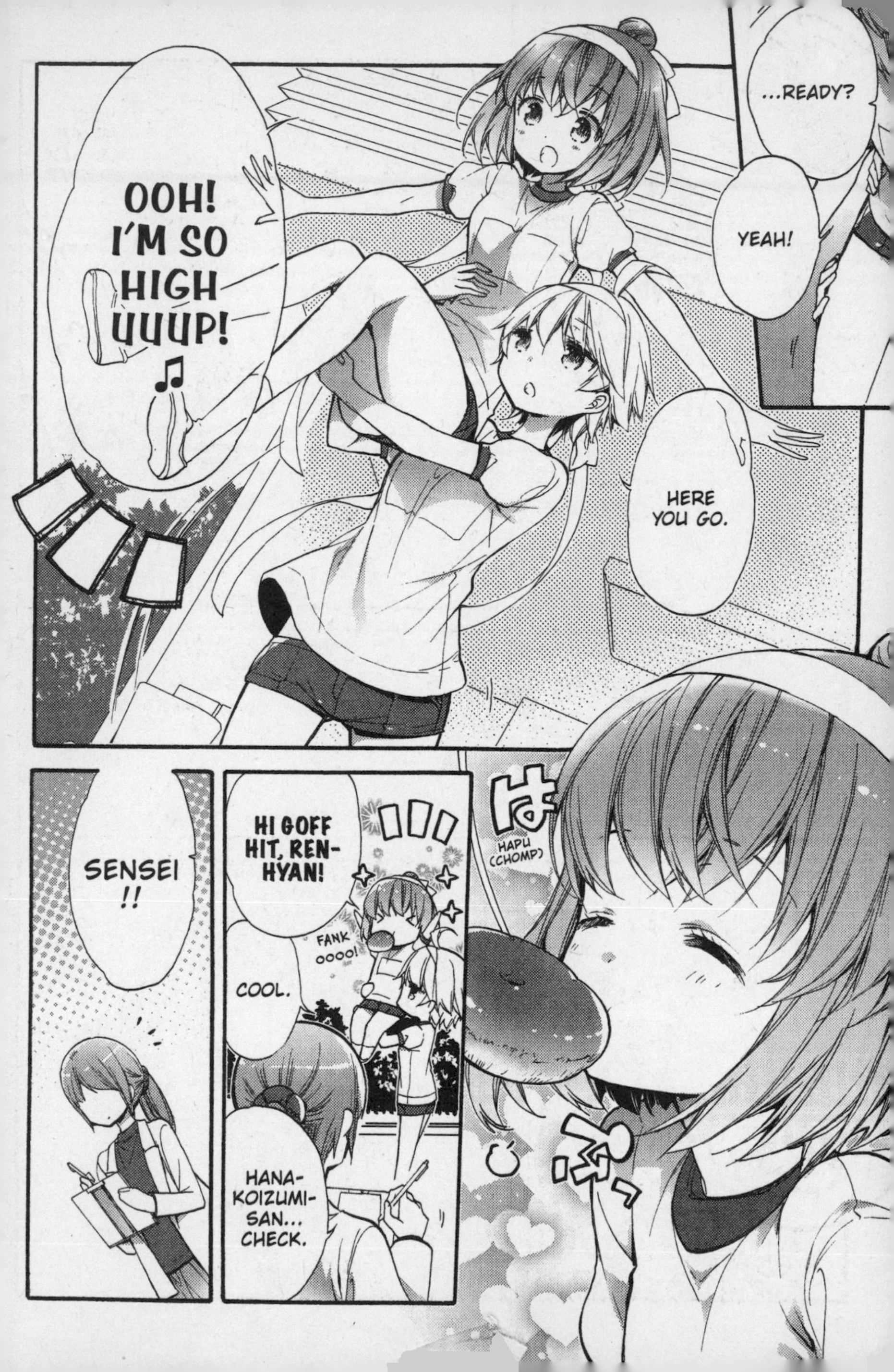

...READY?
YEAH!
HERE YOU GO.
OOH! I'M SO HIGH UUUP! ♪
は
HAPU (CHOMP)
HI GOFF HIT, REN-HYAN!
FANK OOOO!
COOL.
HANA-KOIZUMI-SAN... CHECK.
SENSEI !!

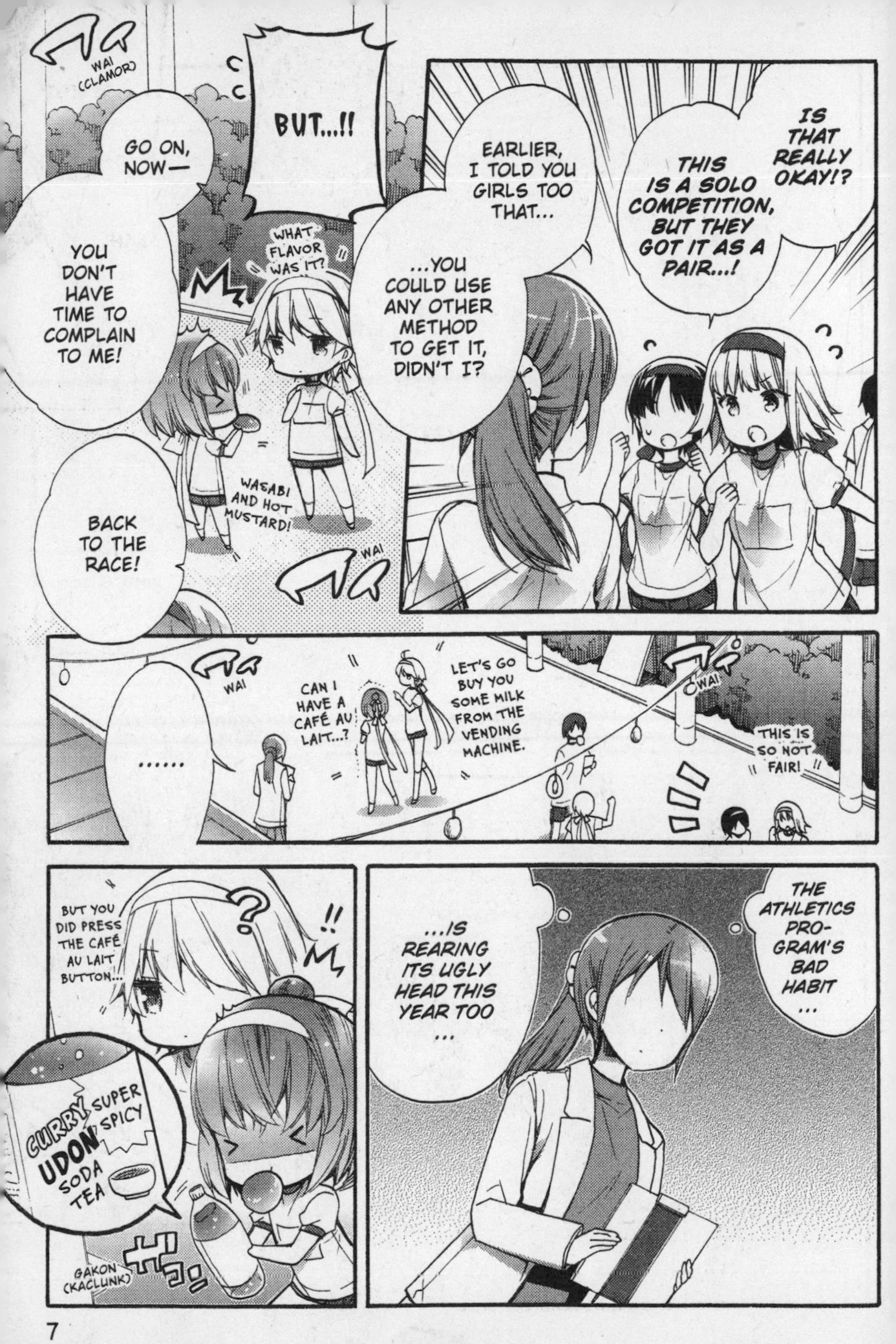

IS THAT REALLY OKAY!?
THIS IS A SOLO COMPETITION, BUT THEY GOT IT AS A PAIR...!
EARLIER, I TOLD YOU GIRLS TOO THAT...
...YOU COULD USE ANY OTHER METHOD TO GET IT, DIDN'T I?
BUT...!!
WAI (CLAMOR)
GO ON, NOW—
YOU DON'T HAVE TIME TO COMPLAIN TO ME!
WHAT FLAVOR WAS IT?
WASABI AND HOT MUSTARD!
WAI
BACK TO THE RACE!
WAI
THIS IS SO NOT FAIR!
LET'S GO BUY YOU SOME MILK FROM THE VENDING MACHINE.
CAN I HAVE A CAFÉ AU LAIT...?
WAI
......
THE ATHLETICS PRO-GRAM'S BAD HABIT...
...IS REARING ITS UGLY HEAD THIS YEAR TOO...
BUT YOU DID PRESS THE CAFÉ AU LAIT BUTTON...
CURRY UDON SUPER SPICY SODA TEA
GAKON (KACLUNK)

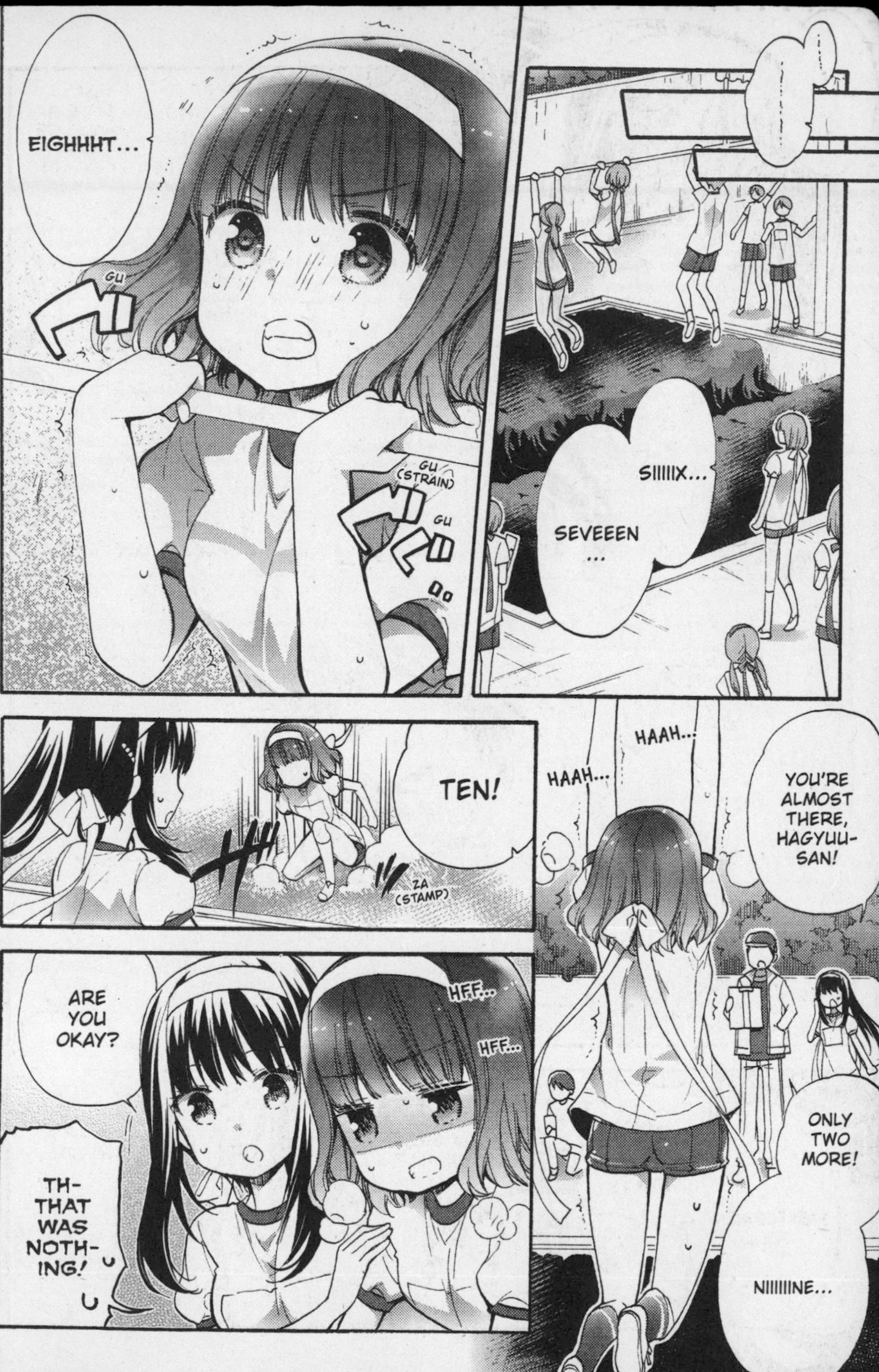
SIIIIX...
SEVEEEN...
EIGHHHT...
GU
GU (STRAIN)
GU
HAAH...
HAAH...
YOU'RE ALMOST THERE, HAGYUU-SAN!
ONLY TWO MORE!
NIIIIINE...
TEN!
ZA (STAMP)
ARE YOU OKAY?
HFF...
HFF...
TH-THAT WAS NOTHING!

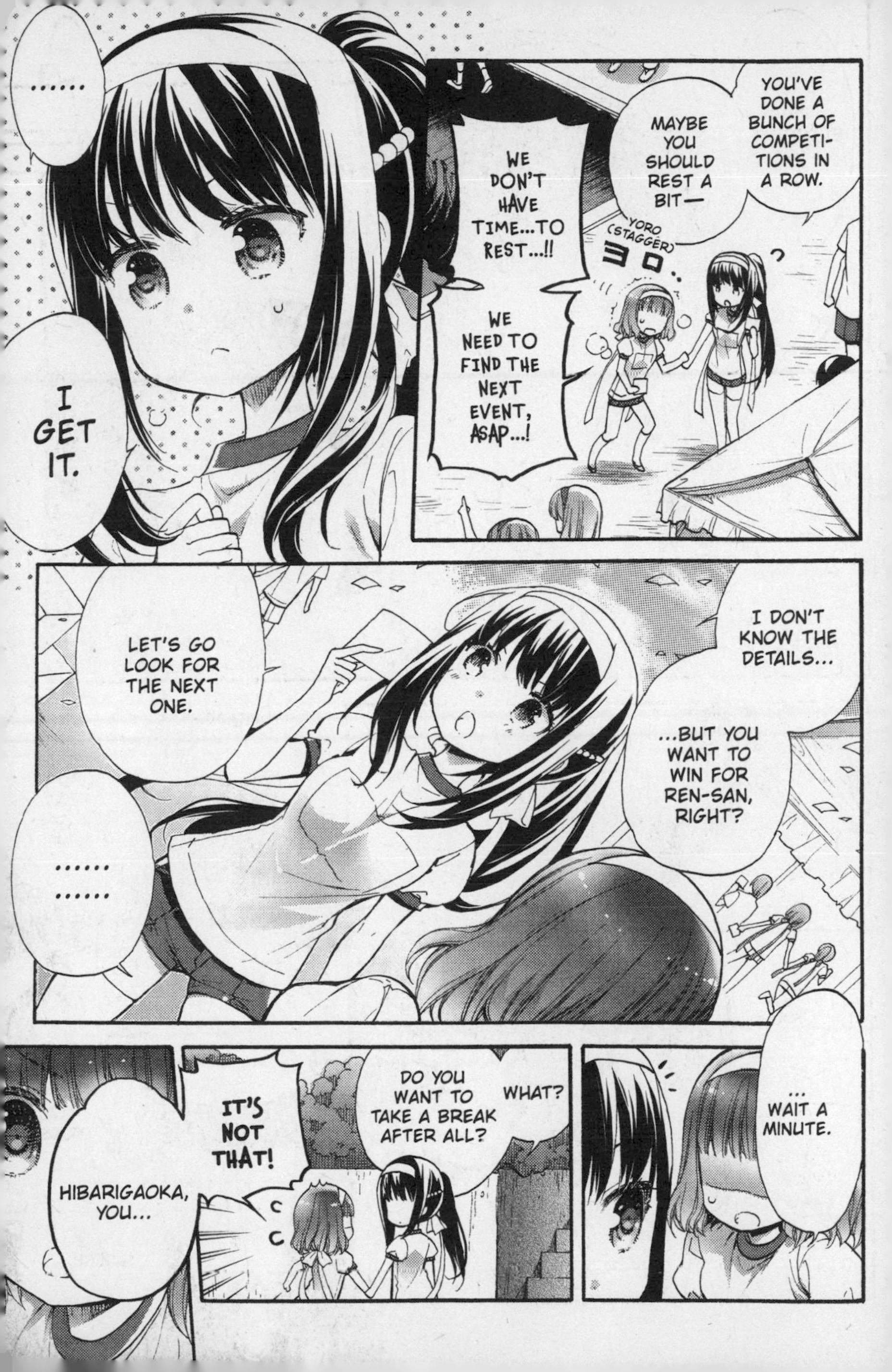
YOU'VE DONE A BUNCH OF COMPETITIONS IN A ROW.
MAYBE YOU SHOULD REST A BIT—
YORO (STAGGER)
ヨロ
WE DON'T HAVE TIME...TO REST...!!
WE NEED TO FIND THE NEXT EVENT, ASAP...!
......
I GET IT.
I DON'T KNOW THE DETAILS...
...BUT YOU WANT TO WIN FOR REN-SAN, RIGHT?
LET'S GO LOOK FOR THE NEXT ONE.
....
... WAIT A MINUTE.
WHAT?
DO YOU WANT TO TAKE A BREAK AFTER ALL?
IT'S NOT THAT!
HIBARIGAOKA, YOU...

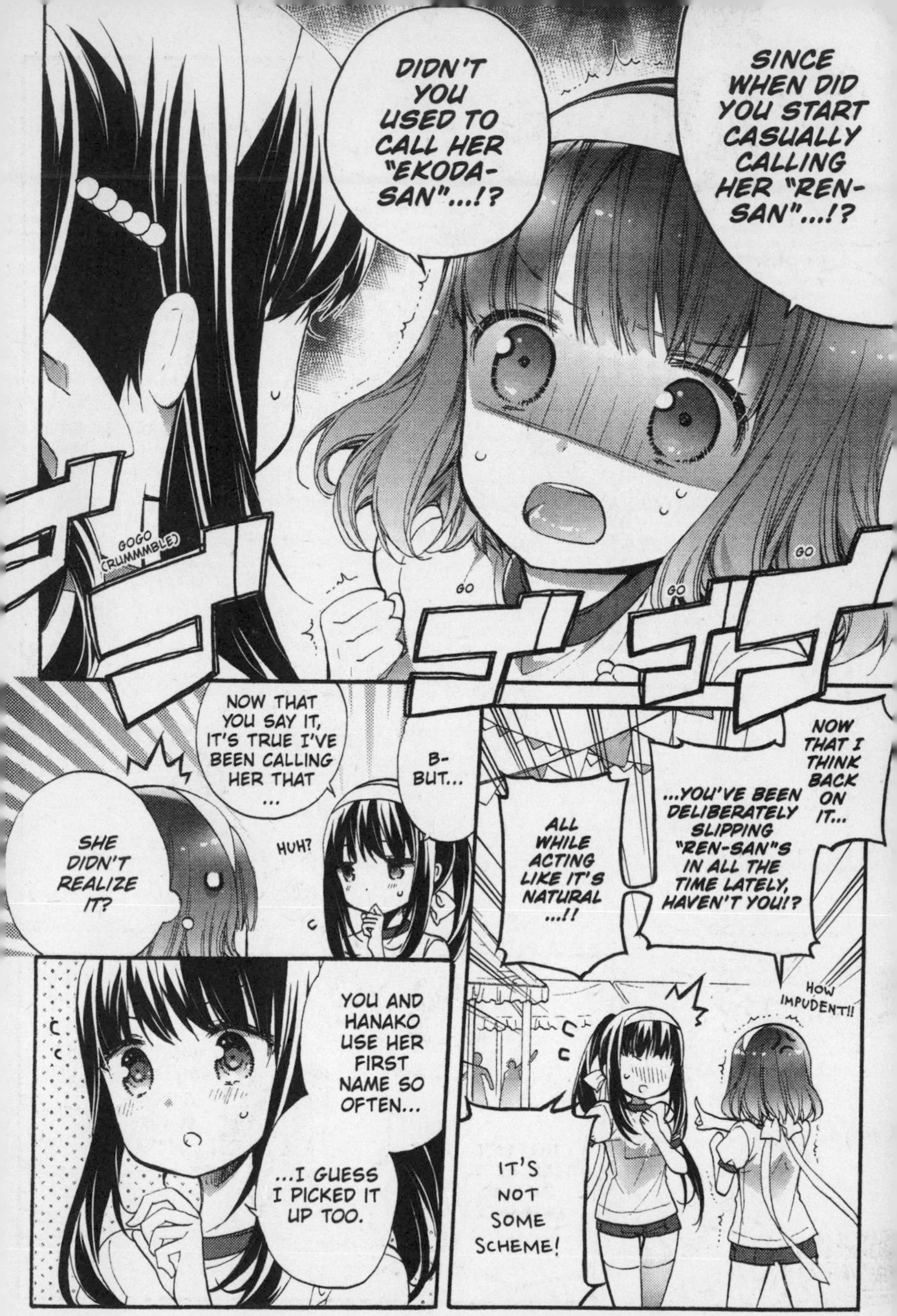
SINCE WHEN DID YOU START CASUALLY CALLING HER "REN-SAN"...!?
DIDN'T YOU USED TO CALL HER "EKODA-SAN"...!?
GO
GO
GO
GOGO (RUMMMBLE)
NOW THAT I THINK BACK ON IT...
...YOU'VE BEEN DELIBERATELY SLIPPING "REN-SAN"S IN ALL THE TIME LATELY, HAVEN'T YOU!?
ALL WHILE ACTING LIKE IT'S NATURAL...!!
HOW IMPUDENT!!
IT'S NOT SOME SCHEME!
B-BUT...
NOW THAT YOU SAY IT, IT'S TRUE I'VE BEEN CALLING HER THAT...
HUH?
SHE DIDN'T REALIZE IT?
YOU AND HANAKO USE HER FIRST NAME SO OFTEN...
...I GUESS I PICKED IT UP TOO.

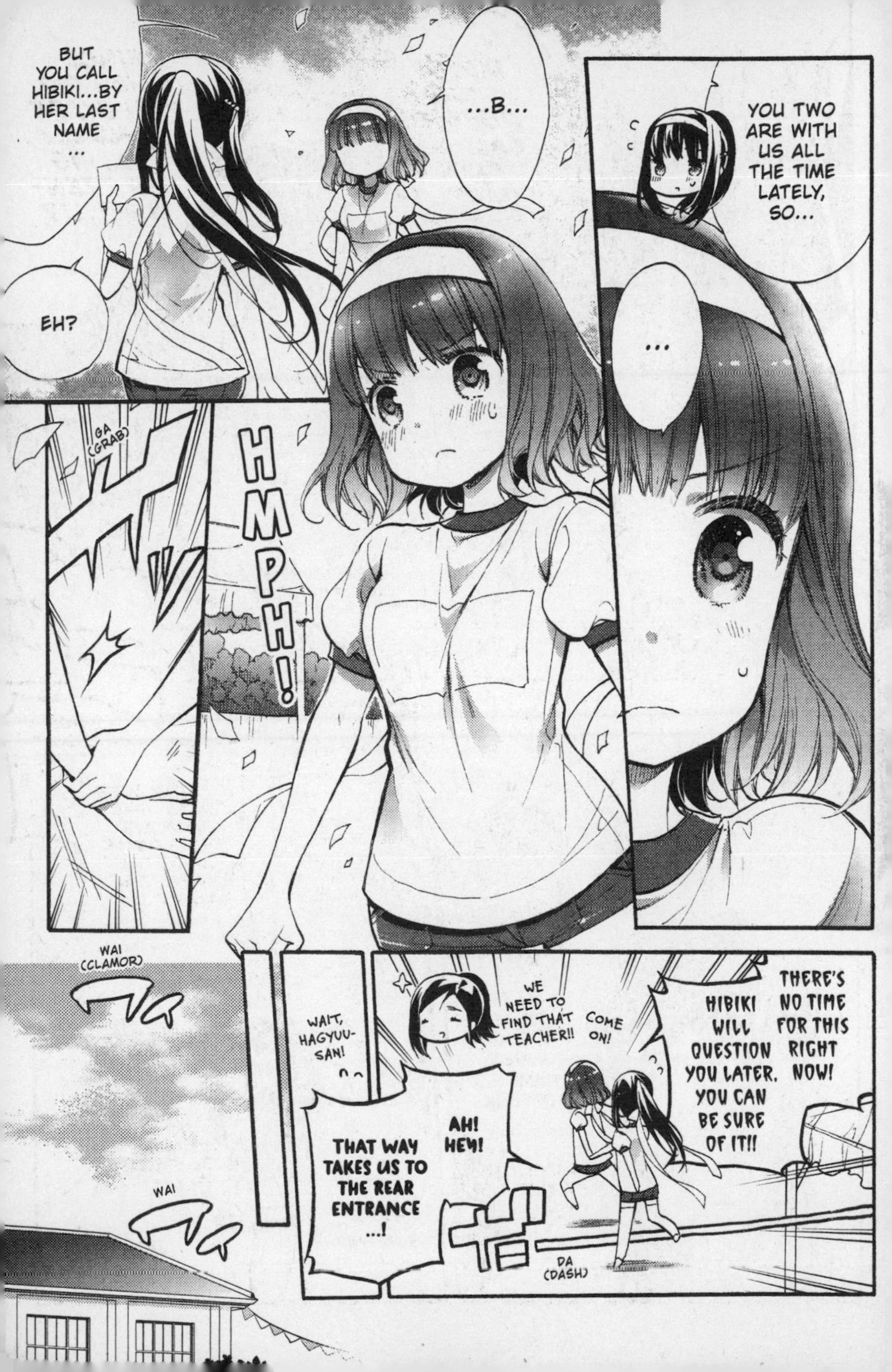

YOU TWO ARE WITH US ALL THE TIME LATELY, SO...
...
...B...
BUT YOU CALL HIBIKI...BY HER LAST NAME ...
EH?
HMPH!
GA (GRAB)
THERE'S NO TIME FOR THIS RIGHT NOW!
HIBIKI WILL QUESTION YOU LATER. YOU CAN BE SURE OF IT!!
COME ON!
WE NEED TO FIND THAT TEACHER!!
WAIT, HAGYUU-SAN!
AH! HEY!
THAT WAY TAKES US TO THE REAR ENTRANCE ...!
DA (DASH)
WAI (CLAMOR)
WAI

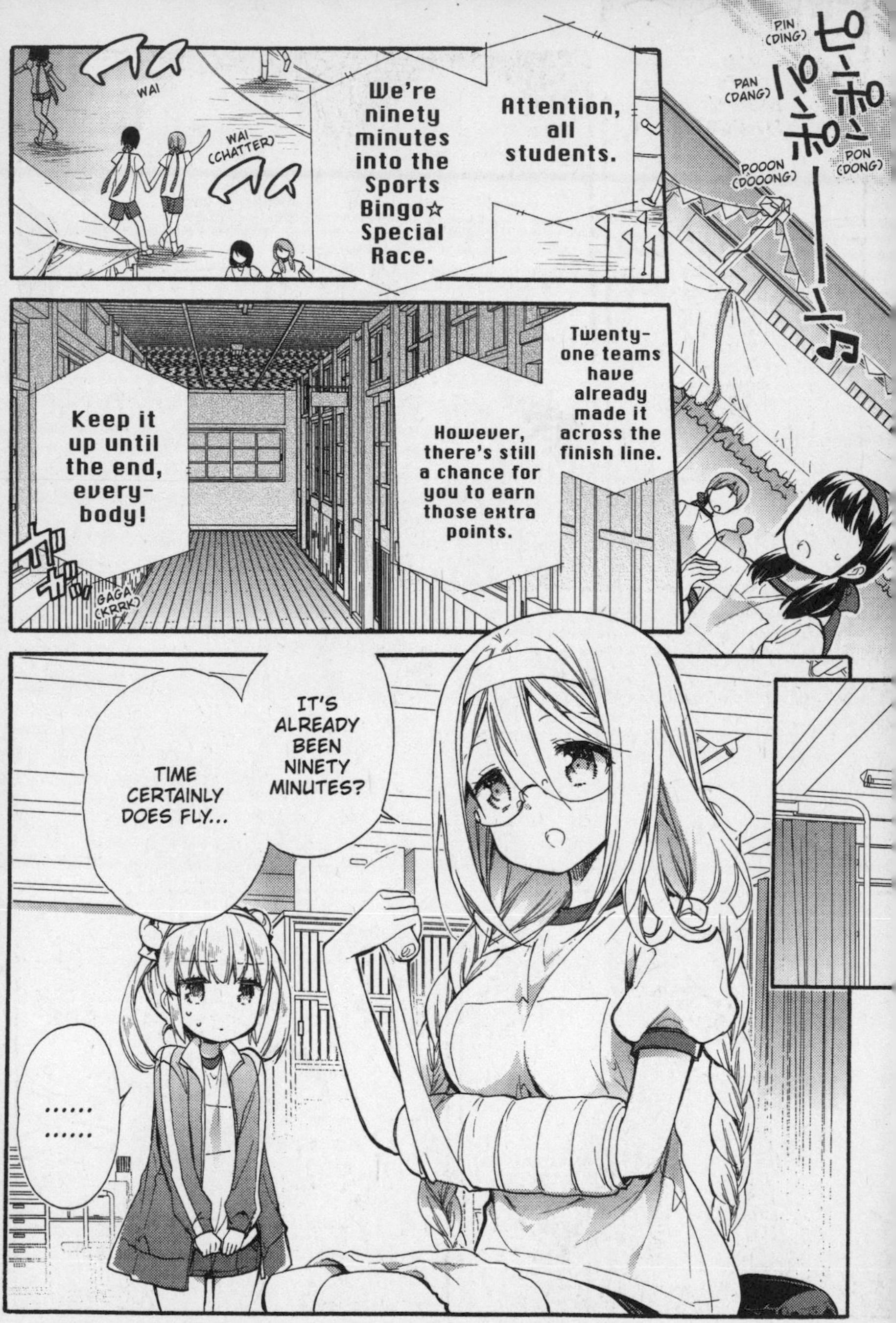
ピンポンパンポーン♪
PIN (DING)
PAN (DANG)
PON (DONG)
POOON (DOOONG)
Attention, all students.
We're ninety minutes into the Sports Bingo☆ Special Race.
WAI
WAI (CHATTER)
Twenty-one teams have already made it across the finish line.
However, there's still a chance for you to earn those extra points.
Keep it up until the end, everybody!
GAGA (KRRK)
IT'S ALREADY BEEN NINETY MINUTES?
TIME CERTAINLY DOES FLY...
....

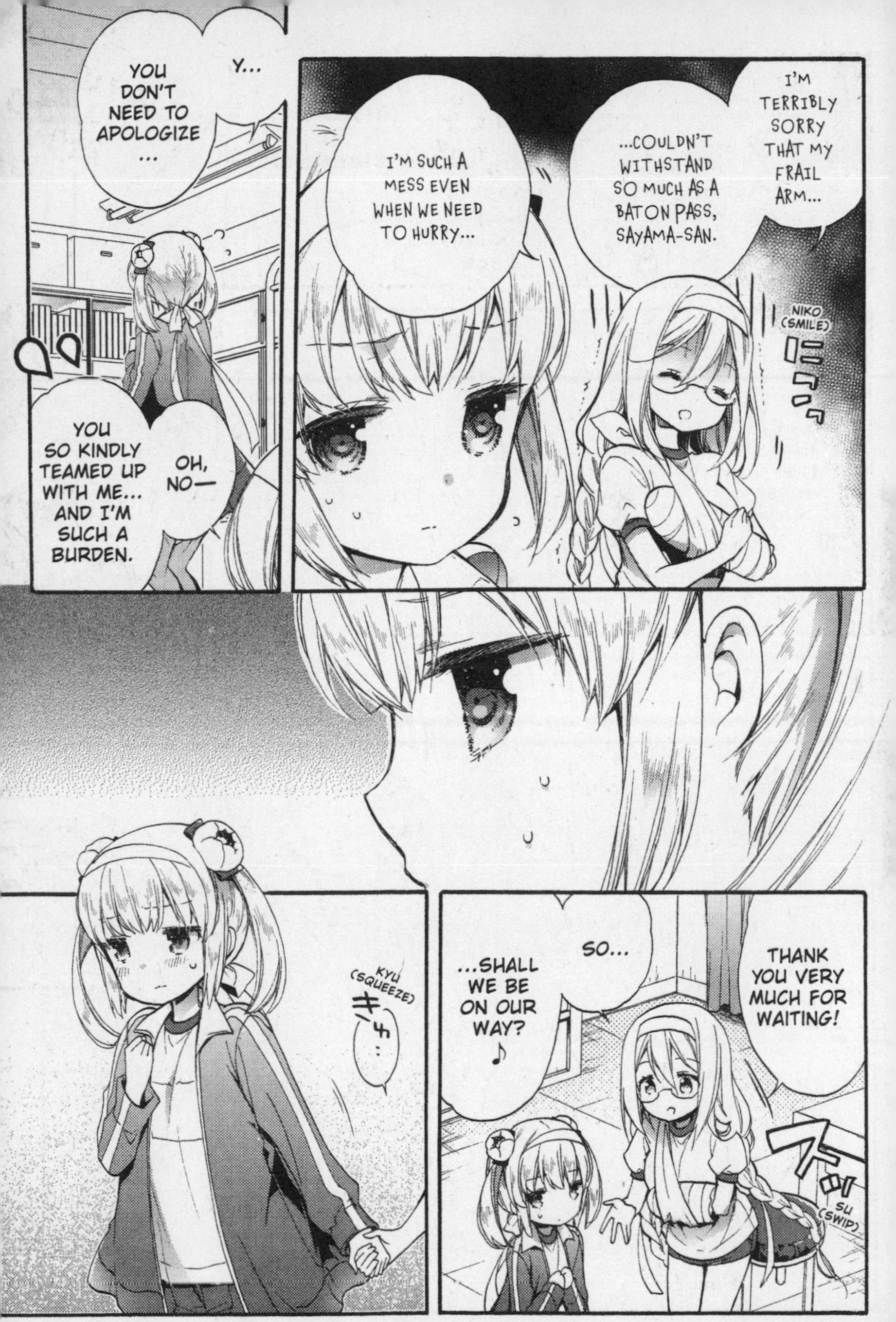
I'M TERRIBLY SORRY THAT MY FRAIL ARM...
...COULDN'T WITHSTAND SO MUCH AS A BATON PASS, SAYAMA-SAN.
NIKO (SMILE)
I'M SUCH A MESS EVEN WHEN WE NEED TO HURRY...
Y...
YOU DON'T NEED TO APOLOGIZE...
OH, NO—
YOU SO KINDLY TEAMED UP WITH ME... AND I'M SUCH A BURDEN.
THANK YOU VERY MUCH FOR WAITING!
SU (SWIP)
SO...
...SHALL WE BE ON OUR WAY? ♪
KYU (SQUEEZE)

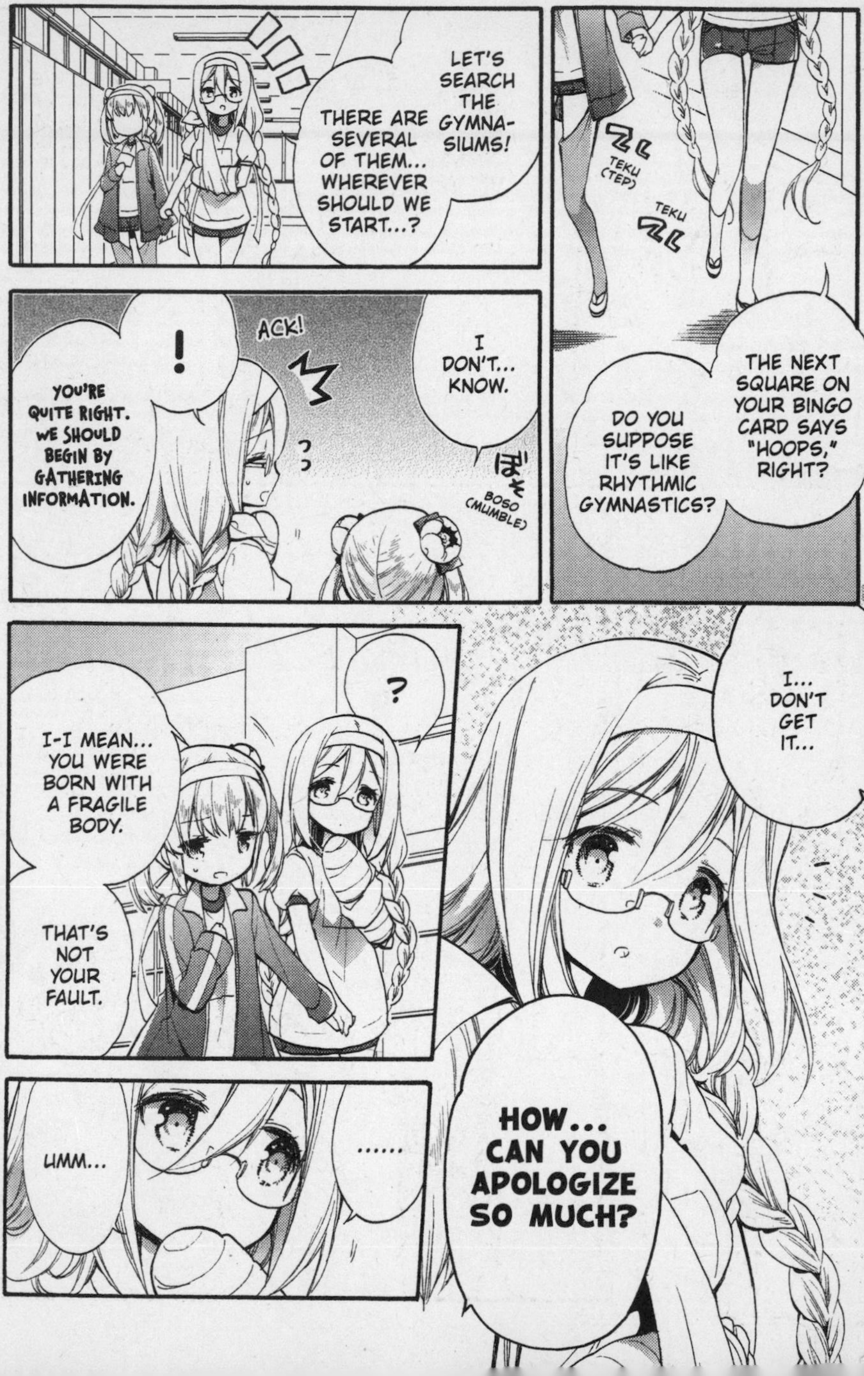
TEKU (TEP)
TEKU
THE NEXT SQUARE ON YOUR BINGO CARD SAYS "HOOPS," RIGHT?
DO YOU SUPPOSE IT'S LIKE RHYTHMIC GYMNASTICS?
LET'S SEARCH THE GYMNASIUMS!
THERE ARE SEVERAL OF THEM... WHEREVER SHOULD WE START...?
I DON'T... KNOW.
ぼそ
BOSO (MUMBLE)
ACK!
!
YOU'RE QUITE RIGHT. WE SHOULD BEGIN BY GATHERING INFORMATION.
I... DON'T GET IT...
HOW... CAN YOU APOLOGIZE SO MUCH?
?
I-I MEAN... YOU WERE BORN WITH A FRAGILE BODY.
THAT'S NOT YOUR FAULT.
......
UMM...

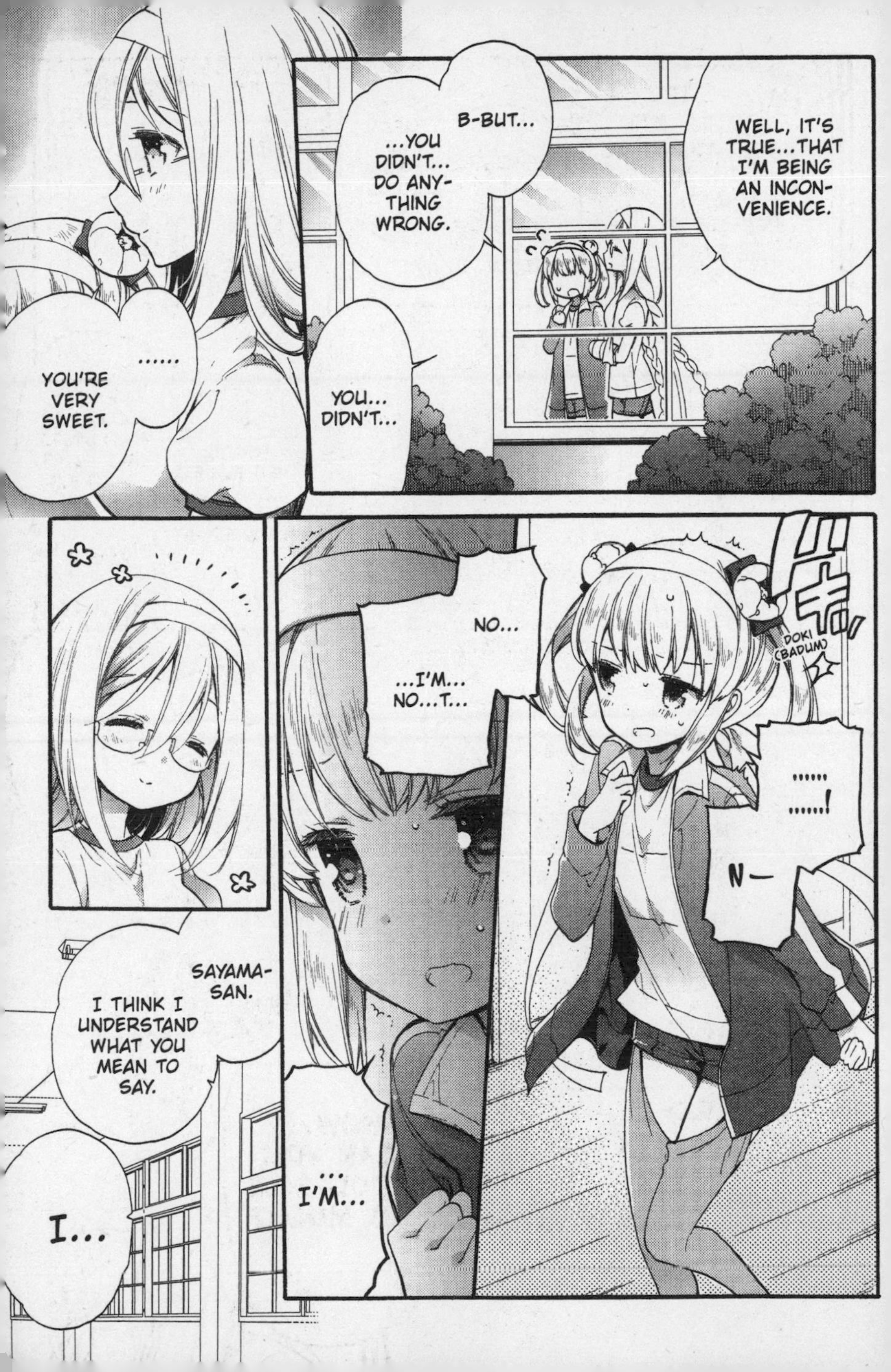
WELL, IT'S TRUE...THAT I'M BEING AN INCONVENIENCE.
B-BUT... ...YOU DIDN'T... DO ANYTHING WRONG.
YOU... DIDN'T...
...... YOU'RE VERY SWEET.
DOKI (BADUM)
......! ......!
N—
NO... ...I'M... NO...T...
... I'M...
SAYAMA-SAN. I THINK I UNDERSTAND WHAT YOU MEAN TO SAY.
I...

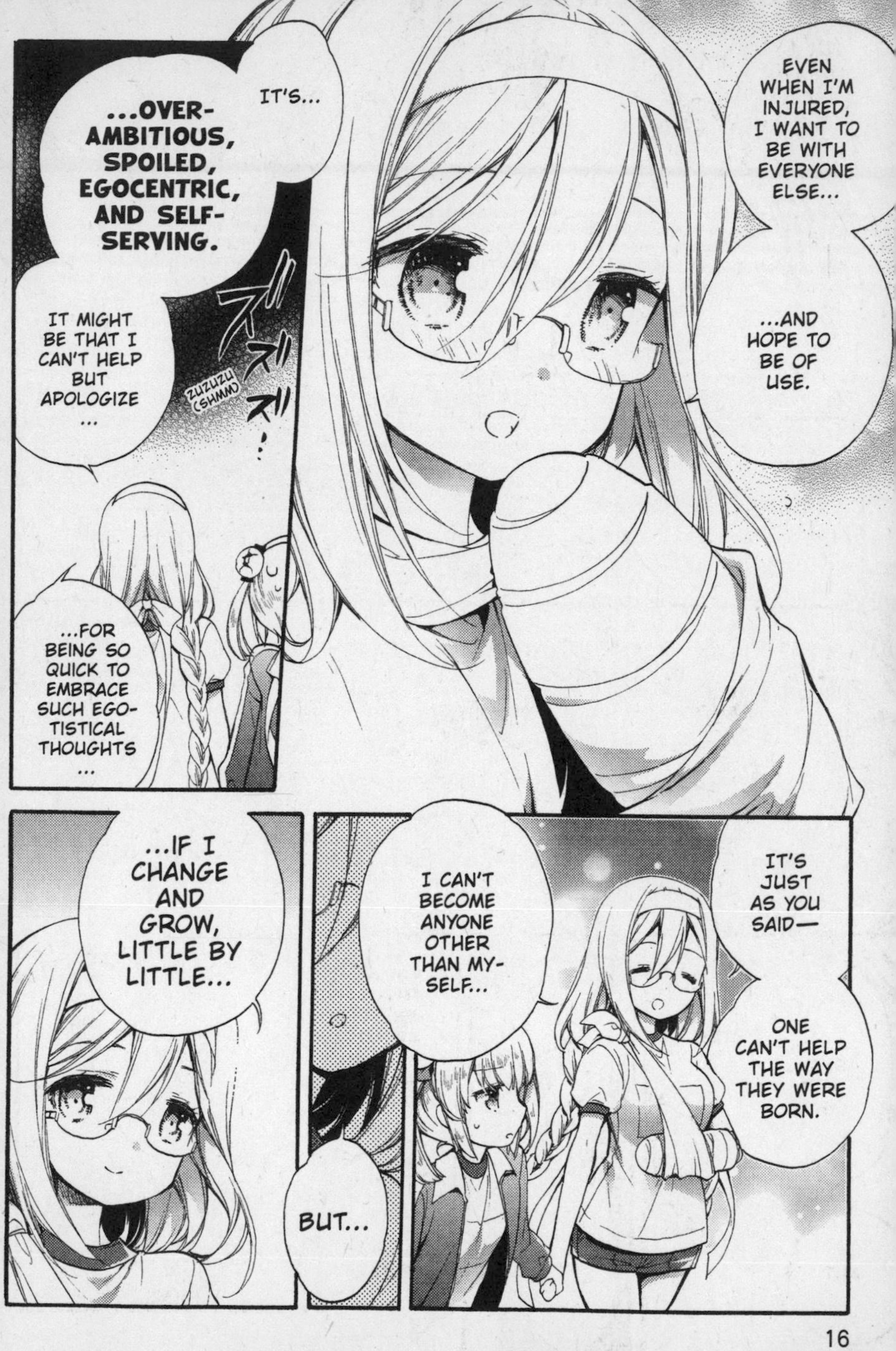
EVEN WHEN I'M INJURED, I WANT TO BE WITH EVERYONE ELSE...
...AND HOPE TO BE OF USE.
IT'S...
...OVER-AMBITIOUS, SPOILED, EGOCENTRIC, AND SELF-SERVING.
ZUZUZU (SHMM)
IT MIGHT BE THAT I CAN'T HELP BUT APOLOGIZE ...
...FOR BEING SO QUICK TO EMBRACE SUCH EGO-TISTICAL THOUGHTS ...
IT'S JUST AS YOU SAID—
ONE CAN'T HELP THE WAY THEY WERE BORN.
I CAN'T BECOME ANYONE OTHER THAN MY-SELF...
BUT...
...IF I CHANGE AND GROW, LITTLE BY LITTLE...

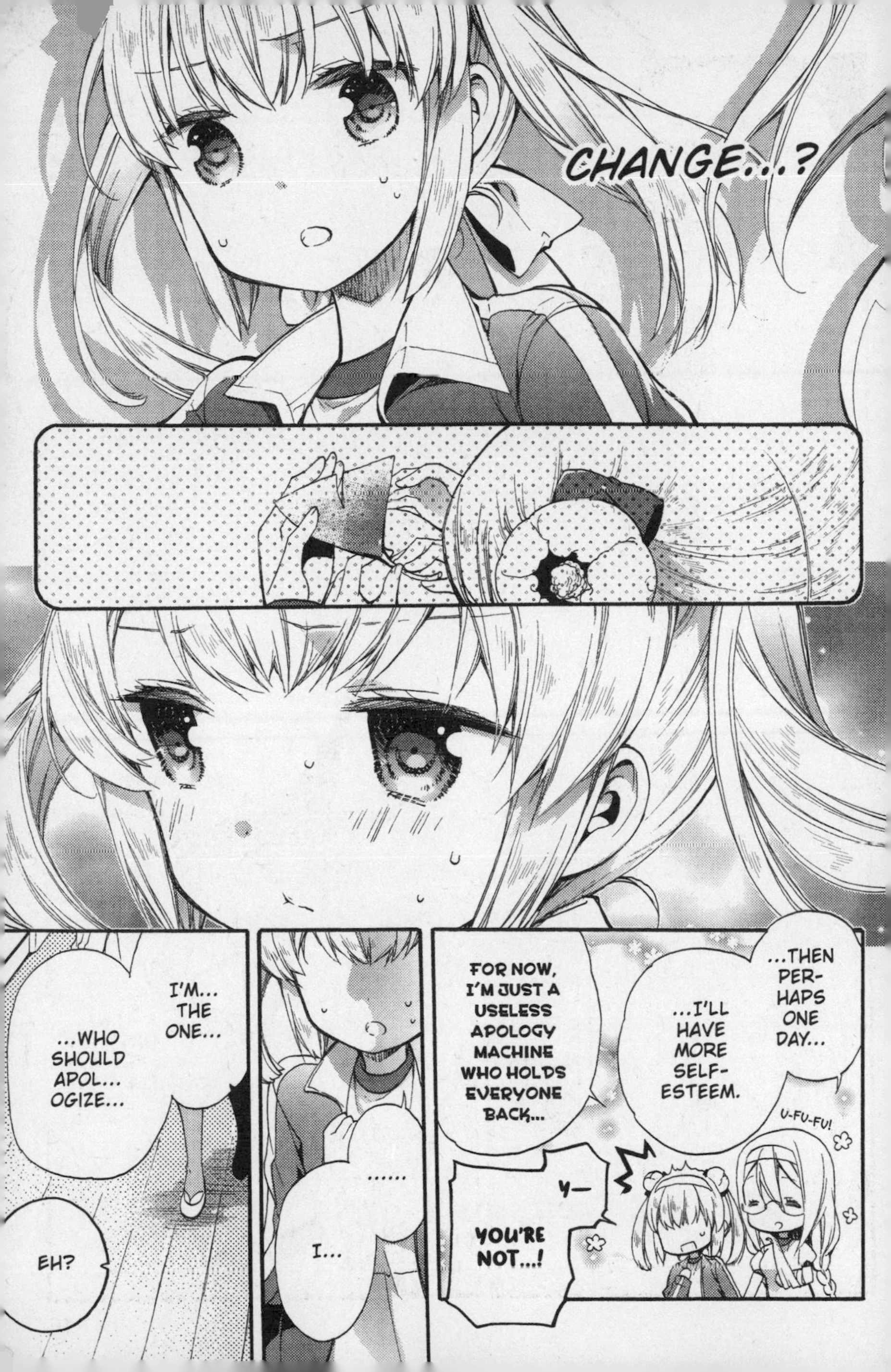
CHANGE...?
...THEN PERHAPS ONE DAY...
...I'LL HAVE MORE SELF-ESTEEM.
FOR NOW, I'M JUST A USELESS APOLOGY MACHINE WHO HOLDS EVERYONE BACK...
U-FU-FU!
Y— YOU'RE NOT...!
......
I...
I'M... THE ONE...
...WHO SHOULD APOL... OGIZE...
EH?

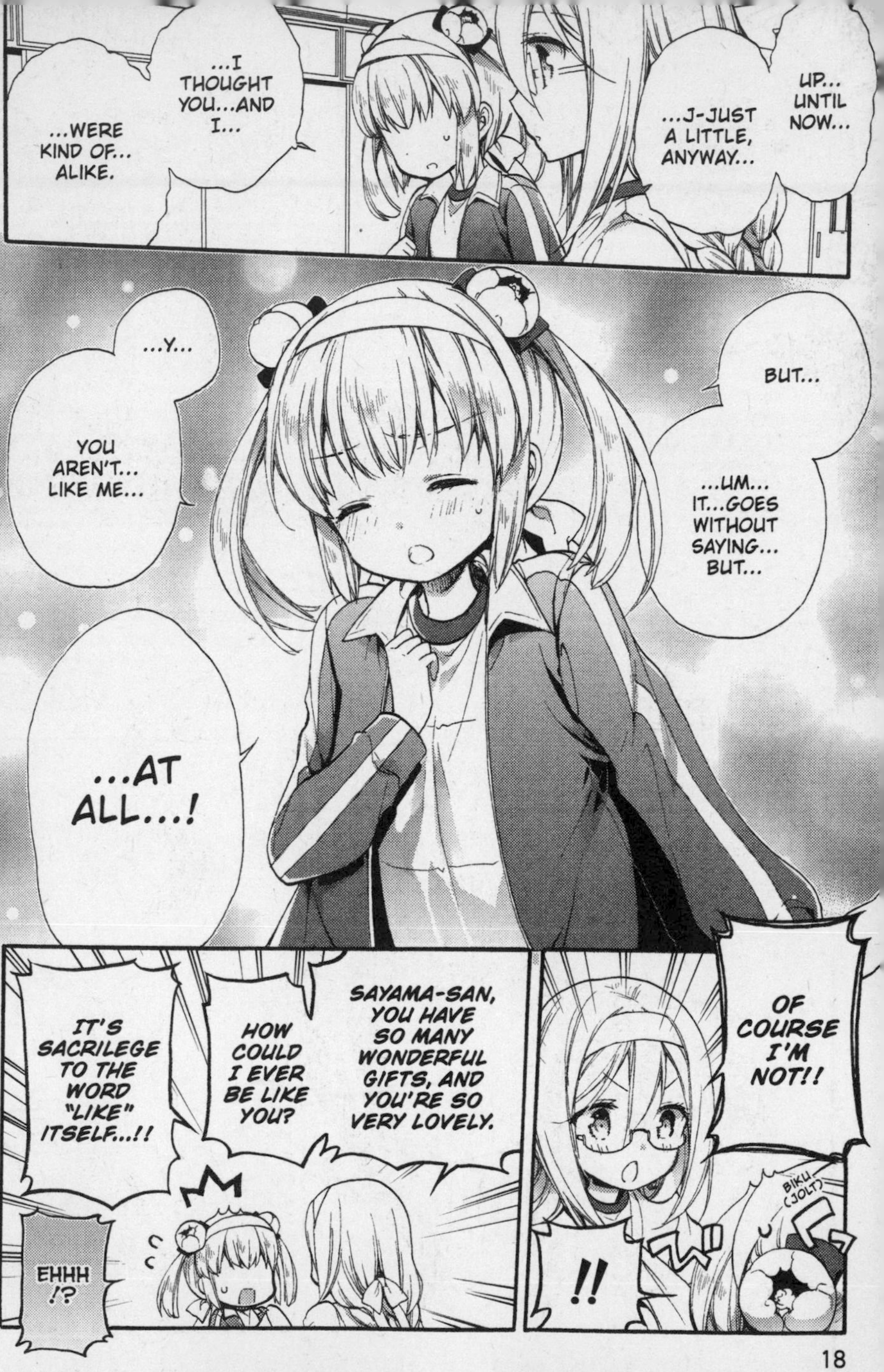
UP... UNTIL NOW...
...J-JUST A LITTLE, ANYWAY...
...I THOUGHT YOU...AND I...
...WERE KIND OF... ALIKE.
BUT...
...UM... IT...GOES WITHOUT SAYING... BUT...
...Y...
YOU AREN'T... LIKE ME...
...AT ALL...!
OF COURSE I'M NOT!!
BIKU (JOLT)
!!
SAYAMA-SAN, YOU HAVE SO MANY WONDERFUL GIFTS, AND YOU'RE SO VERY LOVELY.
HOW COULD I EVER BE LIKE YOU?
IT'S SACRILEGE TO THE WORD "LIKE" ITSELF...!!
EHHH !?

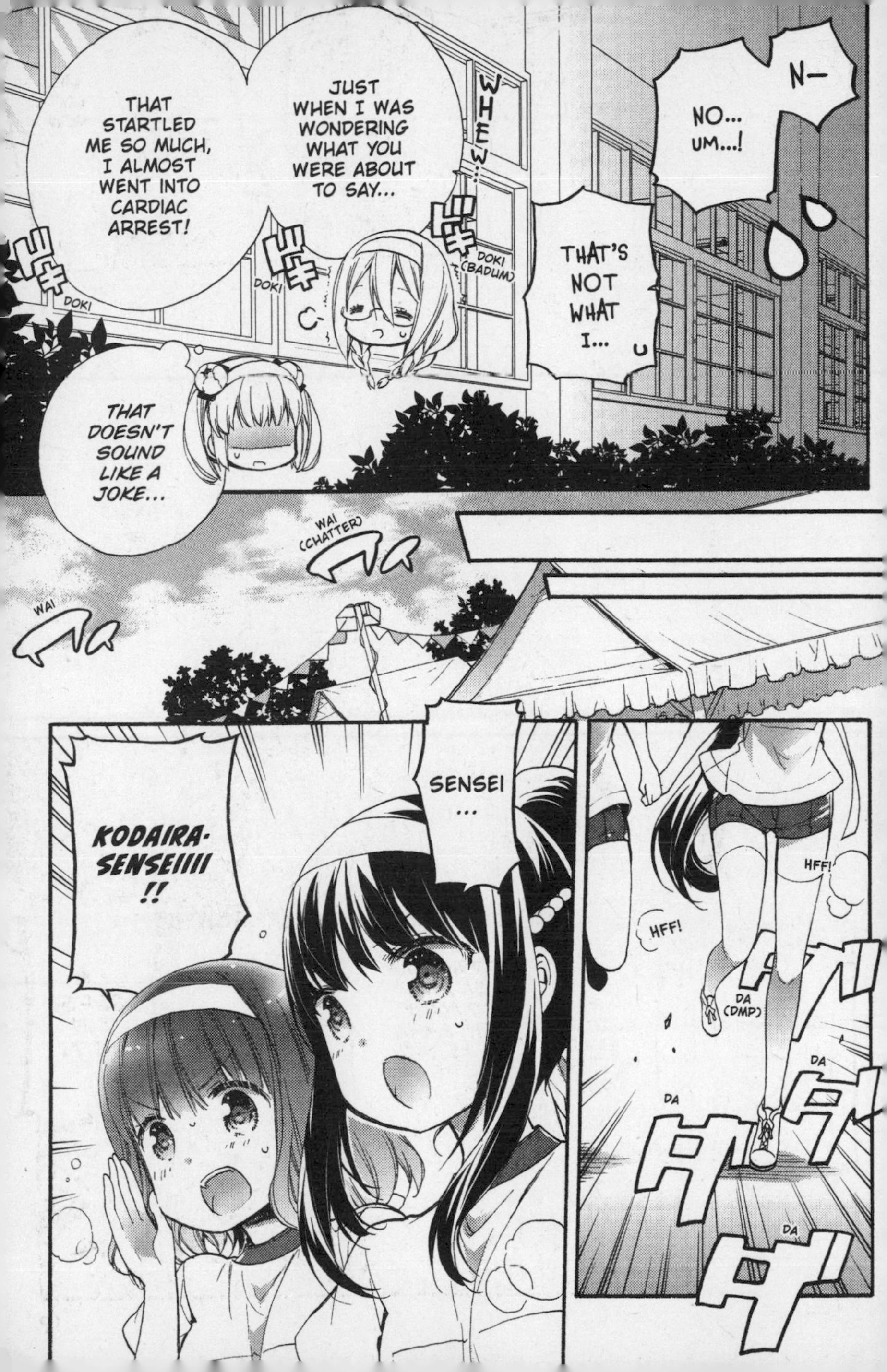
N—
NO... UM...!
THAT'S NOT WHAT I...
WHEW...
JUST WHEN I WAS WONDERING WHAT YOU WERE ABOUT TO SAY...
DOKI (BADUM)
DOKI
DOKI
THAT STARTLED ME SO MUCH, I ALMOST WENT INTO CARDIAC ARREST!
THAT DOESN'T SOUND LIKE A JOKE...
WAI (CHATTER)
WAI
HFF!
HFF!
DA (DMP)
DA
DA
DA
SENSEI...
KODAIRA-SENSEIIIII!!

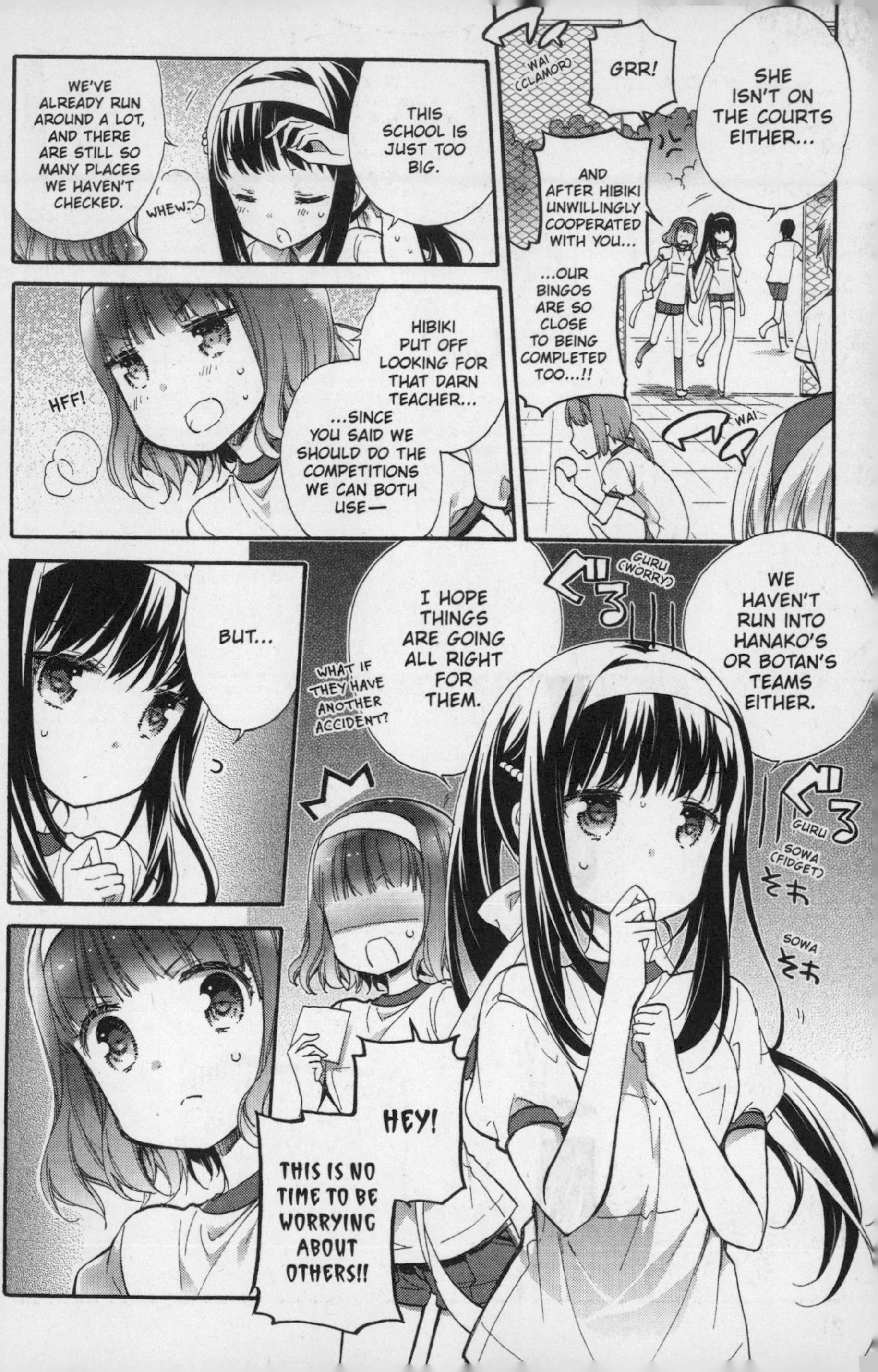

SHE ISN'T ON THE COURTS EITHER...
WAI (CLAMOR)
GRR!
AND AFTER HIBIKI UNWILLINGLY COOPERATED WITH YOU...
...OUR BINGOS ARE SO CLOSE TO BEING COMPLETED TOO...!!
WAI
THIS SCHOOL IS JUST TOO BIG.
WE'VE ALREADY RUN AROUND A LOT, AND THERE ARE STILL SO MANY PLACES WE HAVEN'T CHECKED.
WHEW.
HIBIKI PUT OFF LOOKING FOR THAT DARN TEACHER...
...SINCE YOU SAID WE SHOULD DO THE COMPETITIONS WE CAN BOTH USE—
HFF!
GURU (WORRY)
WE HAVEN'T RUN INTO HANAKO'S OR BOTAN'S TEAMS EITHER.
GURU
SOWA (FIDGET)
SOWA
I HOPE THINGS ARE GOING ALL RIGHT FOR THEM.
WHAT IF THEY HAVE ANOTHER ACCIDENT?
BUT...
HEY!
THIS IS NO TIME TO BE WORRYING ABOUT OTHERS!!

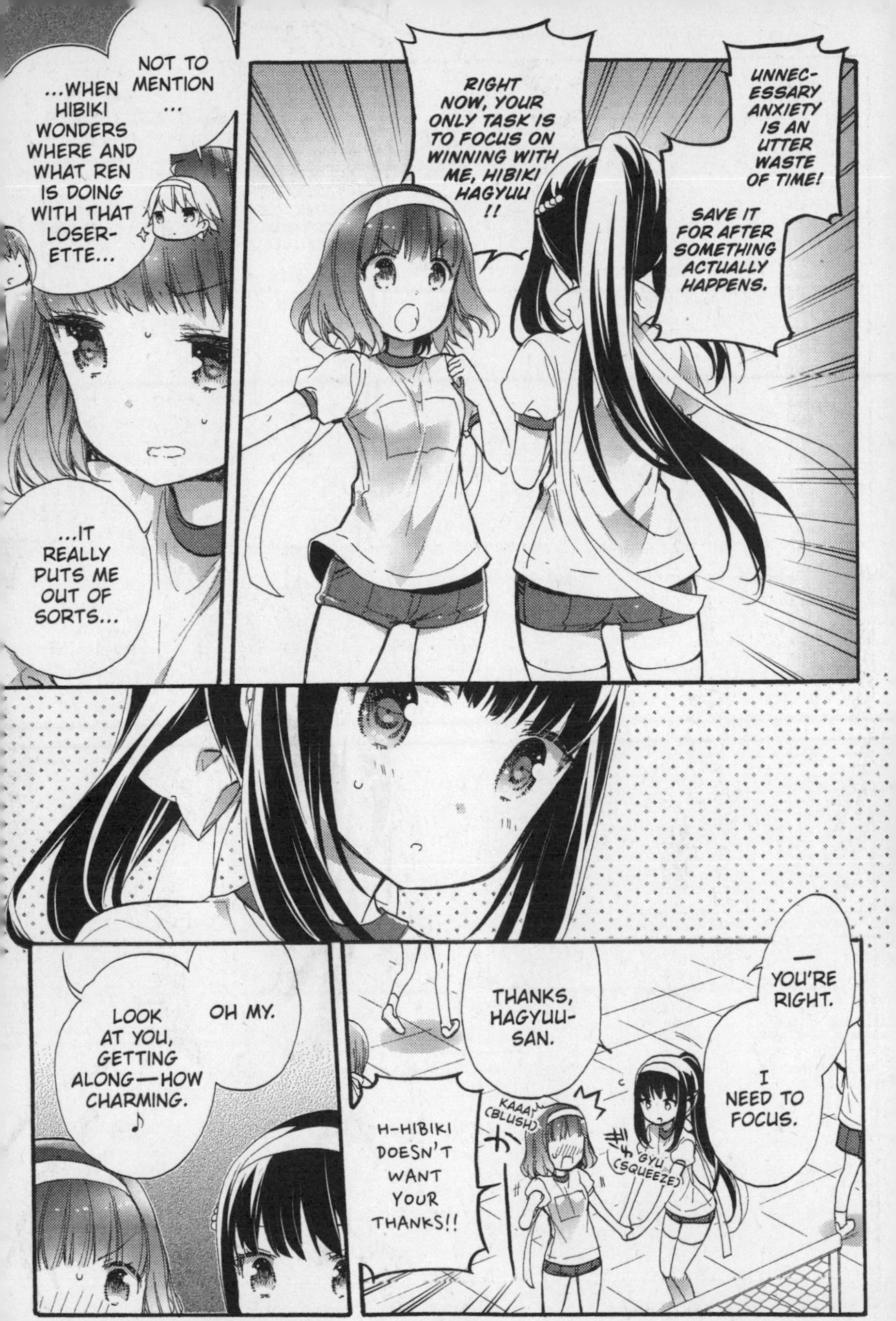
UNNECESSARY ANXIETY IS AN UTTER WASTE OF TIME!
SAVE IT FOR AFTER SOMETHING ACTUALLY HAPPENS.
RIGHT NOW, YOUR ONLY TASK IS TO FOCUS ON WINNING WITH ME, HIBIKI HAGYUU!!
NOT TO MENTION...
...WHEN HIBIKI WONDERS WHERE AND WHAT REN IS DOING WITH THAT LOSERETTE...
...IT REALLY PUTS ME OUT OF SORTS...
—YOU'RE RIGHT.
I NEED TO FOCUS.
THANKS, HAGYUU-SAN.
GYU (SQUEEZE)
KAAA (BLUSH)
H-HIBIKI DOESN'T WANT YOUR THANKS!!
OH MY.
LOOK AT YOU, GETTING ALONG—HOW CHARMING. ♪

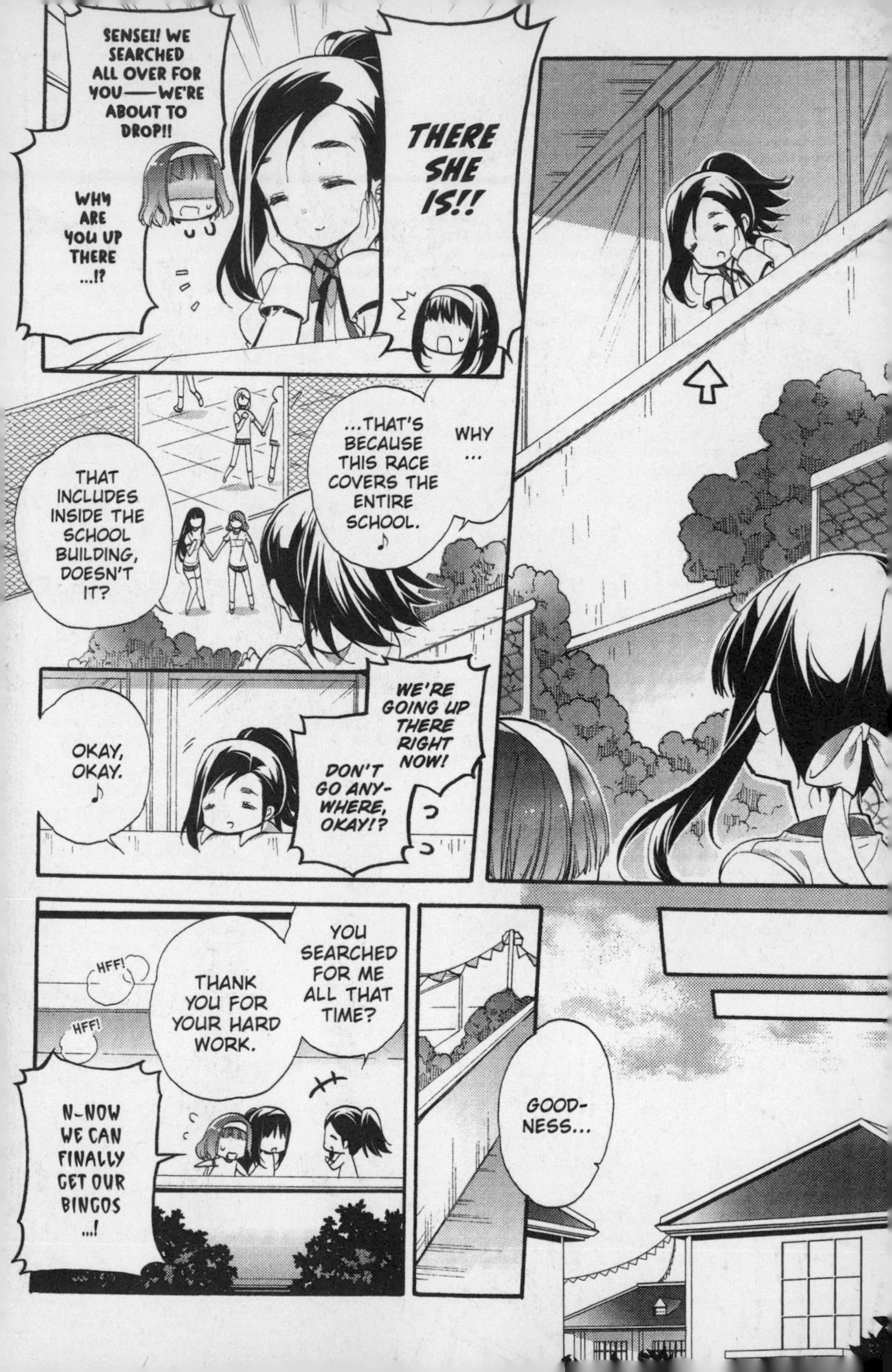
THERE SHE IS!!
SENSEI! WE SEARCHED ALL OVER FOR YOU—WE'RE ABOUT TO DROP!!
WHY ARE YOU UP THERE ...!?
WHY ...
...THAT'S BECAUSE THIS RACE COVERS THE ENTIRE SCHOOL. ♪
THAT INCLUDES INSIDE THE SCHOOL BUILDING, DOESN'T IT?
WE'RE GOING UP THERE RIGHT NOW!
DON'T GO ANY-WHERE, OKAY!?
OKAY, OKAY. ♪
GOOD-NESS...
YOU SEARCHED FOR ME ALL THAT TIME?
THANK YOU FOR YOUR HARD WORK.
HFF!
HFF!
N-NOW WE CAN FINALLY GET OUR BINGOS ...!

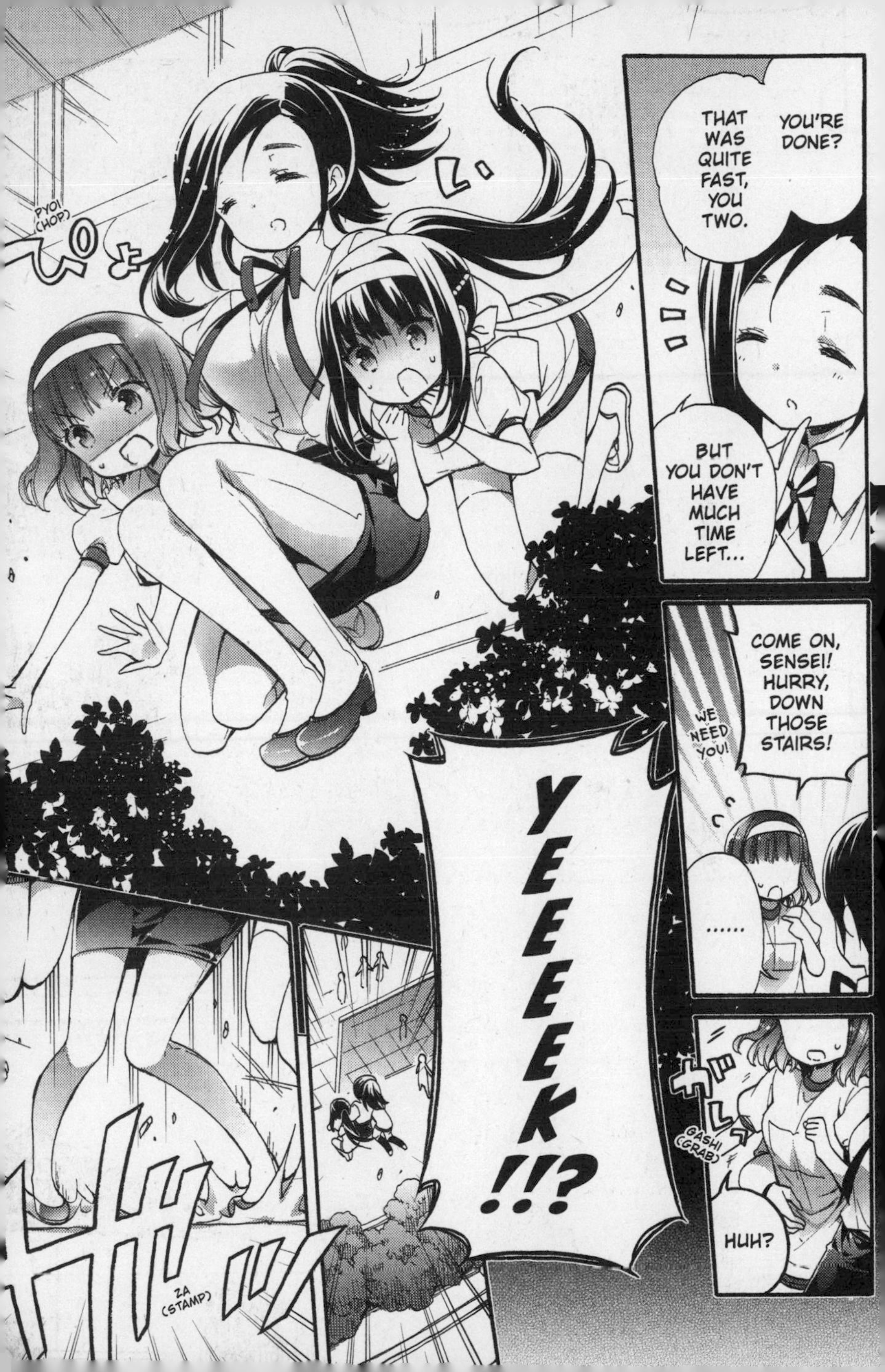
YOU'RE DONE?
THAT WAS QUITE FAST, YOU TWO.
BUT YOU DON'T HAVE MUCH TIME LEFT...
COME ON, SENSEI! HURRY, DOWN THOSE STAIRS!
WE NEED YOU!
......
GASHI (GRAB)
HUH?
PYOI (HOP)
YEEEEK!!?
ZA (STAMP)

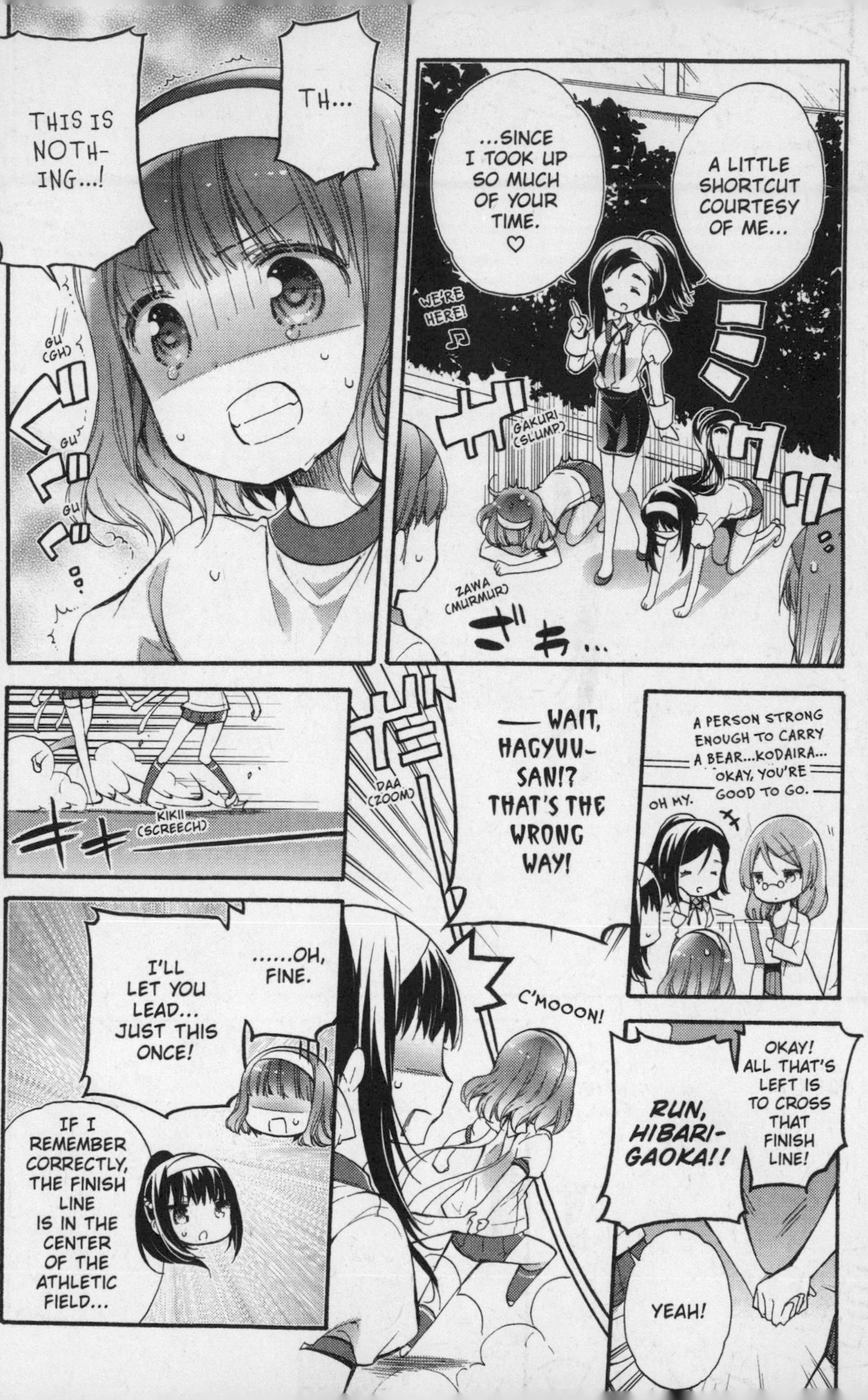
A LITTLE SHORTCUT COURTESY OF ME...
...SINCE I TOOK UP SO MUCH OF YOUR TIME. ♡
WE'RE HERE! ♪
GAKURI (SLUMP)
ZAWA (MURMUR)
TH...
THIS IS NOTH-ING...!
GU (GH)
GU
GU
A PERSON STRONG ENOUGH TO CARRY A BEAR...KODAIRA... OKAY, YOU'RE GOOD TO GO.
OH MY.
— WAIT, HAGYUU-SAN!? THAT'S THE WRONG WAY!
DAA (ZOOM)
KIKII (SCREECH)
OKAY! ALL THAT'S LEFT IS TO CROSS THAT FINISH LINE!
RUN, HIBARI-GAOKA!!
YEAH!
C'MOOOON!
......OH, FINE.
I'LL LET YOU LEAD... JUST THIS ONCE!
IF I REMEMBER CORRECTLY, THE FINISH LINE IS IN THE CENTER OF THE ATHLETIC FIELD...

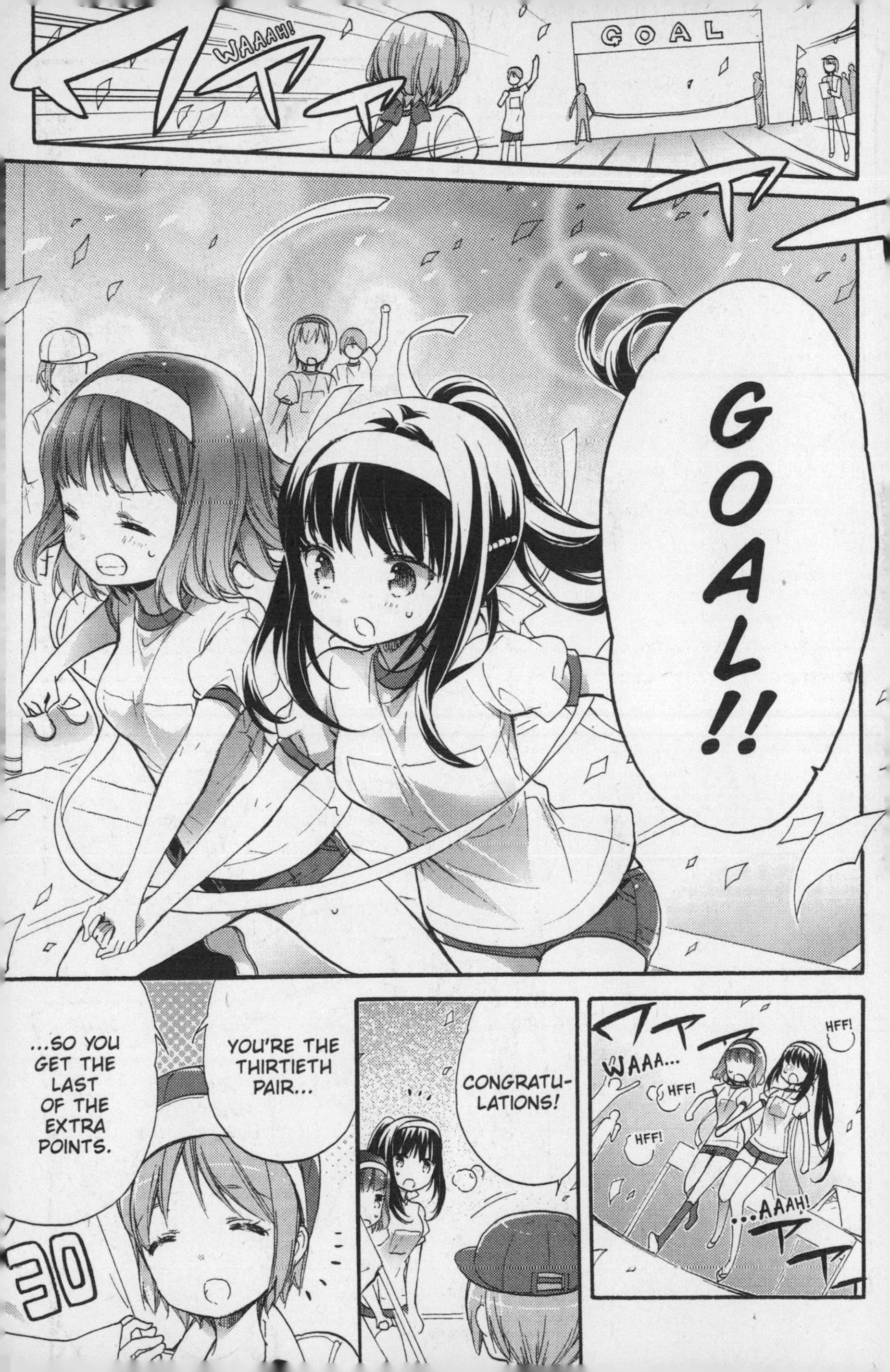
WAAAH!
GOAL
GOAL!!
HFF!
WAAA...
HFF!
HFF!
...AAAH!
CONGRATU-LATIONS!
YOU'RE THE THIRTIETH PAIR...
...SO YOU GET THE LAST OF THE EXTRA POINTS.
30

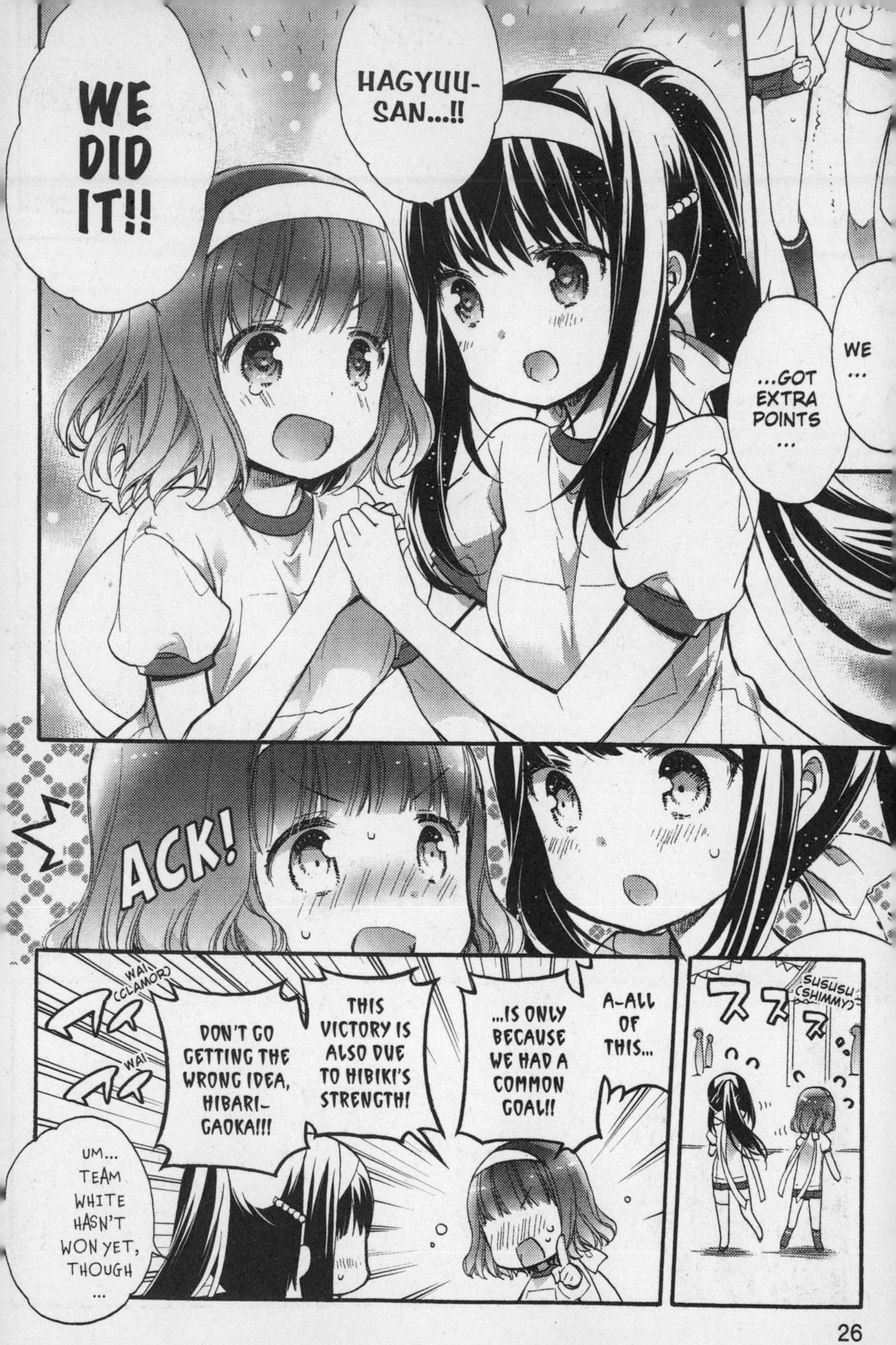
WE ...
...GOT EXTRA POINTS ...
HAGYUU-SAN...!!
WE DID IT!!
ACK!
SUSUSU (SHIMMY)
A-ALL OF THIS...
...IS ONLY BECAUSE WE HAD A COMMON GOAL!!
THIS VICTORY IS ALSO DUE TO HIBIKI'S STRENGTH!
DON'T GO GETTING THE WRONG IDEA, HIBARIGAOKA!!!
WAI (CLAMOR)
WAI
UM... TEAM WHITE HASN'T WON YET, THOUGH ...

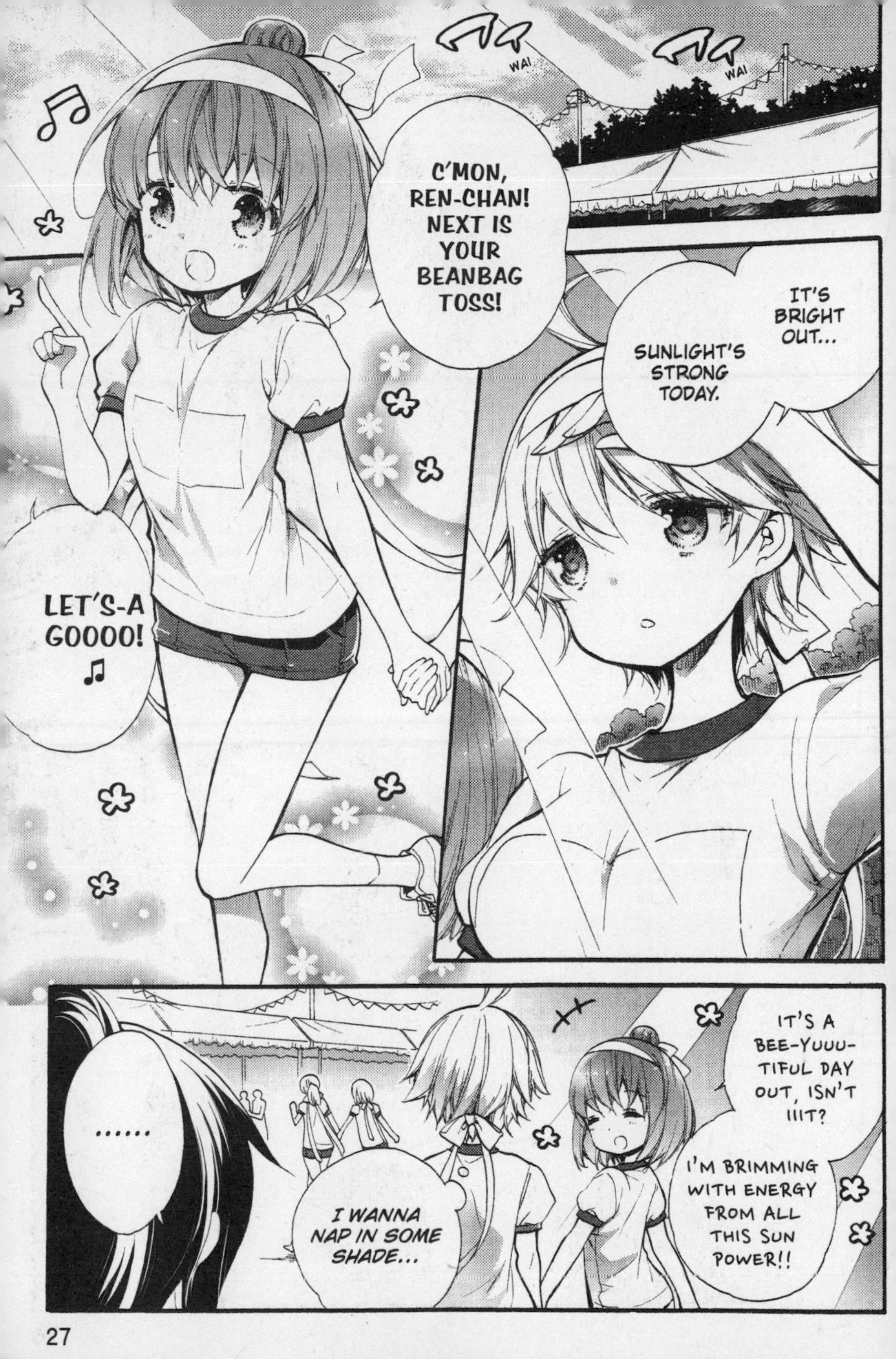
WAI
WAI
IT'S BRIGHT OUT...
SUNLIGHT'S STRONG TODAY.
C'MON, REN-CHAN! NEXT IS YOUR BEANBAG TOSS!
LET'S-A GOOOO! ♫
IT'S A BEE-YUUU-TIFUL DAY OUT, ISN'T IIIT?
I'M BRIMMING WITH ENERGY FROM ALL THIS SUN POWER!!
I WANNA NAP IN SOME SHADE...
......

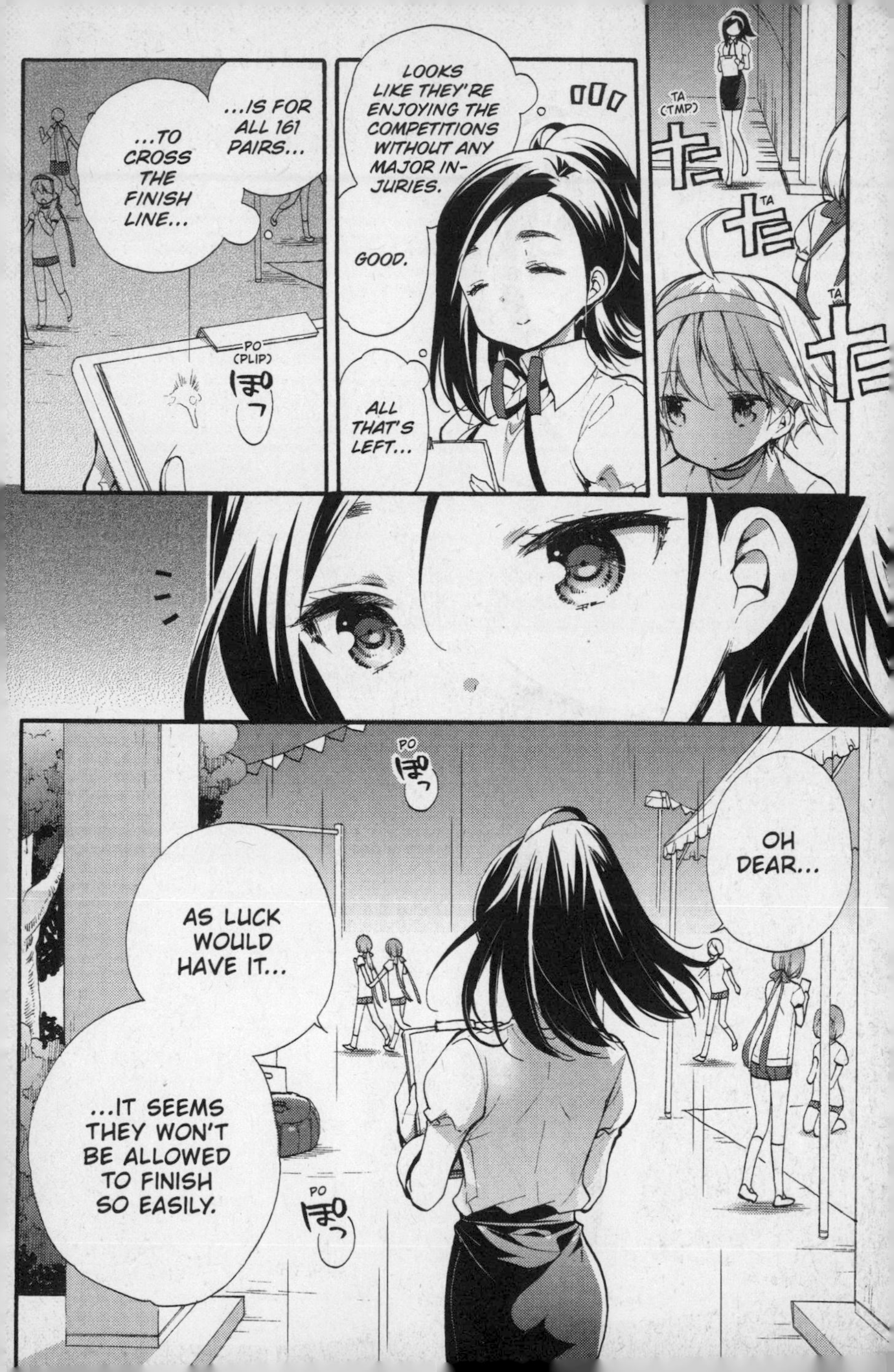

TA (TMP)
た
TA
た
TA
た
LOOKS LIKE THEY'RE ENJOYING THE COMPETITIONS WITHOUT ANY MAJOR INJURIES.
GOOD.
ALL THAT'S LEFT...
...IS FOR ALL 161 PAIRS...
...TO CROSS THE FINISH LINE...
PO (PLIP)
ぽっ
PO
ぽっ
OH DEAR...
AS LUCK WOULD HAVE IT...
...IT SEEMS THEY WON'T BE ALLOWED TO FINISH SO EASILY.
PO
ぽっ

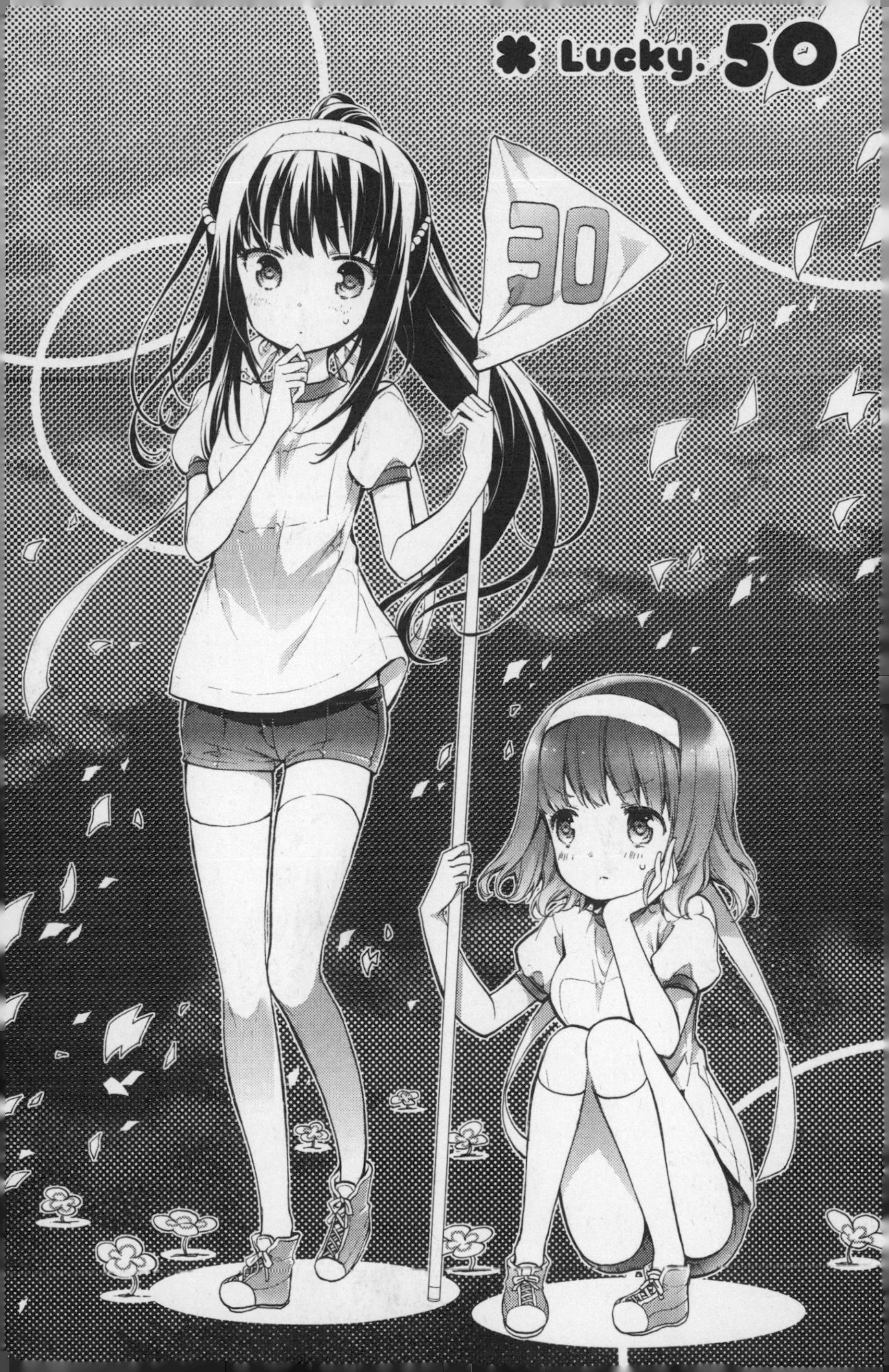

Lucky. 50
30

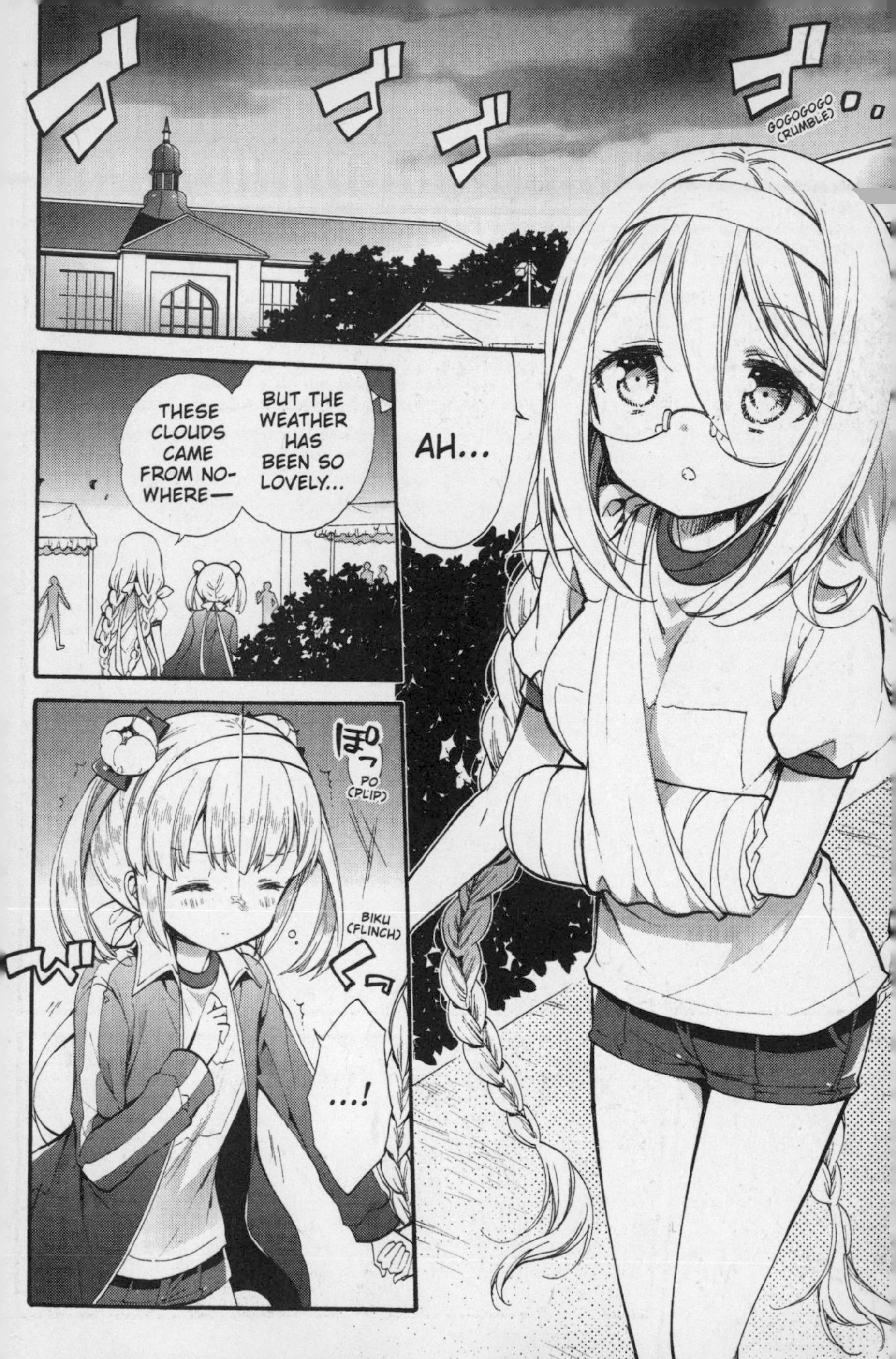
GOGOGOGO
(RUMBLE)
AH...
BUT THE WEATHER HAS BEEN SO LOVELY...
THESE CLOUDS CAME FROM NO-WHERE—
ぽっ
PO
(PLIP)
BIKU
(FLINCH)
...!

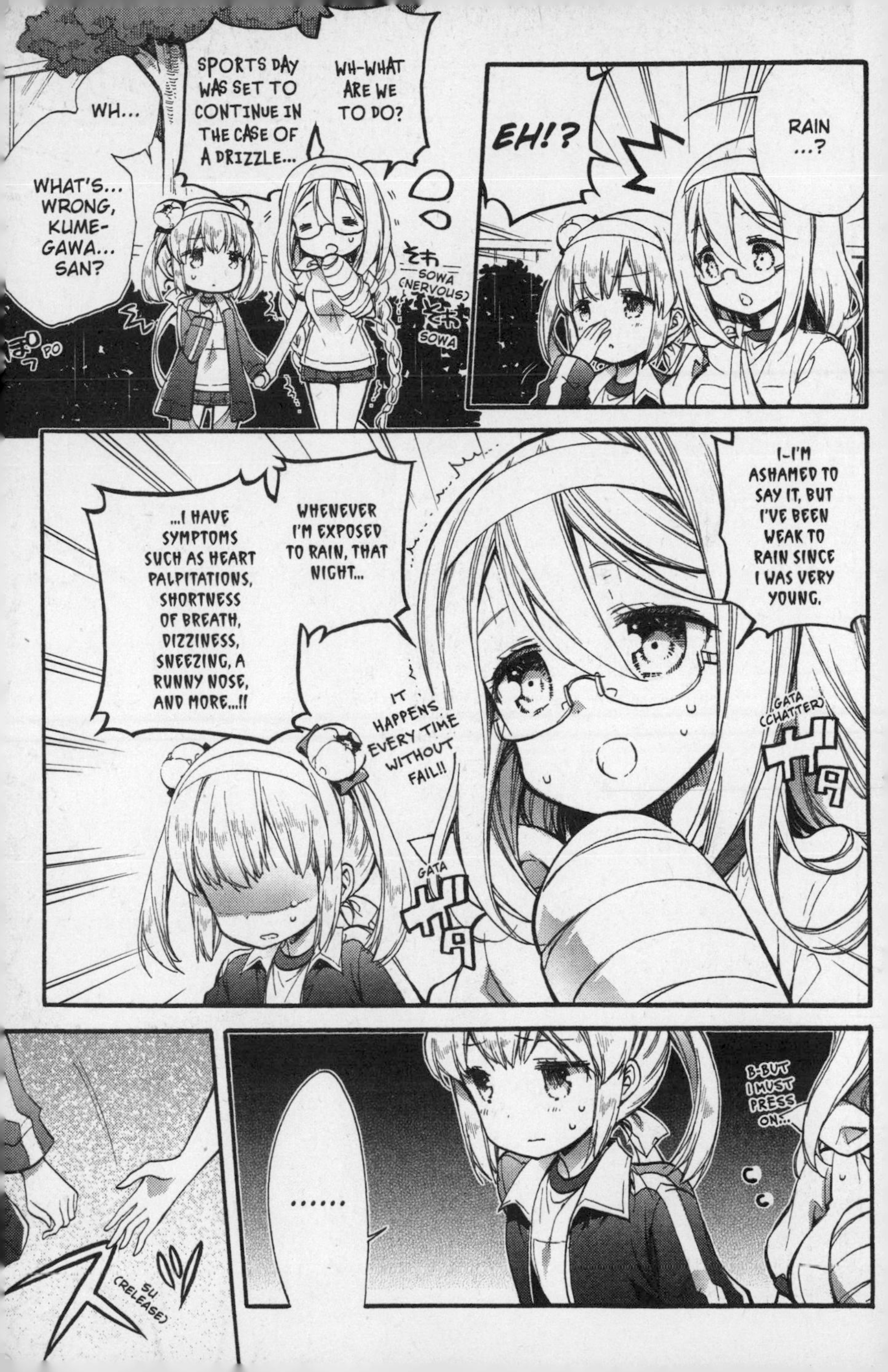
RAIN ...?
EH!?
WH-WHAT ARE WE TO DO?
SPORTS DAY WAS SET TO CONTINUE IN THE CASE OF A DRIZZLE...
WH...
WHAT'S... WRONG, KUME-GAWA... SAN?
そわ SOWA (NERVOUS)
そわ SOWA
ぽつ PO
I-I'M ASHAMED TO SAY IT, BUT I'VE BEEN WEAK TO RAIN SINCE I WAS VERY YOUNG.
GATA (CHATTER)
WHENEVER I'M EXPOSED TO RAIN, THAT NIGHT...
...I HAVE SYMPTOMS SUCH AS HEART PALPITATIONS, SHORTNESS OF BREATH, DIZZINESS, SNEEZING, A RUNNY NOSE, AND MORE...!!
IT HAPPENS EVERY TIME WITHOUT FAIL!!
GATA
B-BUT I MUST PRESS ON...
......
SU (RELEASE)

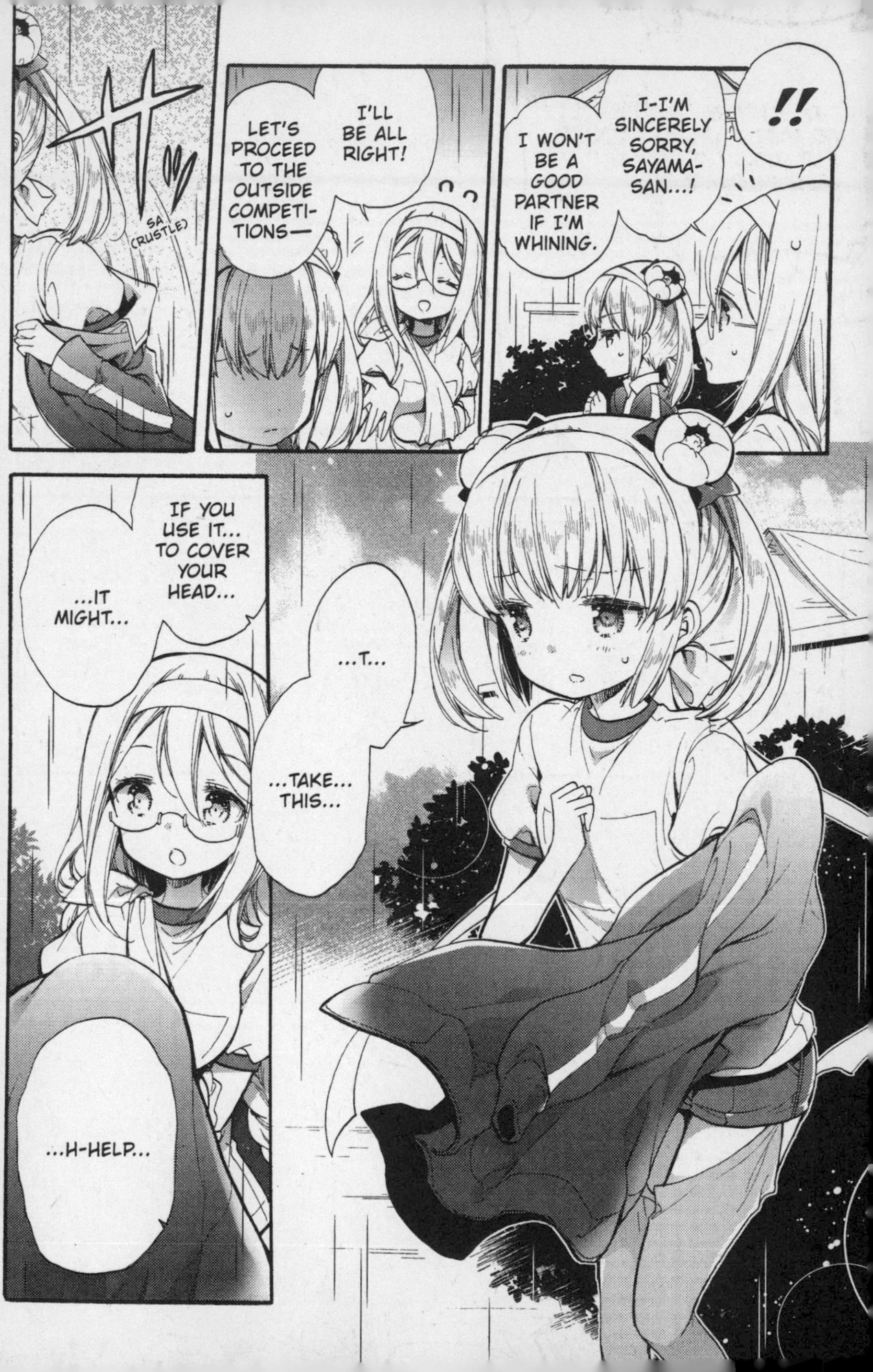
!!
I-I'M SINCERELY SORRY, SAYAMA-SAN...!
I WON'T BE A GOOD PARTNER IF I'M WHINING.
I'LL BE ALL RIGHT!
LET'S PROCEED TO THE OUTSIDE COMPETITIONS—
SA (RUSTLE)
...T...
...TAKE... THIS...
IF YOU USE IT... TO COVER YOUR HEAD...
...IT MIGHT...
...H-HELP...

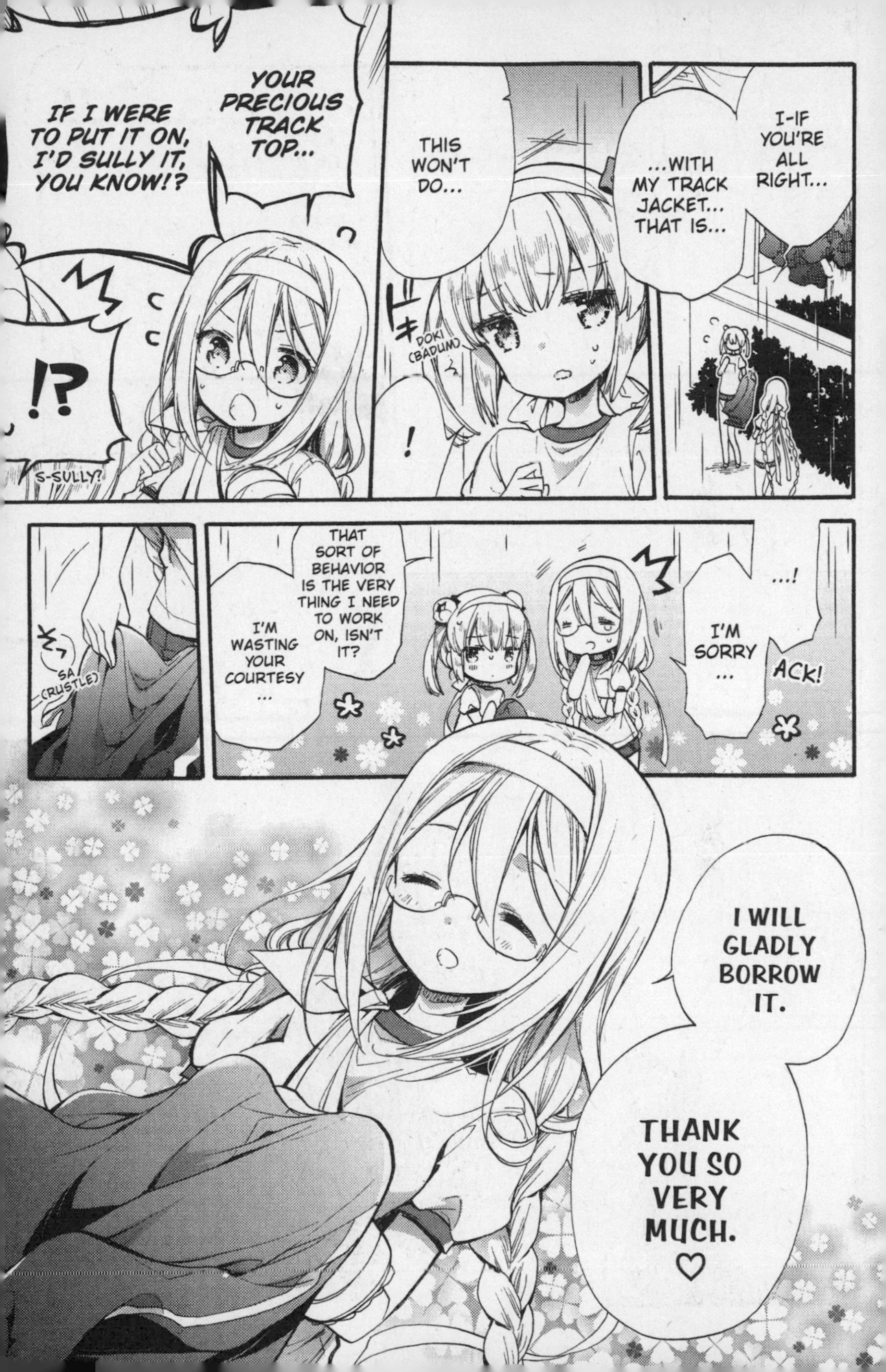
I-IF YOU'RE ALL RIGHT...
...WITH MY TRACK JACKET... THAT IS...
THIS WON'T DO...
DOKI (BADUMP)
!
YOUR PRECIOUS TRACK TOP...
IF I WERE TO PUT IT ON, I'D SULLY IT, YOU KNOW!?
!?
S-SULLY?
...!
I'M SORRY ...
ACK!
THAT SORT OF BEHAVIOR IS THE VERY THING I NEED TO WORK ON, ISN'T IT?
I'M WASTING YOUR COURTESY ...
SA (RUSTLE)
I WILL GLADLY BORROW IT.
THANK YOU SO VERY MUCH. ♡

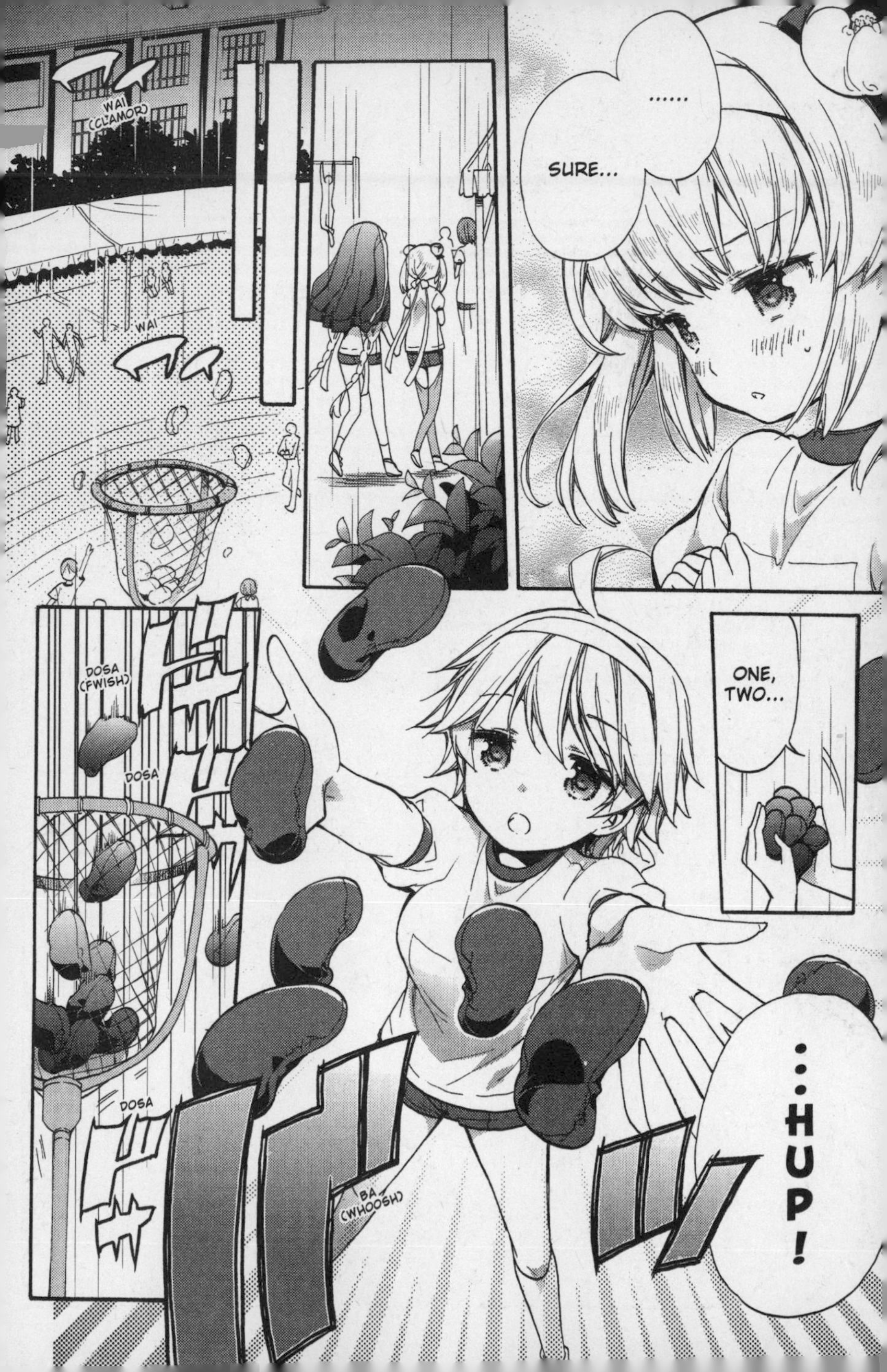
......
SURE...
WAI (CLAMOR)
WAI
ONE, TWO...
...HUP!
BA (WHOOSH)
DOSA (FWISH)
DOSA
DOSA

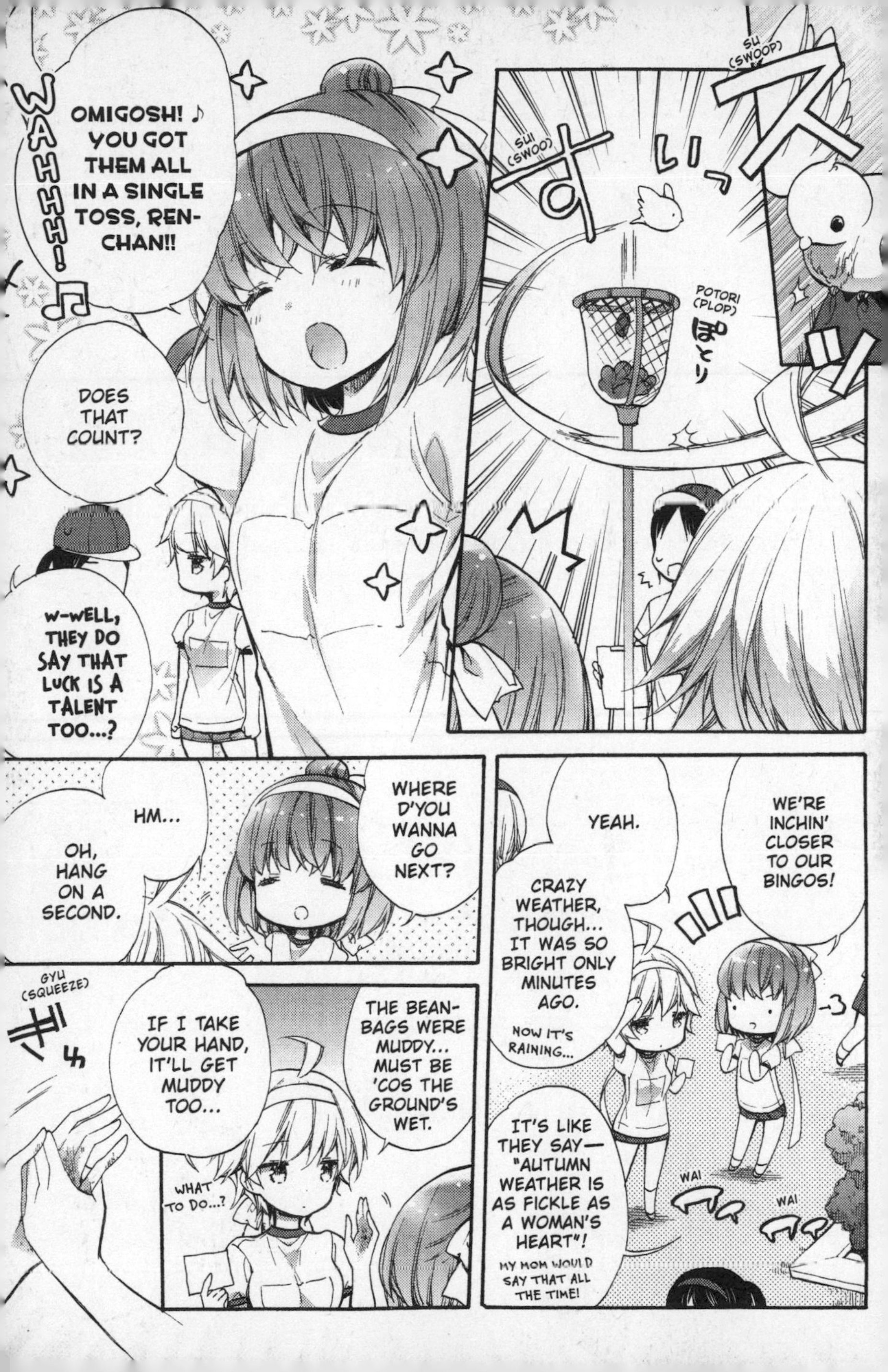
SU (SWOOP)
SUI (SWOO)
POTORI (PLOP)
WAHHHH!
OMIGOSH! ♪ YOU GOT THEM ALL IN A SINGLE TOSS, REN-CHAN!!
DOES THAT COUNT?
W-WELL, THEY DO SAY THAT LUCK IS A TALENT TOO...?
WE'RE INCHIN' CLOSER TO OUR BINGOS!
YEAH.
CRAZY WEATHER, THOUGH... IT WAS SO BRIGHT ONLY MINUTES AGO.
NOW IT'S RAINING...
IT'S LIKE THEY SAY—"AUTUMN WEATHER IS AS FICKLE AS A WOMAN'S HEART"!
MY MOM WOULD SAY THAT ALL THE TIME!
WAI
WAI
WHERE D'YOU WANNA GO NEXT?
HM...
OH, HANG ON A SECOND.
GYU (SQUEEZE)
THE BEAN-BAGS WERE MUDDY... MUST BE 'COS THE GROUND'S WET.
IF I TAKE YOUR HAND, IT'LL GET MUDDY TOO...
WHAT TO DO...?

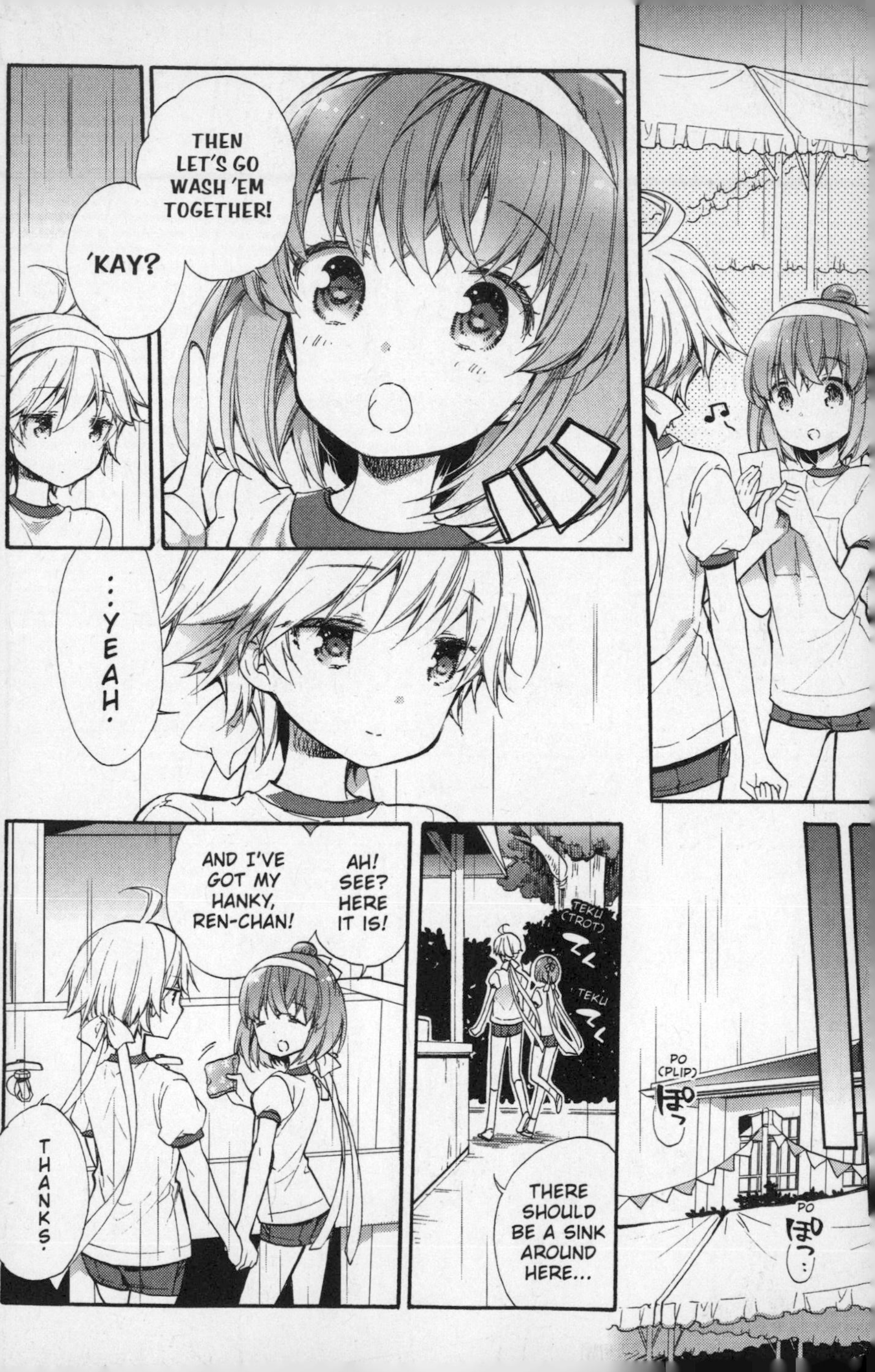

♪
THEN LET'S GO WASH 'EM TOGETHER!
'KAY?
...YEAH.
PO (PLIP)
ぽっ
PO
ぽっ...
TEKU (TROT)
てく
TEKU
てく
THERE SHOULD BE A SINK AROUND HERE...
AH! SEE? HERE IT IS!
AND I'VE GOT MY HANKY, REN-CHAN!
THANKS.

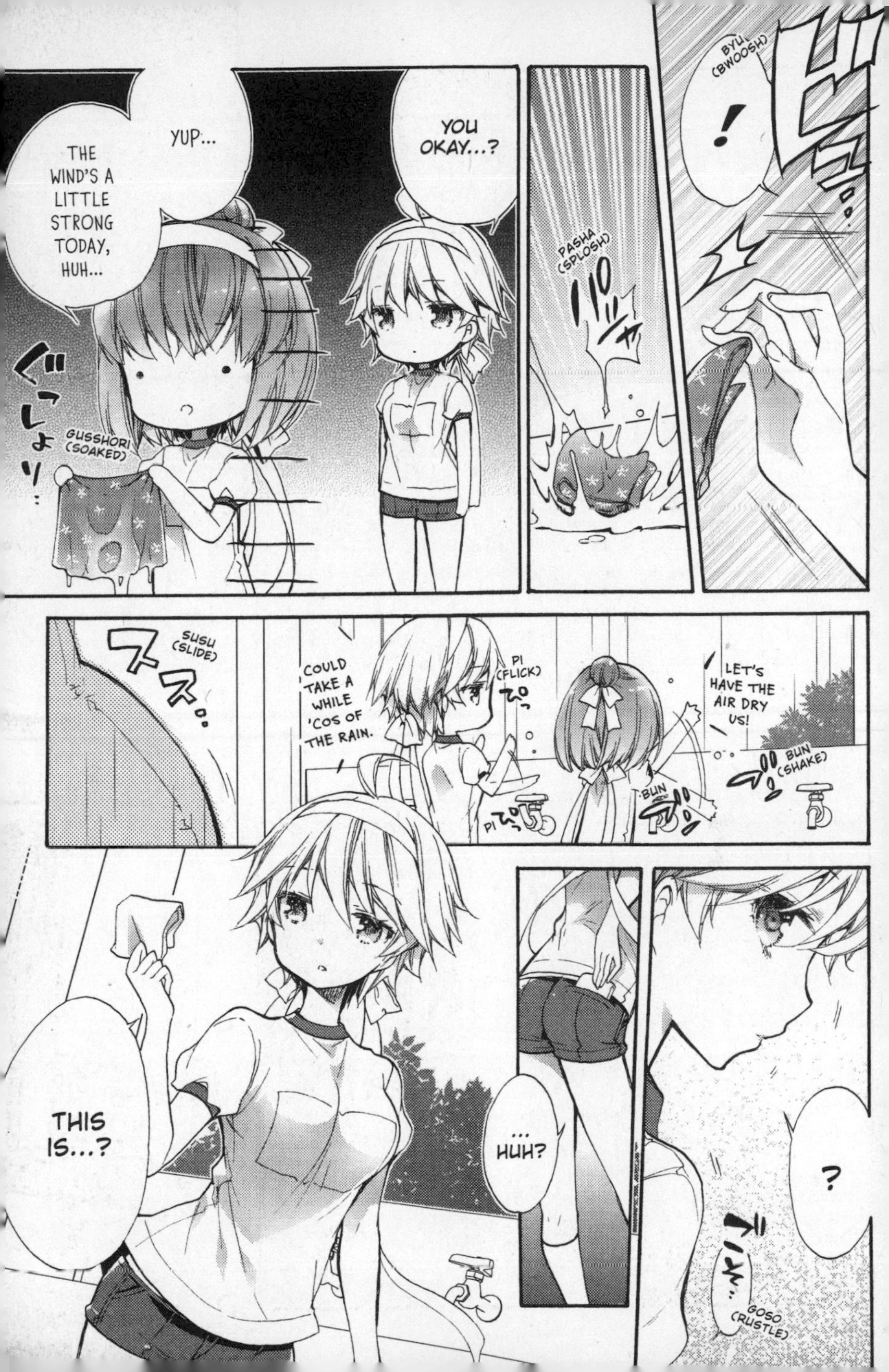
BYU (BWOOSH)
!
PASHA (SPLOSH)
YOU OKAY...?
YUP...
THE WIND'S A LITTLE STRONG TODAY, HUH...
GUSSHORI (SOAKED)
LET'S HAVE THE AIR DRY US!
BUN (SHAKE)
BUN
PI (FLICK)
COULD TAKE A WHILE 'COS OF THE RAIN.
PI
SUSU (SLIDE)
?
GOSO (RUSTLE)
...HUH?
THIS IS...?

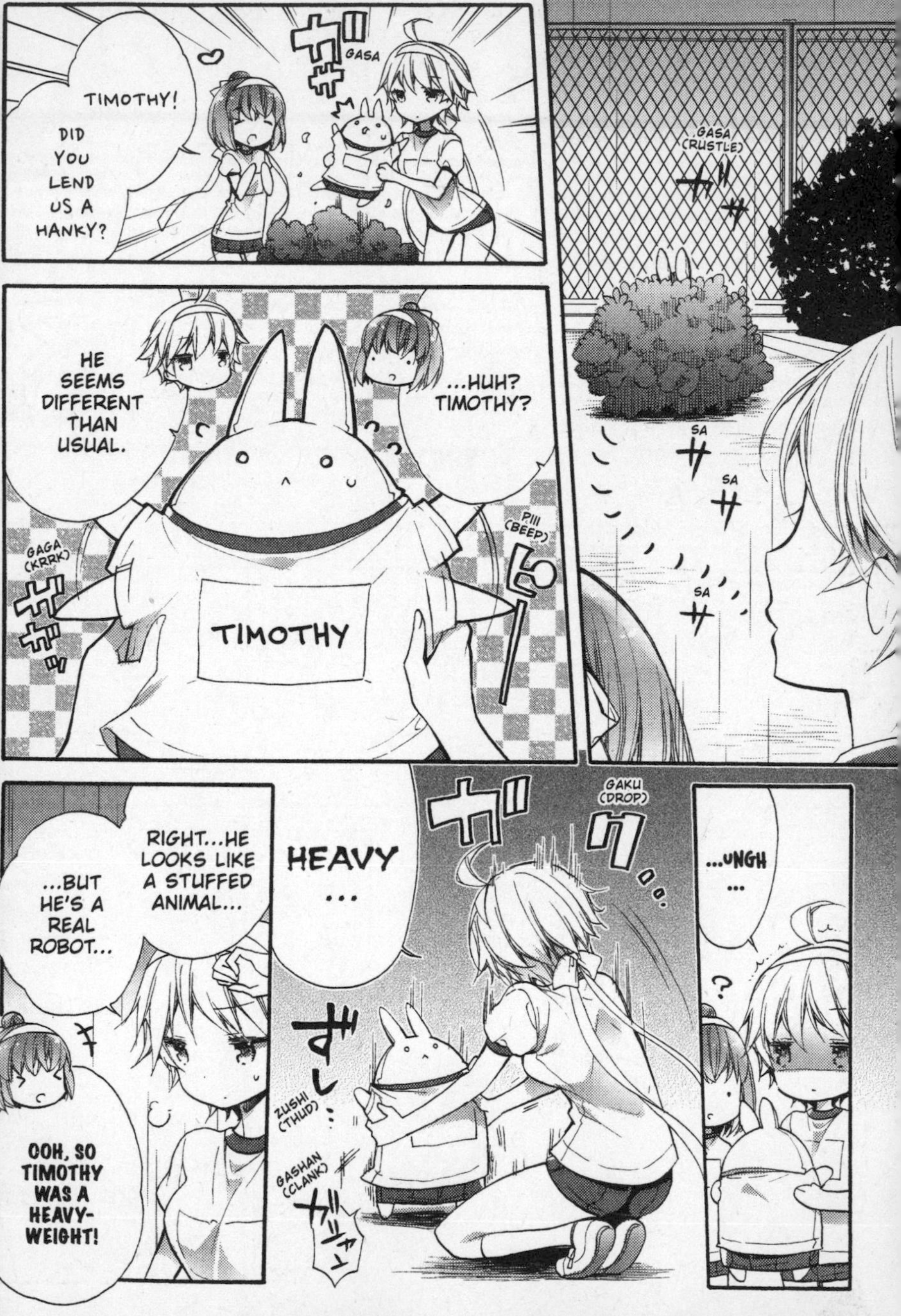
GASA (RUSTLE)
SA
SA
SA
GASA
TIMOTHY!
DID YOU LEND US A HANKY?
...HUH? TIMOTHY?
HE SEEMS DIFFERENT THAN USUAL.
PIII (BEEP)
GAGA (KRRK)
TIMOTHY
...UNGH ...
GAKU (DROP)
HEAVY ...
ZUSHI (THUD)
GASHAN (CLANK)
RIGHT...HE LOOKS LIKE A STUFFED ANIMAL...
...BUT HE'S A REAL ROBOT...
OOH, SO TIMOTHY WAS A HEAVY-WEIGHT!

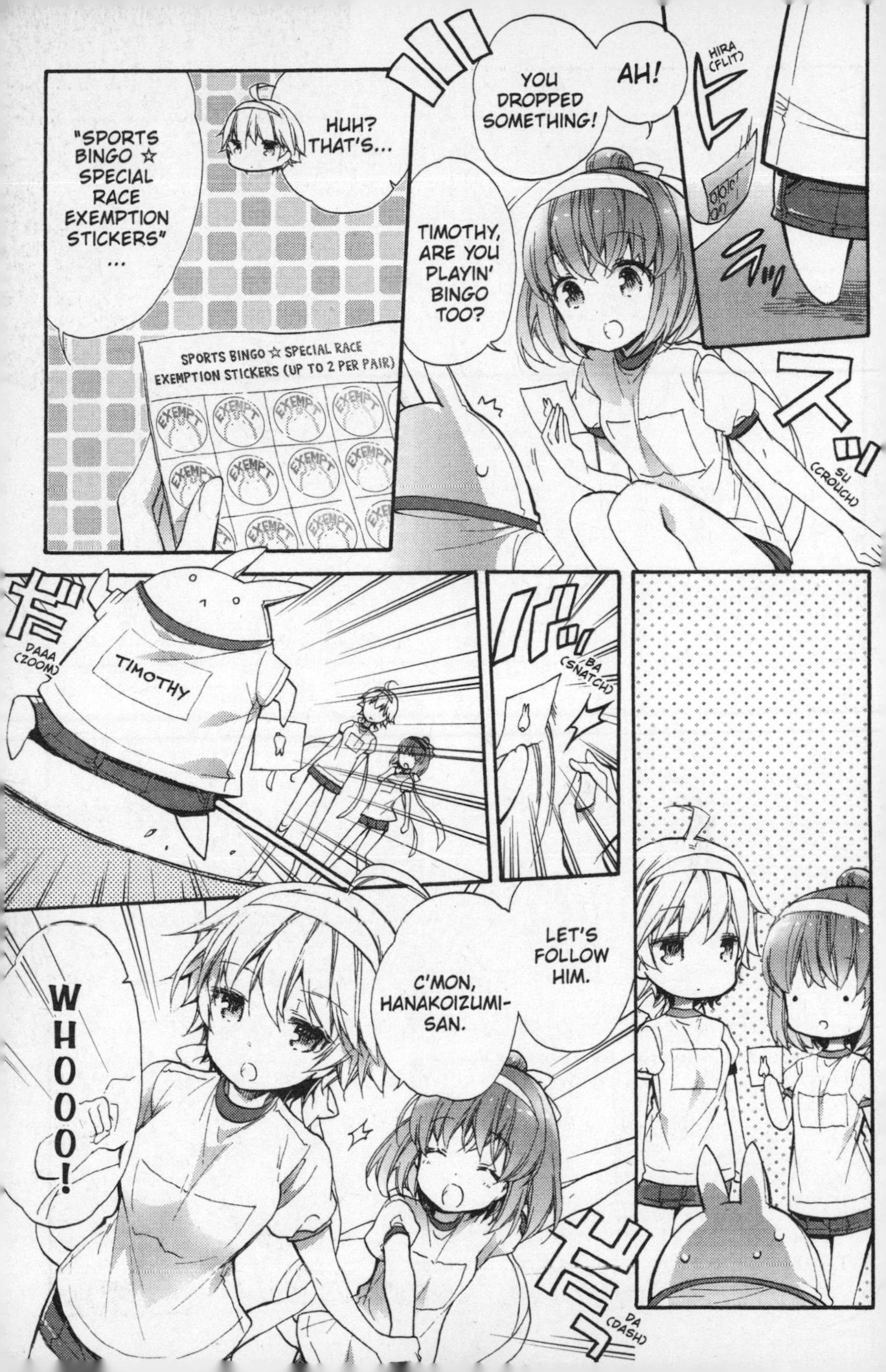
HIRA (FLIT)
AH!
YOU DROPPED SOMETHING!
TIMOTHY, ARE YOU PLAYIN' BINGO TOO?
SU (CROUCH)
HUH? THAT'S...
"SPORTS BINGO ☆ SPECIAL RACE EXEMPTION STICKERS" ...
SPORTS BINGO ☆ SPECIAL RACE EXEMPTION STICKERS (UP TO 2 PER PAIR)
EXEMPT
BA (SNATCH)
DAAA (ZOOM)
TIMOTHY
DA (DASH)
LET'S FOLLOW HIM.
C'MON, HANAKOIZUMI-SAN.
WHOOOO!

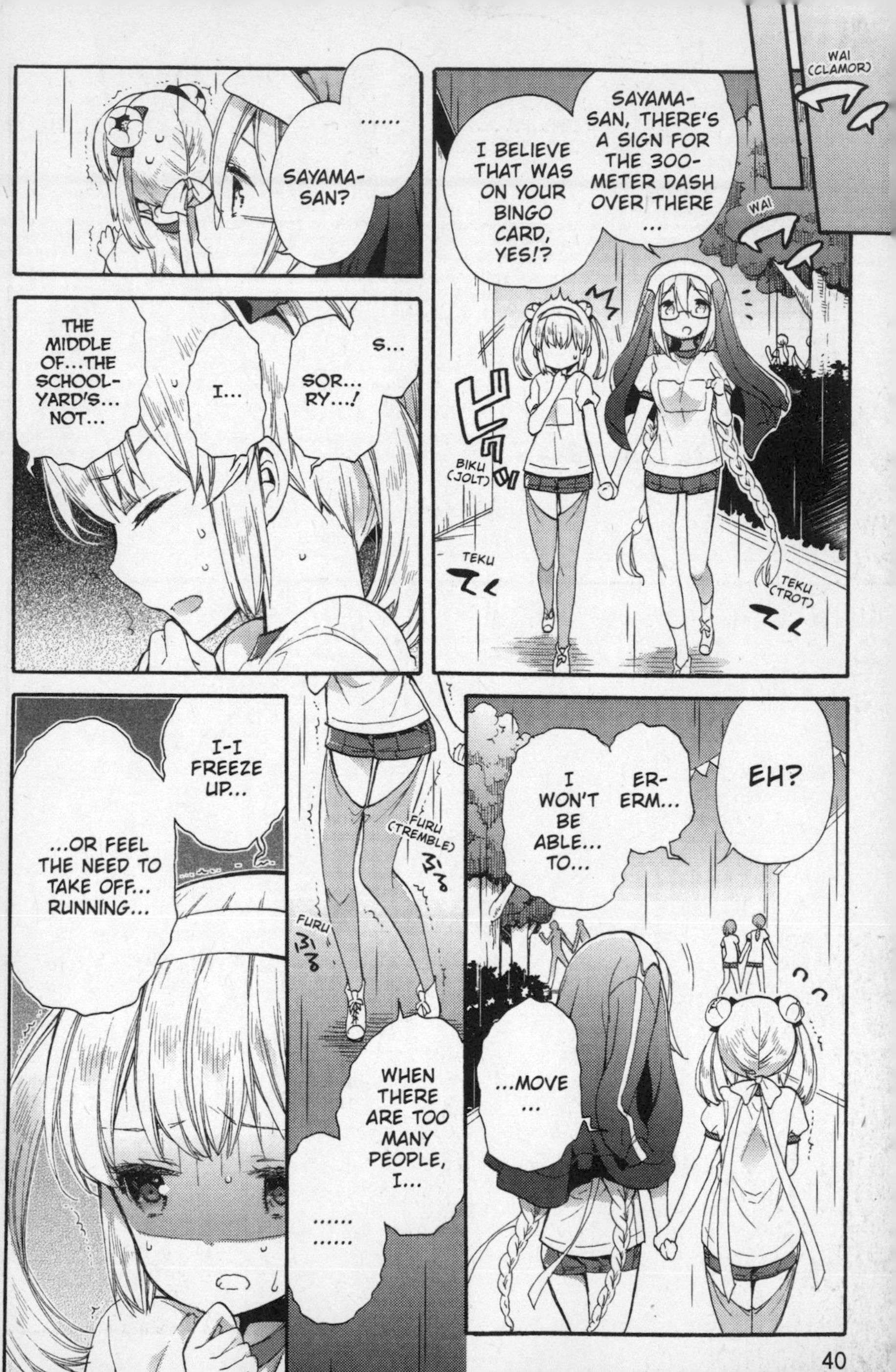
WAI (CLAMOR)
SAYAMA-SAN, THERE'S A SIGN FOR THE 300-METER DASH OVER THERE ...
I BELIEVE THAT WAS ON YOUR BINGO CARD, YES!?
WAI
BIKU (JOLT)
TEKU (TROT)
TEKU
......
SAYAMA-SAN?
S... SOR... RY...!
I...
THE MIDDLE OF...THE SCHOOLYARD'S... NOT...
EH?
ER- ERM...
I WON'T BE ABLE... TO...
...MOVE ...
FURU (TREMBLE)
FURU
WHEN THERE ARE TOO MANY PEOPLE, I...
....
I-I FREEZE UP...
...OR FEEL THE NEED TO TAKE OFF... RUNNING...

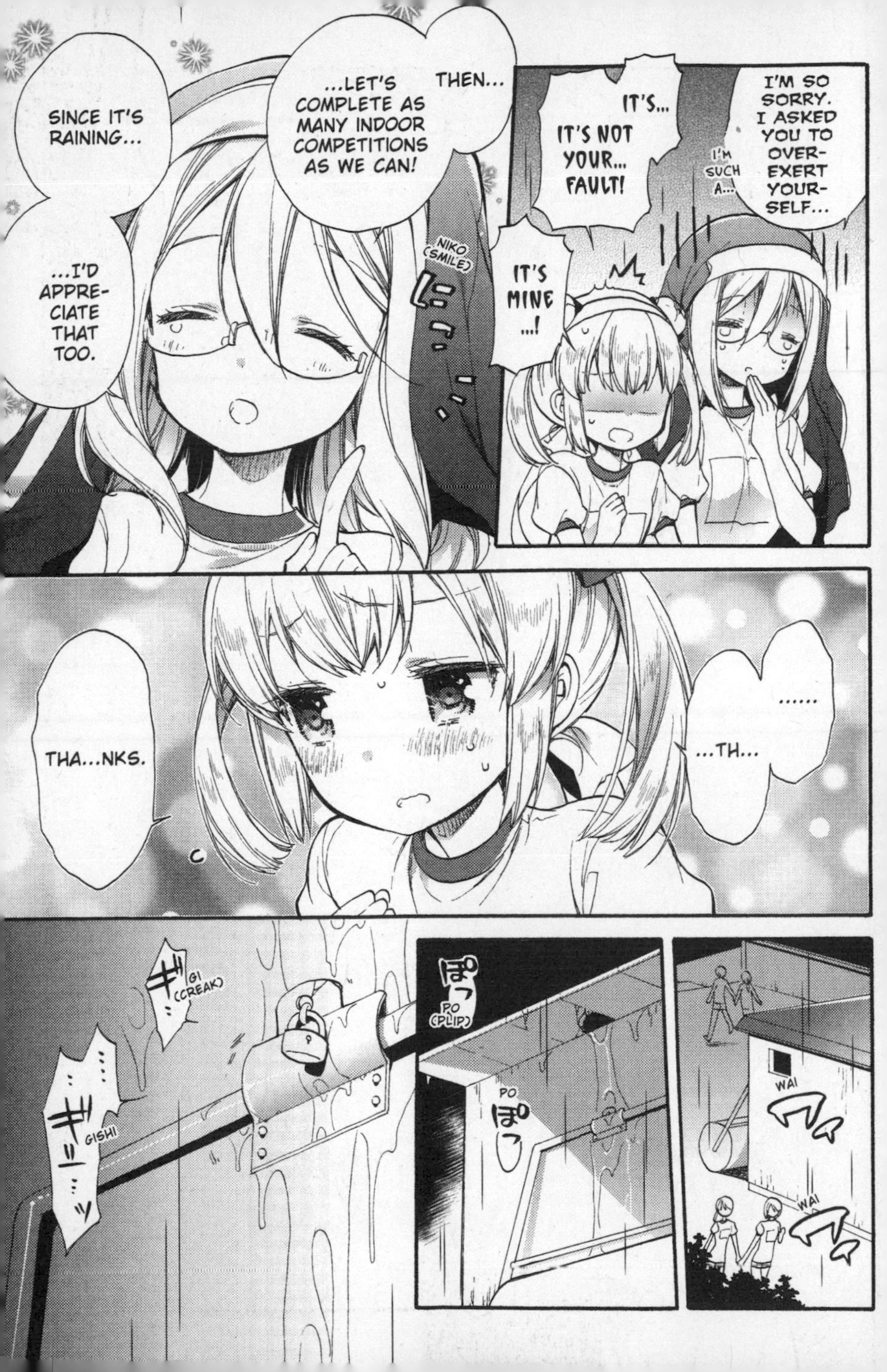
I'M SO SORRY. I ASKED YOU TO OVER-EXERT YOURSELF...
I'M SUCH A...
IT'S... IT'S NOT YOUR... FAULT!
IT'S MINE...!
THEN...
...LET'S COMPLETE AS MANY INDOOR COMPETITIONS AS WE CAN!
NIKO (SMILE)
SINCE IT'S RAINING...
...I'D APPRECIATE THAT TOO.
......
...TH...
THA...NKS.
WAI
WAI
ぽっ
PO (PLIP)
ぽっ
PO
ギ
GI (CREAK)
ギシッ
GISHI

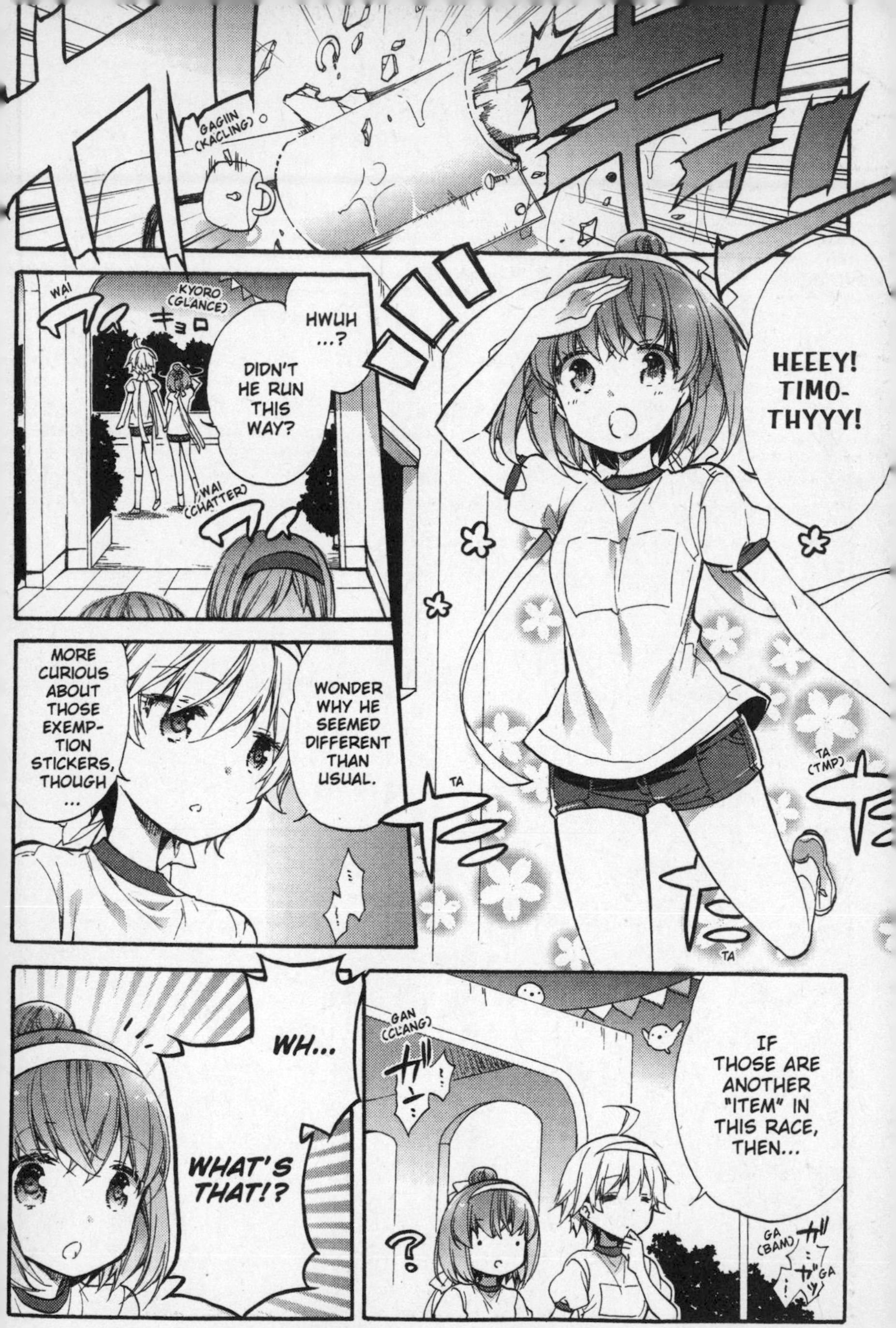
GAGIIN (KACLING)
HEEEY! TIMOTHYYY!
TA (TMP)
TA
TA
KYORO (GLANCE)
キョロ
HWUH ...?
DIDN'T HE RUN THIS WAY?
WAI
WAI (CHATTER)
WONDER WHY HE SEEMED DIFFERENT THAN USUAL.
MORE CURIOUS ABOUT THOSE EXEMPTION STICKERS, THOUGH ...
IF THOSE ARE ANOTHER "ITEM" IN THIS RACE, THEN...
GAN (CLANG)
GA (BAM)
GA
WH...
WHAT'S THAT!?

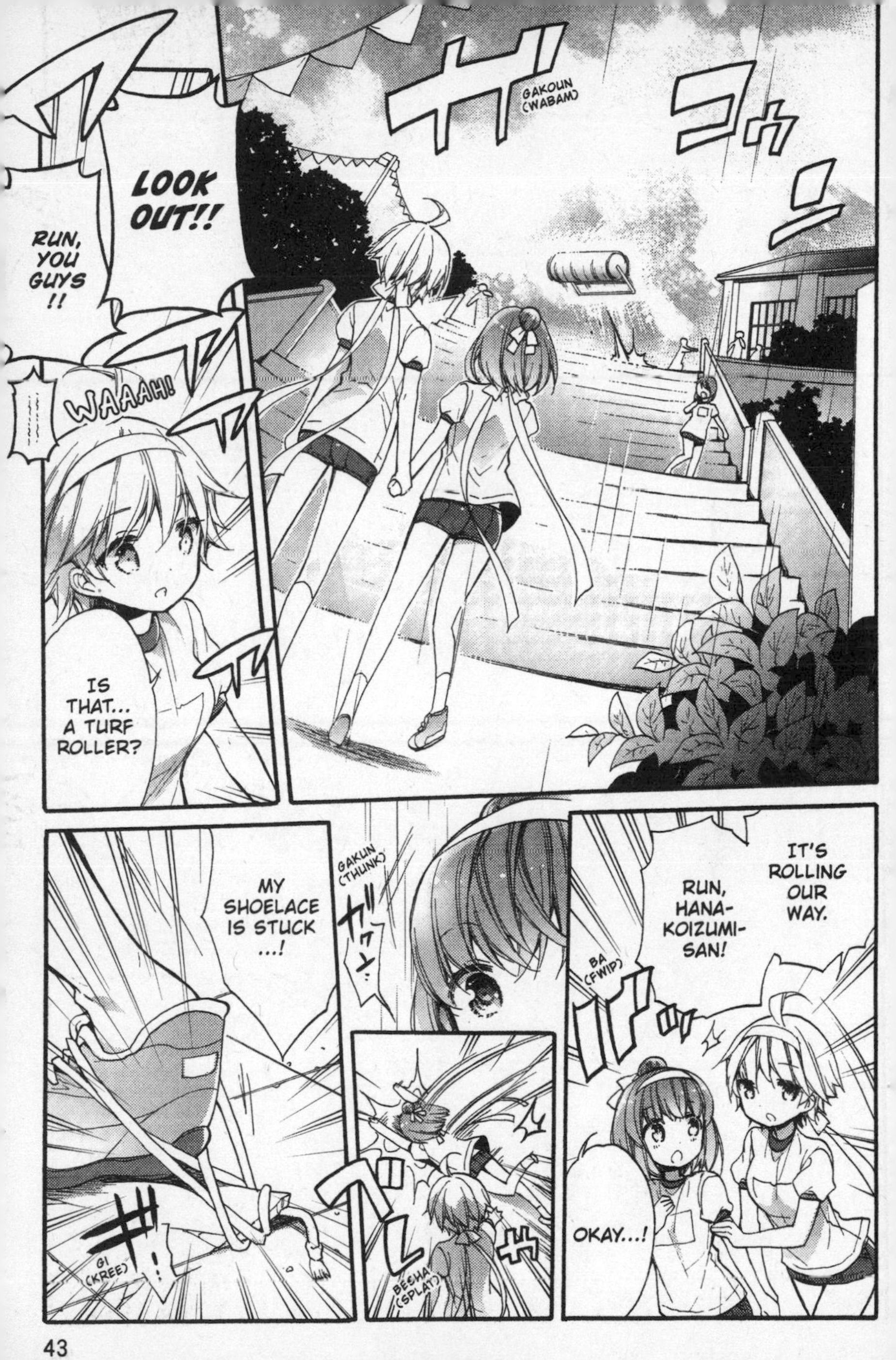
GAKOUN (WABAM)
LOOK OUT!!
RUN, YOU GUYS !!
WAAAH!
IS THAT... A TURF ROLLER?
IT'S ROLLING OUR WAY.
RUN, HANA-KOIZUMI-SAN!
BA (FWIP)
OKAY...!
GAKUN (THUNK)
BESHA (SPLAT)
MY SHOELACE IS STUCK ...!
GI (KREE)

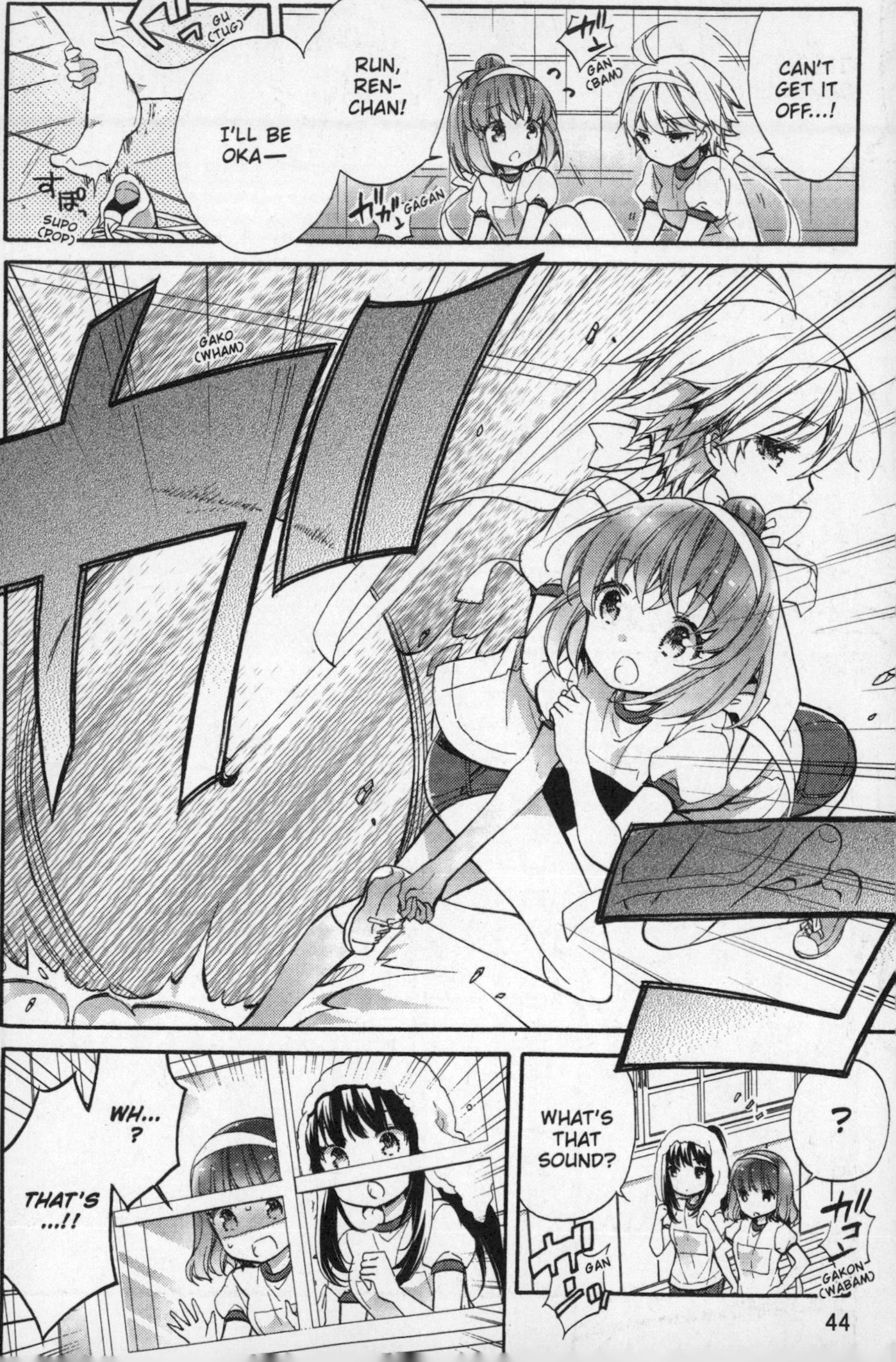
CAN'T GET IT OFF...!
GAN (BAM)
RUN, REN-CHAN!
I'LL BE OKA—
GAGAN
GU (TUG)
すぽ、
SUPO (POP)
GAKO (WHAM)
?
WHAT'S THAT SOUND?
GAKON (WABAM)
GAN
WH... ?
THAT'S ...!!

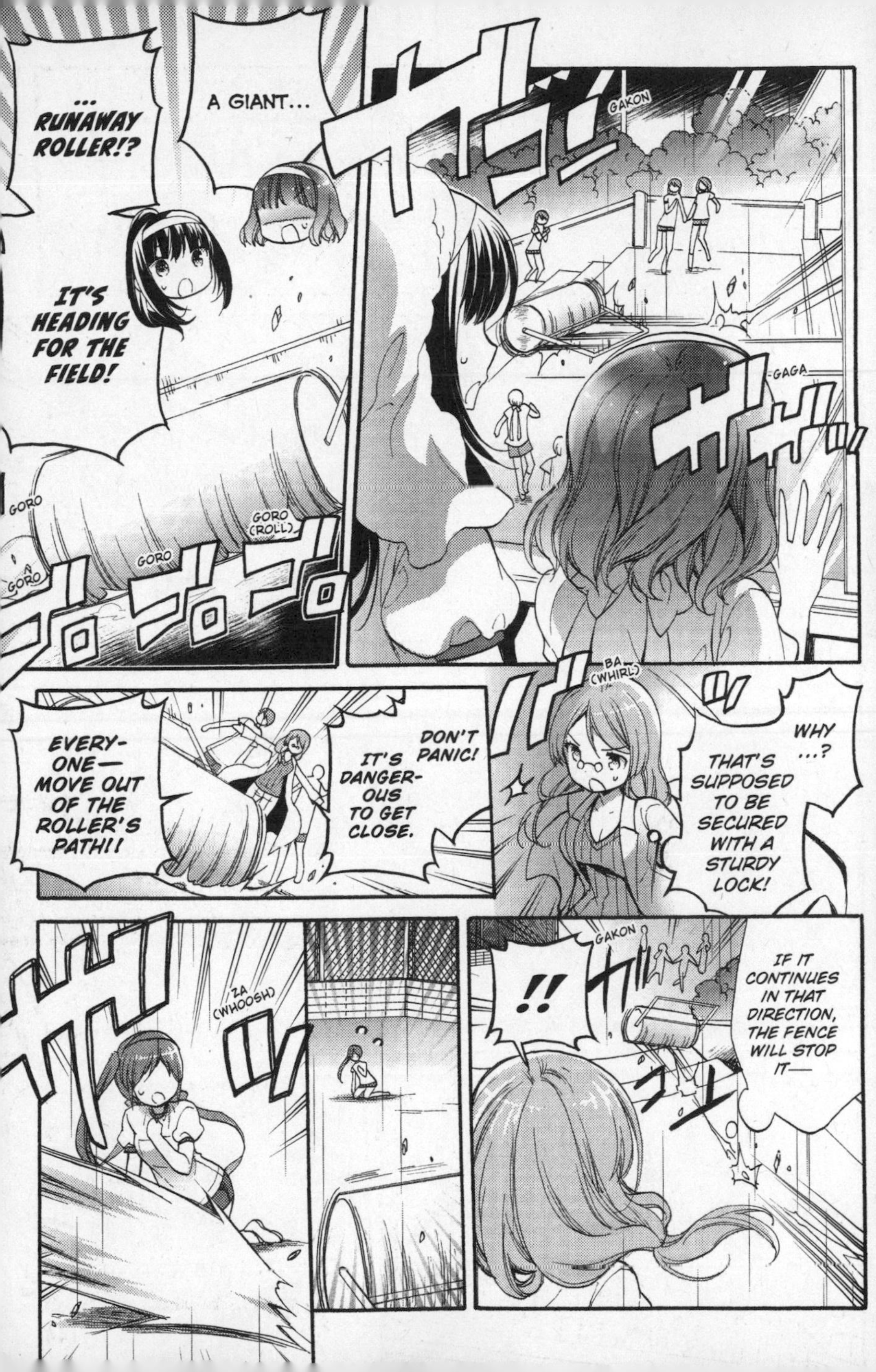
GAKON
GAGA
A GIANT...
... RUNAWAY ROLLER!?
IT'S HEADING FOR THE FIELD!
GORO
GORO (ROLL)
GORO
GORO
BA (WHIRL)
WHY ...?
THAT'S SUPPOSED TO BE SECURED WITH A STURDY LOCK!
DON'T PANIC!
IT'S DANGER-OUS TO GET CLOSE.
EVERY-ONE— MOVE OUT OF THE ROLLER'S PATH!!
GAKON
IF IT CONTINUES IN THAT DIRECTION, THE FENCE WILL STOP IT—
!!
ZA (WHOOSH)

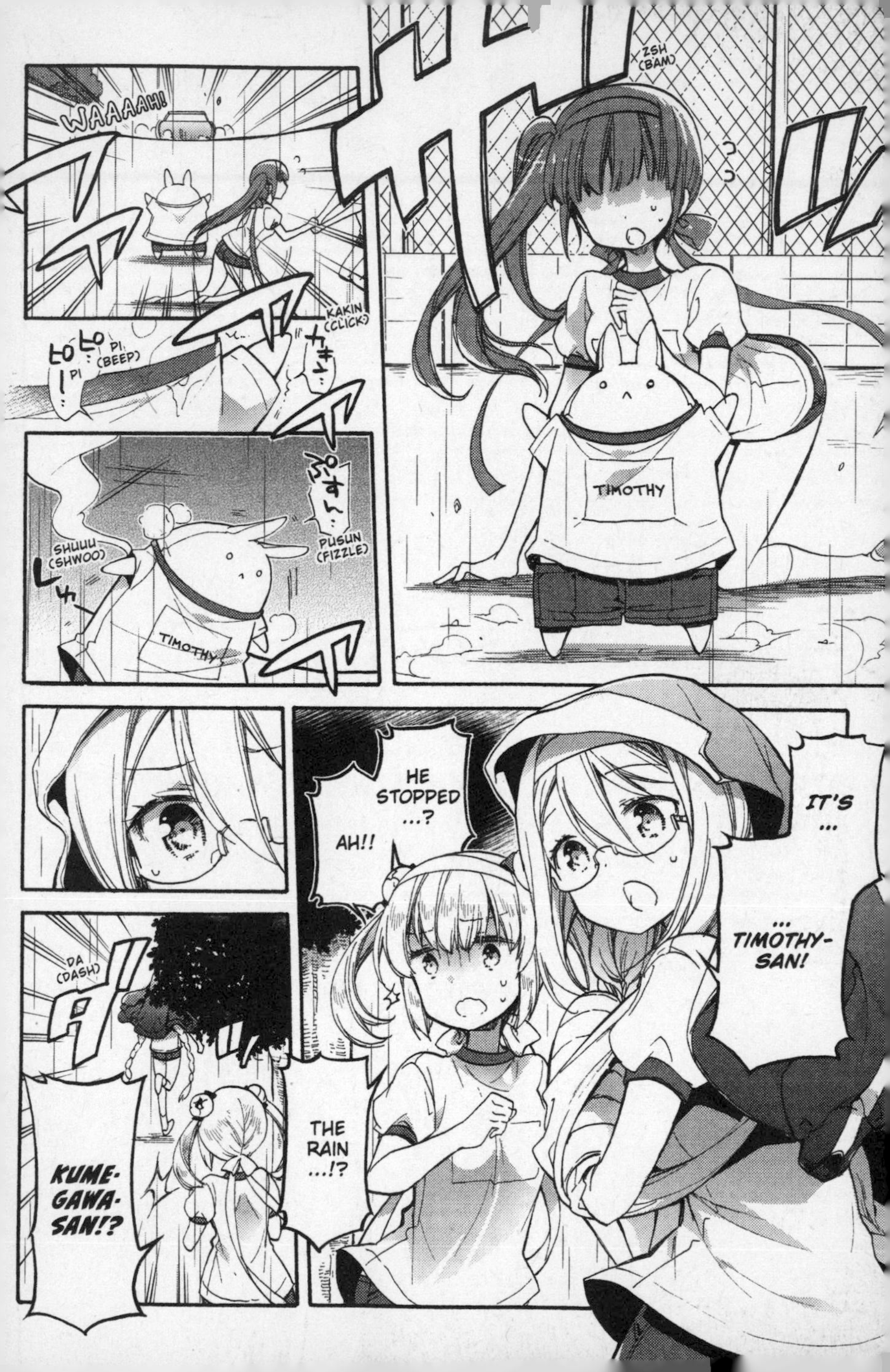
ZSH (BAM)
WAAAAH!
KAKIN (CLICK)
PI PI (BEEP) PI
ぷすん…
PUSUN (FIZZLE)
SHUUU (SHWOO)
IT'S ...
... TIMOTHY-SAN!
HE STOPPED ...?
AH!!
THE RAIN ...!?
DA (DASH)
KUME-GAWA-SAN!?

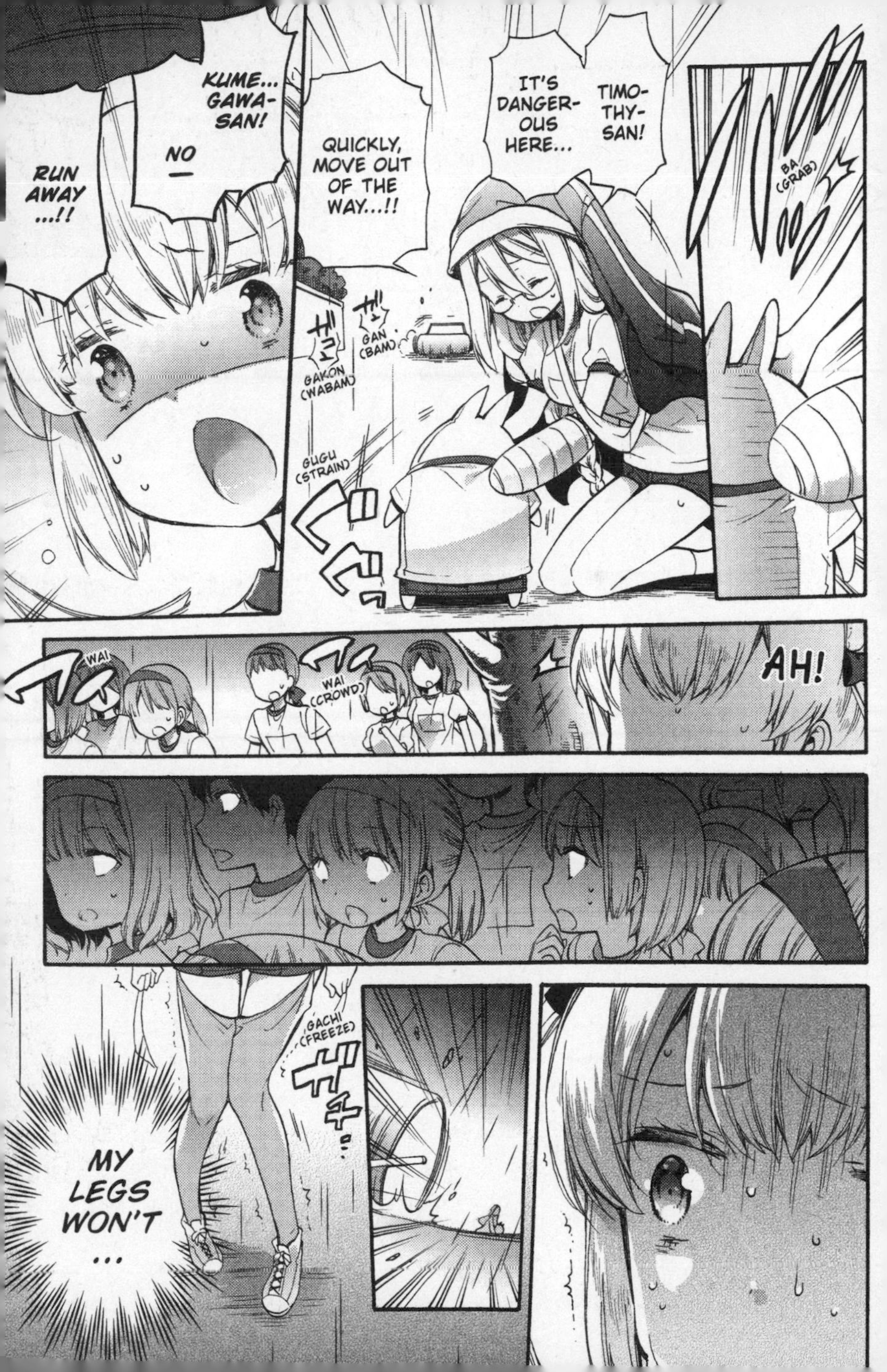
BA (GRAB)
TIMO-THY-SAN!
IT'S DANGER-OUS HERE...
QUICKLY, MOVE OUT OF THE WAY...!!
GAN (BAM)
GAKON (WABAM)
GUGU (STRAIN)
KUME... GAWA-SAN!
NO—
RUN AWAY ...!!
AH!
WAI (CROWD)
WAI
GACHI (FREEZE)
MY LEGS WON'T ...

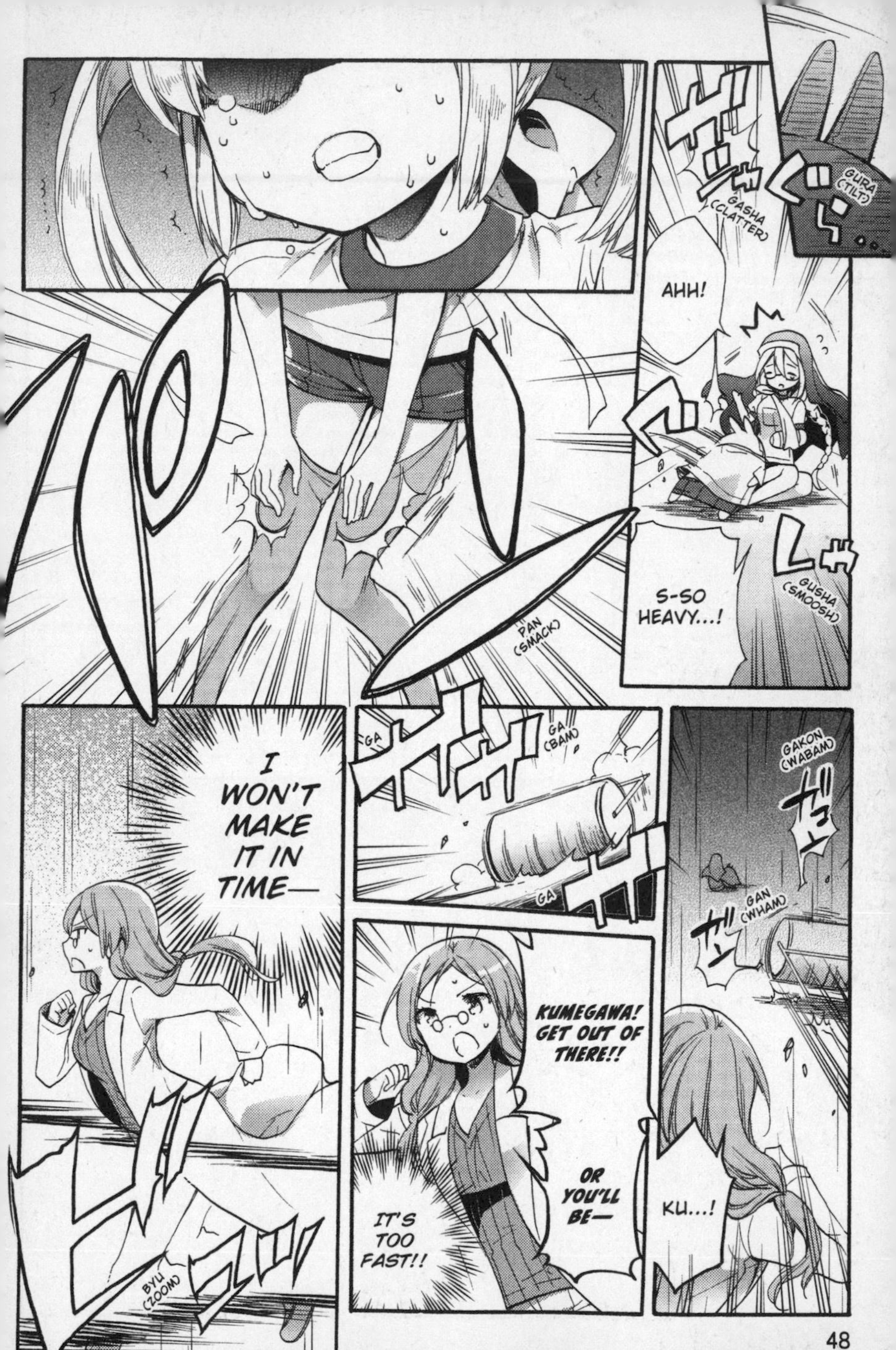
GURA (TILT)
GASHA (CLATTER)
AHH!
GUSHA (SMOOSH)
S-SO HEAVY...!
PAN (SMACK)
GAKON (WABAM)
GAN (WHAM)
KU...!
GA
GA (BAM)
GA
KUMEGAWA! GET OUT OF THERE!!
OR YOU'LL BE—
IT'S TOO FAST!!
I WON'T MAKE IT IN TIME—
BYU (ZOOM)

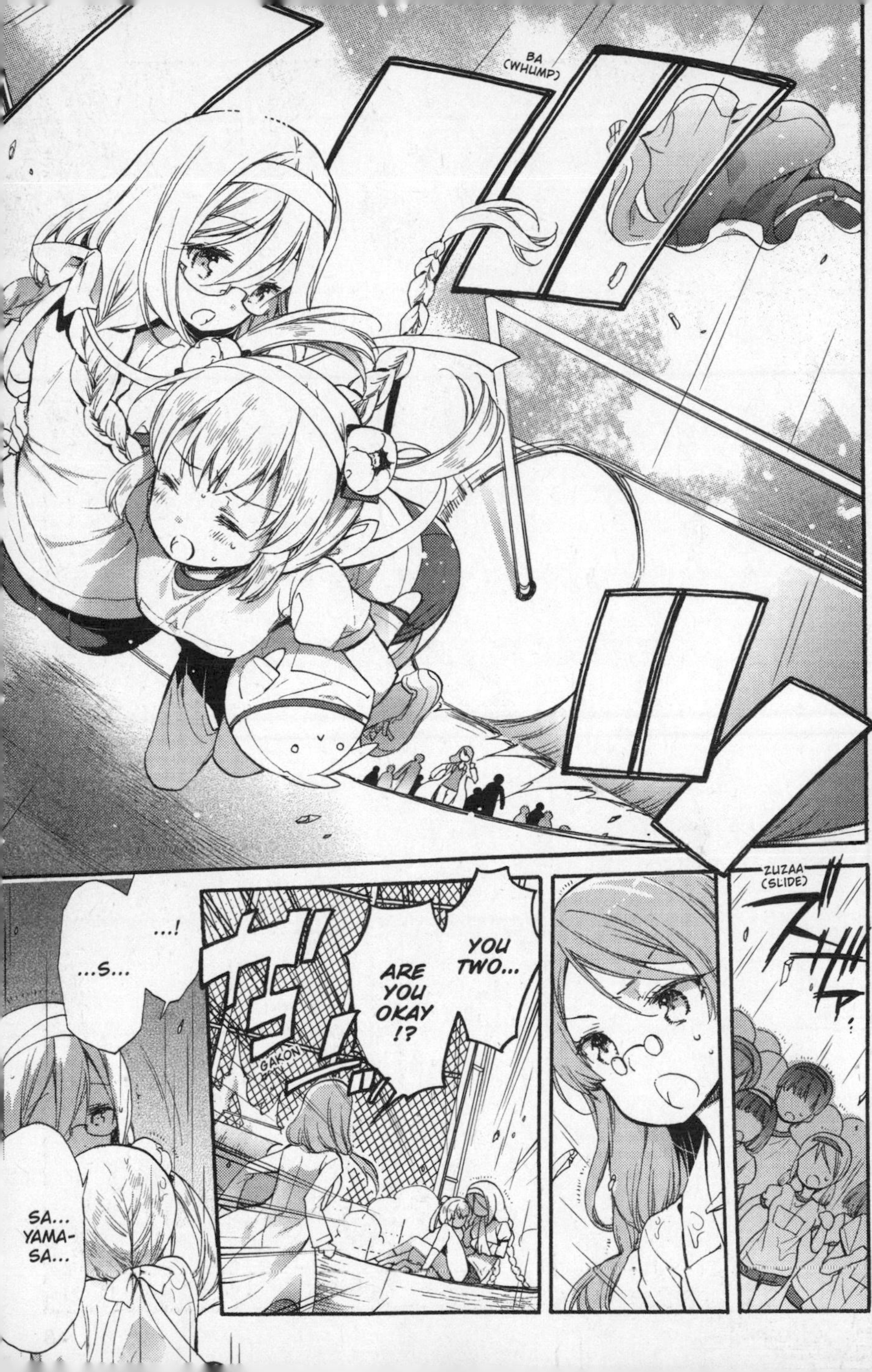
BA (WHUMP)
ZUZAA (SLIDE)
YOU TWO...
ARE YOU OKAY !?
GAKON
...!
...S...
SA... YAMA-SA...

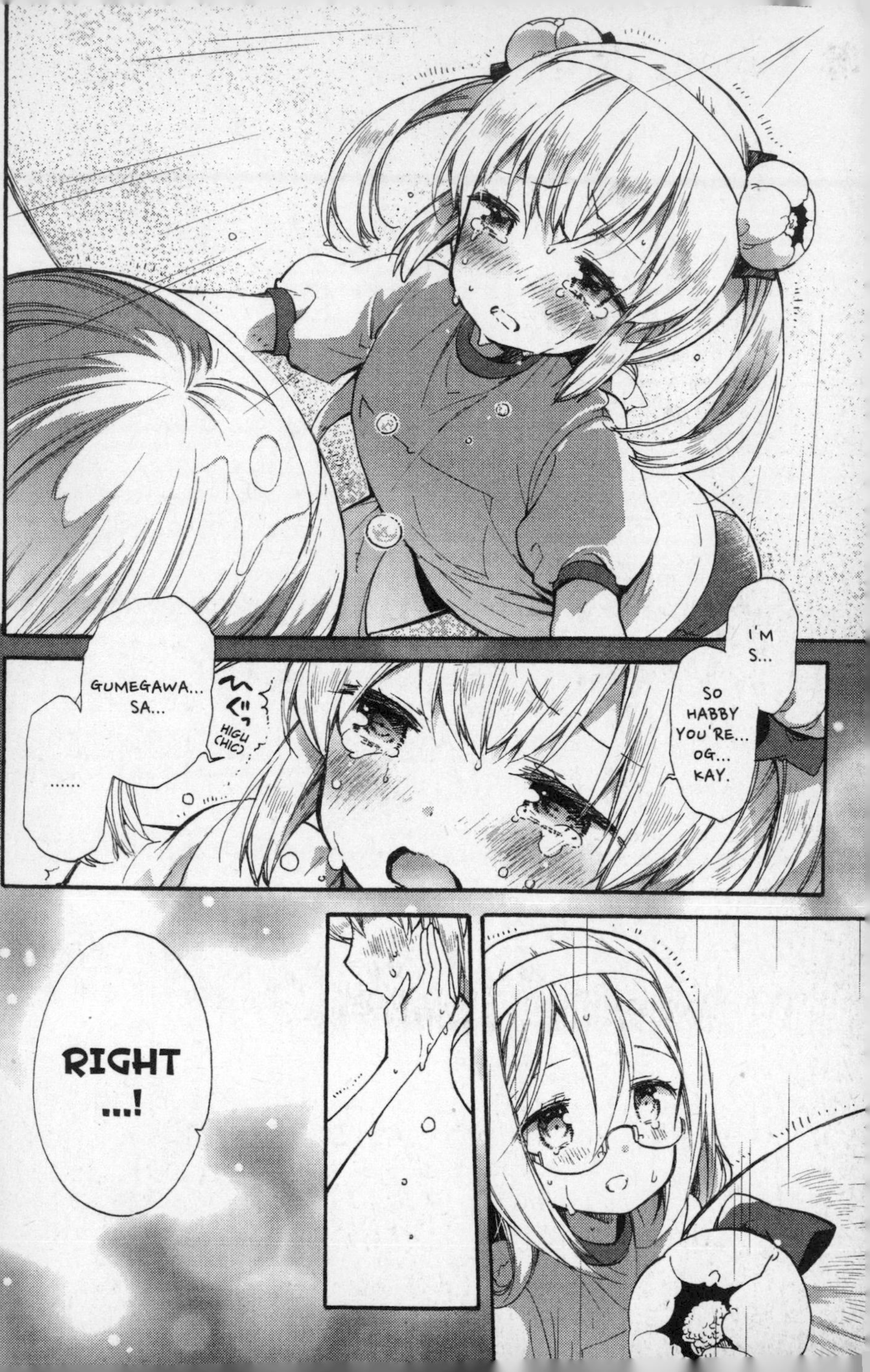

I'M S...
SO HABBY YOU'RE... OG... KAY.
HIGU (HIC)
GUMEGAWA... SA...
......
RIGHT ...!

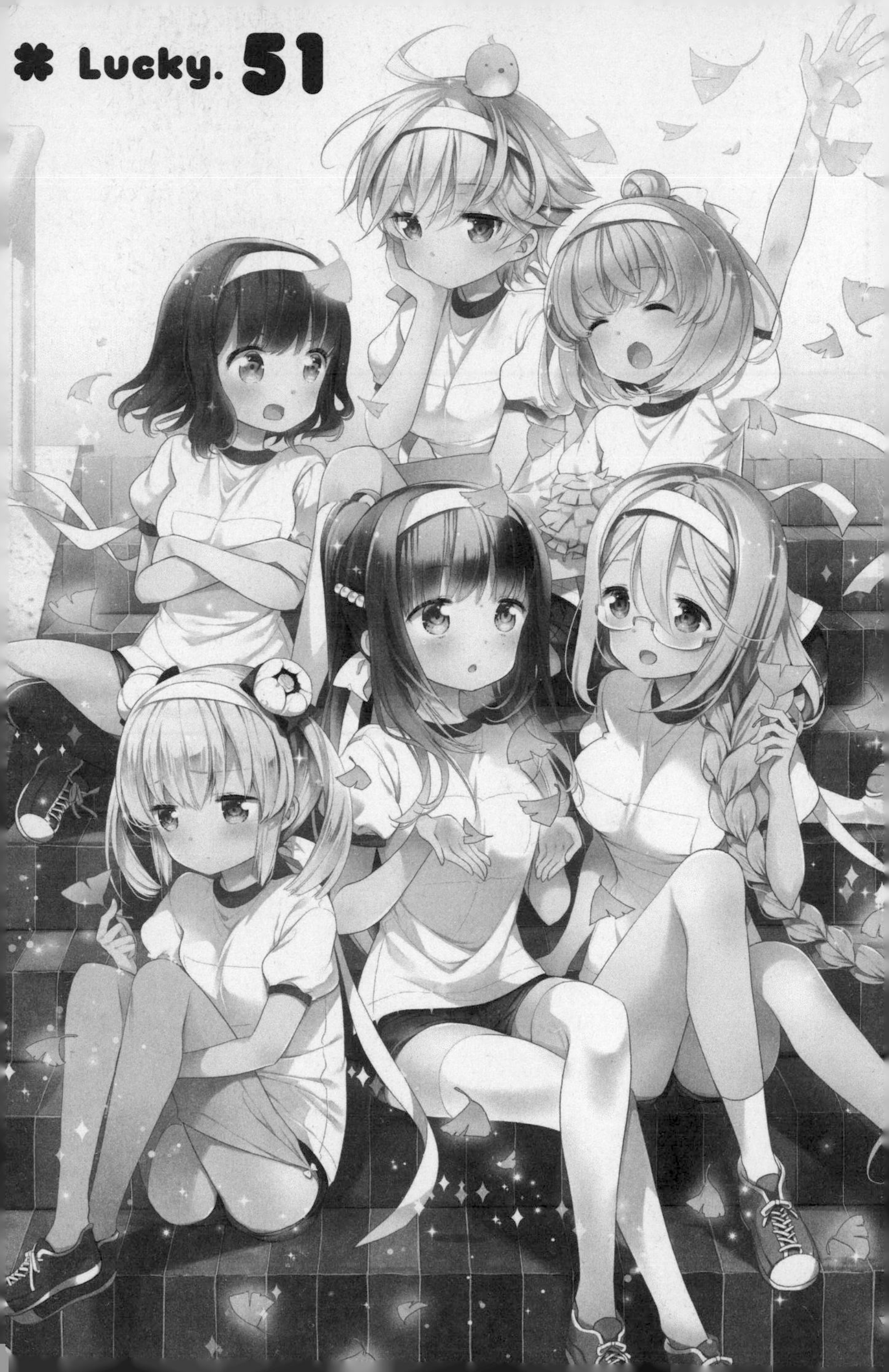
Lucky. 51

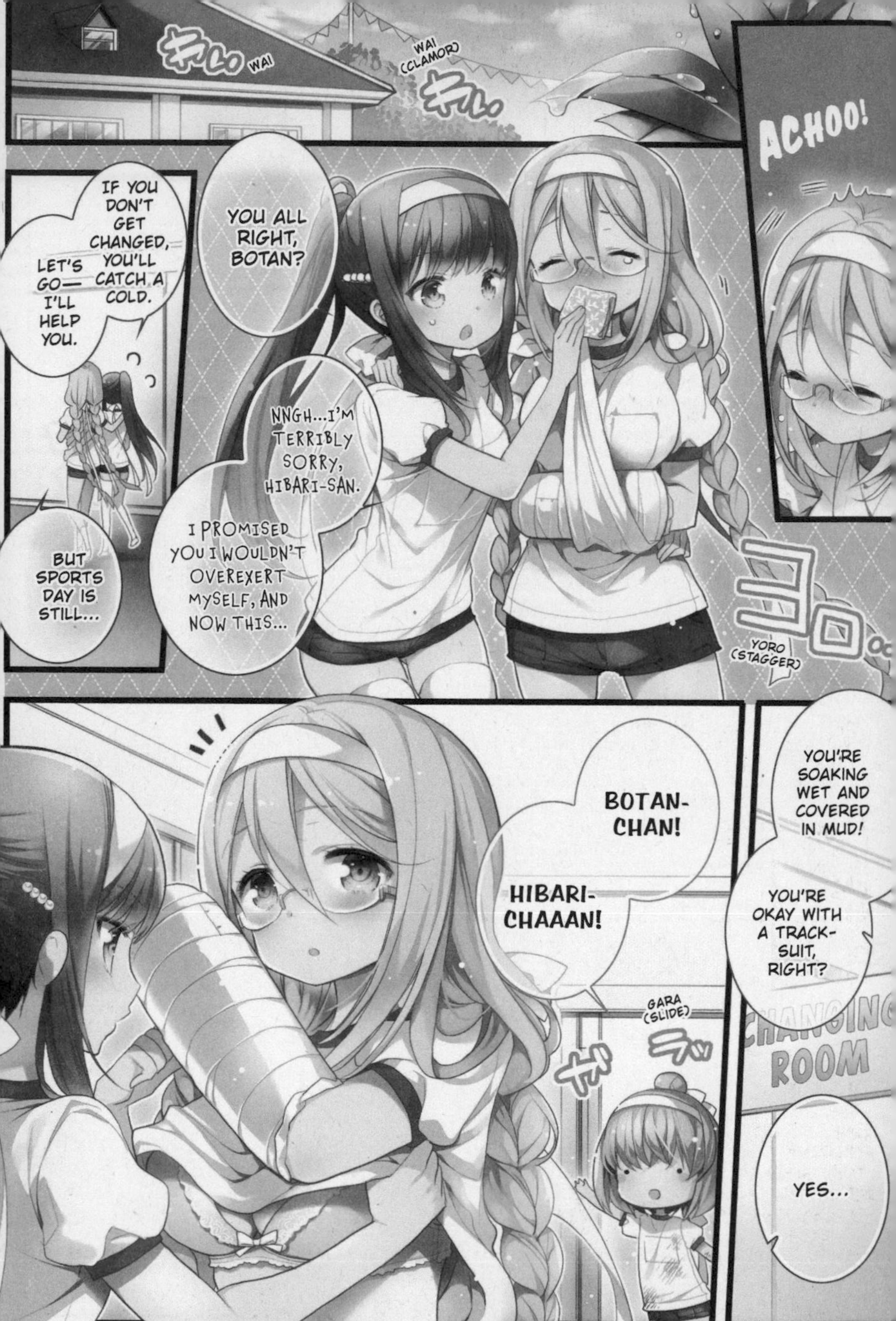
ACHOO!
WAI
WAI (CLAMOR)
YOU ALL RIGHT, BOTAN?
NNGH...I'M TERRIBLY SORRY, HIBARI-SAN.
I PROMISED YOU I WOULDN'T OVEREXERT MYSELF, AND NOW THIS...
YORO (STAGGER)
IF YOU DON'T GET CHANGED, YOU'LL CATCH A COLD.
LET'S GO— I'LL HELP YOU.
BUT SPORTS DAY IS STILL...
YOU'RE SOAKING WET AND COVERED IN MUD!
YOU'RE OKAY WITH A TRACK-SUIT, RIGHT?
CHANGING ROOM
YES...
BOTAN-CHAN!
HIBARI-CHAAAN!
GARA (SLIDE)

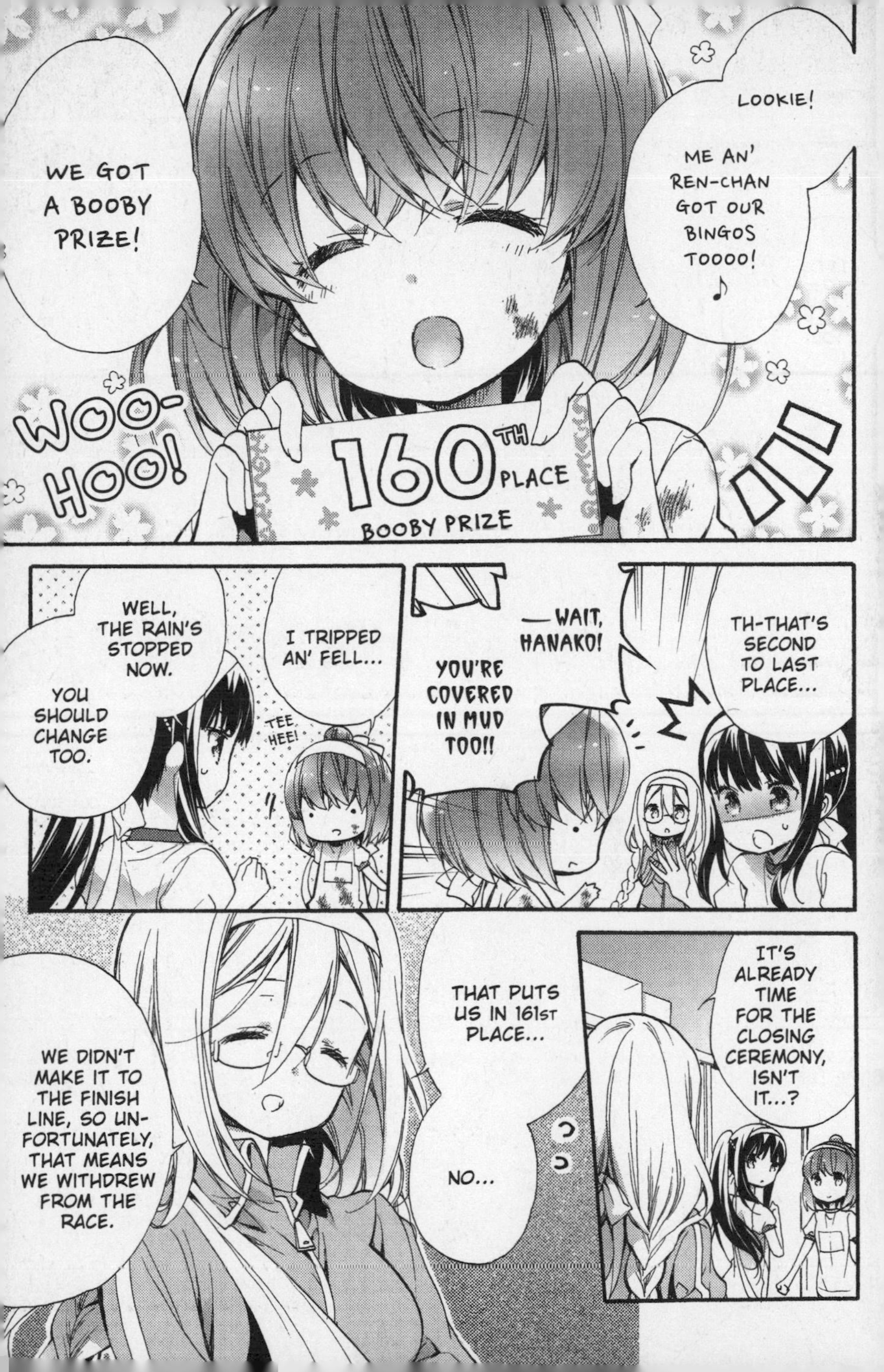
LOOKIE!
ME AN' REN-CHAN GOT OUR BINGOS TOOOO! ♪
WE GOT A BOOBY PRIZE!
WOO-HOO!
160TH PLACE
BOOBY PRIZE
TH-THAT'S SECOND TO LAST PLACE...
—WAIT, HANAKO!
YOU'RE COVERED IN MUD TOO!!
I TRIPPED AN' FELL...
TEE HEE!
WELL, THE RAIN'S STOPPED NOW.
YOU SHOULD CHANGE TOO.
IT'S ALREADY TIME FOR THE CLOSING CEREMONY, ISN'T IT...?
THAT PUTS US IN 161ST PLACE...
NO...
WE DIDN'T MAKE IT TO THE FINISH LINE, SO UN-FORTUNATELY, THAT MEANS WE WITHDREW FROM THE RACE.

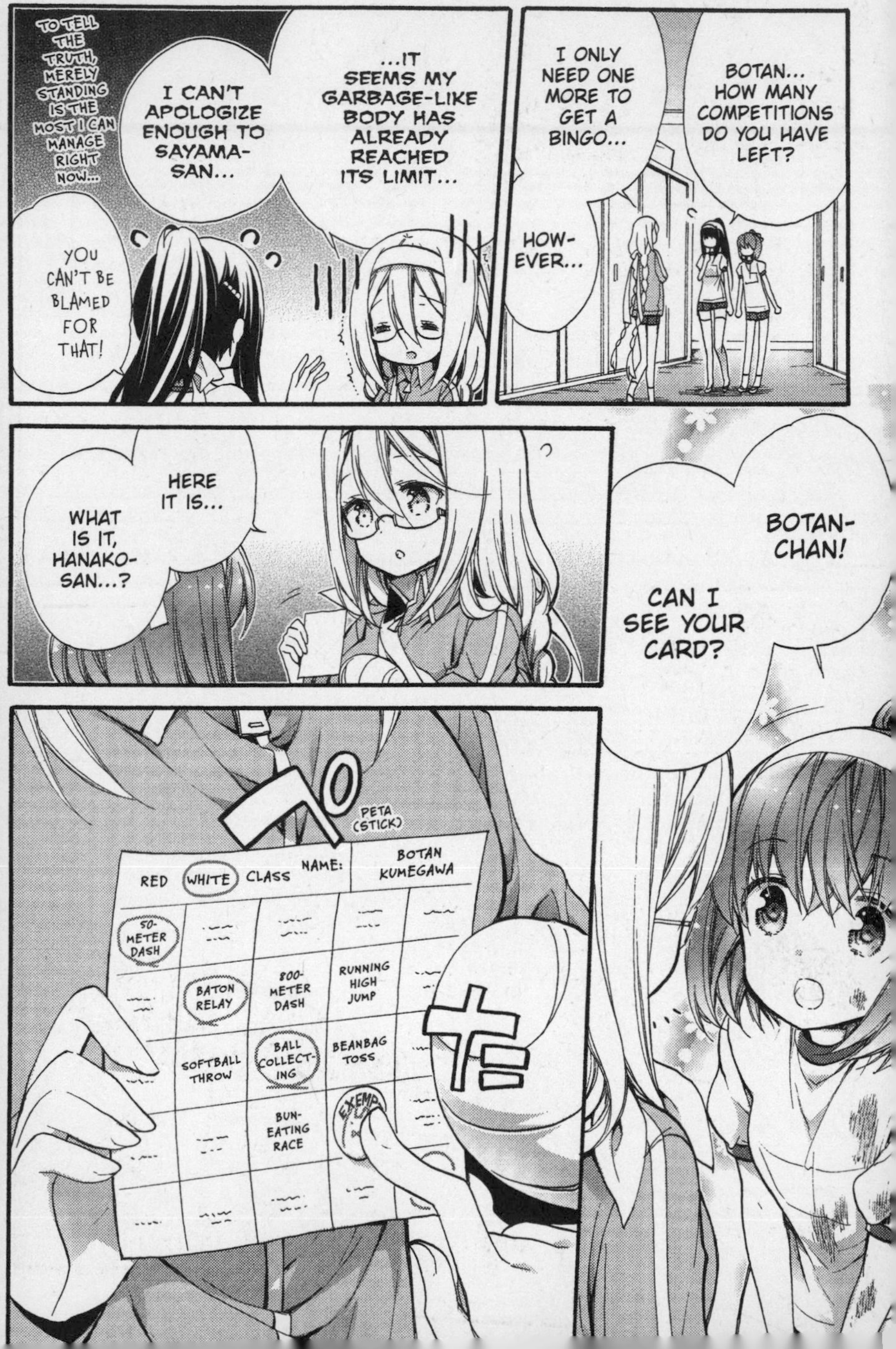
BOTAN... HOW MANY COMPETITIONS DO YOU HAVE LEFT?
I ONLY NEED ONE MORE TO GET A BINGO...
HOW-EVER...
...IT SEEMS MY GARBAGE-LIKE BODY HAS ALREADY REACHED ITS LIMIT...
I CAN'T APOLOGIZE ENOUGH TO SAYAMA-SAN...
TO TELL THE TRUTH, MERELY STANDING IS THE MOST I CAN MANAGE RIGHT NOW...
YOU CAN'T BE BLAMED FOR THAT!
BOTAN-CHAN!
CAN I SEE YOUR CARD?
HERE IT IS...
WHAT IS IT, HANAKO-SAN...?
PETA (STICK)
RED WHITE CLASS
NAME: BOTAN KUMEGAWA
50-METER DASH
BATON RELAY
800-METER DASH
RUNNING HIGH JUMP
SOFTBALL THROW
BALL COLLECTING
BEANBAG TOSS
BUN-EATING RACE
EXEMP

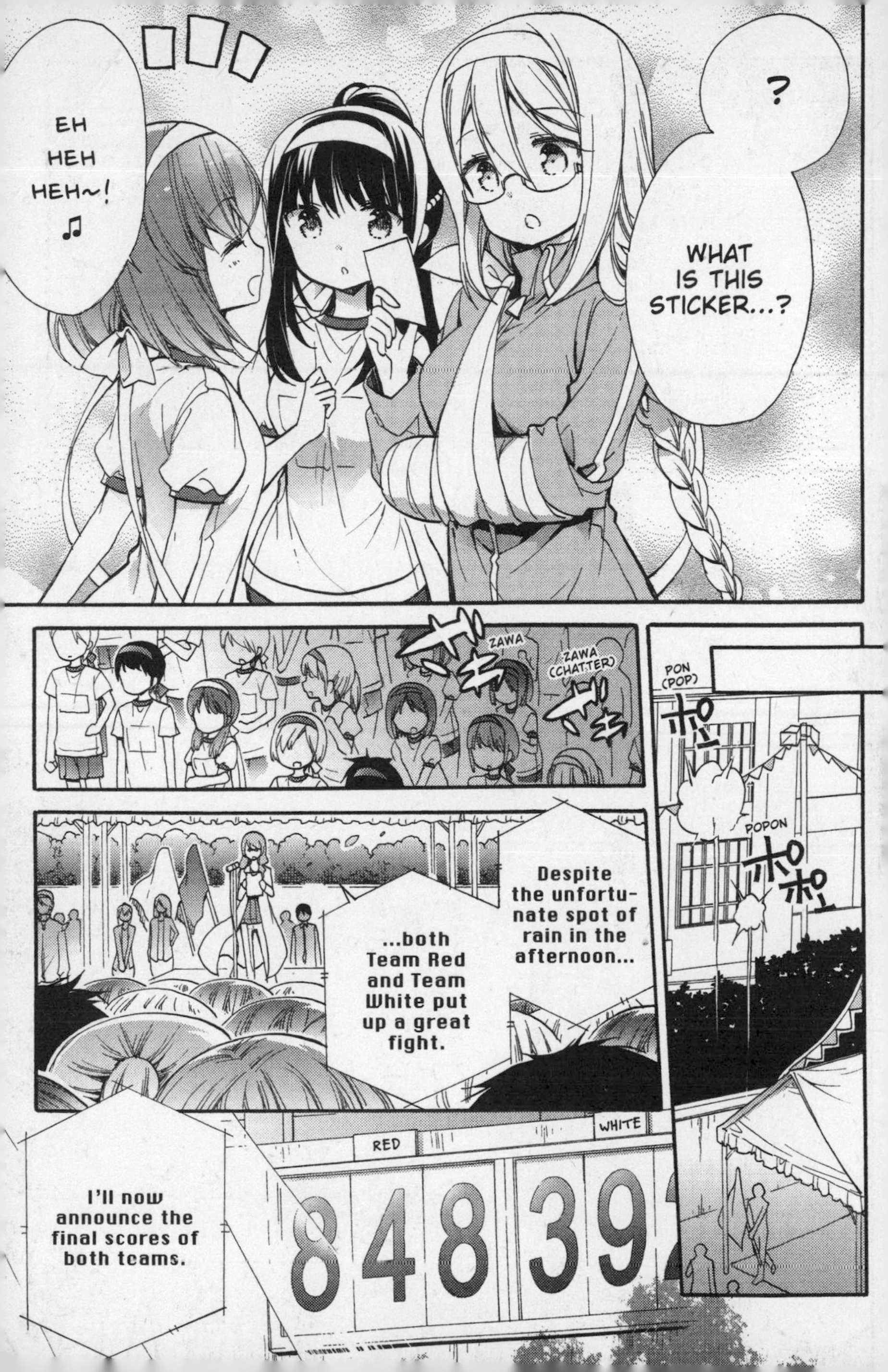
?
WHAT IS THIS STICKER...?
EH HEH HEH~! ♫
PON (POP)
POPON
ZAWA
ZAWA (CHATTER)
Despite the unfortunate spot of rain in the afternoon...
...both Team Red and Team White put up a great fight.
WHITE
RED
848
39
I'll now announce the final scores of both teams.

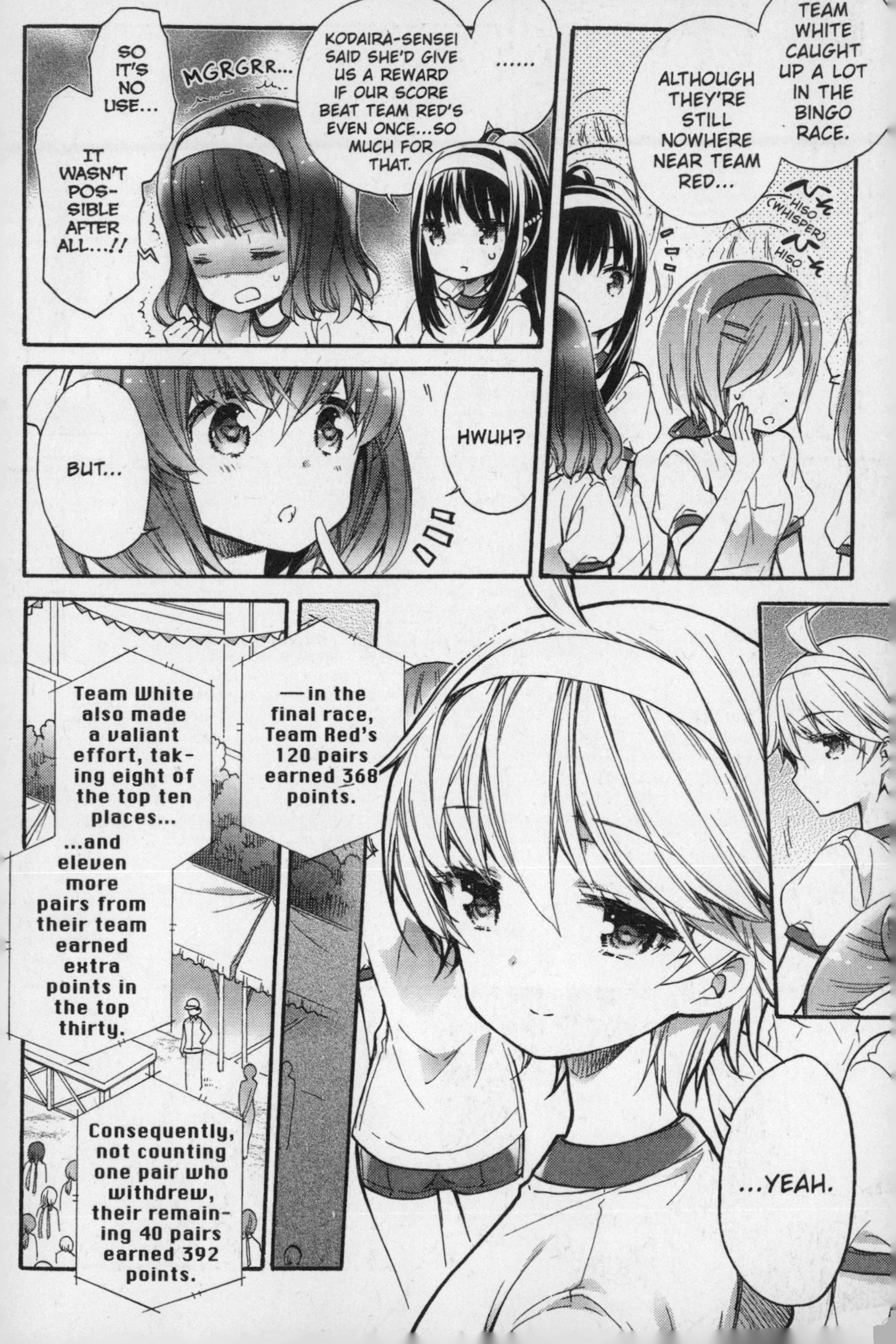
TEAM WHITE CAUGHT UP A LOT IN THE BINGO RACE.
ALTHOUGH THEY'RE STILL NOWHERE NEAR TEAM RED...
HISO (WHISPER)
HISO
KODAIRA-SENSEI SAID SHE'D GIVE US A REWARD IF OUR SCORE BEAT TEAM RED'S EVEN ONCE...SO MUCH FOR THAT.
......
MGRGRR...
SO IT'S NO USE...
IT WASN'T POS-SIBLE AFTER ALL...!!
HWUH?
BUT...
...YEAH.
—in the final race, Team Red's 120 pairs earned 368 points.
Team White also made a valiant effort, tak-ing eight of the top ten places...
...and eleven more pairs from their team earned extra points in the top thirty.
Consequently, not counting one pair who withdrew, their remain-ing 40 pairs earned 392 points.

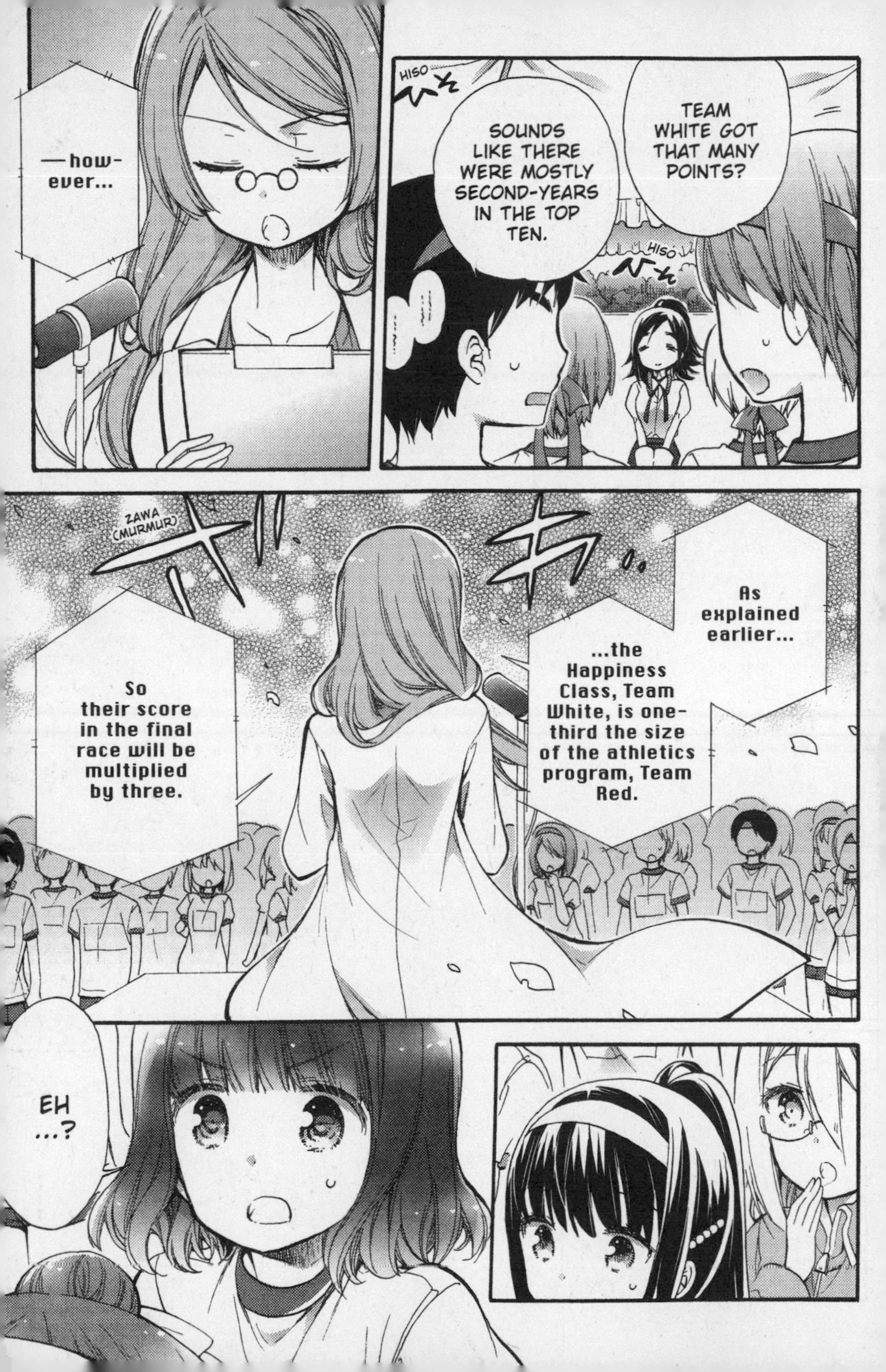
HISO
TEAM WHITE GOT THAT MANY POINTS?
SOUNDS LIKE THERE WERE MOSTLY SECOND-YEARS IN THE TOP TEN.
HISO
—how-ever...
ZAWA (MURMUR)
As explained earlier...
...the Happiness Class, Team White, is one-third the size of the athletics program, Team Red.
So their score in the final race will be multiplied by three.
EH ...?

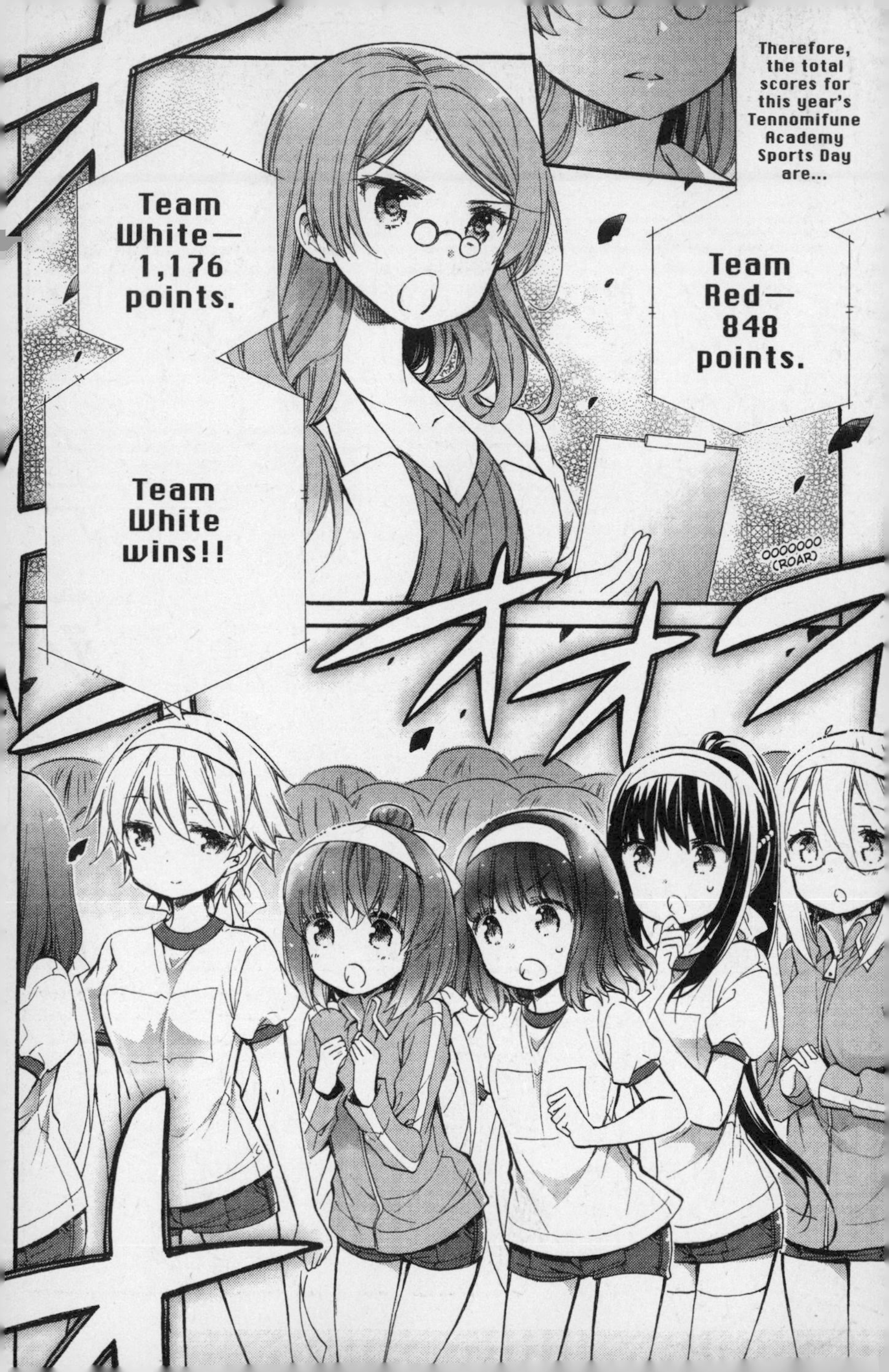
Therefore, the total scores for this year's Tennomifune Academy Sports Day are...
Team Red—848 points.
Team White—1,176 points.
Team White wins!!
OOOOOOO (ROAR)

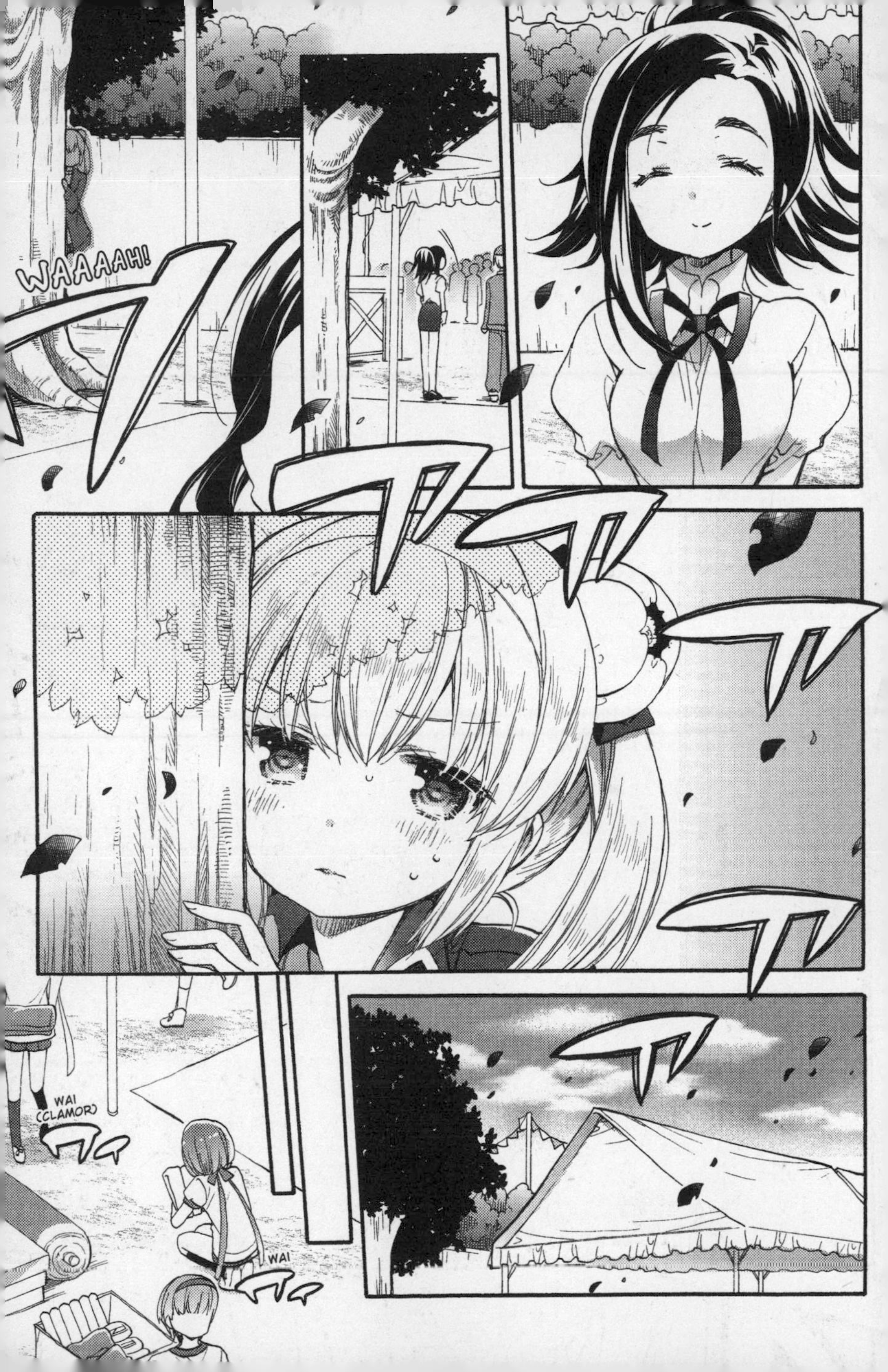
WAAAAH!
WAI (CLAMOR)
WAI

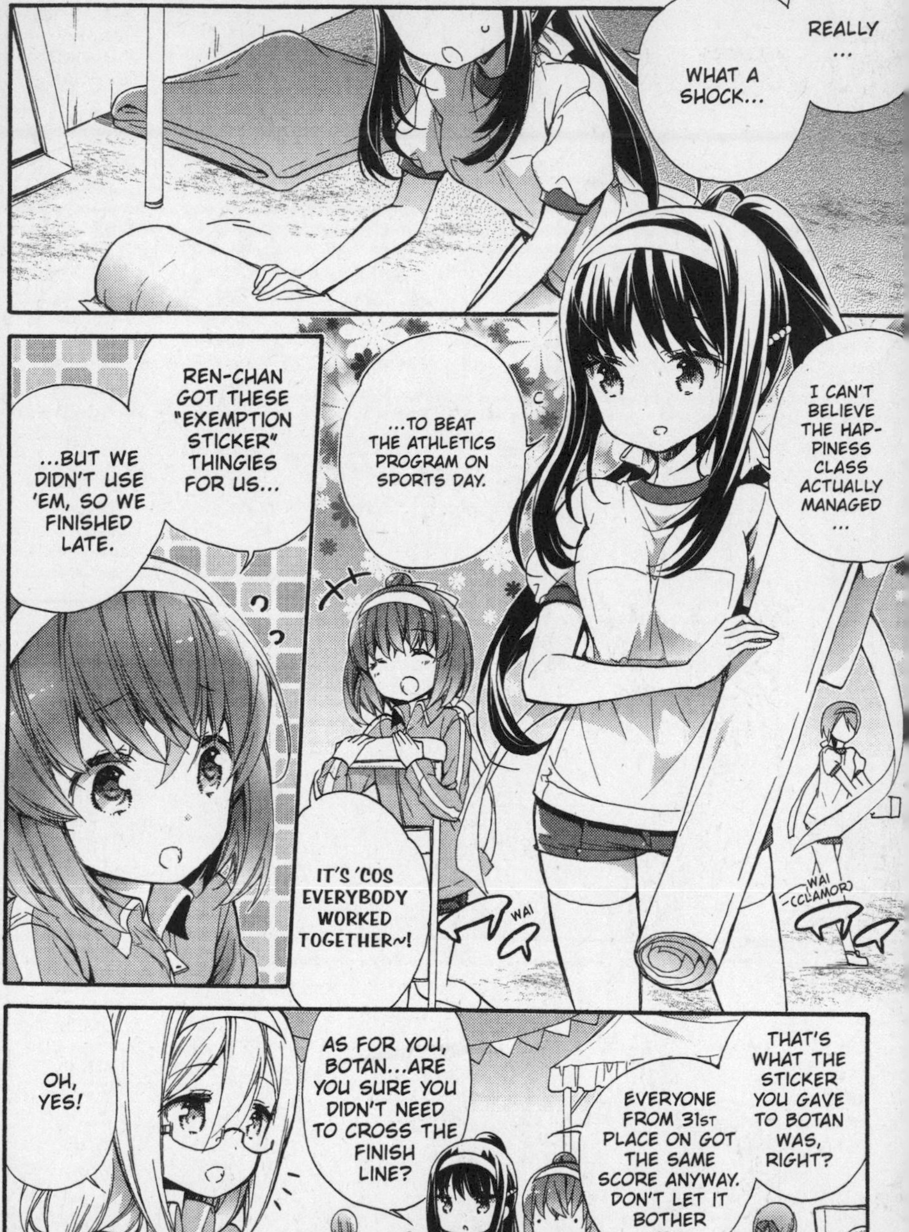
REALLY...
WHAT A SHOCK...
I CAN'T BELIEVE THE HAPPINESS CLASS ACTUALLY MANAGED...
...TO BEAT THE ATHLETICS PROGRAM ON SPORTS DAY.
IT'S 'COS EVERYBODY WORKED TOGETHER~!
WAI
WAI (CLAMOR)
REN-CHAN GOT THESE "EXEMPTION STICKER" THINGIES FOR US...
...BUT WE DIDN'T USE 'EM, SO WE FINISHED LATE.
THAT'S WHAT THE STICKER YOU GAVE TO BOTAN WAS, RIGHT?
EVERYONE FROM 31ST PLACE ON GOT THE SAME SCORE ANYWAY. DON'T LET IT BOTHER YOU.
AS FOR YOU, BOTAN...ARE YOU SURE YOU DIDN'T NEED TO CROSS THE FINISH LINE?
OH, YES!

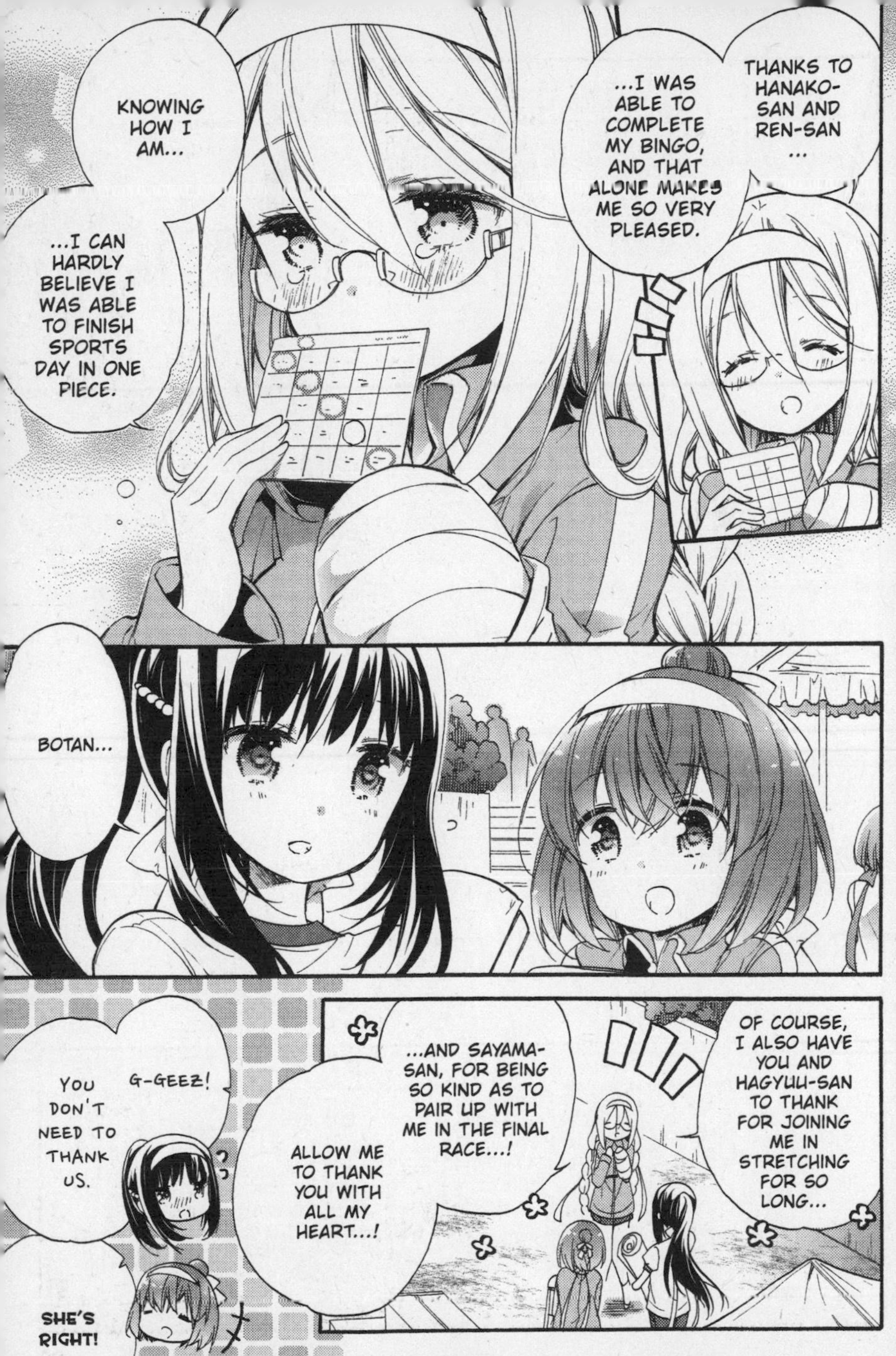
THANKS TO HANAKO-SAN AND REN-SAN...
...I WAS ABLE TO COMPLETE MY BINGO, AND THAT ALONE MAKES ME SO VERY PLEASED.
KNOWING HOW I AM...
...I CAN HARDLY BELIEVE I WAS ABLE TO FINISH SPORTS DAY IN ONE PIECE.
BOTAN...
OF COURSE, I ALSO HAVE YOU AND HAGYUU-SAN TO THANK FOR JOINING ME IN STRETCHING FOR SO LONG...
...AND SAYAMA-SAN, FOR BEING SO KIND AS TO PAIR UP WITH ME IN THE FINAL RACE...!
ALLOW ME TO THANK YOU WITH ALL MY HEART...!
G-GEEZ!
YOU DON'T NEED TO THANK US.
SHE'S RIGHT!

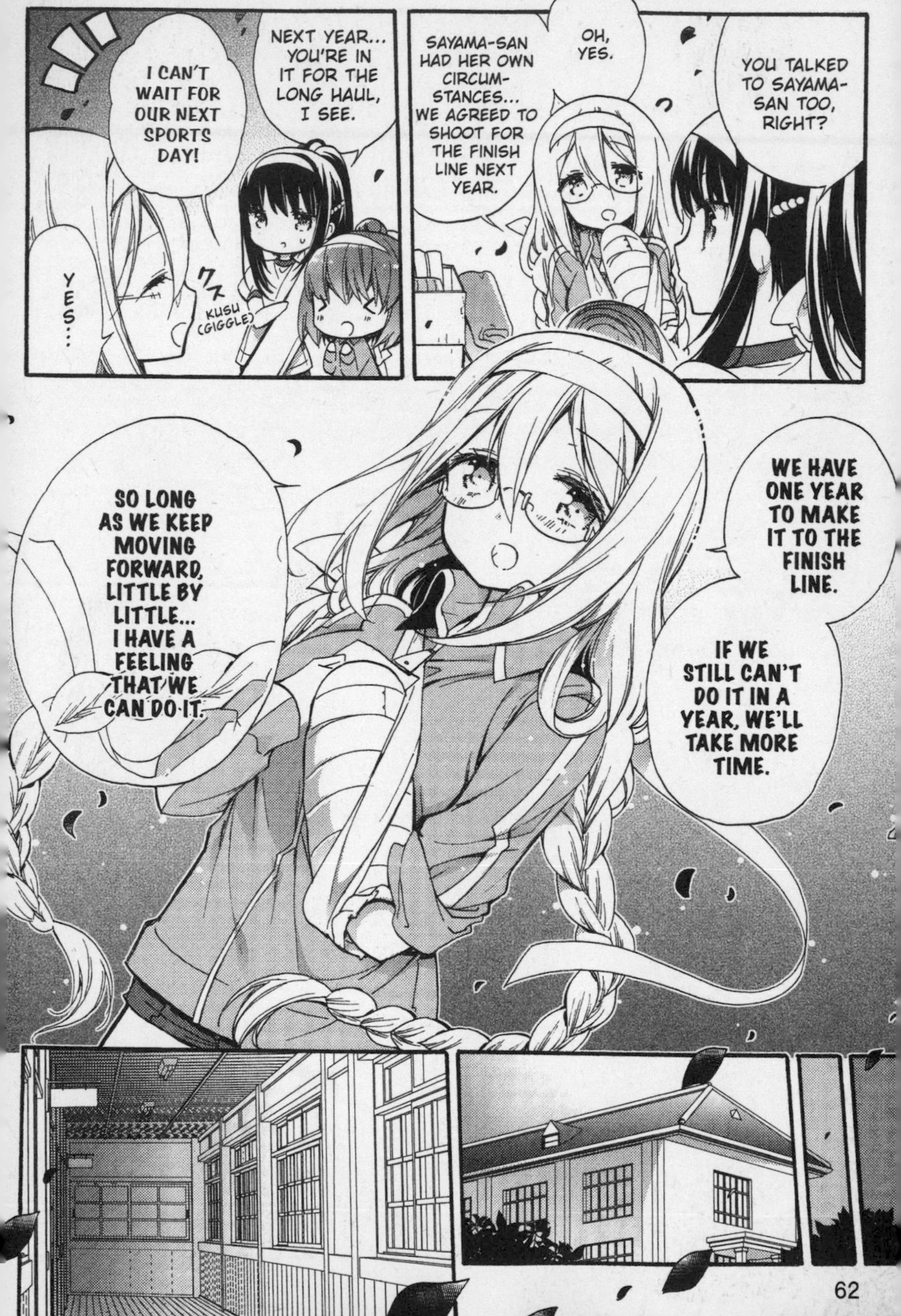
YOU TALKED TO SAYAMA-SAN TOO, RIGHT?
OH, YES.
SAYAMA-SAN HAD HER OWN CIRCUM-STANCES... WE AGREED TO SHOOT FOR THE FINISH LINE NEXT YEAR.
NEXT YEAR... YOU'RE IN IT FOR THE LONG HAUL, I SEE.
I CAN'T WAIT FOR OUR NEXT SPORTS DAY!
クス
KUSU (GIGGLE)
YES...
WE HAVE ONE YEAR TO MAKE IT TO THE FINISH LINE.
IF WE STILL CAN'T DO IT IN A YEAR, WE'LL TAKE MORE TIME.
SO LONG AS WE KEEP MOVING FORWARD, LITTLE BY LITTLE... I HAVE A FEELING THAT WE CAN DO IT.

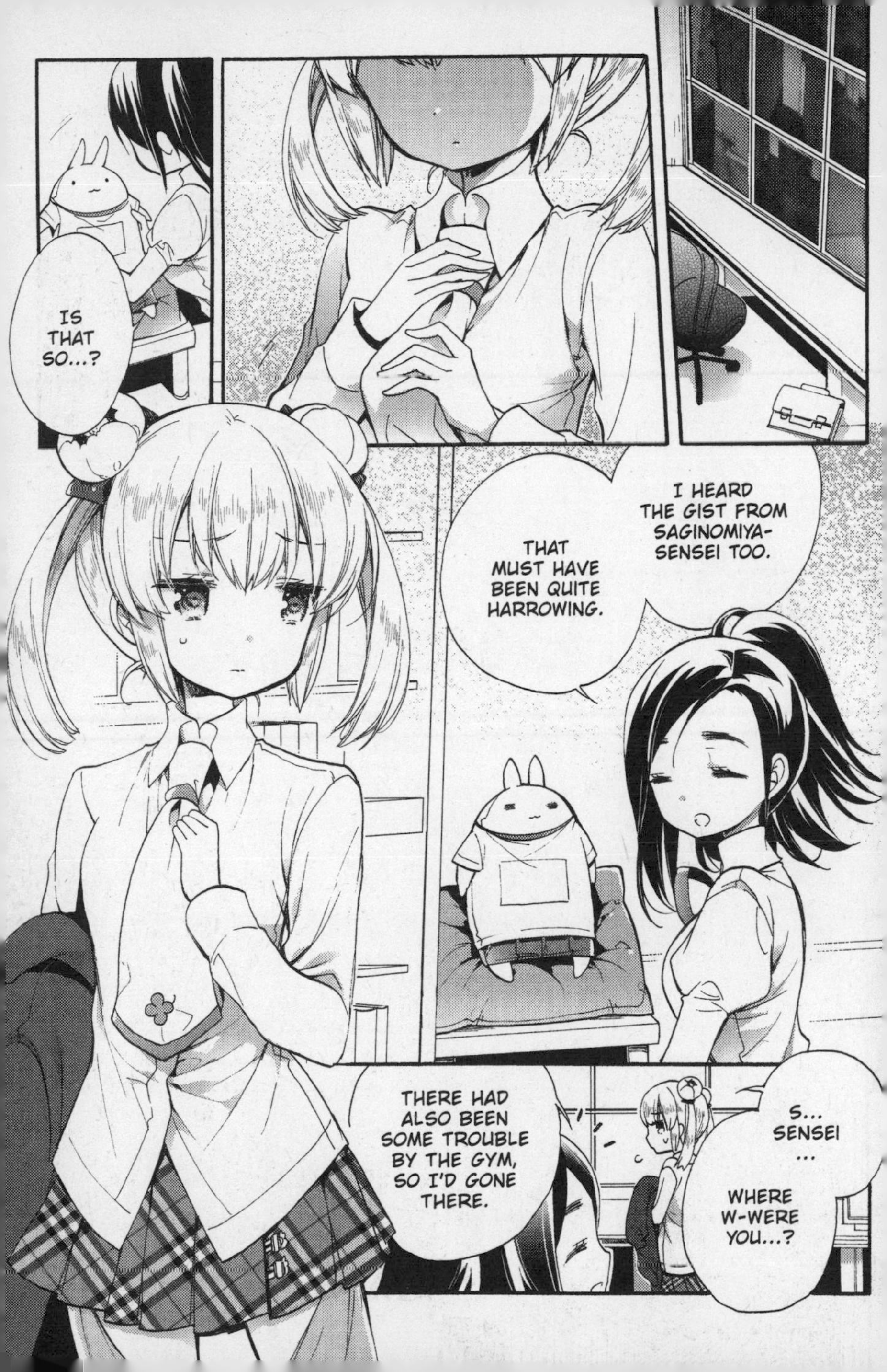
IS THAT SO...?
I HEARD THE GIST FROM SAGINOMIYA-SENSEI TOO.
THAT MUST HAVE BEEN QUITE HARROWING.
S... SENSEI... WHERE W-WERE YOU...?
THERE HAD ALSO BEEN SOME TROUBLE BY THE GYM, SO I'D GONE THERE.

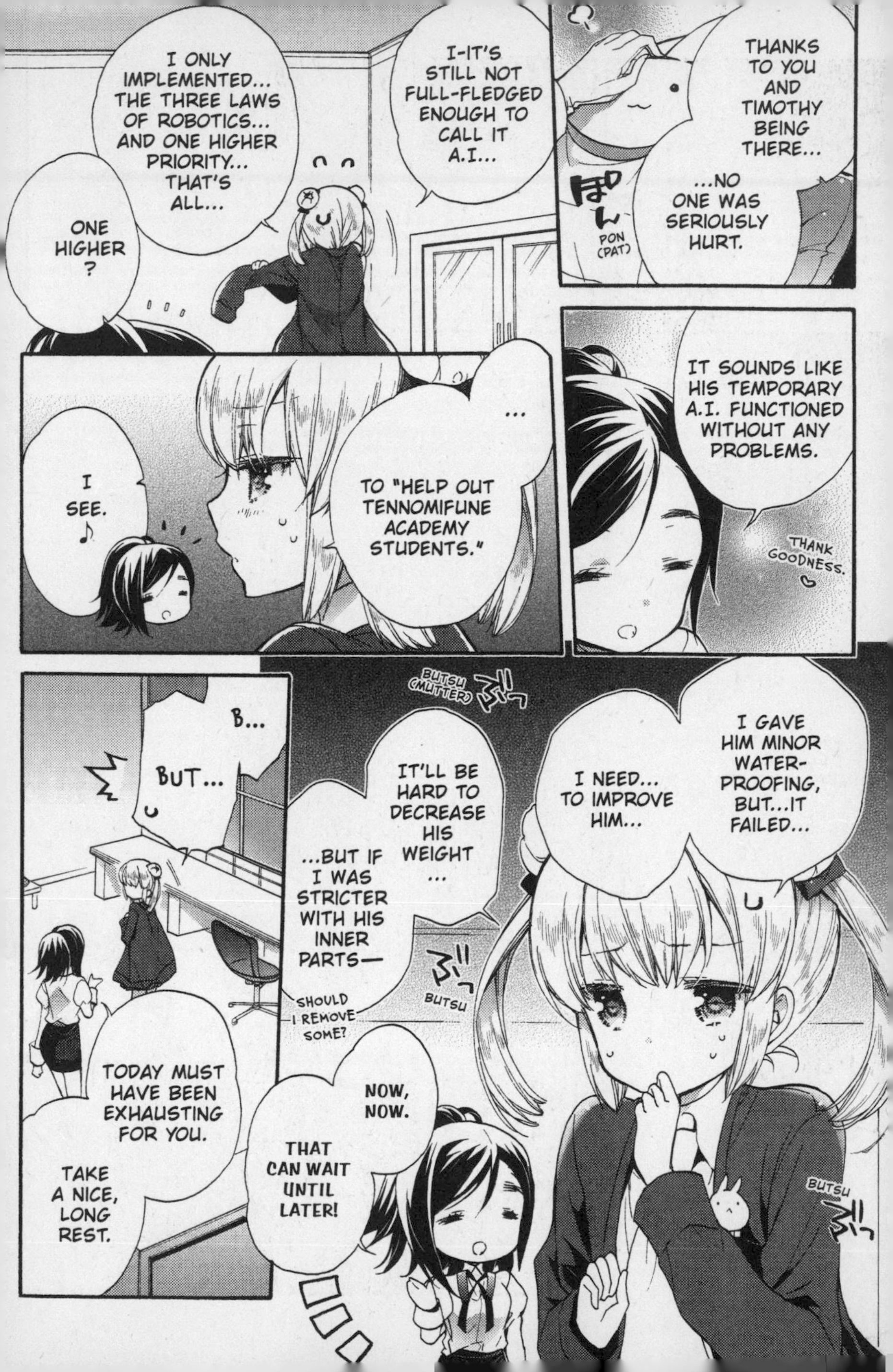

THANKS TO YOU AND TIMOTHY BEING THERE...
ぽん
PON (PAT)
...NO ONE WAS SERIOUSLY HURT.
I-IT'S STILL NOT FULL-FLEDGED ENOUGH TO CALL IT A.I...
I ONLY IMPLEMENTED... THE THREE LAWS OF ROBOTICS... AND ONE HIGHER PRIORITY... THAT'S ALL...
ONE HIGHER?
IT SOUNDS LIKE HIS TEMPORARY A.I. FUNCTIONED WITHOUT ANY PROBLEMS.
THANK GOODNESS.
...
TO "HELP OUT TENNOMIFUNE ACADEMY STUDENTS."
I SEE. ♪
BUTSU (MUTTER) ぶつ
I GAVE HIM MINOR WATER-PROOFING, BUT...IT FAILED...
I NEED... TO IMPROVE HIM...
IT'LL BE HARD TO DECREASE HIS WEIGHT...
...BUT IF I WAS STRICTER WITH HIS INNER PARTS—
ぶつ
BUTSU
SHOULD I REMOVE SOME?
BUTSU
ぶつ
NOW, NOW.
THAT CAN WAIT UNTIL LATER!
TODAY MUST HAVE BEEN EXHAUSTING FOR YOU.
TAKE A NICE, LONG REST.
B...
BUT...

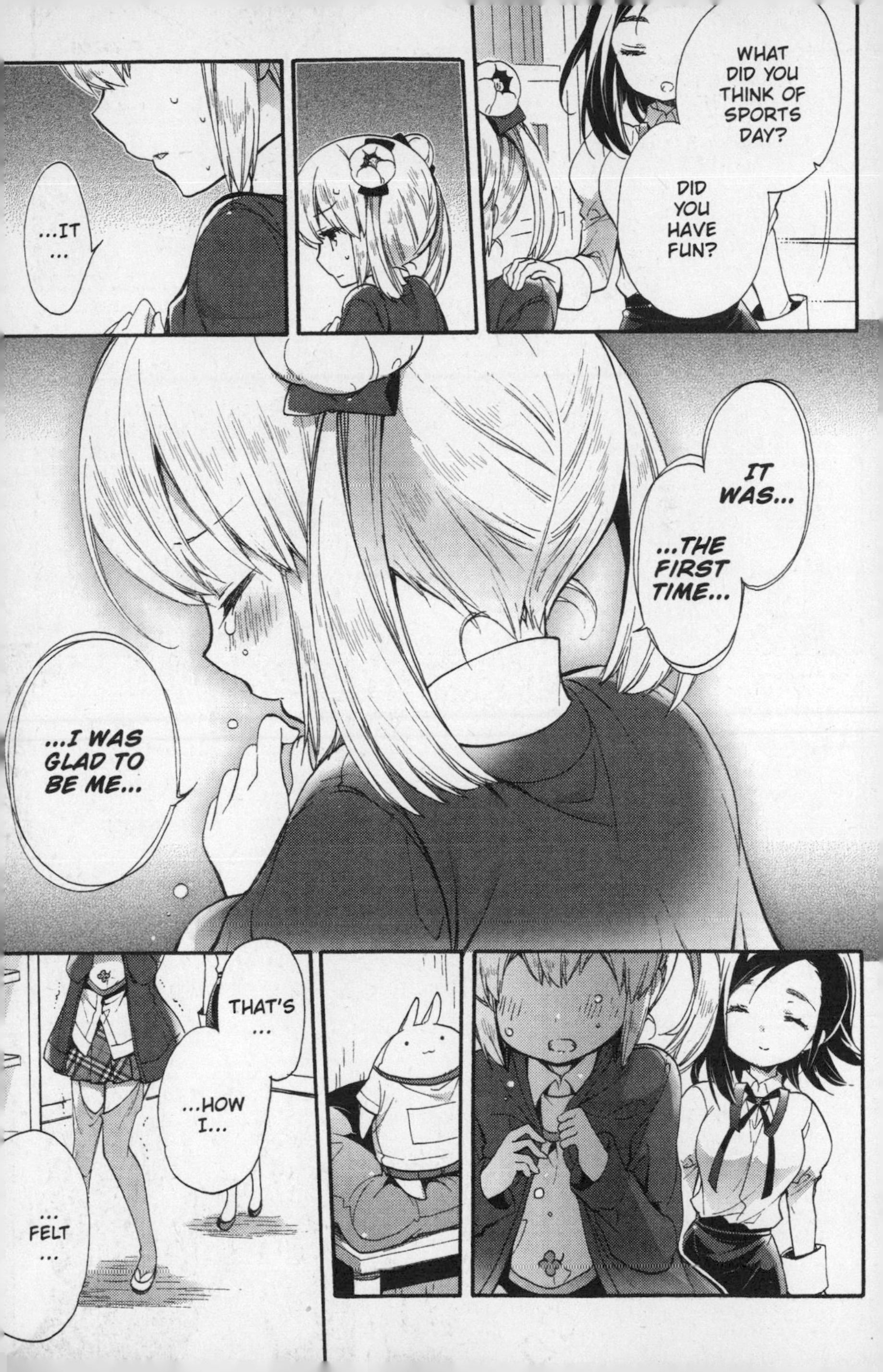
WHAT DID YOU THINK OF SPORTS DAY?
DID YOU HAVE FUN?
...IT ...
IT WAS...
...THE FIRST TIME...
...I WAS GLAD TO BE ME...
THAT'S ...
...HOW I...
... FELT ...

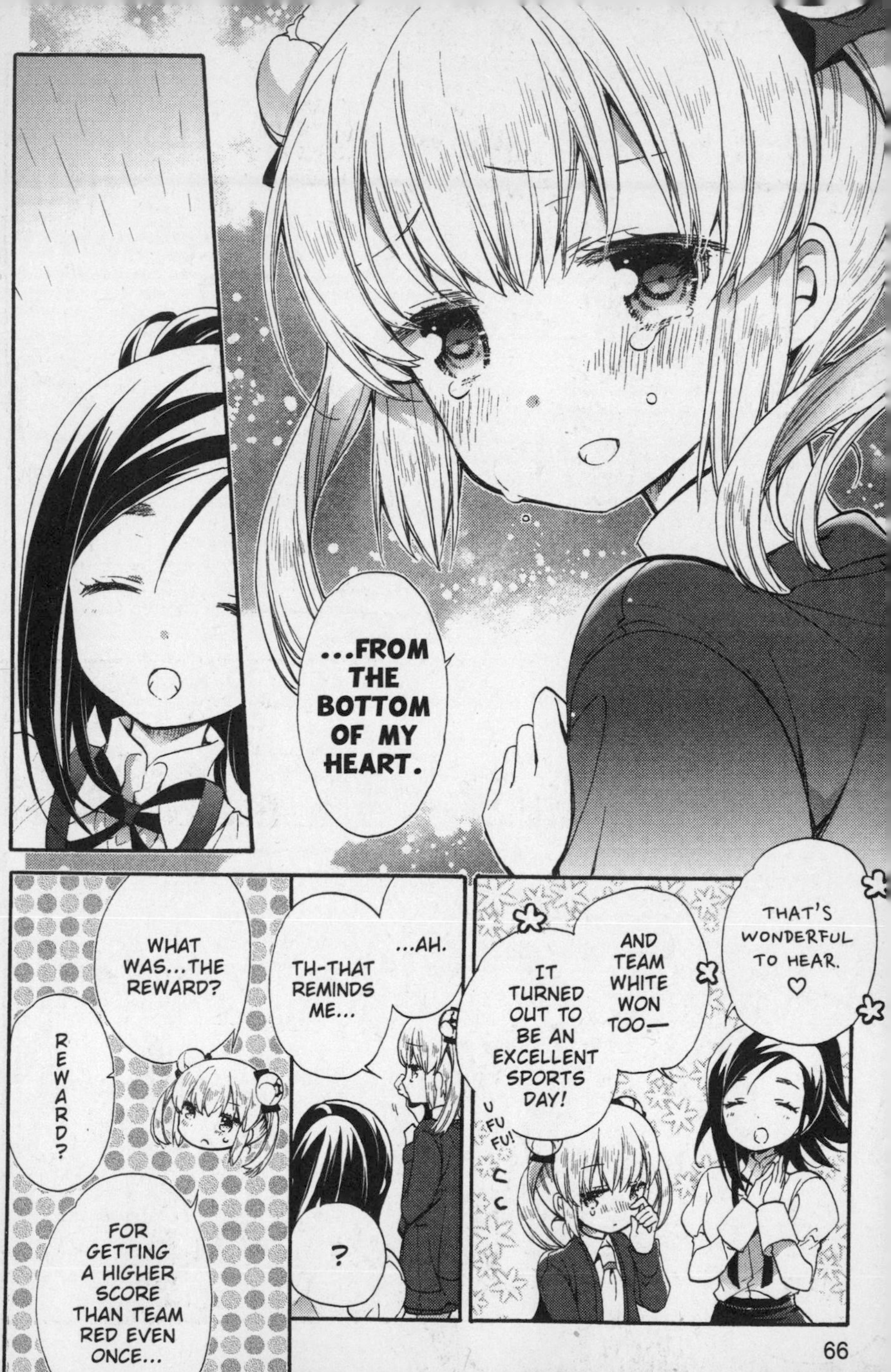

...FROM THE BOTTOM OF MY HEART.
THAT'S WONDERFUL TO HEAR. ♡
AND TEAM WHITE WON TOO—
IT TURNED OUT TO BE AN EXCELLENT SPORTS DAY!
UFU FU!
...AH.
TH-THAT REMINDS ME...
?
WHAT WAS...THE REWARD?
REWARD?
FOR GETTING A HIGHER SCORE THAN TEAM RED EVEN ONCE...

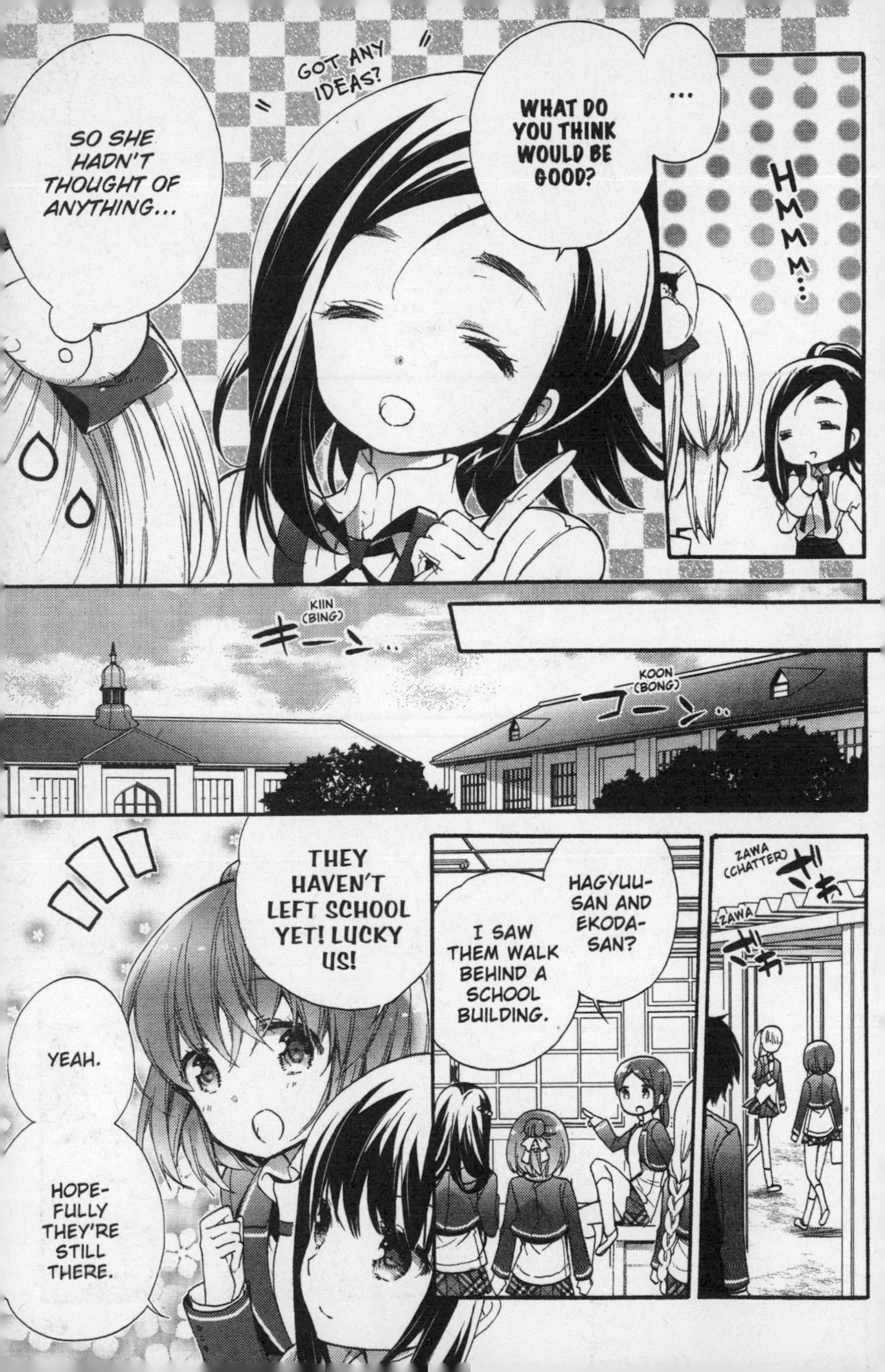
...
HMMMM...
WHAT DO YOU THINK WOULD BE GOOD?
GOT ANY IDEAS?
SO SHE HADN'T THOUGHT OF ANYTHING...
KIIN (BING)
KOON (BONG)
ZAWA (CHATTER)
ZAWA
HAGYUU-SAN AND EKODA-SAN?
I SAW THEM WALK BEHIND A SCHOOL BUILDING.
THEY HAVEN'T LEFT SCHOOL YET! LUCKY US!
YEAH.
HOPE-FULLY THEY'RE STILL THERE.

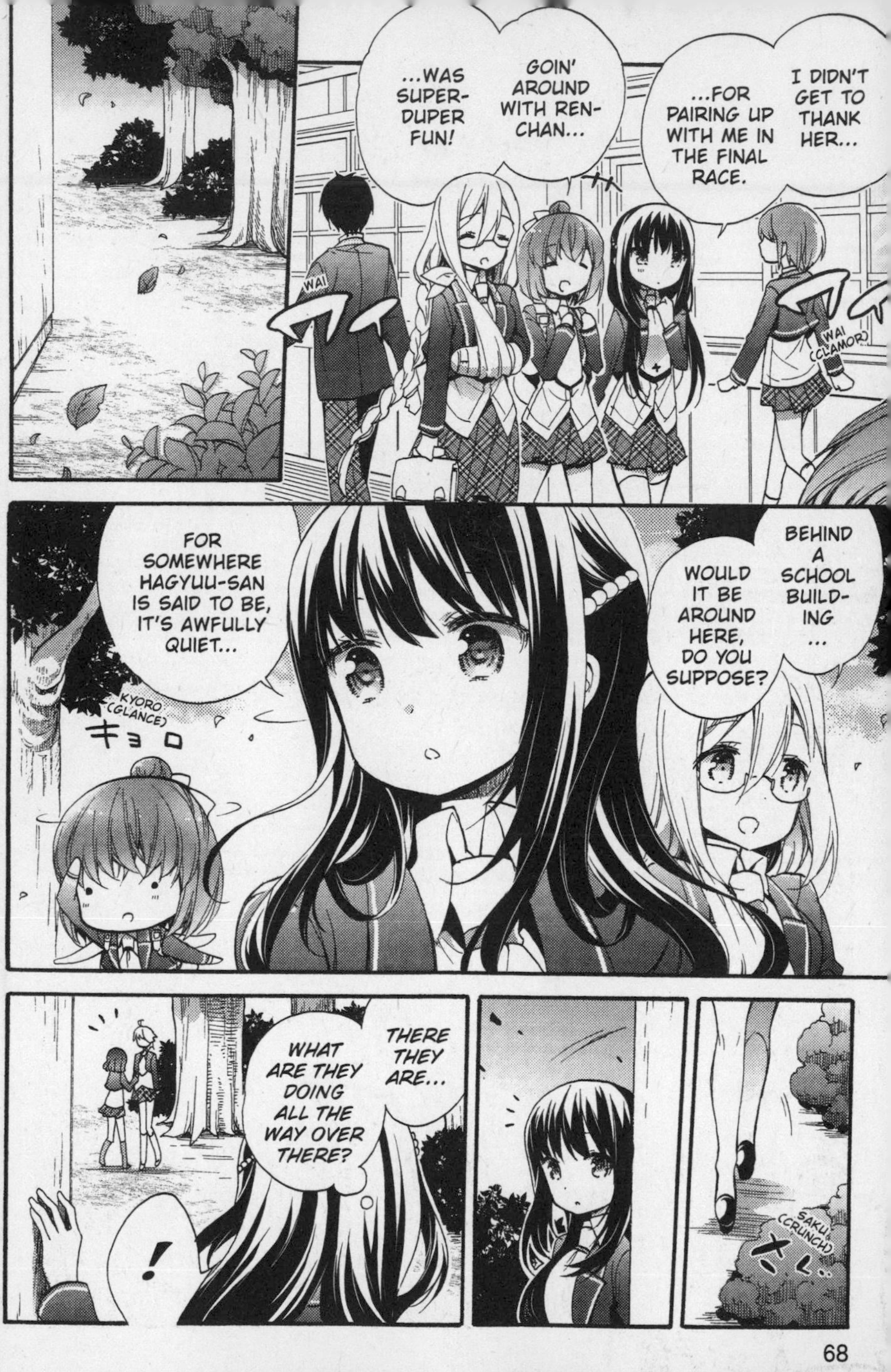

I DIDN'T GET TO THANK HER...
...FOR PAIRING UP WITH ME IN THE FINAL RACE.
GOIN' AROUND WITH REN-CHAN...
...WAS SUPER-DUPER FUN!
WAI (CLAMOR)
WAI
BEHIND A SCHOOL BUILD-ING...
WOULD IT BE AROUND HERE, DO YOU SUPPOSE?
FOR SOMEWHERE HAGYUU-SAN IS SAID TO BE, IT'S AWFULLY QUIET...
KYORO (GLANCE)
SAKU (CRUNCH)
THERE THEY ARE...
WHAT ARE THEY DOING ALL THE WAY OVER THERE?
!

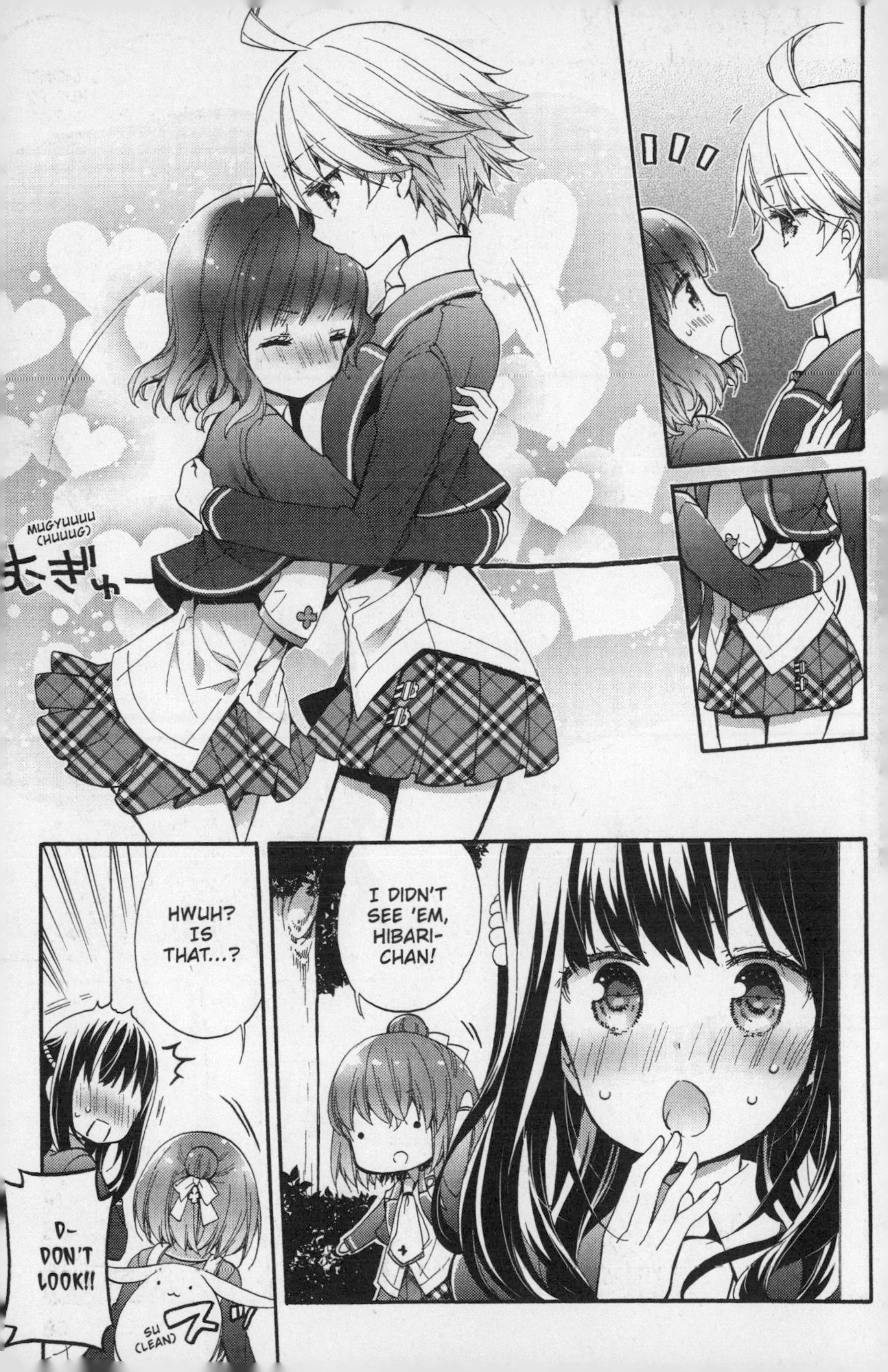
MUGYUUUU (HUUUG)
むぎゅー
I DIDN'T SEE 'EM, HIBARI-CHAN!
HWUH? IS THAT...?
D-DON'T LOOK!!
SU (LEAN)

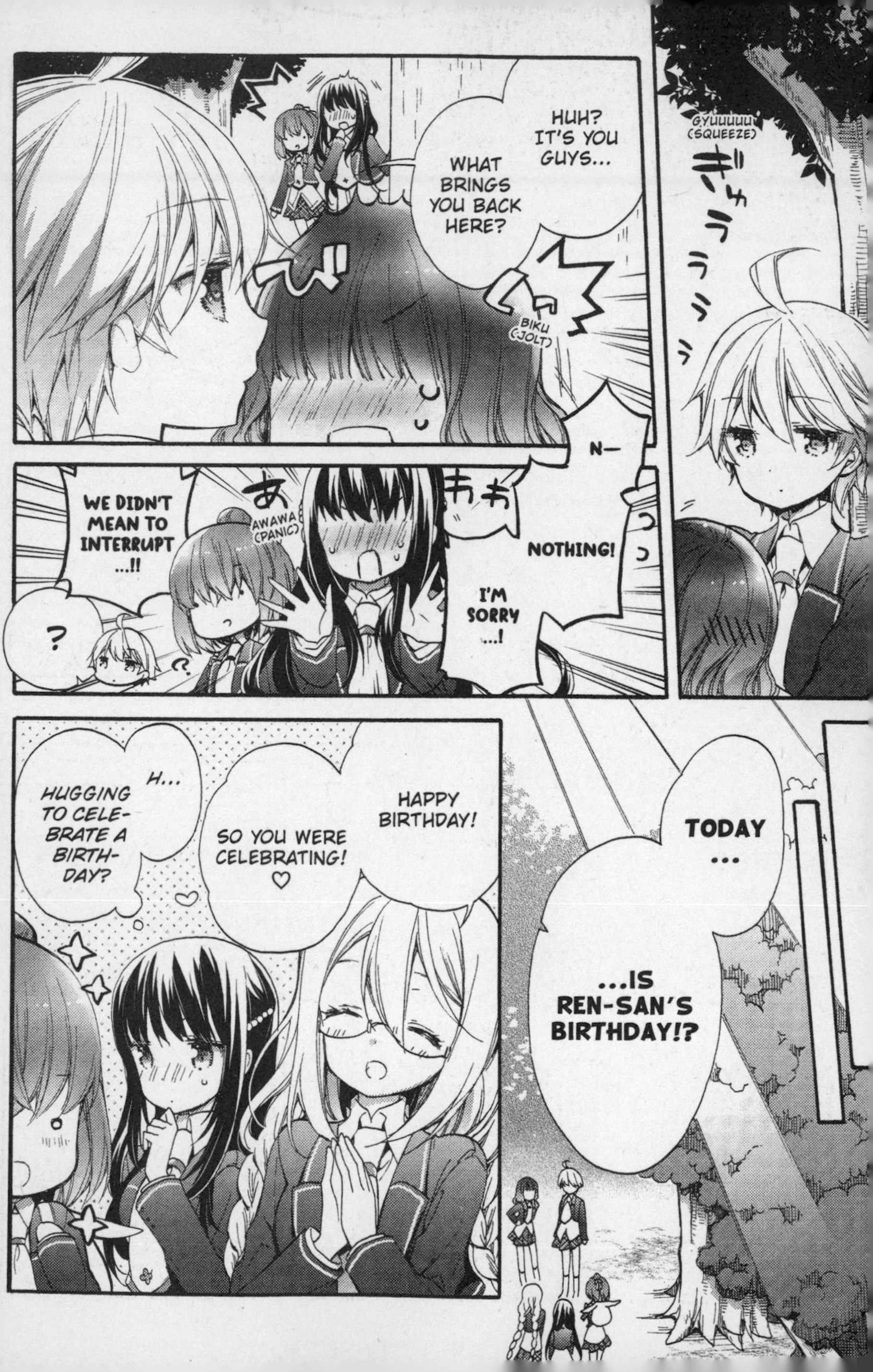
GYUUUUU (SQUEEZE)
HUH? IT'S YOU GUYS...
WHAT BRINGS YOU BACK HERE?
BIKU (JOLT)
N—
NOTHING!
I'M SORRY ...!
AWAWA (PANIC)
WE DIDN'T MEAN TO INTERRUPT ...!!
?
TODAY ...
...IS REN-SAN'S BIRTHDAY!?
HAPPY BIRTHDAY!
SO YOU WERE CELEBRATING! ♡
H... HUGGING TO CELE-BRATE A BIRTH-DAY?

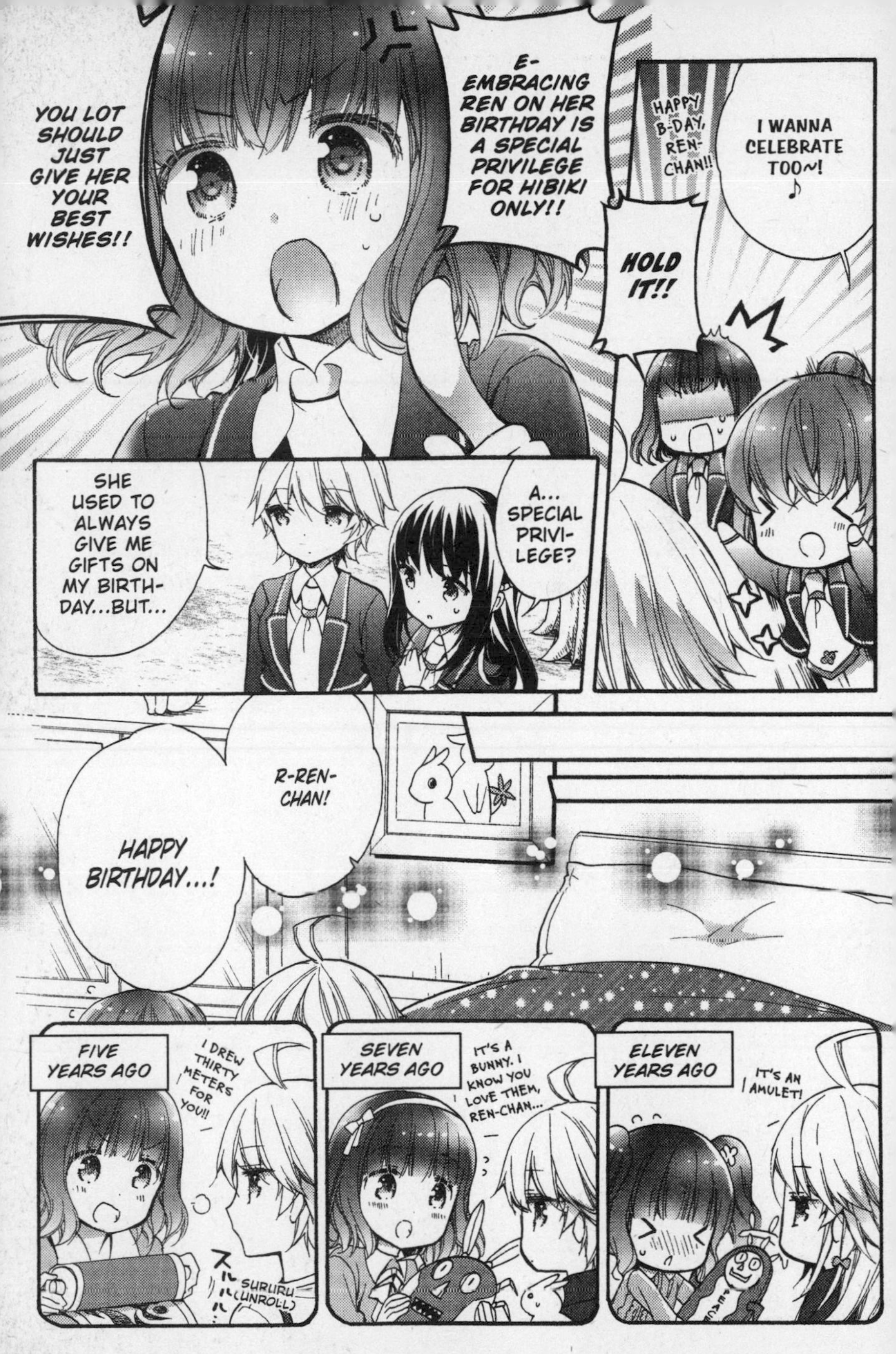
I WANNA CELEBRATE TOO~! ♪
HAPPY B-DAY, REN-CHAN!!
HOLD IT!!
E-EMBRACING REN ON HER BIRTHDAY IS A SPECIAL PRIVILEGE FOR HIBIKI ONLY!!
YOU LOT SHOULD JUST GIVE HER YOUR BEST WISHES!!
A... SPECIAL PRIVI-LEGE?
SHE USED TO ALWAYS GIVE ME GIFTS ON MY BIRTH-DAY...BUT...
R-REN-CHAN!
HAPPY BIRTHDAY...!
ELEVEN YEARS AGO
IT'S AN AMULET!
SEVEN YEARS AGO
IT'S A BUNNY. I KNOW YOU LOVE THEM, REN-CHAN...
FIVE YEARS AGO
I DREW THIRTY METERS FOR YOU!!
スルルル…
SURURU (UNROLL)

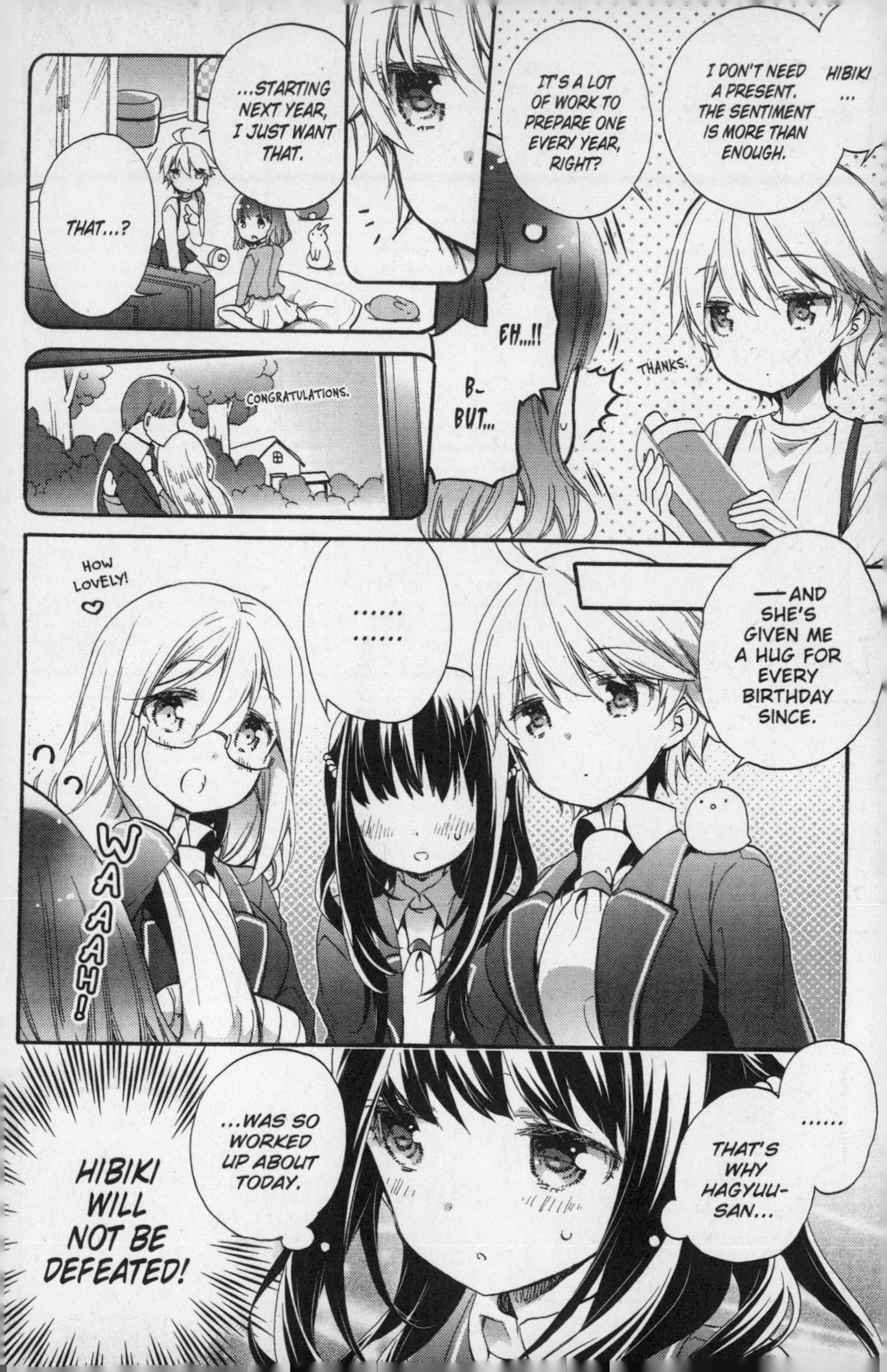
I DON'T NEED A PRESENT. THE SENTIMENT IS MORE THAN ENOUGH.
HIBIKI ...
IT'S A LOT OF WORK TO PREPARE ONE EVERY YEAR, RIGHT?
EH...!!
B- BUT...
THANKS.
...STARTING NEXT YEAR, I JUST WANT THAT.
THAT...?
CONGRATULATIONS.
—AND SHE'S GIVEN ME A HUG FOR EVERY BIRTHDAY SINCE.
....
HOW LOVELY! ♡
WAAAAH!
...... THAT'S WHY HAGYUU-SAN...
...WAS SO WORKED UP ABOUT TODAY.
HIBIKI WILL NOT BE DEFEATED!

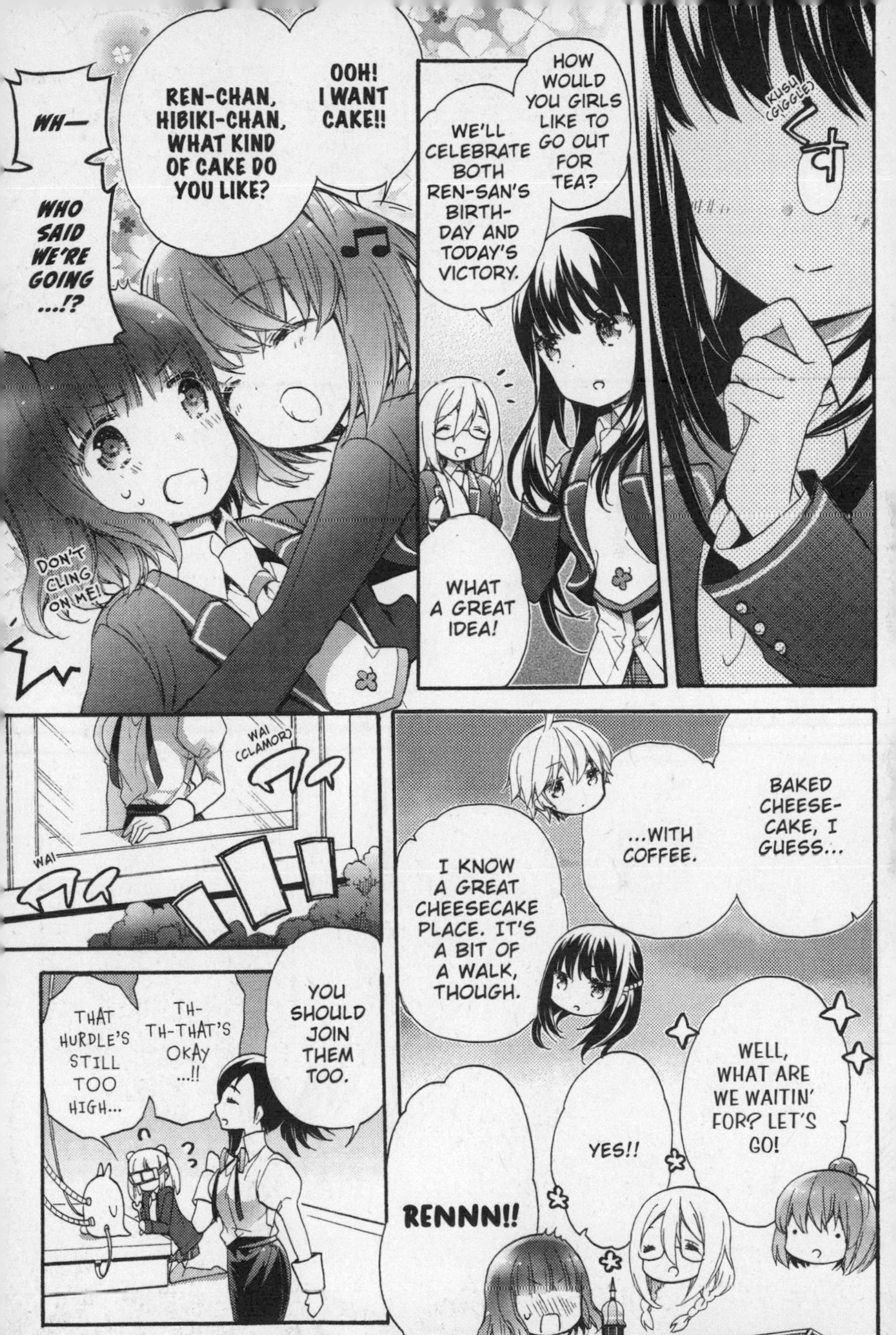
KUSU (GIGGLE)
HOW WOULD YOU GIRLS LIKE TO GO OUT FOR TEA?
WE'LL CELEBRATE BOTH REN-SAN'S BIRTHDAY AND TODAY'S VICTORY.
WHAT A GREAT IDEA!
OOH! I WANT CAKE!!
REN-CHAN, HIBIKI-CHAN, WHAT KIND OF CAKE DO YOU LIKE?
WH—
WHO SAID WE'RE GOING...!?
DON'T CLING ON ME!
BAKED CHEESE-CAKE, I GUESS...
...WITH COFFEE.
I KNOW A GREAT CHEESECAKE PLACE. IT'S A BIT OF A WALK, THOUGH.
WELL, WHAT ARE WE WAITIN' FOR? LET'S GO!
YES!!
RENNN!!
WAI (CLAMOR)
WAI
YOU SHOULD JOIN THEM TOO.
TH-TH-THAT'S OKAY ...!!
THAT HURDLE'S STILL TOO HIGH...

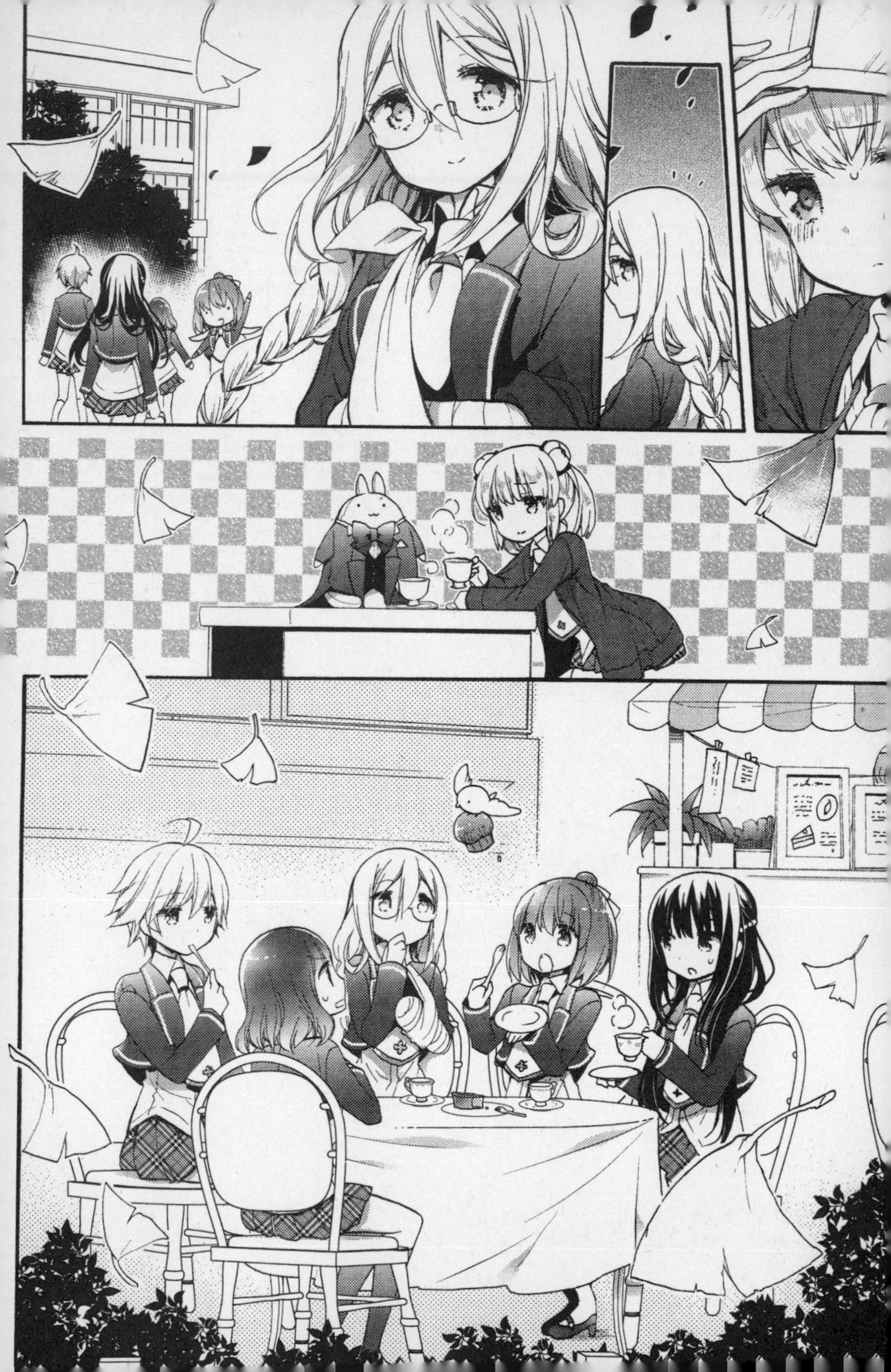

Anne Happy♪

unhappy go lucky!

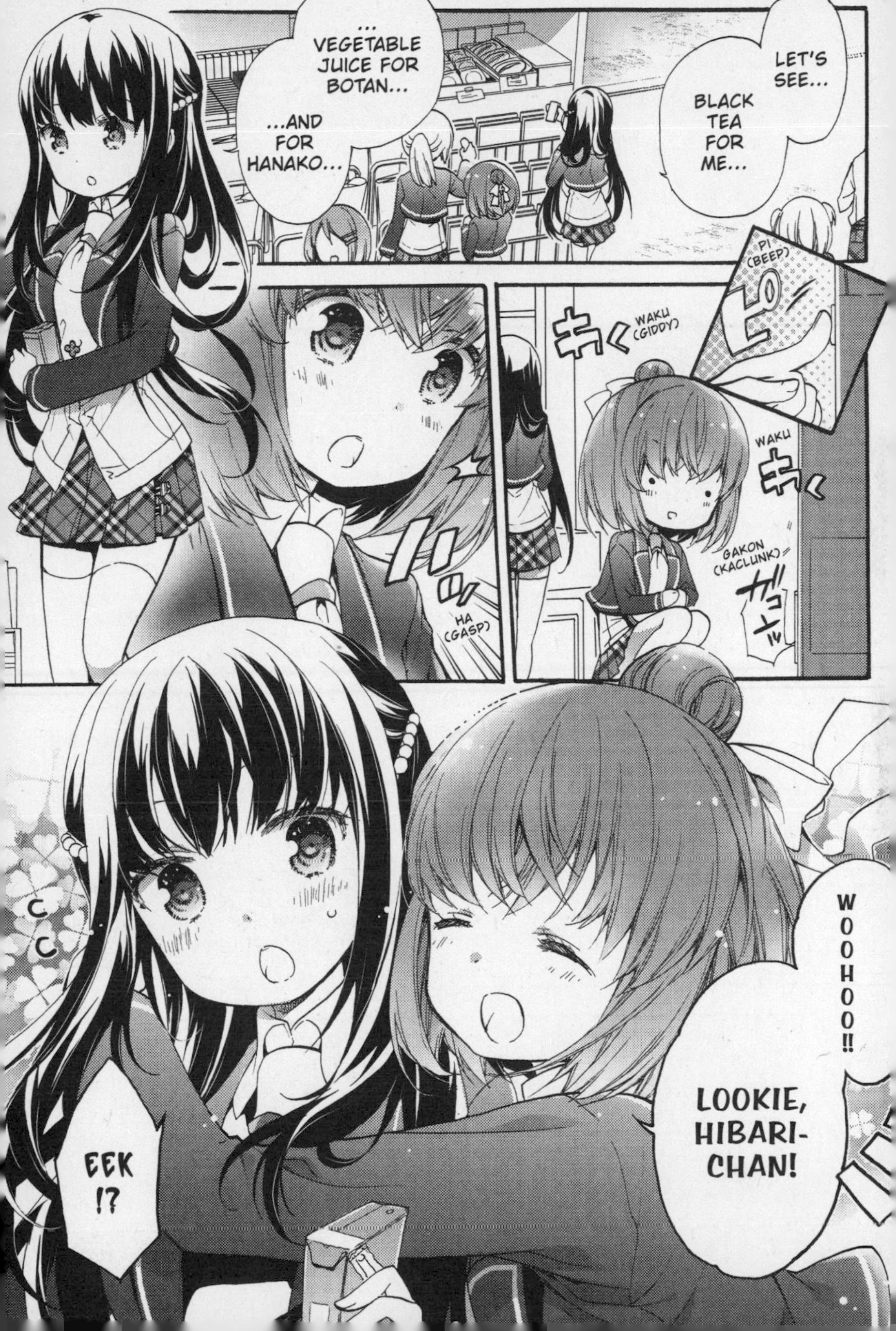
LET'S SEE...
BLACK TEA FOR ME...
... VEGETABLE JUICE FOR BOTAN...
...AND FOR HANAKO...
PI (BEEP)
WAKU (GIDDY)
WAKU
GAKON (KACLUNK)
HA (GASP)
WOOHOO!!
LOOKIE, HIBARI-CHAN!
EEK !?

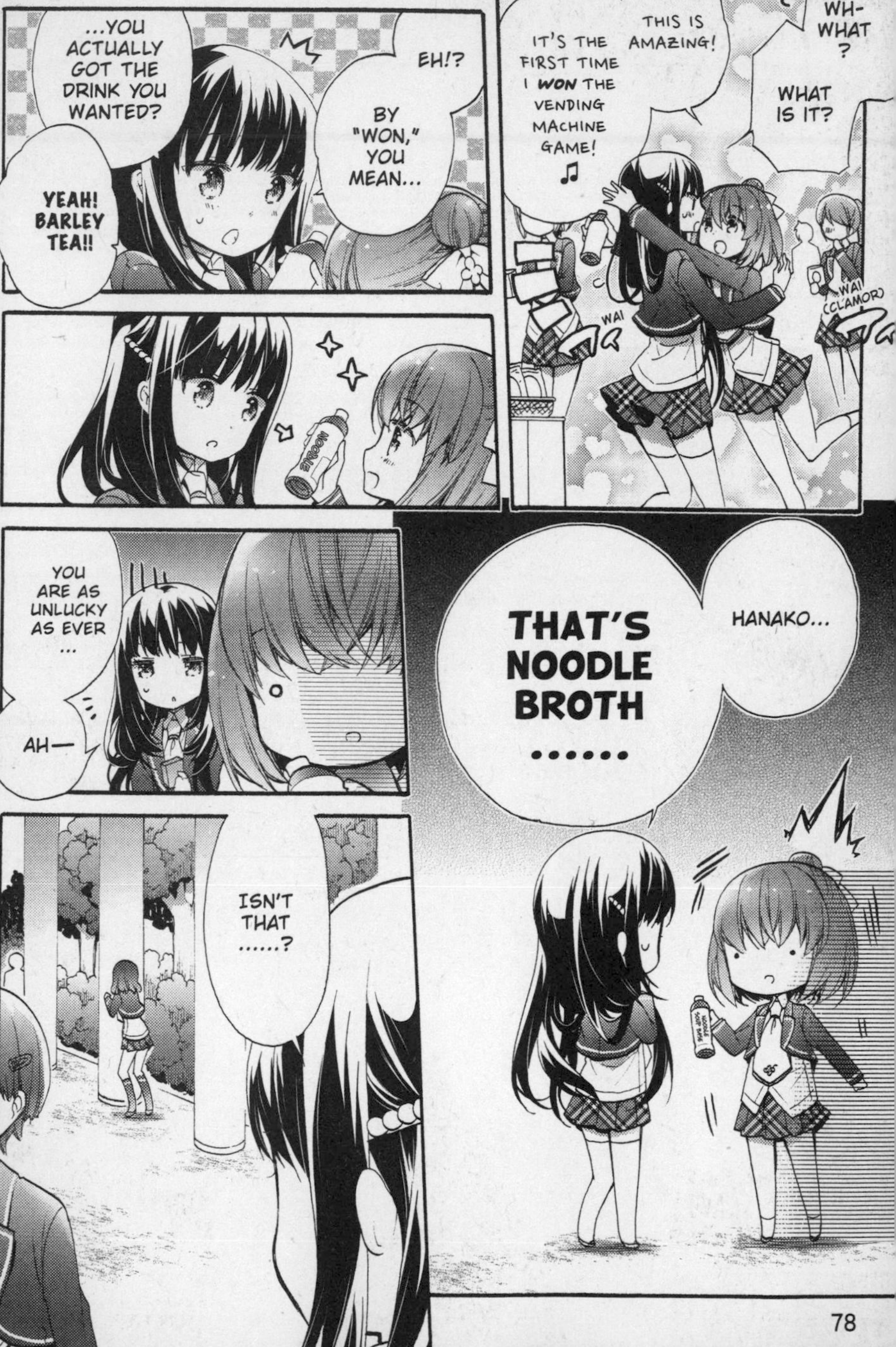
WH-WHAT? WHAT IS IT?
THIS IS AMAZING! IT'S THE FIRST TIME I **WON** THE VENDING MACHINE GAME! ♫
WAI
WAI (CLAMOR)
EH!? BY "WON," YOU MEAN...
...YOU ACTUALLY GOT THE DRINK YOU WANTED?
YEAH! BARLEY TEA!!
NOODLE
HANAKO... THAT'S NOODLE BROTH ......
YOU ARE AS UNLUCKY AS EVER ...
AH—
ISN'T THAT ......?

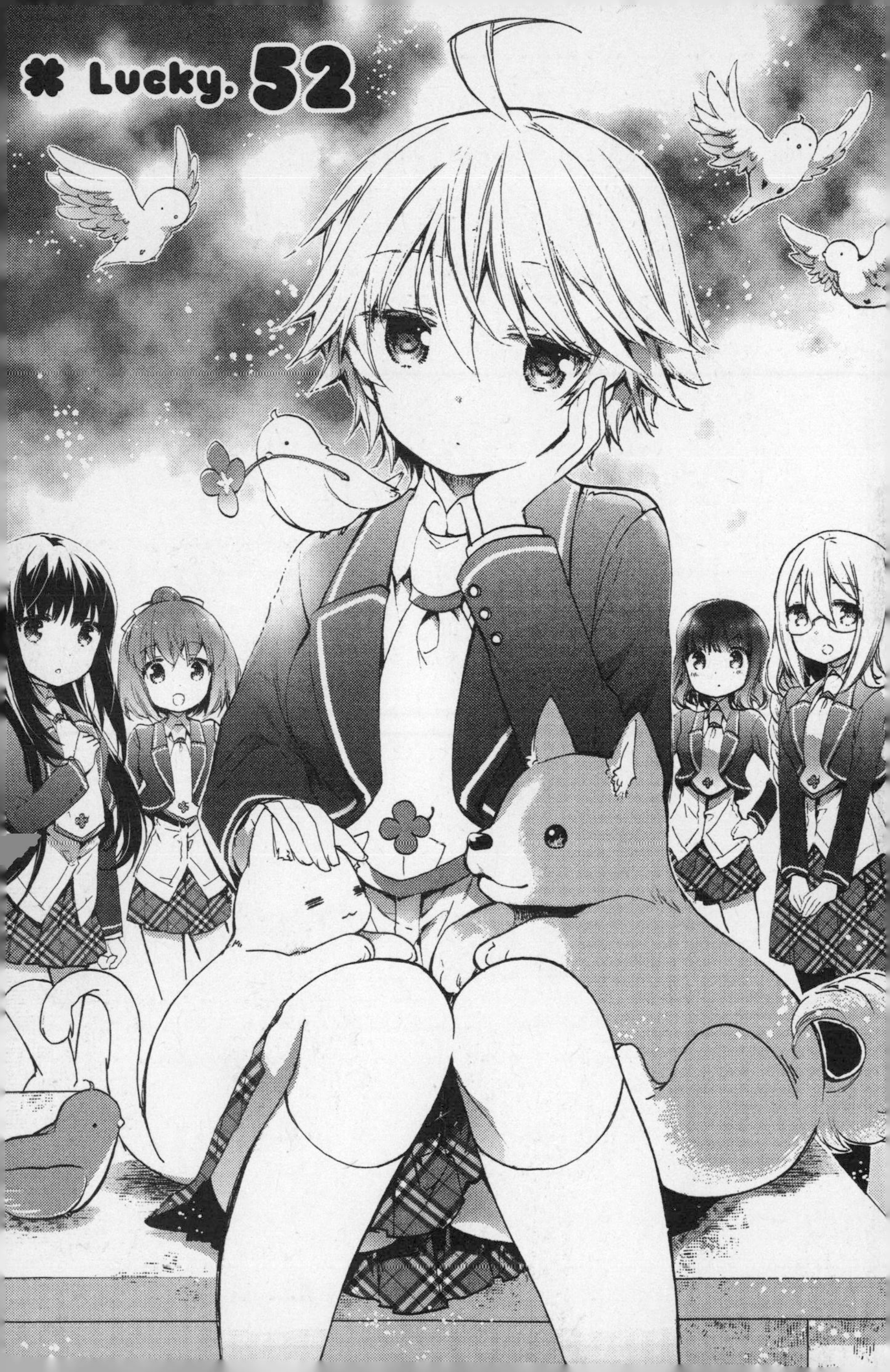
Lucky. 52

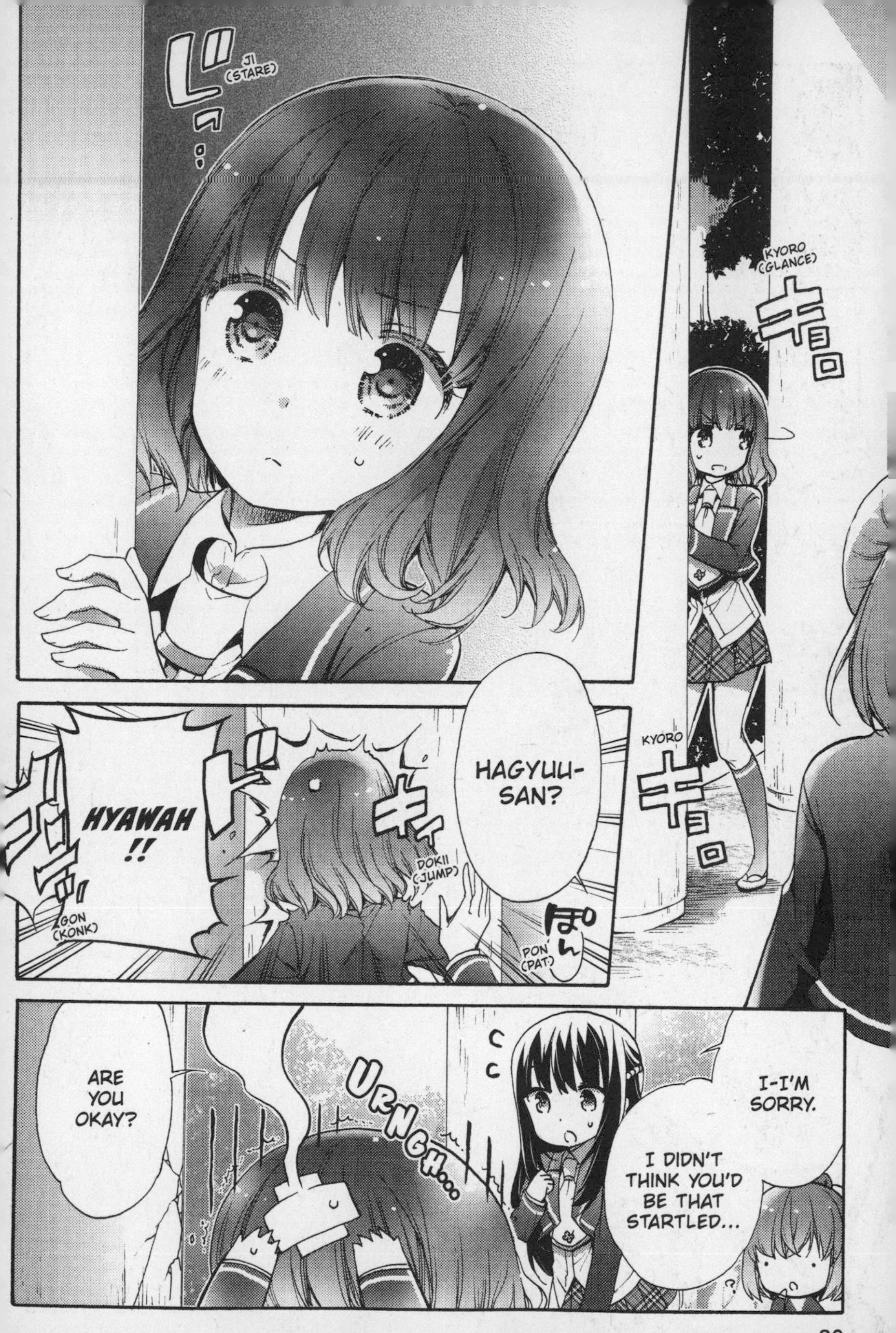
KYORO (GLANCE)
KYORO
JI (STARE)
HAGYUU-SAN?
PON (PAT)
DOKII (JUMP)
HYAWAH!!
GON (KONK)
I-I'M SORRY.
I DIDN'T THINK YOU'D BE THAT STARTLED...
URNGH...
ARE YOU OKAY?

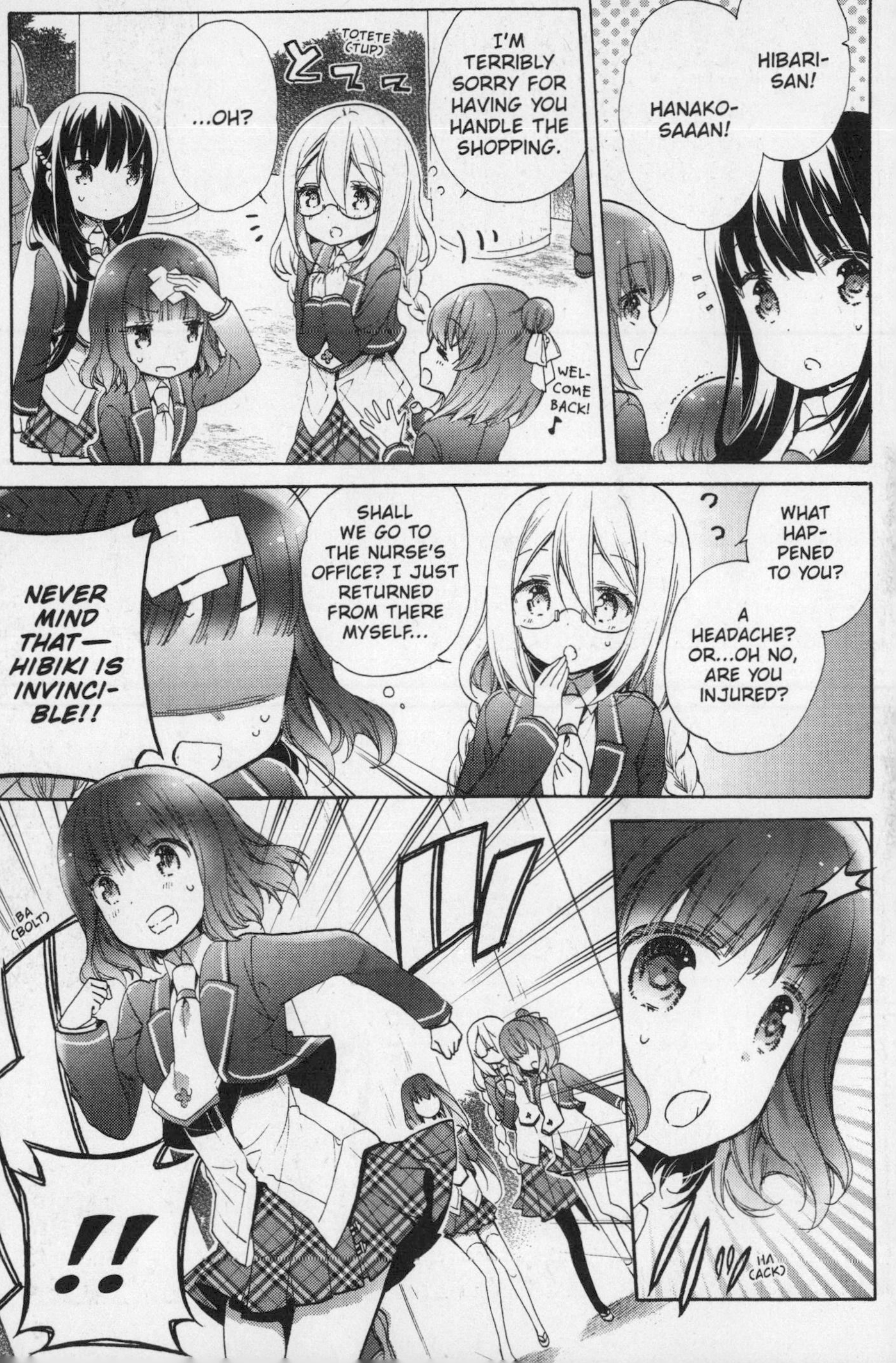
HIBARI-SAN!
HANAKO-SAAAN!
I'M TERRIBLY SORRY FOR HAVING YOU HANDLE THE SHOPPING.
TOTETE (TUP)
...OH?
WEL-COME BACK!
WHAT HAP-PENED TO YOU?
A HEADACHE? OR...OH NO, ARE YOU INJURED?
SHALL WE GO TO THE NURSE'S OFFICE? I JUST RETURNED FROM THERE MYSELF...
NEVER MIND THAT— HIBIKI IS INVINCI-BLE!!
HA (ACK)
BA (BOLT)
!!

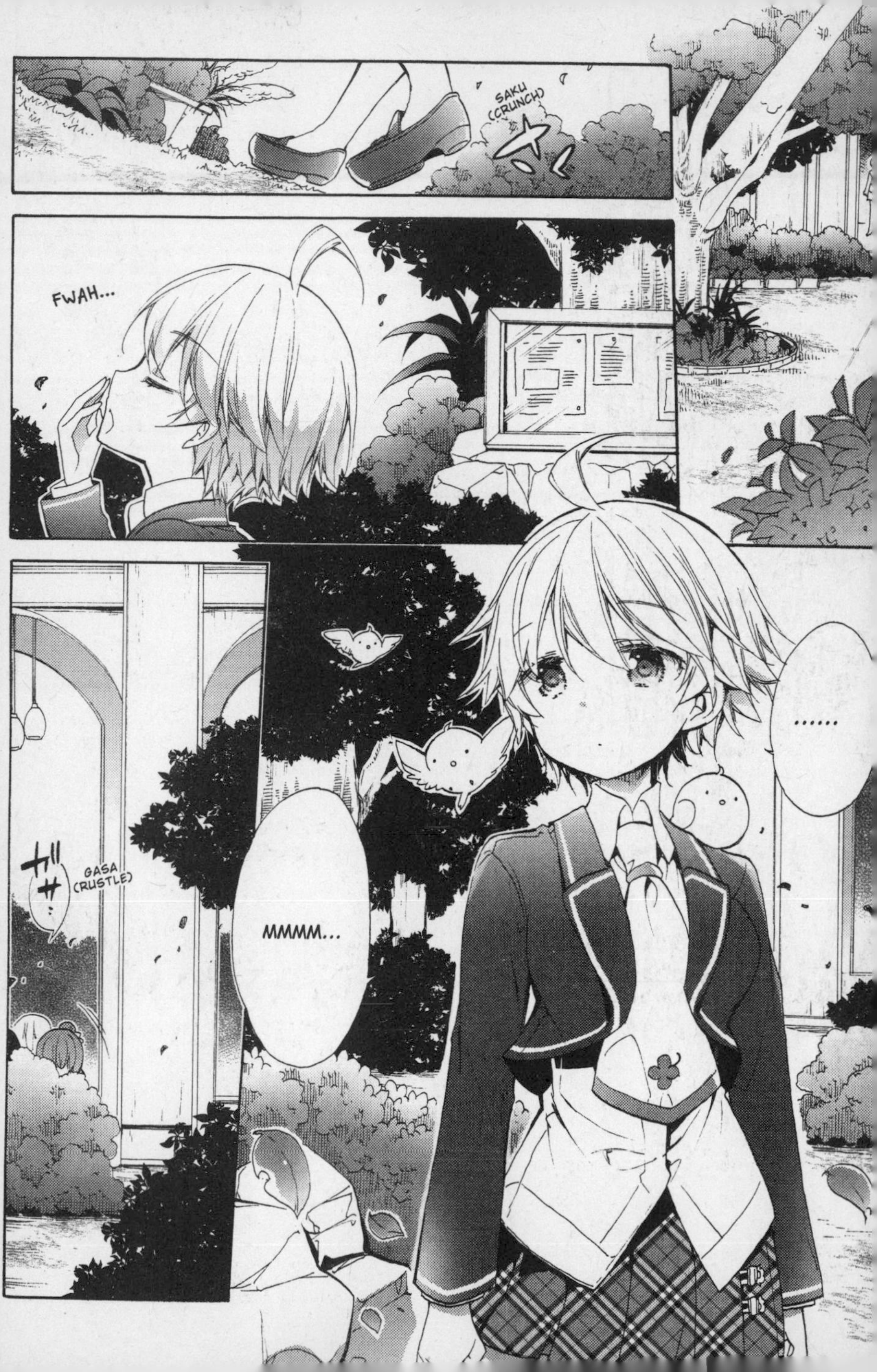
SAKU (CRUNCH)
FWAH...
......
MMMM...
GASA (RUSTLE)

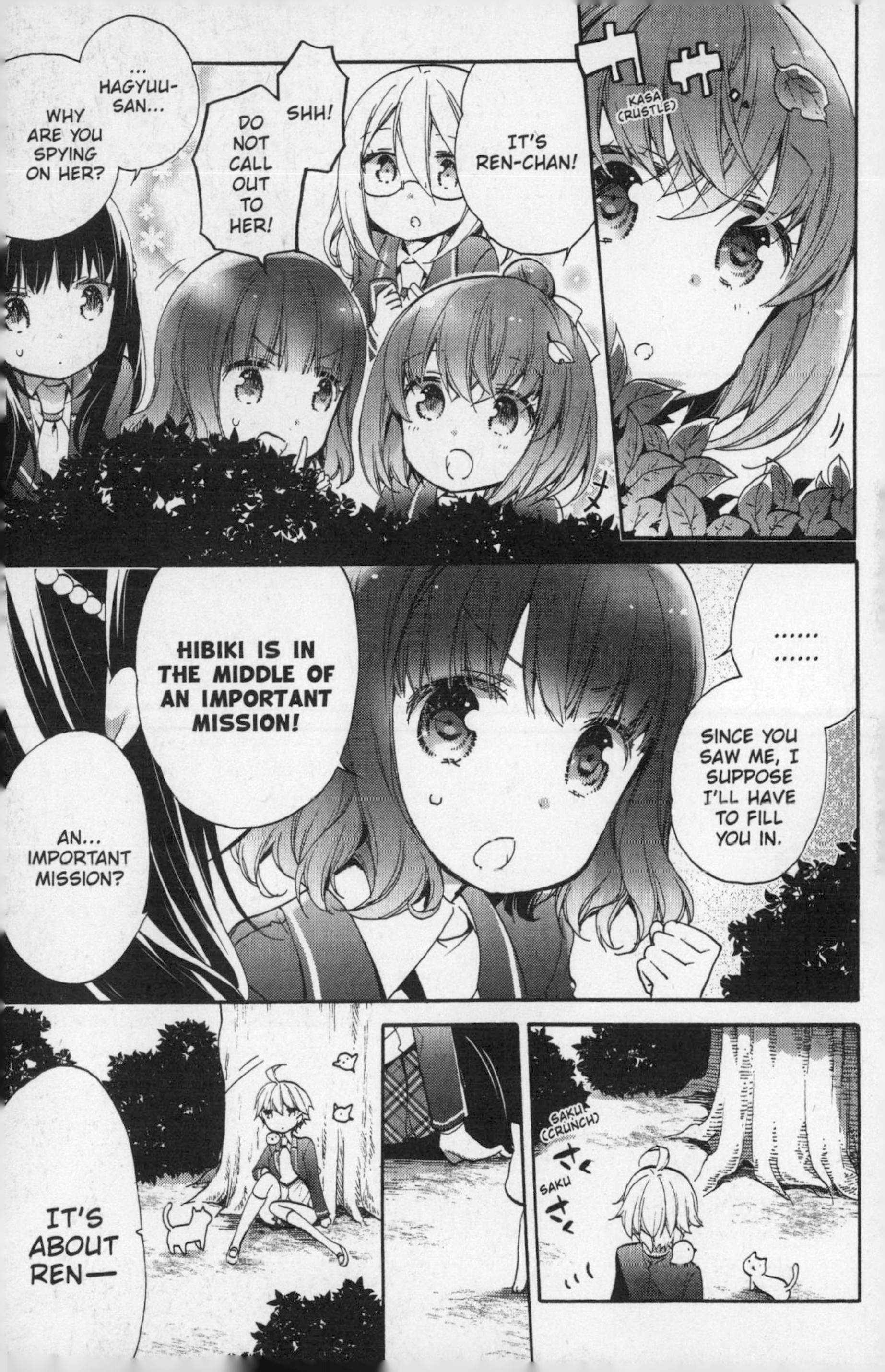
KASA (RUSTLE)
IT'S REN-CHAN!
SHH!
DO NOT CALL OUT TO HER!
... HAGYUU-SAN... WHY ARE YOU SPYING ON HER?
....
SINCE YOU SAW ME, I SUPPOSE I'LL HAVE TO FILL YOU IN.
HIBIKI IS IN THE MIDDLE OF AN IMPORTANT MISSION!
AN... IMPORTANT MISSION?
SAKU (CRUNCH)
SAKU
IT'S ABOUT REN—

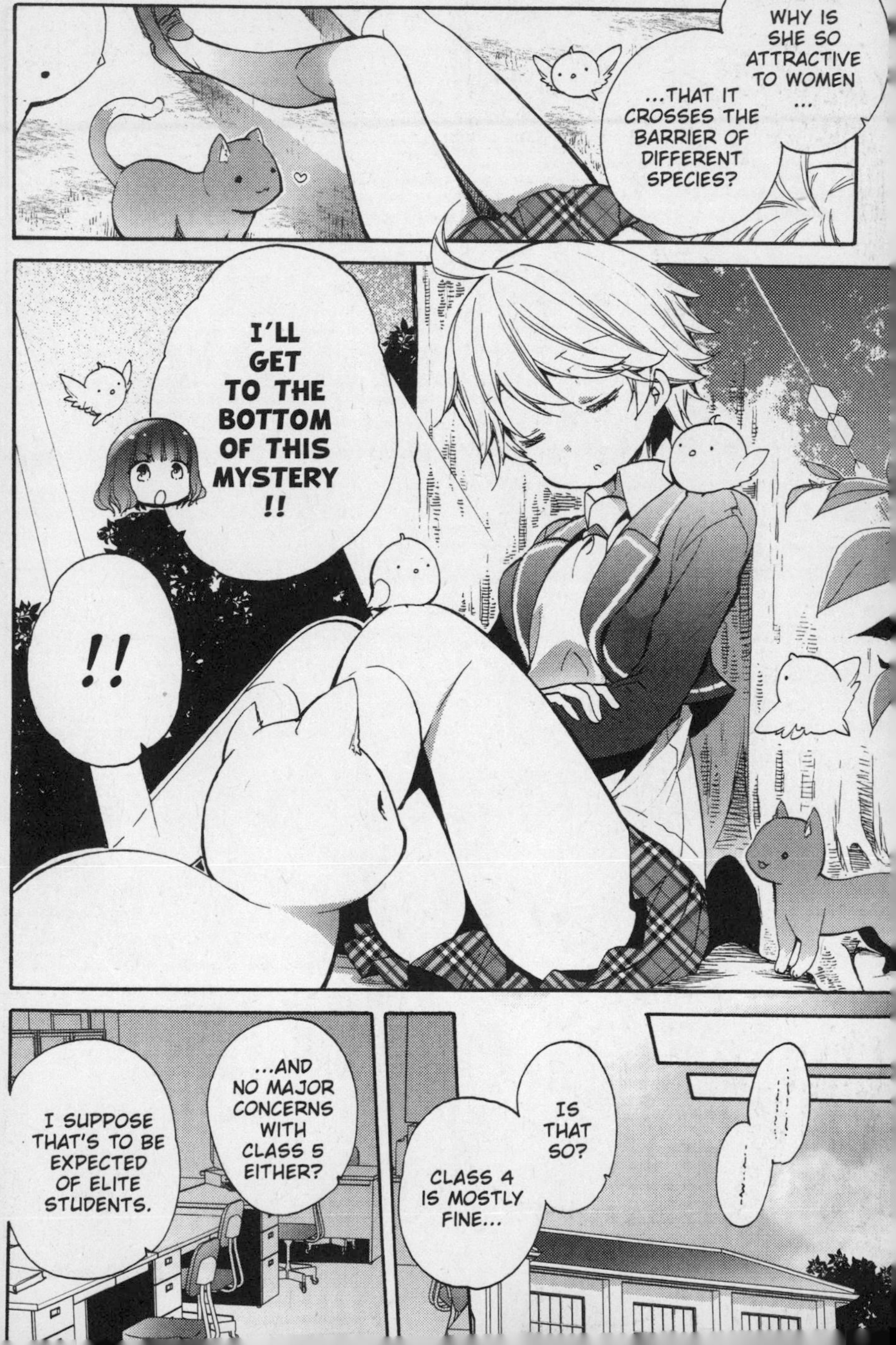
WHY IS SHE SO ATTRACTIVE TO WOMEN ...
...THAT IT CROSSES THE BARRIER OF DIFFERENT SPECIES?
.
I'LL GET TO THE BOTTOM OF THIS MYSTERY !!
!!
......
IS THAT SO?
CLASS 4 IS MOSTLY FINE...
...AND NO MAJOR CONCERNS WITH CLASS 5 EITHER?
I SUPPOSE THAT'S TO BE EXPECTED OF ELITE STUDENTS.

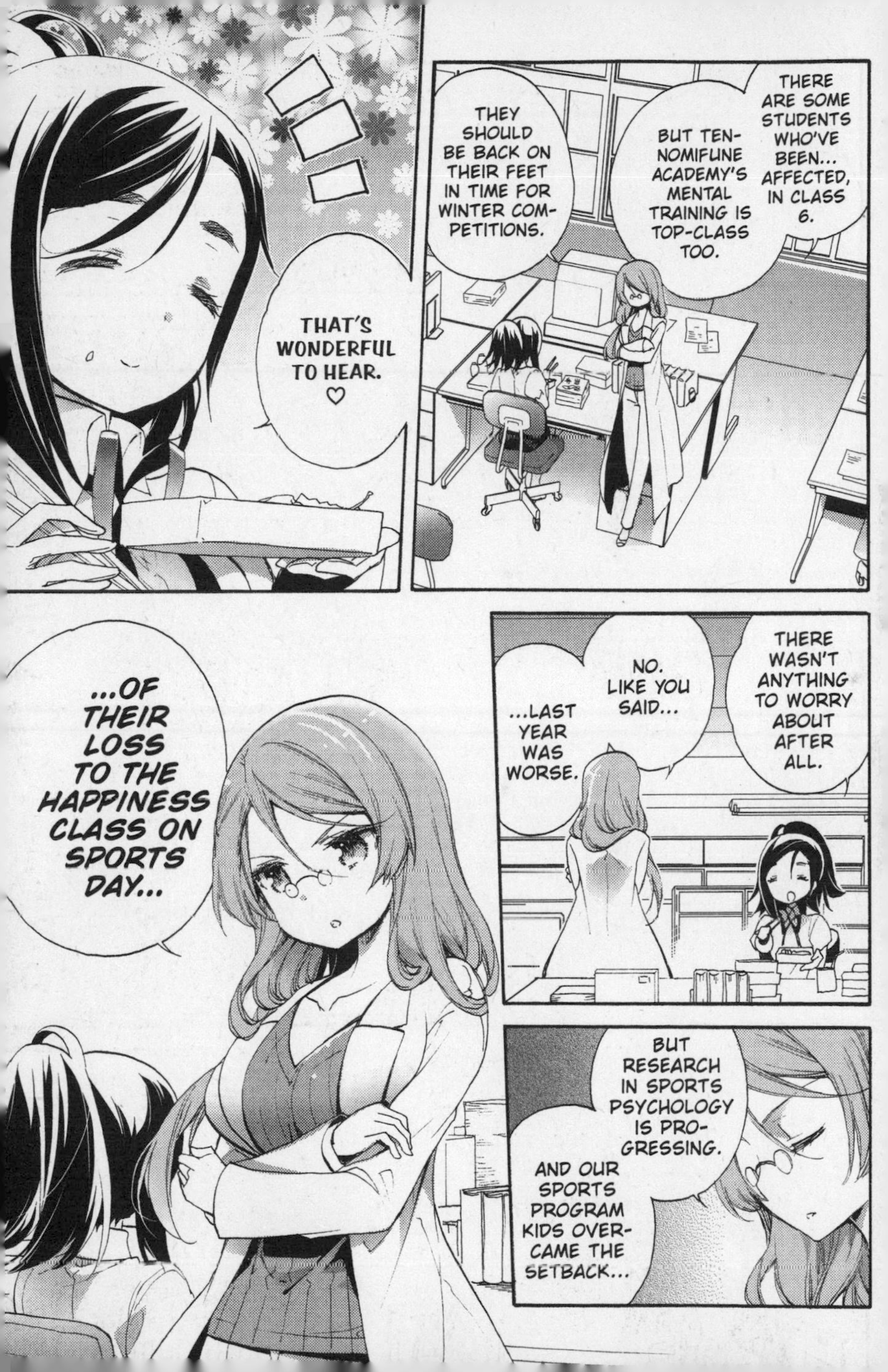
THERE ARE SOME STUDENTS WHO'VE BEEN... AFFECTED, IN CLASS 6.
BUT TENNOMIFUNE ACADEMY'S MENTAL TRAINING IS TOP-CLASS TOO.
THEY SHOULD BE BACK ON THEIR FEET IN TIME FOR WINTER COMPETITIONS.
THAT'S WONDERFUL TO HEAR. ♡
THERE WASN'T ANYTHING TO WORRY ABOUT AFTER ALL.
NO. LIKE YOU SAID...
...LAST YEAR WAS WORSE.
BUT RESEARCH IN SPORTS PSYCHOLOGY IS PROGRESSING.
AND OUR SPORTS PROGRAM KIDS OVERCAME THE SETBACK...
...OF THEIR LOSS TO THE HAPPINESS CLASS ON SPORTS DAY...

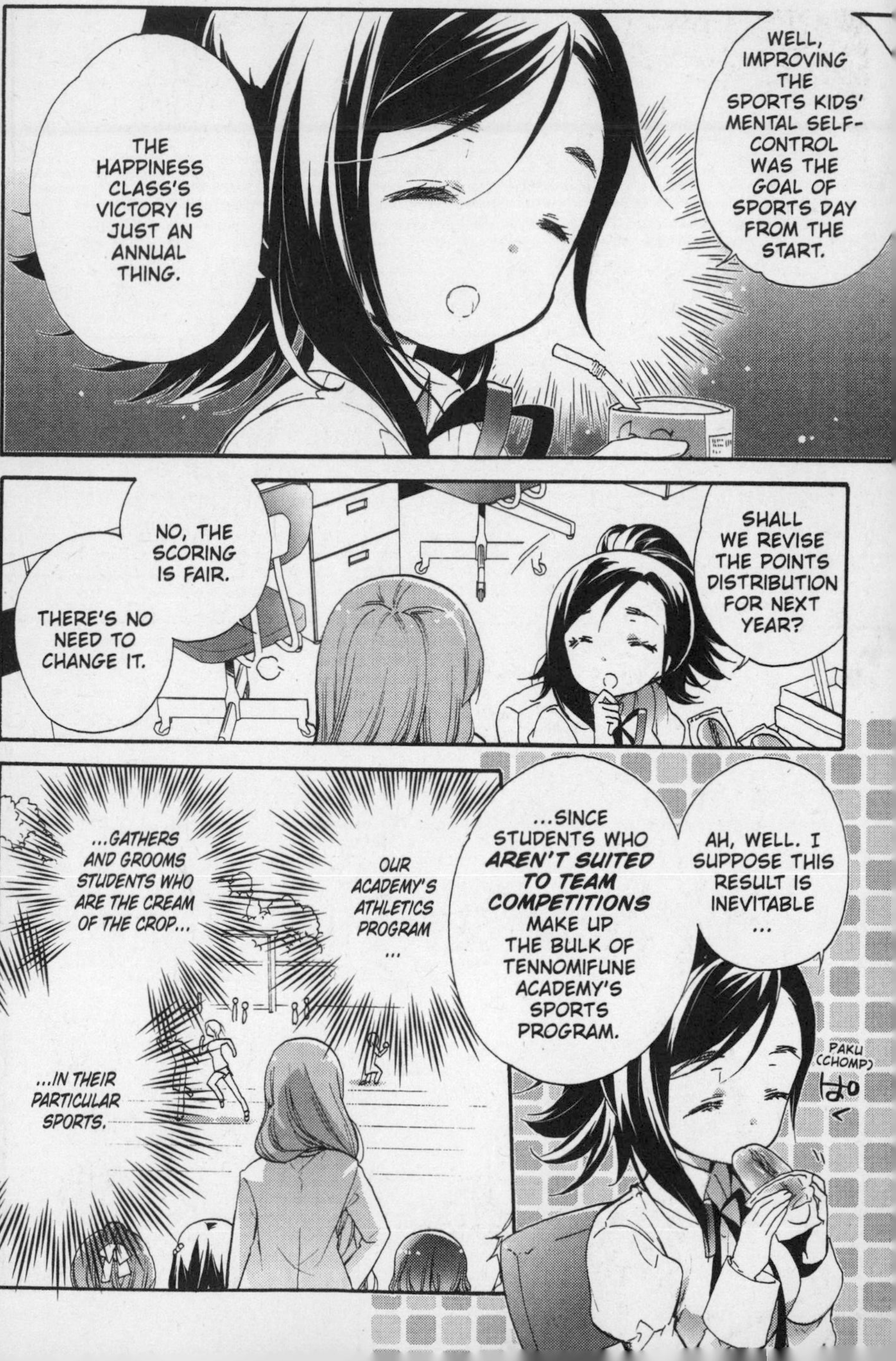
WELL, IMPROVING THE SPORTS KIDS' MENTAL SELF-CONTROL WAS THE GOAL OF SPORTS DAY FROM THE START.
THE HAPPINESS CLASS'S VICTORY IS JUST AN ANNUAL THING.
SHALL WE REVISE THE POINTS DISTRIBUTION FOR NEXT YEAR?
NO, THE SCORING IS FAIR.
THERE'S NO NEED TO CHANGE IT.
AH, WELL. I SUPPOSE THIS RESULT IS INEVITABLE...
...SINCE STUDENTS WHO **AREN'T SUITED TO TEAM COMPETITIONS** MAKE UP THE BULK OF TENNOMIFUNE ACADEMY'S SPORTS PROGRAM.
PAKU (CHOMP)
OUR ACADEMY'S ATHLETICS PROGRAM...
...GATHERS AND GROOMS STUDENTS WHO ARE THE CREAM OF THE CROP...
...IN THEIR PARTICULAR SPORTS.

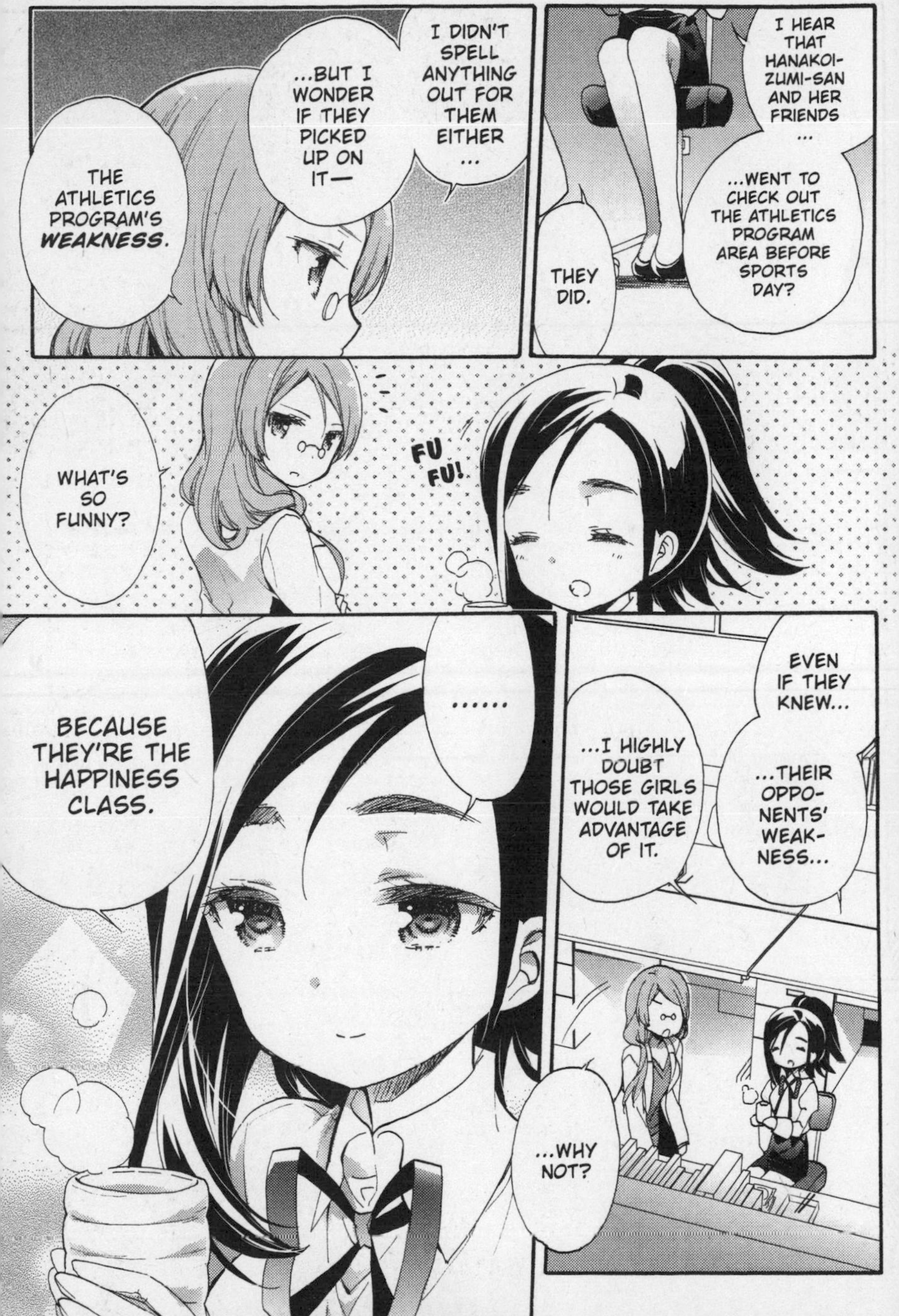
I HEAR THAT HANAKOIZUMI-SAN AND HER FRIENDS ...
...WENT TO CHECK OUT THE ATHLETICS PROGRAM AREA BEFORE SPORTS DAY?
THEY DID.
I DIDN'T SPELL ANYTHING OUT FOR THEM EITHER ...
...BUT I WONDER IF THEY PICKED UP ON IT—
THE ATHLETICS PROGRAM'S ***WEAKNESS***.
FU FU!
WHAT'S SO FUNNY?
EVEN IF THEY KNEW...
...THEIR OPPONENTS' WEAKNESS...
...I HIGHLY DOUBT THOSE GIRLS WOULD TAKE ADVANTAGE OF IT.
...WHY NOT?
......
BECAUSE THEY'RE THE HAPPINESS CLASS.

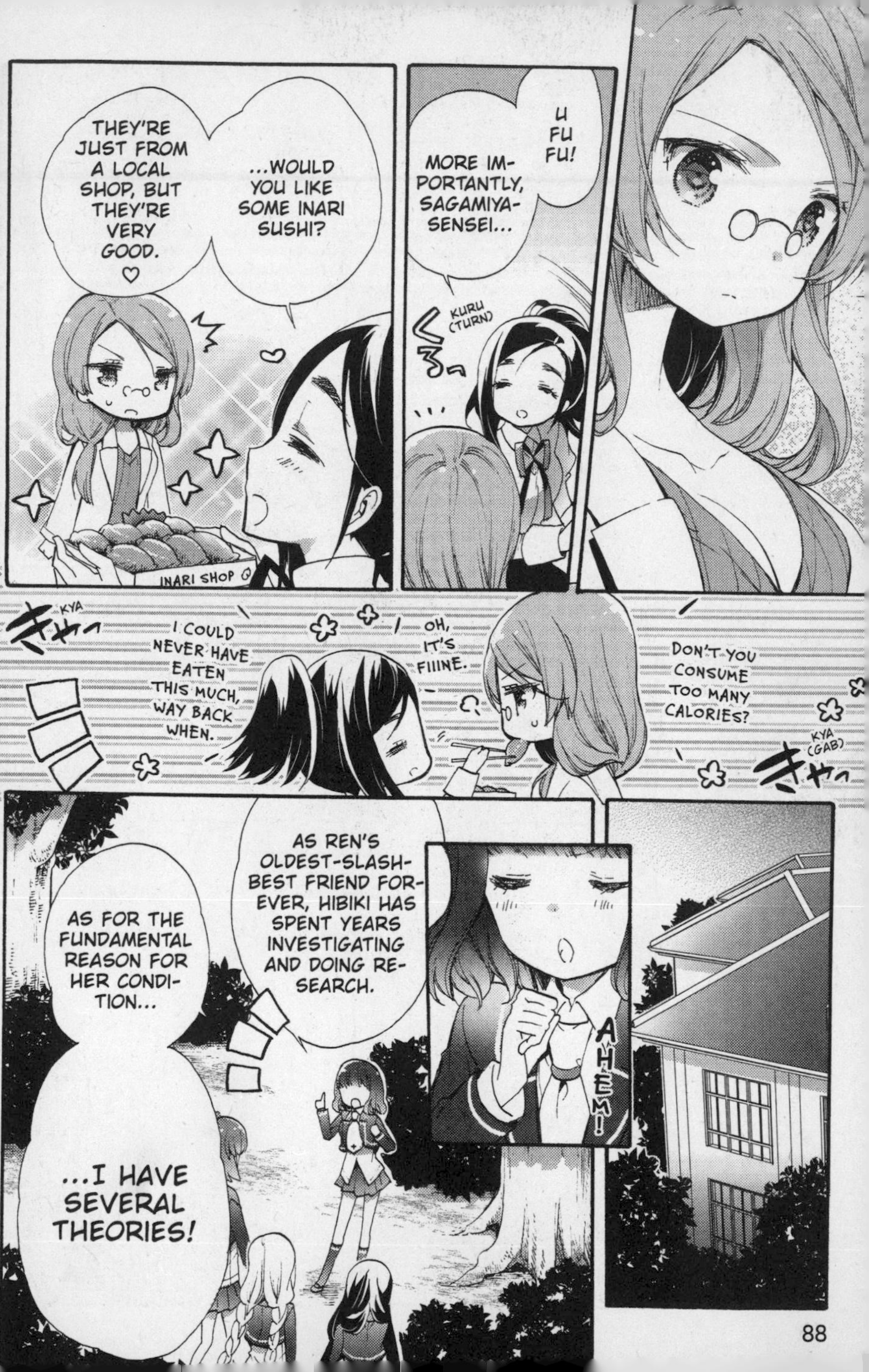
U FU FU!
MORE IMPORTANTLY, SAGAMIYA-SENSEI...
くるっ
KURU (TURN)
...WOULD YOU LIKE SOME INARI SUSHI?
THEY'RE JUST FROM A LOCAL SHOP, BUT THEY'RE VERY GOOD. ♡
INARI SHOP
きゃっ
KYA (GAB)
DON'T YOU CONSUME TOO MANY CALORIES?
OH, IT'S FIIINE.
I COULD NEVER HAVE EATEN THIS MUCH, WAY BACK WHEN.
きゃっ
KYA
AHEM!
AS REN'S OLDEST-SLASH-BEST FRIEND FOREVER, HIBIKI HAS SPENT YEARS INVESTIGATING AND DOING RESEARCH.
AS FOR THE FUNDAMENTAL REASON FOR HER CONDITION...
...I HAVE SEVERAL THEORIES!

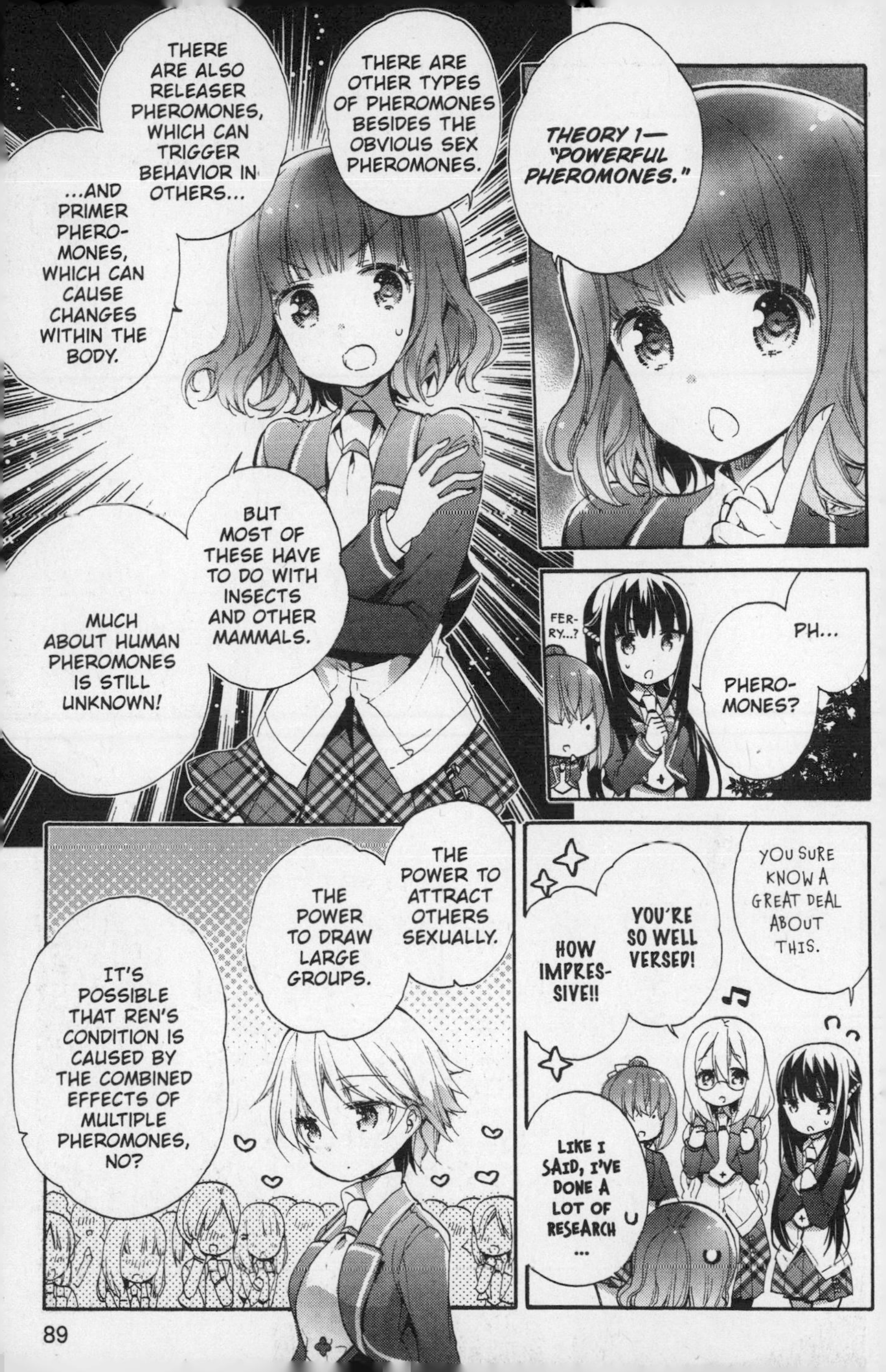
THEORY 1— "POWERFUL PHEROMONES."
PH... PHERO-MONES?
FER-RY...?
THERE ARE OTHER TYPES OF PHEROMONES BESIDES THE OBVIOUS SEX PHEROMONES.
THERE ARE ALSO RELEASER PHEROMONES, WHICH CAN TRIGGER BEHAVIOR IN OTHERS...
...AND PRIMER PHERO-MONES, WHICH CAN CAUSE CHANGES WITHIN THE BODY.
BUT MOST OF THESE HAVE TO DO WITH INSECTS AND OTHER MAMMALS.
MUCH ABOUT HUMAN PHEROMONES IS STILL UNKNOWN!
YOU SURE KNOW A GREAT DEAL ABOUT THIS.
YOU'RE SO WELL VERSED!
HOW IMPRES-SIVE!!
LIKE I SAID, I'VE DONE A LOT OF RESEARCH ...
THE POWER TO ATTRACT OTHERS SEXUALLY.
THE POWER TO DRAW LARGE GROUPS.
IT'S POSSIBLE THAT REN'S CONDITION IS CAUSED BY THE COMBINED EFFECTS OF MULTIPLE PHEROMONES, NO?

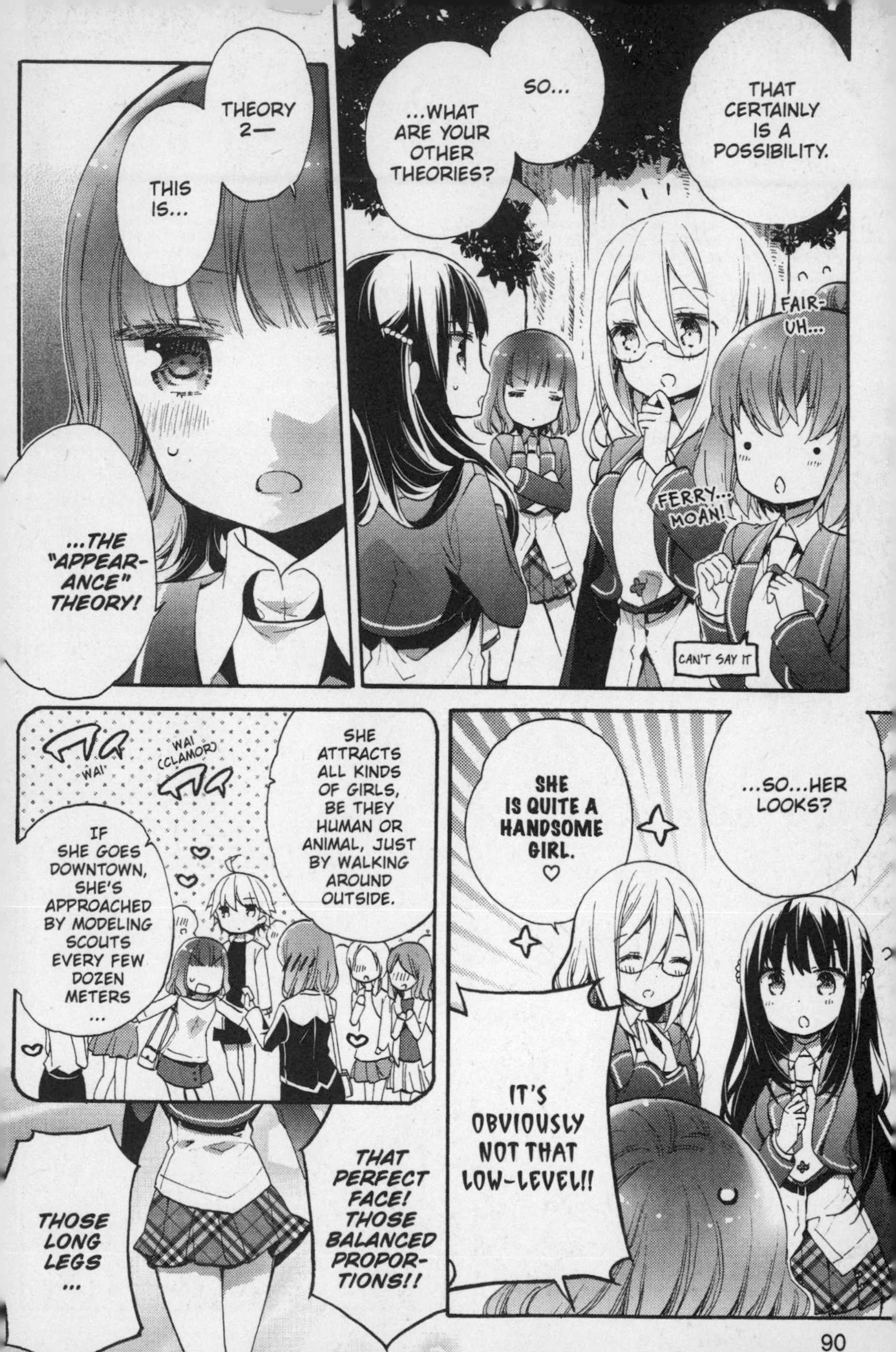
THAT CERTAINLY IS A POSSIBILITY.
SO...
...WHAT ARE YOUR OTHER THEORIES?
FAIR- UH...
FERRY... MOAN!
CAN'T SAY IT
THEORY 2—
THIS IS...
...THE "APPEARANCE" THEORY!
...SO...HER LOOKS?
SHE IS QUITE A HANDSOME GIRL.
IT'S OBVIOUSLY NOT THAT LOW-LEVEL!!
SHE ATTRACTS ALL KINDS OF GIRLS, BE THEY HUMAN OR ANIMAL, JUST BY WALKING AROUND OUTSIDE.
WAI (CLAMOR)
WAI
IF SHE GOES DOWNTOWN, SHE'S APPROACHED BY MODELING SCOUTS EVERY FEW DOZEN METERS ...
THAT PERFECT FACE! THOSE BALANCED PROPORTIONS!!
THOSE LONG LEGS ...

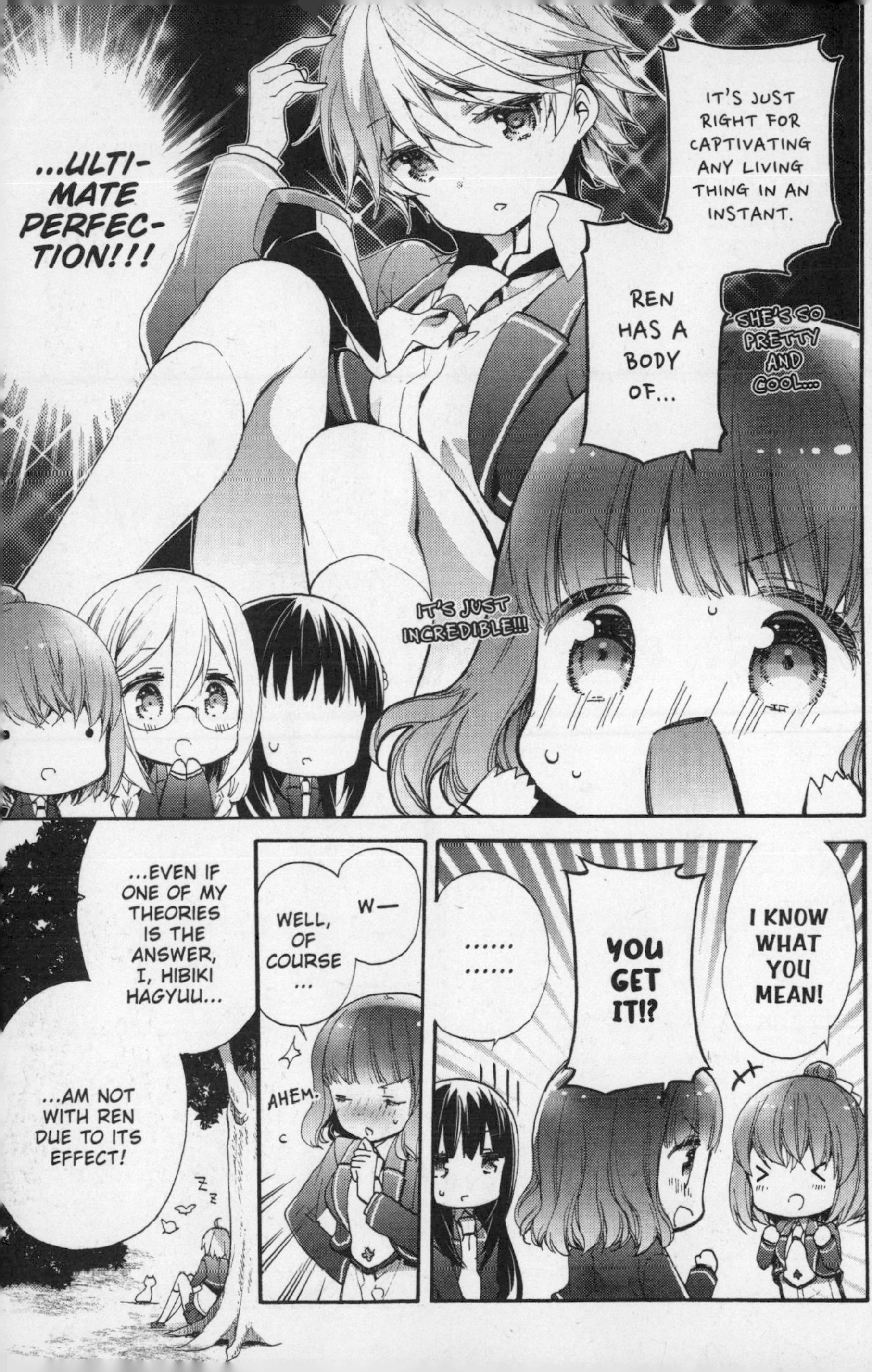
IT'S JUST RIGHT FOR CAPTIVATING ANY LIVING THING IN AN INSTANT.
REN HAS A BODY OF...
SHE'S SO PRETTY AND COOL...
...ULTIMATE PERFECTION!!!
IT'S JUST INCREDIBLE!!!
I KNOW WHAT YOU MEAN!
YOU GET IT!?
......
......
W— WELL, OF COURSE...
AHEM.
...EVEN IF ONE OF MY THEORIES IS THE ANSWER, I, HIBIKI HAGYUU...
...AM NOT WITH REN DUE TO ITS EFFECT!

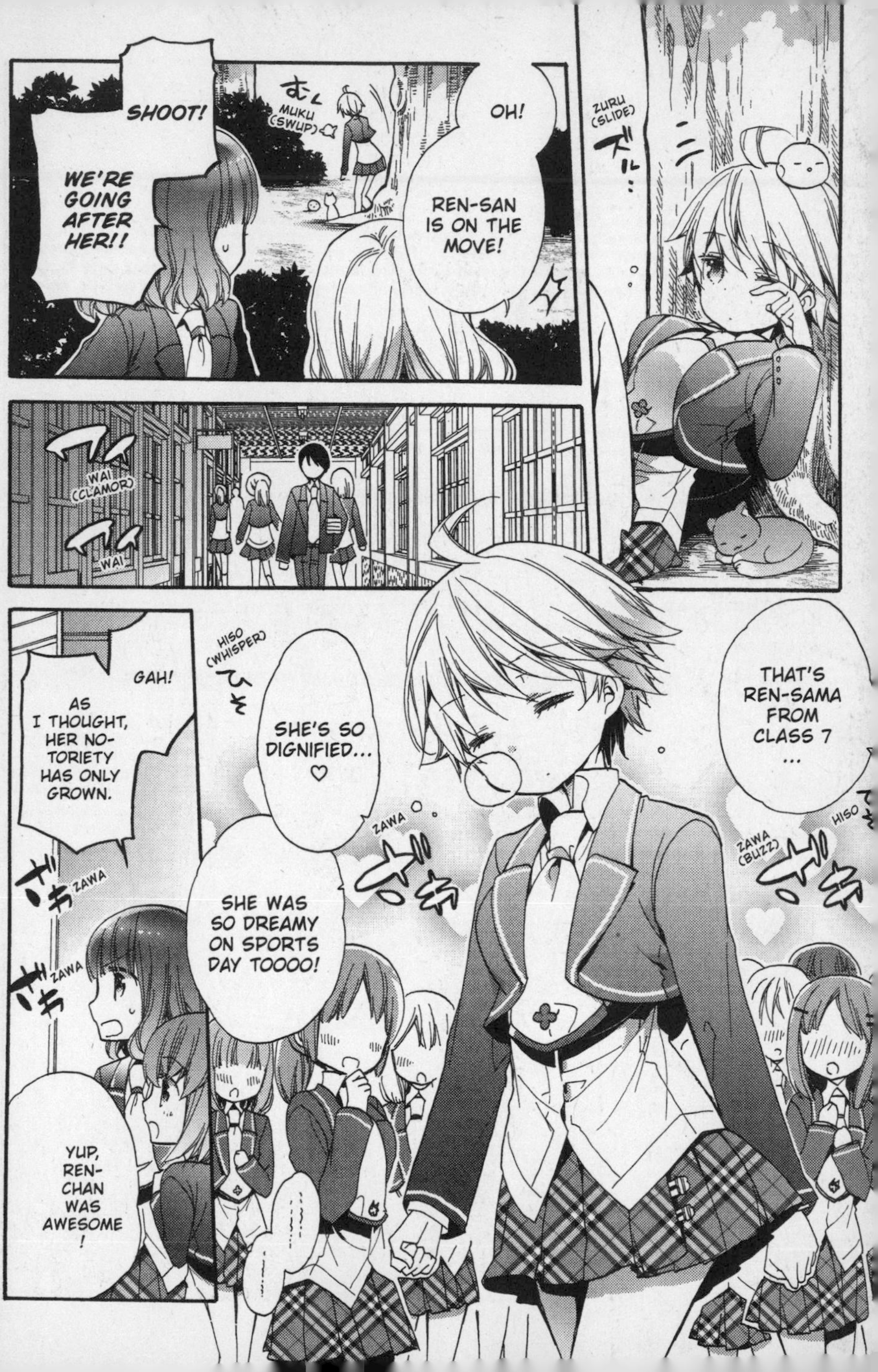
ZURU (SLIDE)
OH!
REN-SAN IS ON THE MOVE!
MUKU (SWUP)
SHOOT!
WE'RE GOING AFTER HER!!
WAI (CLAMOR)
WAI
THAT'S REN-SAMA FROM CLASS 7 ...
HISO
ZAWA (BUZZ)
HISO (WHISPER)
SHE'S SO DIGNIFIED... ♡
ZAWA
SHE WAS SO DREAMY ON SPORTS DAY TOOOO!
GAH!
AS I THOUGHT, HER NO-TORIETY HAS ONLY GROWN.
ZAWA
ZAWA
YUP, REN-CHAN WAS AWESOME!

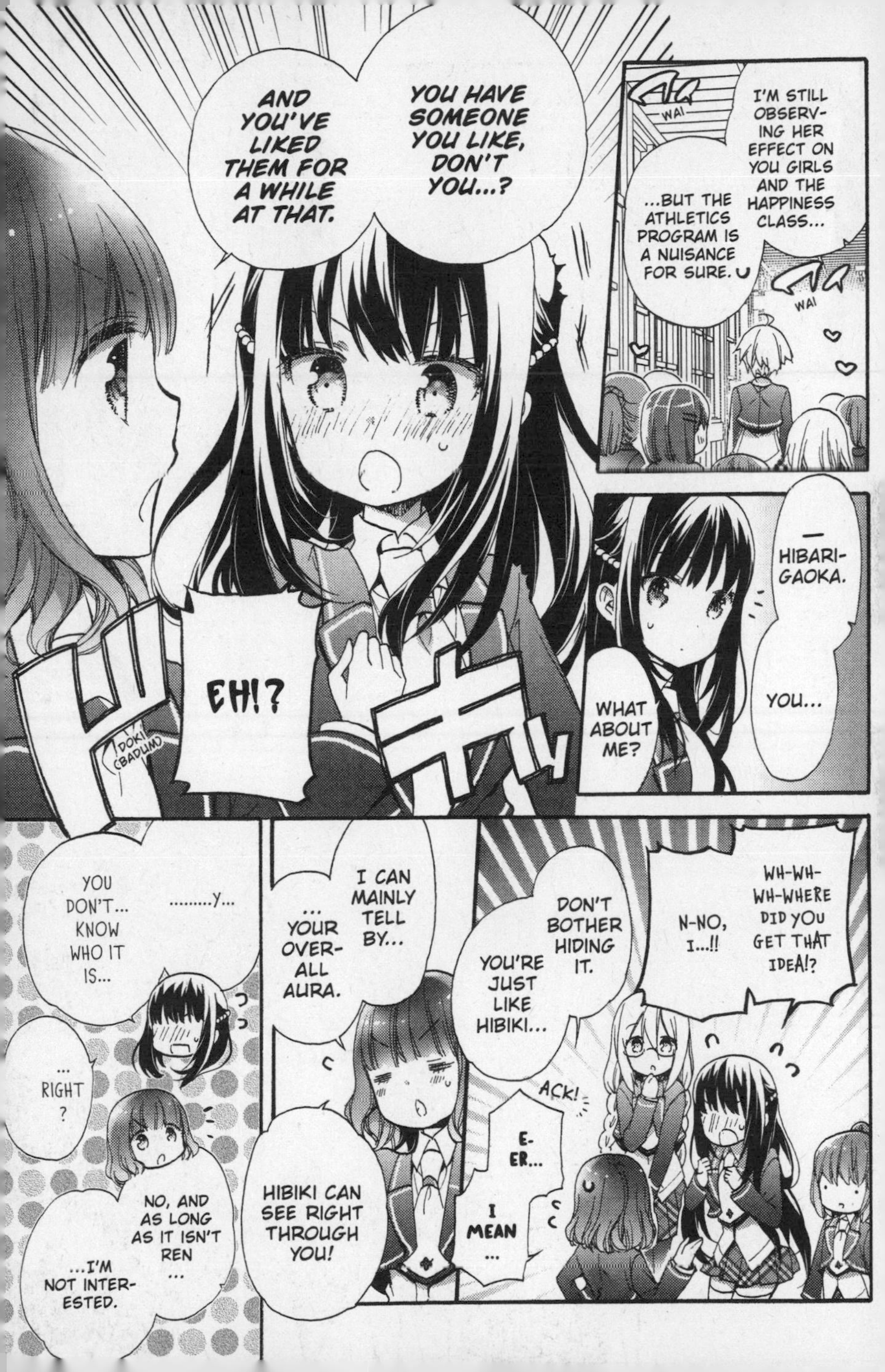

WAI
I'M STILL OBSERVING HER EFFECT ON YOU GIRLS AND THE HAPPINESS CLASS...
...BUT THE ATHLETICS PROGRAM IS A NUISANCE FOR SURE.
WAI
—HIBARIGAOKA.
YOU...
WHAT ABOUT ME?
YOU HAVE SOMEONE YOU LIKE, DON'T YOU...?
AND YOU'VE LIKED THEM FOR A WHILE AT THAT.
DOKI (BADUM)
EH!?
WH-WH-WH-WHERE DID YOU GET THAT IDEA!?
N-NO, I...!!
DON'T BOTHER HIDING IT.
YOU'RE JUST LIKE HIBIKI...
ACK!
E-ER...
I MEAN...
I CAN MAINLY TELL BY...
...YOUR OVERALL AURA.
HIBIKI CAN SEE RIGHT THROUGH YOU!
.........Y...
YOU DON'T... KNOW WHO IT IS...
...RIGHT?
NO, AND AS LONG AS IT ISN'T REN...
...I'M NOT INTERESTED.

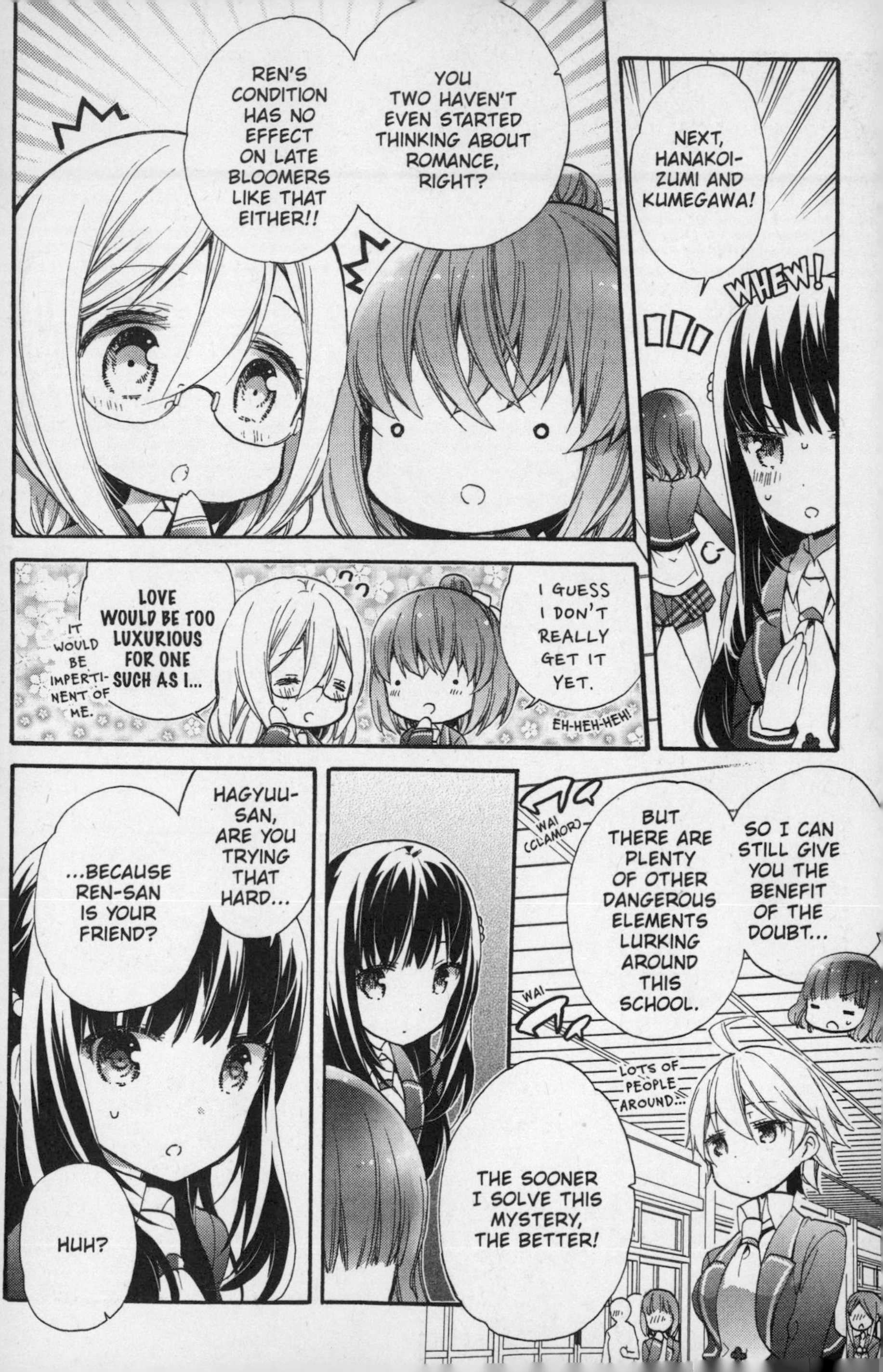
NEXT, HANAKOIZUMI AND KUMEGAWA!
WHEW!
YOU TWO HAVEN'T EVEN STARTED THINKING ABOUT ROMANCE, RIGHT?
REN'S CONDITION HAS NO EFFECT ON LATE BLOOMERS LIKE THAT EITHER!!
I GUESS I DON'T REALLY GET IT YET.
EH-HEH-HEH!
LOVE WOULD BE TOO LUXURIOUS FOR ONE SUCH AS I...
IT WOULD BE IMPERTINENT OF ME.
WAI (CLAMOR)
SO I CAN STILL GIVE YOU THE BENEFIT OF THE DOUBT...
BUT THERE ARE PLENTY OF OTHER DANGEROUS ELEMENTS LURKING AROUND THIS SCHOOL.
WAI
LOTS OF PEOPLE AROUND...
THE SOONER I SOLVE THIS MYSTERY, THE BETTER!
HAGYUU-SAN, ARE YOU TRYING THAT HARD...
...BECAUSE REN-SAN IS YOUR FRIEND?
HUH?

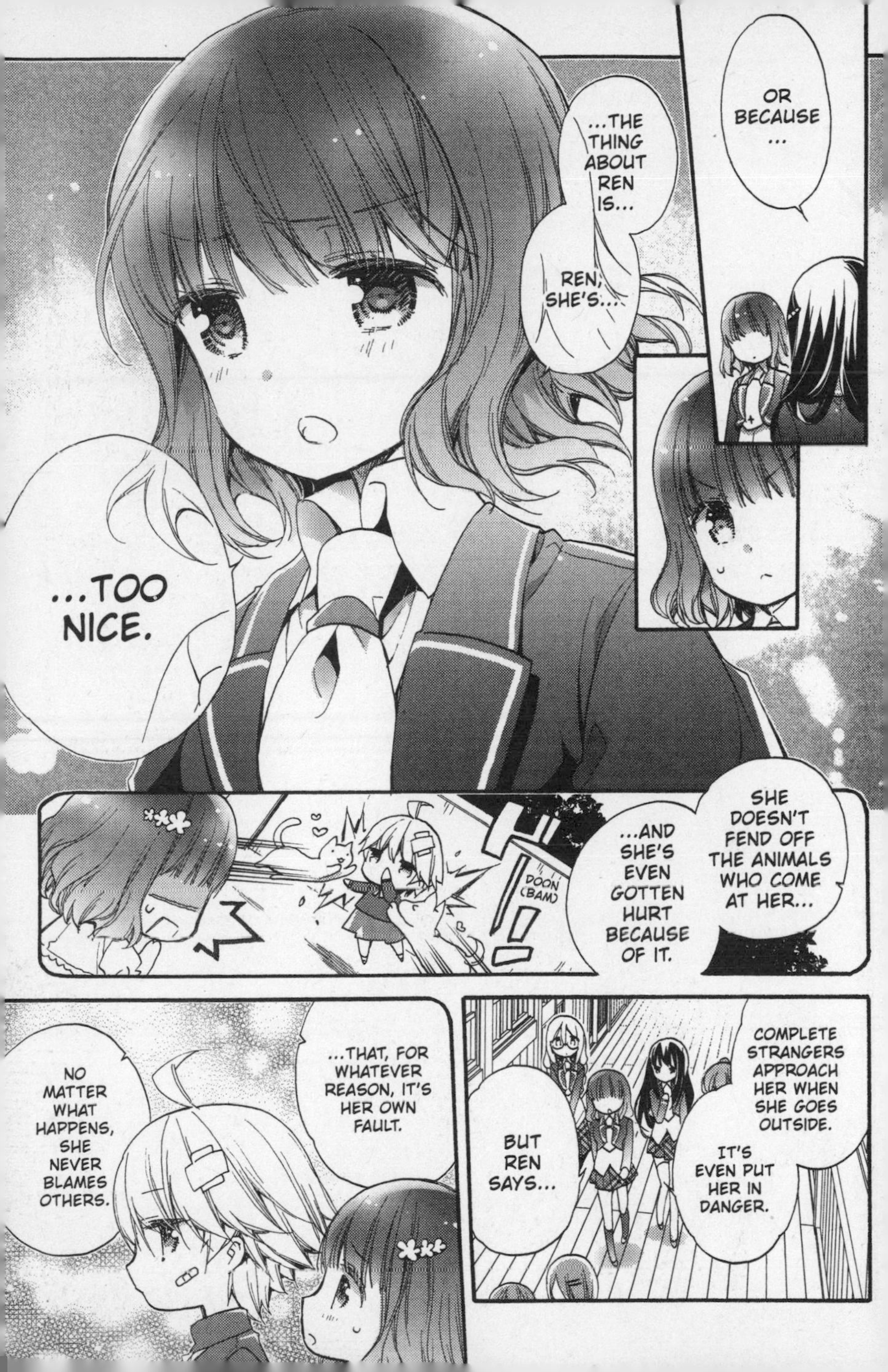
OR BECAUSE ...
...THE THING ABOUT REN IS...
REN, SHE'S...
...TOO NICE.
SHE DOESN'T FEND OFF THE ANIMALS WHO COME AT HER...
...AND SHE'S EVEN GOTTEN HURT BECAUSE OF IT.
DOON (BAM)
COMPLETE STRANGERS APPROACH HER WHEN SHE GOES OUTSIDE.
IT'S EVEN PUT HER IN DANGER.
BUT REN SAYS...
...THAT, FOR WHATEVER REASON, IT'S HER OWN FAULT.
NO MATTER WHAT HAPPENS, SHE NEVER BLAMES OTHERS.

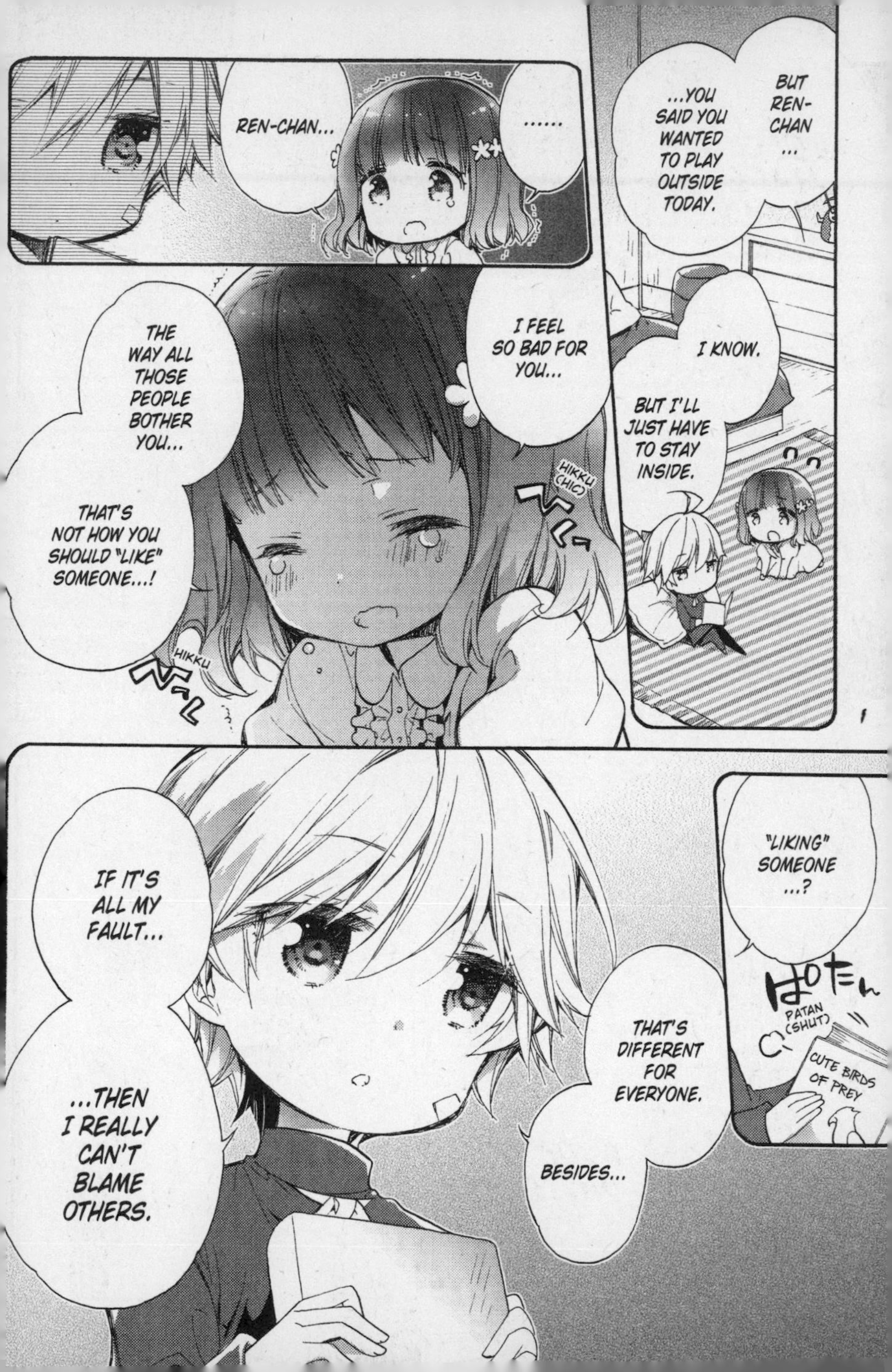
BUT REN-CHAN...
...YOU SAID YOU WANTED TO PLAY OUTSIDE TODAY.
I KNOW.
BUT I'LL JUST HAVE TO STAY INSIDE.
......
REN-CHAN...
I FEEL SO BAD FOR YOU...
HIKKU (HIC)
THE WAY ALL THOSE PEOPLE BOTHER YOU...
THAT'S NOT HOW YOU SHOULD "LIKE" SOMEONE...!
HIKKU
"LIKING" SOMEONE...?
ぱたん
PATAN (SHUT)
CUTE BIRDS OF PREY
THAT'S DIFFERENT FOR EVERYONE.
BESIDES...
IF IT'S ALL MY FAULT...
...THEN I REALLY CAN'T BLAME OTHERS.

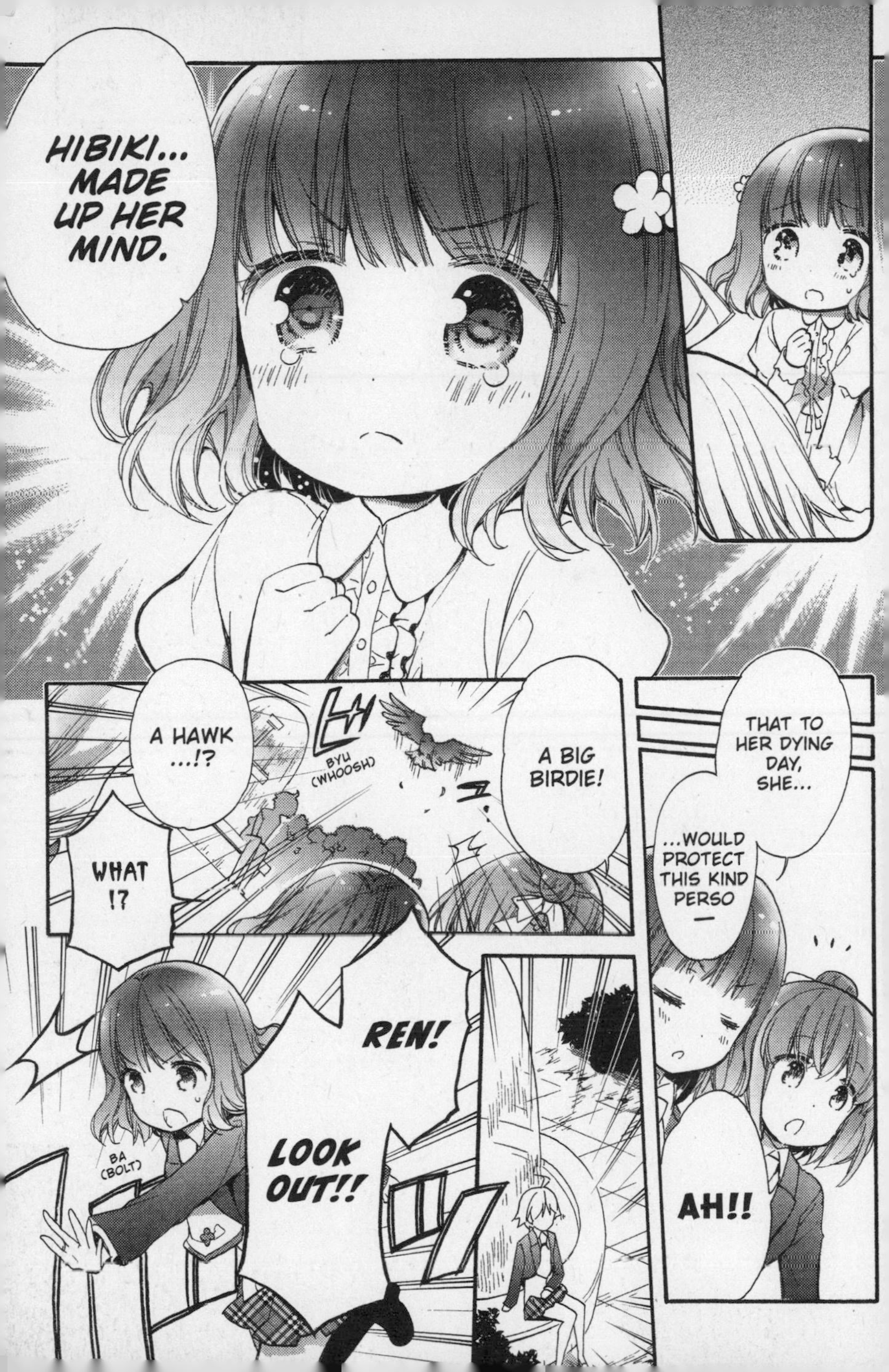
HIBIKI... MADE UP HER MIND.
THAT TO HER DYING DAY, SHE...
...WOULD PROTECT THIS KIND PERSO—
A BIG BIRDIE!
BYU (WHOOSH)
A HAWK ...!?
WHAT !?
AH!!
REN!
LOOK OUT!!
BA (BOLT)

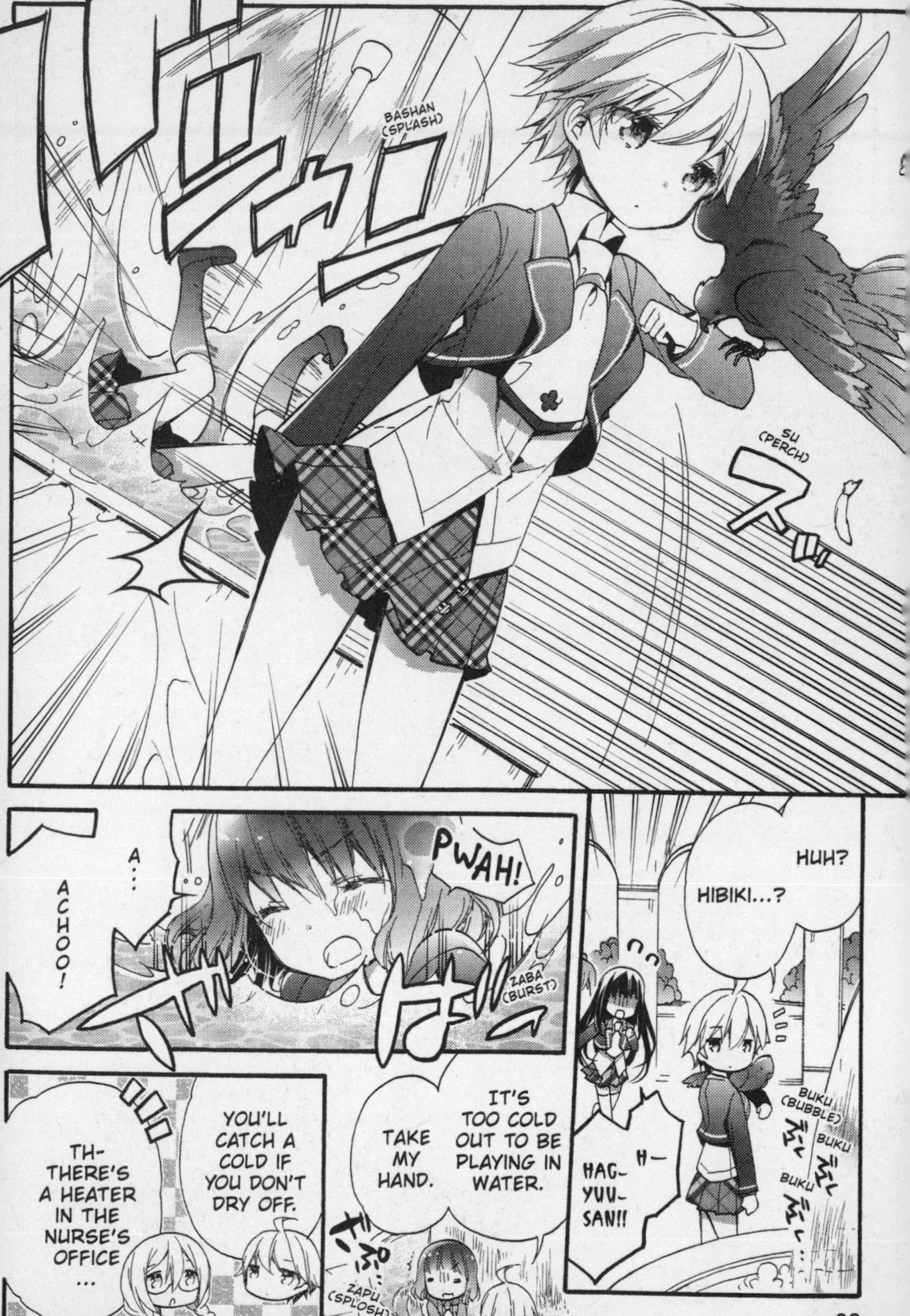
BASHAN (SPLASH)
SU (PERCH)
HUH?
HIBIKI...?
H—
HAG-YUU-SAN!!
BUKU (BUBBLE)
BUKU
BUKU
PWAH!
ZABA (BURST)
A...
ACHOO!
IT'S TOO COLD OUT TO BE PLAYING IN WATER.
TAKE MY HAND.
ZAPU (SPLOSH)
YOU'LL CATCH A COLD IF YOU DON'T DRY OFF.
TH-THERE'S A HEATER IN THE NURSE'S OFFICE ...

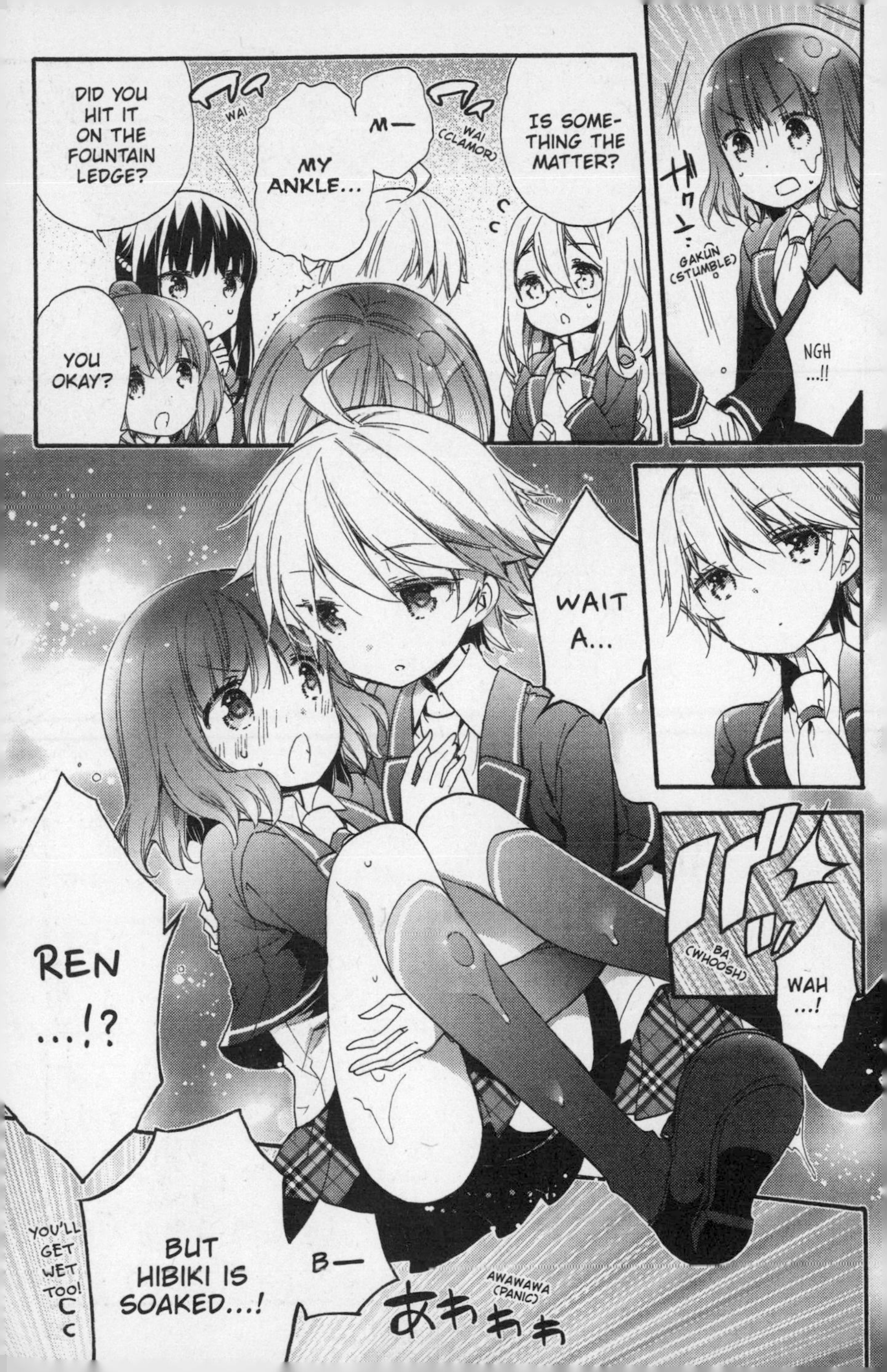
GAKUN (STUMBLE)
NGH ...!!
IS SOMETHING THE MATTER?
WAI (CLAMOR)
M—
MY ANKLE...
WAI
DID YOU HIT IT ON THE FOUNTAIN LEDGE?
YOU OKAY?
WAIT A...
BA (WHOOSH)
WAH ...!
REN ...!?
B—
AWAWAWA (PANIC)
BUT HIBIKI IS SOAKED...!
YOU'LL GET WET TOO!

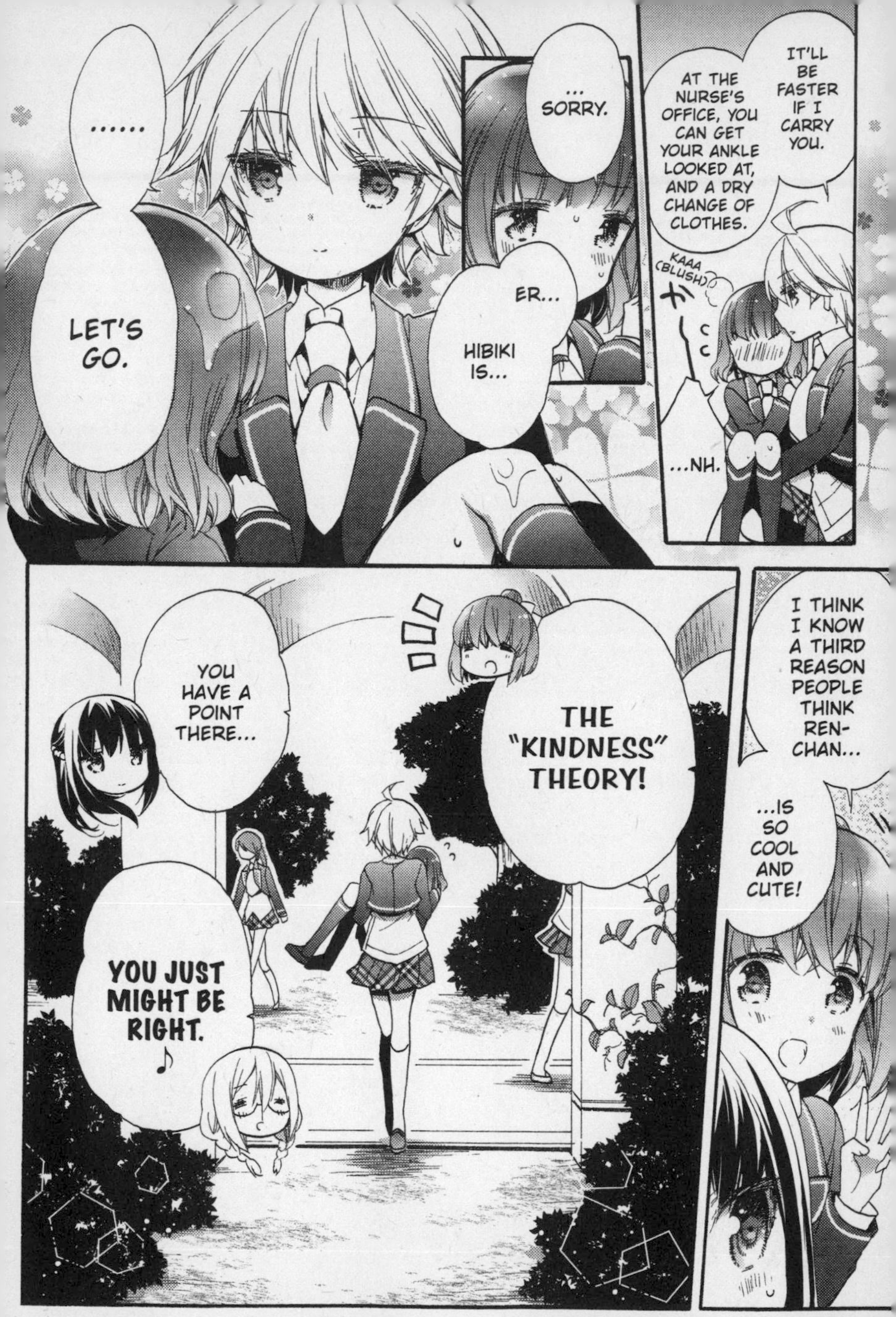
IT'LL BE FASTER IF I CARRY YOU.
AT THE NURSE'S OFFICE, YOU CAN GET YOUR ANKLE LOOKED AT, AND A DRY CHANGE OF CLOTHES.
KAAA (BLUSH)
...NH.
... SORRY.
ER...
HIBIKI IS...
......
LET'S GO.
I THINK I KNOW A THIRD REASON PEOPLE THINK REN-CHAN...
...IS SO COOL AND CUTE!
THE "KINDNESS" THEORY!
YOU HAVE A POINT THERE...
YOU JUST MIGHT BE RIGHT. ♪

Anne Happy

unhappy go lucky!

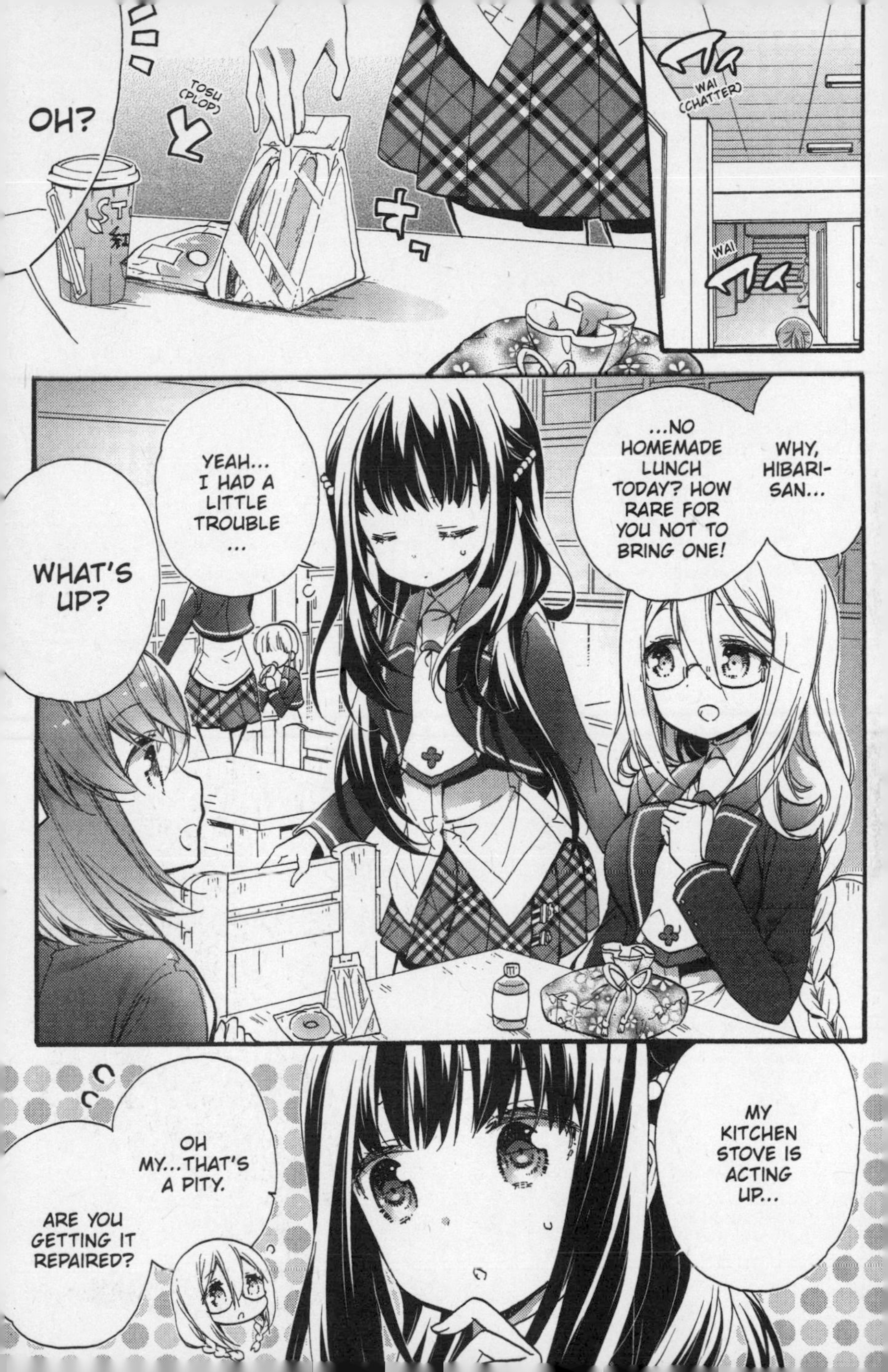
WAI (CHATTER)
WAI
OH?
TOSU (PLOP)
WHY, HIBARI-SAN...
...NO HOMEMADE LUNCH TODAY? HOW RARE FOR YOU NOT TO BRING ONE!
YEAH... I HAD A LITTLE TROUBLE...
WHAT'S UP?
MY KITCHEN STOVE IS ACTING UP...
OH MY...THAT'S A PITY.
ARE YOU GETTING IT REPAIRED?

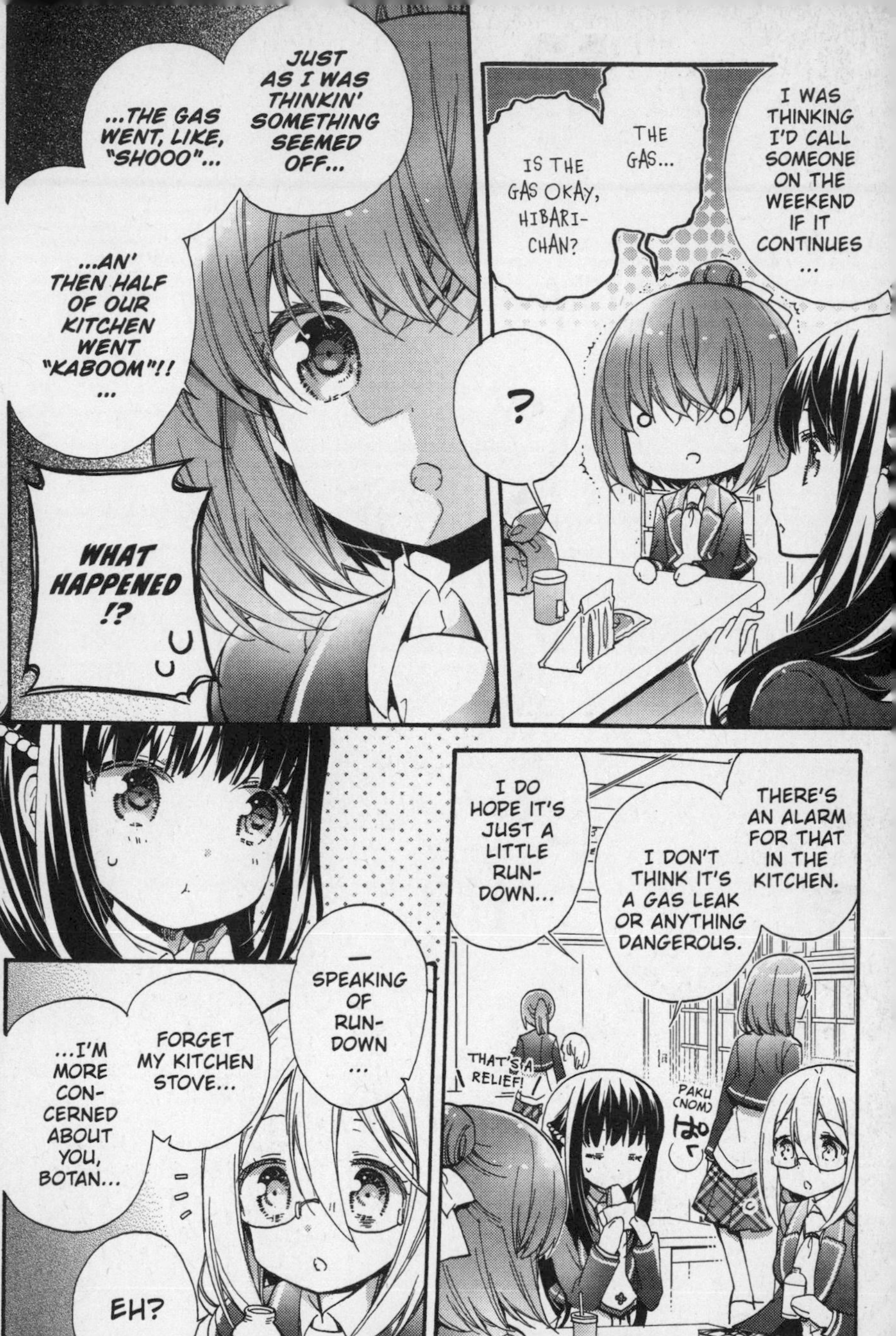
I WAS THINKING I'D CALL SOMEONE ON THE WEEKEND IF IT CONTINUES...
THE GAS...
IS THE GAS OKAY, HIBARI-CHAN?
?
JUST AS I WAS THINKIN' SOMETHING SEEMED OFF...
...THE GAS WENT, LIKE, "SHOOO"...
...AN' THEN HALF OF OUR KITCHEN WENT "KABOOM"!! ...
WHAT HAPPENED!?
THERE'S AN ALARM FOR THAT IN THE KITCHEN.
I DON'T THINK IT'S A GAS LEAK OR ANYTHING DANGEROUS.
I DO HOPE IT'S JUST A LITTLE RUN-DOWN...
THAT'S A RELIEF!
PAKU (NOM)
ぱく
—SPEAKING OF RUN-DOWN...
FORGET MY KITCHEN STOVE...
...I'M MORE CONCERNED ABOUT YOU, BOTAN...
EH?

Lucky. 53

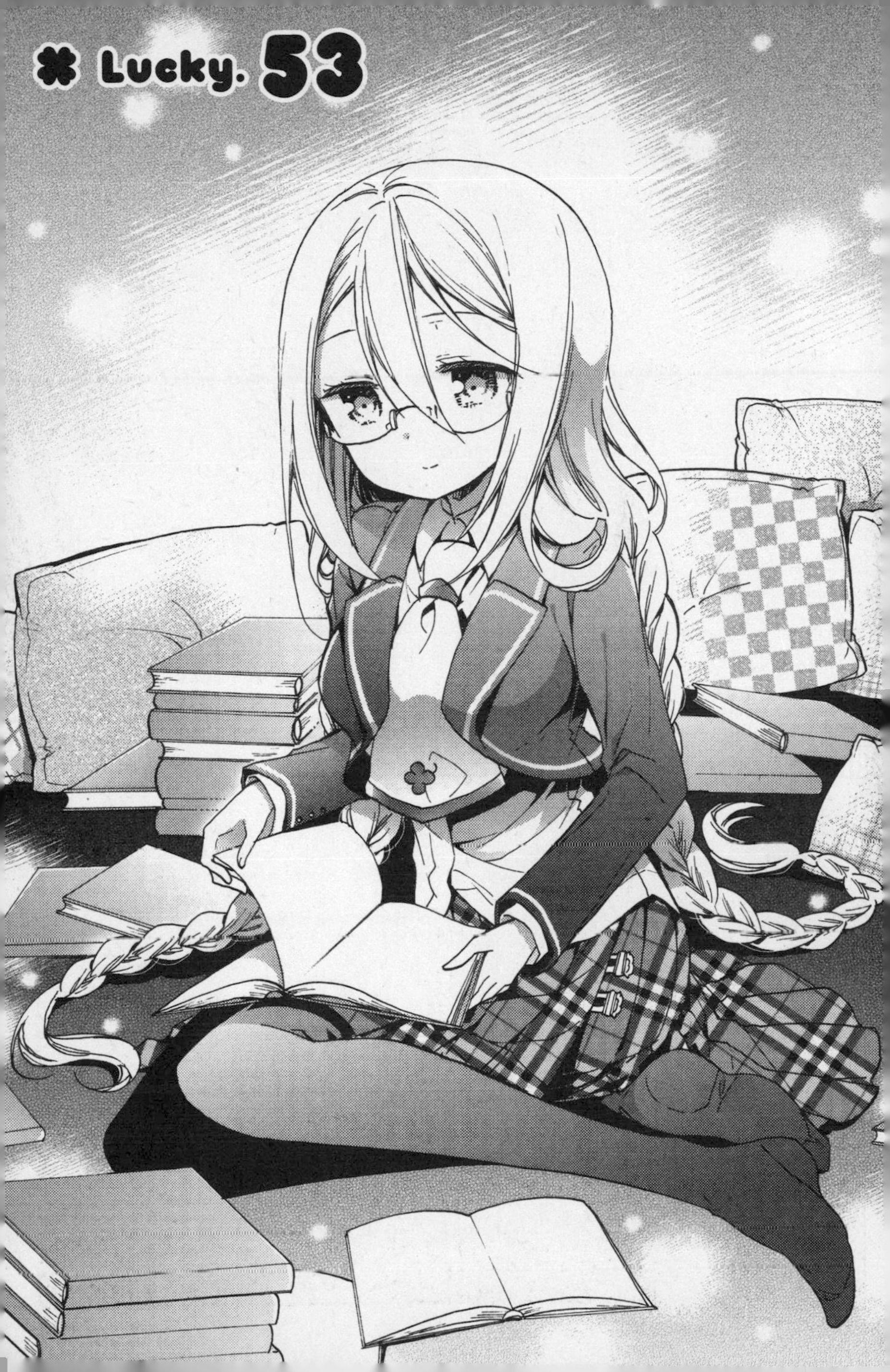

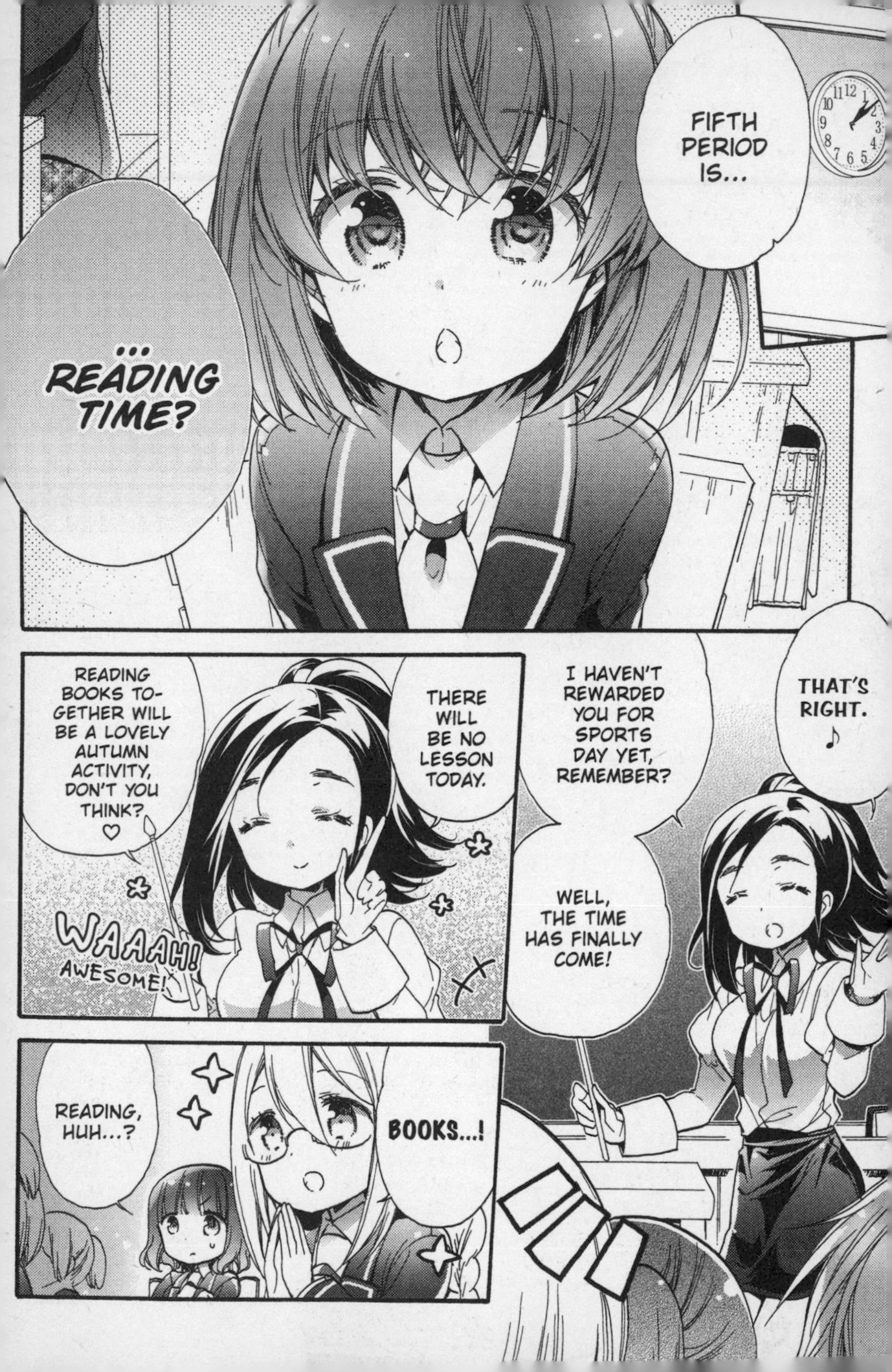
FIFTH PERIOD IS...
...READING TIME?
THAT'S RIGHT. ♪
I HAVEN'T REWARDED YOU FOR SPORTS DAY YET, REMEMBER?
WELL, THE TIME HAS FINALLY COME!
THERE WILL BE NO LESSON TODAY.
READING BOOKS TO-GETHER WILL BE A LOVELY AUTUMN ACTIVITY, DON'T YOU THINK? ♡
WAAAH! AWESOME!
BOOKS...!
READING, HUH...?

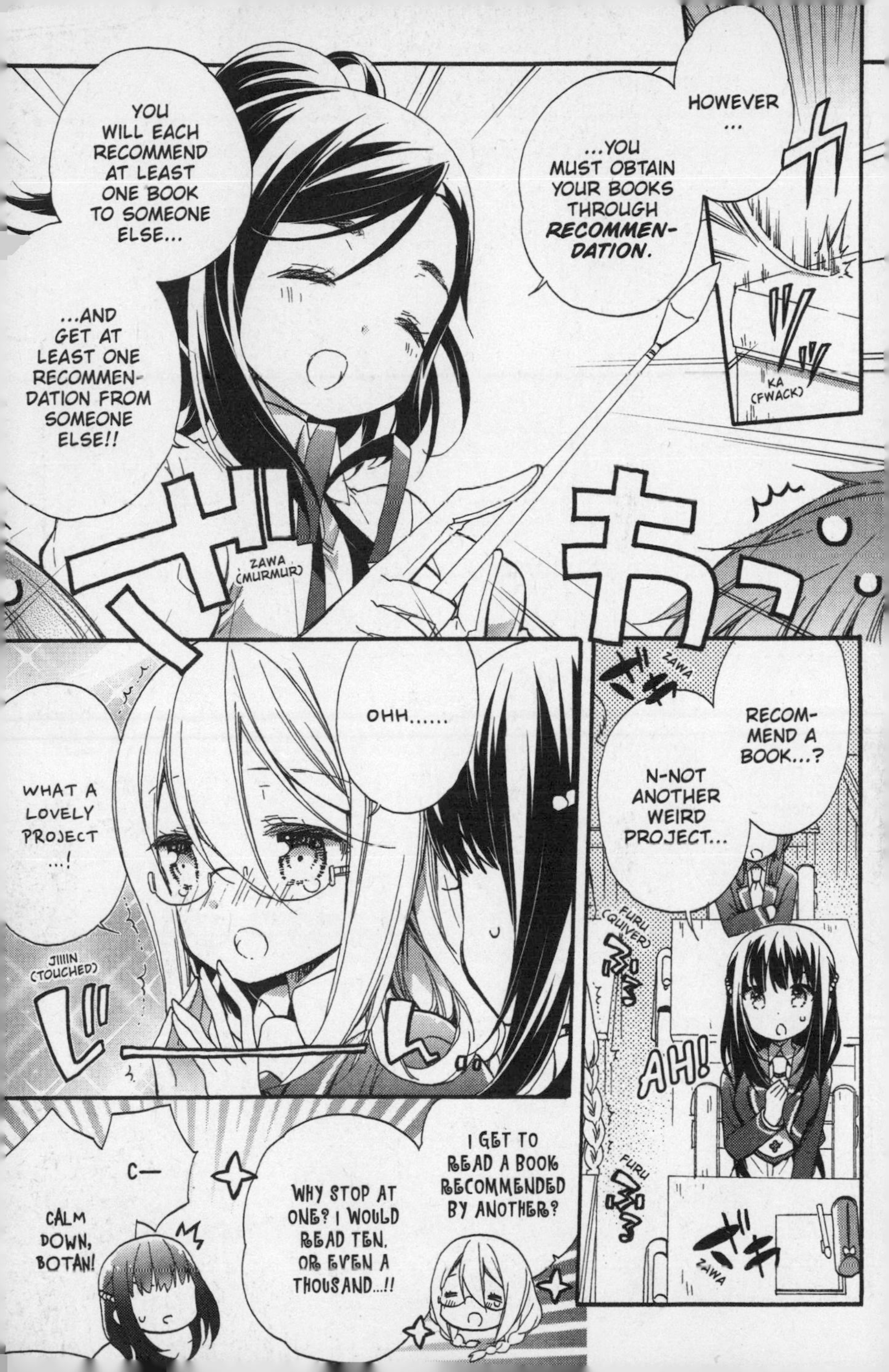
HOWEVER...
...YOU MUST OBTAIN YOUR BOOKS THROUGH RECOMMENDATION.
KA (FWACK)
YOU WILL EACH RECOMMEND AT LEAST ONE BOOK TO SOMEONE ELSE...
...AND GET AT LEAST ONE RECOMMENDATION FROM SOMEONE ELSE!!
ZAWA (MURMUR)
ZAWA
RECOMMEND A BOOK...?
N-NOT ANOTHER WEIRD PROJECT...
FURU (QUIVER)
AH!
FURU
ZAWA
OHH......
WHAT A LOVELY PROJECT...!
JIIIN (TOUCHED)
I GET TO READ A BOOK RECOMMENDED BY ANOTHER?
WHY STOP AT ONE? I WOULD READ TEN, OR EVEN A THOUSAND...!!
C—
CALM DOWN, BOTAN!

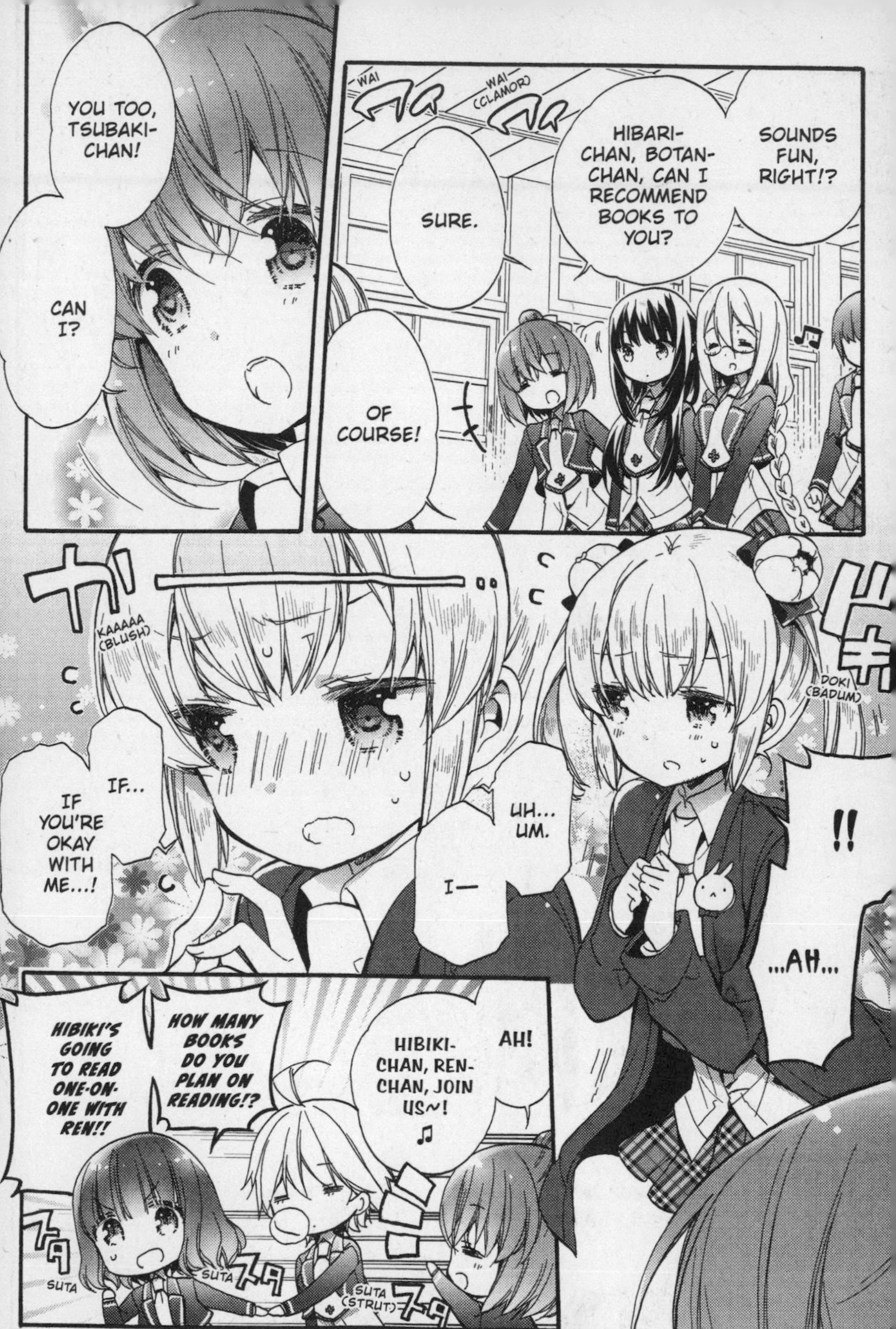
SOUNDS FUN, RIGHT!?
HIBARI-CHAN, BOTAN-CHAN, CAN I RECOMMEND BOOKS TO YOU?
WAI (CLAMOR)
WAI
SURE.
OF COURSE!
YOU TOO, TSUBAKI-CHAN!
CAN I?
DOKI (BADUM)
!!
UH... UM.
I—
KAAAAA (BLUSH)
IF...
IF YOU'RE OKAY WITH ME...!
...AH...
AH!
HIBIKI-CHAN, REN-CHAN, JOIN US~! ♫
HOW MANY BOOKS DO YOU PLAN ON READING!?
HIBIKI'S GOING TO READ ONE-ON-ONE WITH REN!!
SUTA (STRUT)
SUTA
SUTA

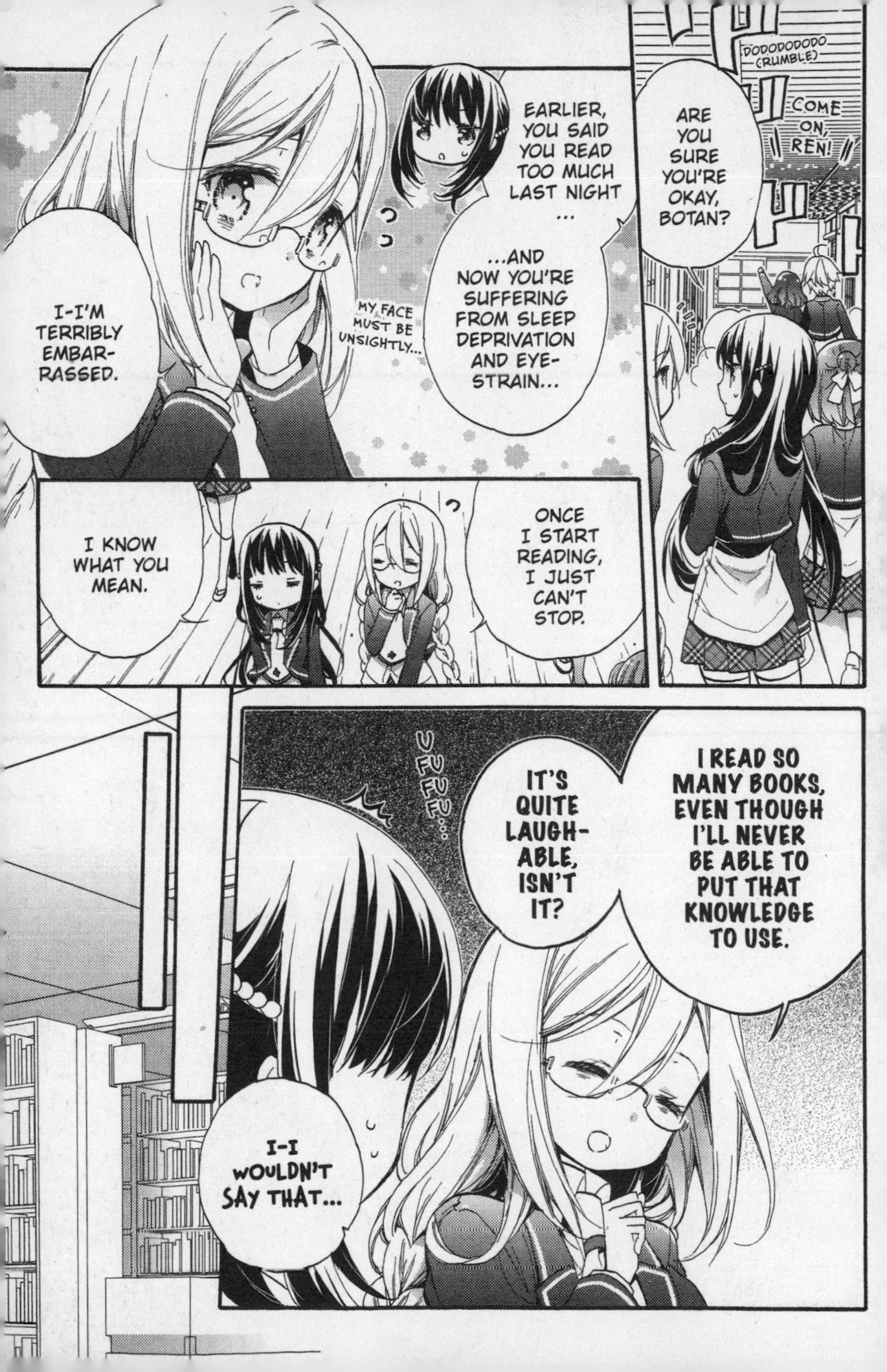
DODODODODO (RUMBLE)
COME ON, REN!
ARE YOU SURE YOU'RE OKAY, BOTAN?
EARLIER, YOU SAID YOU READ TOO MUCH LAST NIGHT ...
...AND NOW YOU'RE SUFFERING FROM SLEEP DEPRIVATION AND EYE-STRAIN...
MY FACE MUST BE UNSIGHTLY...
I-I'M TERRIBLY EMBARRASSED.
ONCE I START READING, I JUST CAN'T STOP.
I KNOW WHAT YOU MEAN.
I READ SO MANY BOOKS, EVEN THOUGH I'LL NEVER BE ABLE TO PUT THAT KNOWLEDGE TO USE.
IT'S QUITE LAUGHABLE, ISN'T IT?
UFUFUFU...
I-I WOULDN'T SAY THAT...

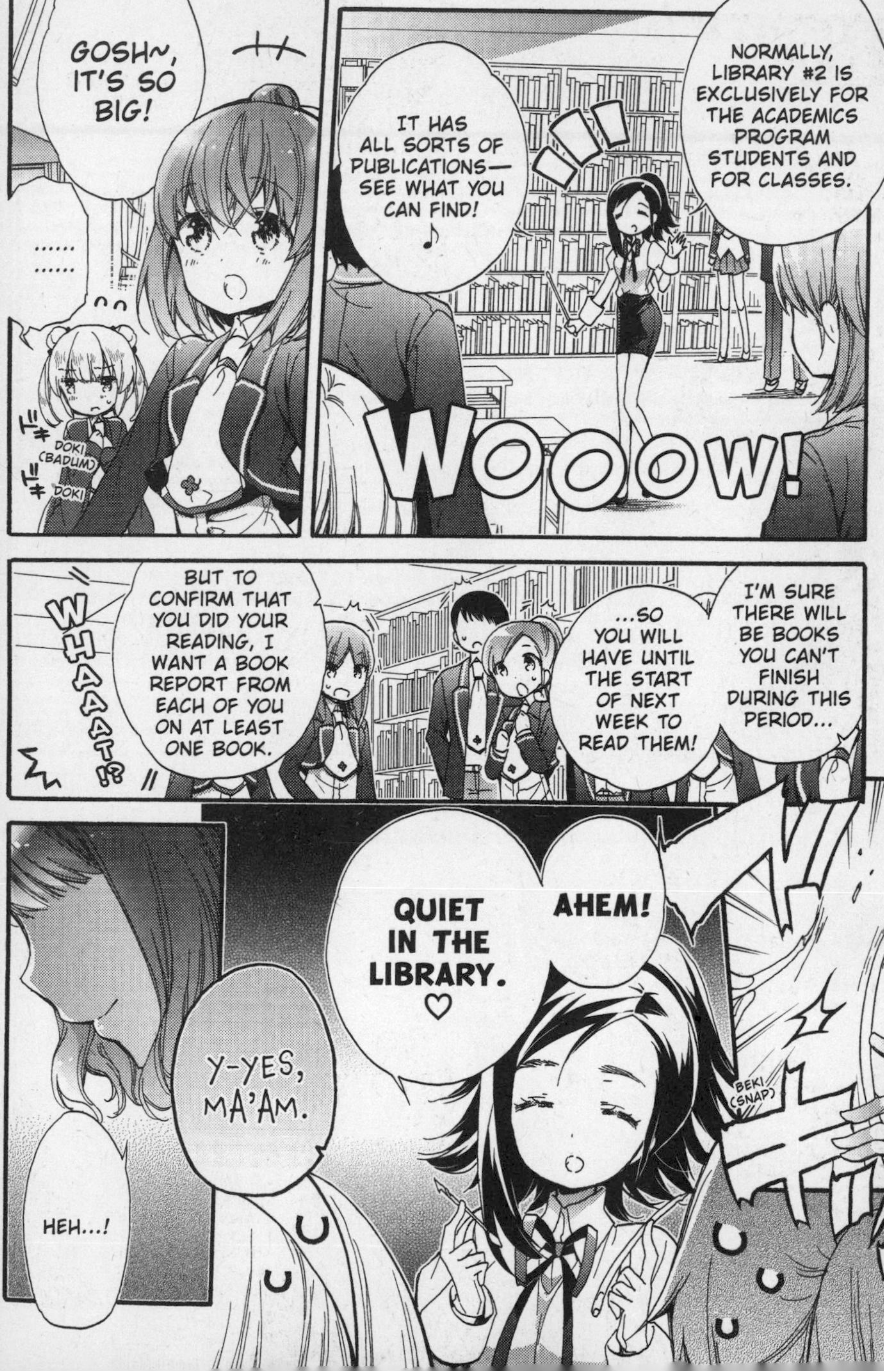
NORMALLY, LIBRARY #2 IS EXCLUSIVELY FOR THE ACADEMICS PROGRAM STUDENTS AND FOR CLASSES.
IT HAS ALL SORTS OF PUBLICATIONS—SEE WHAT YOU CAN FIND! ♪
WOOOW!
GOSH~, IT'S SO BIG!
……
……
DOKI (BADUM)
DOKI
I'M SURE THERE WILL BE BOOKS YOU CAN'T FINISH DURING THIS PERIOD...
...SO YOU WILL HAVE UNTIL THE START OF NEXT WEEK TO READ THEM!
BUT TO CONFIRM THAT YOU DID YOUR READING, I WANT A BOOK REPORT FROM EACH OF YOU ON AT LEAST ONE BOOK.
WHAAAT!?
BEKI (SNAP)
AHEM!
QUIET IN THE LIBRARY. ♡
Y-YES, MA'AM.
HEH...!

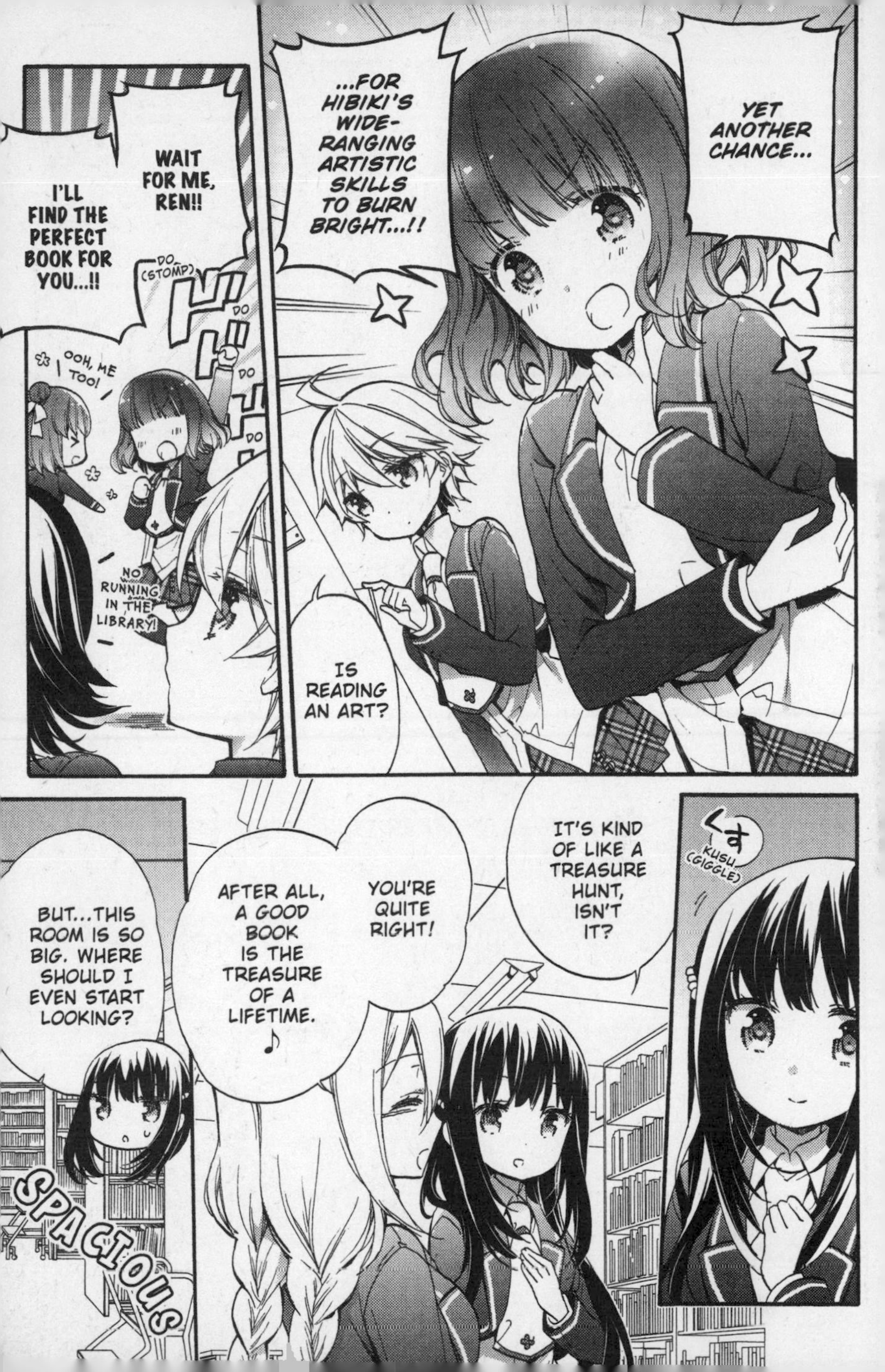
YET ANOTHER CHANCE...
...FOR HIBIKI'S WIDE-RANGING ARTISTIC SKILLS TO BURN BRIGHT...!!
IS READING AN ART?
WAIT FOR ME, REN!!
I'LL FIND THE PERFECT BOOK FOR YOU...!!
DO (STOMP)
DO
DO
DO
OOH, ME TOO!
NO RUNNING IN THE LIBRARY!
くす
KUSU (GIGGLE)
IT'S KIND OF LIKE A TREASURE HUNT, ISN'T IT?
YOU'RE QUITE RIGHT!
AFTER ALL, A GOOD BOOK IS THE TREASURE OF A LIFETIME. ♪
BUT...THIS ROOM IS SO BIG. WHERE SHOULD I EVEN START LOOKING?
SPACIOUS

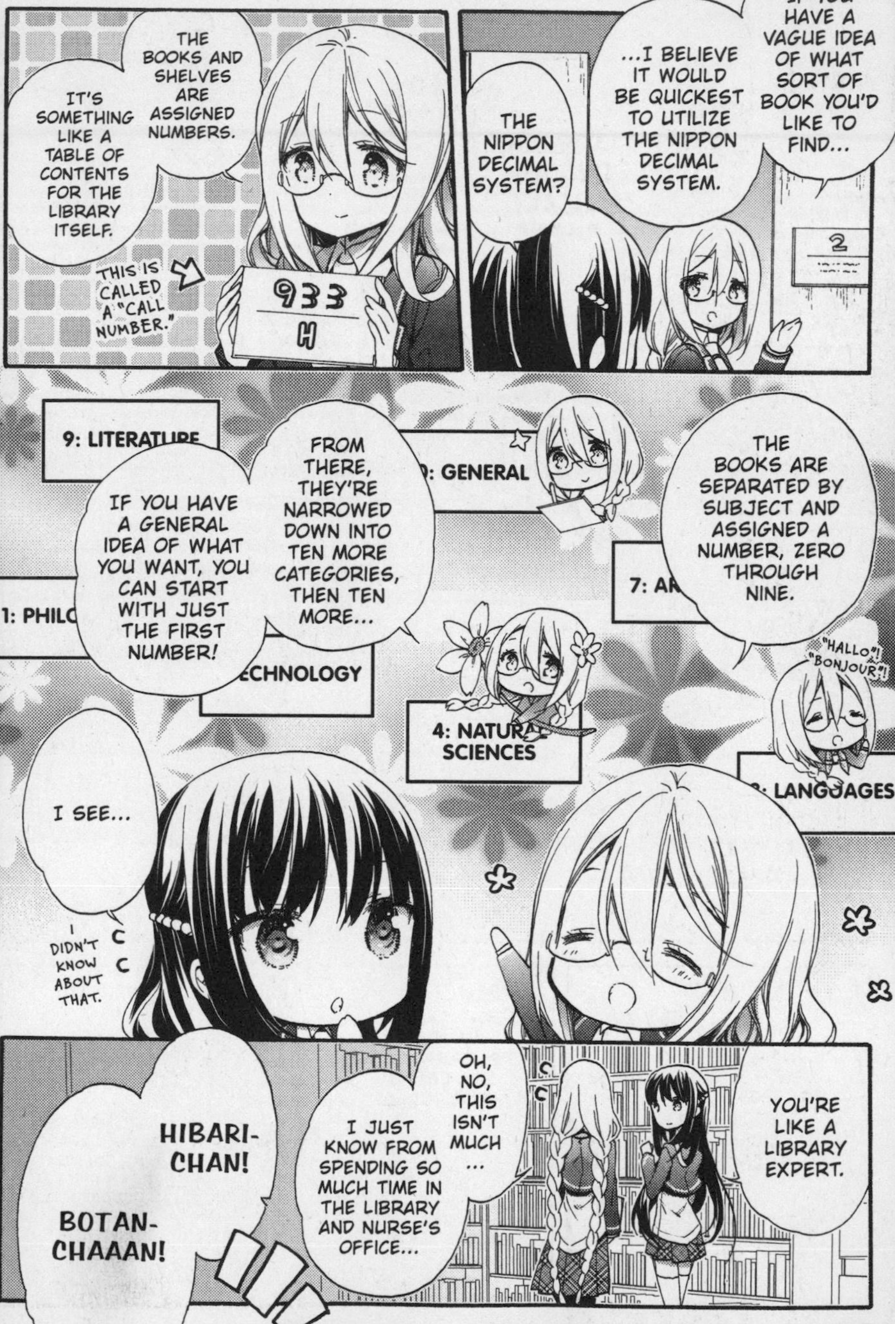
IF YOU HAVE A VAGUE IDEA OF WHAT SORT OF BOOK YOU'D LIKE TO FIND...
...I BELIEVE IT WOULD BE QUICKEST TO UTILIZE THE NIPPON DECIMAL SYSTEM.
THE NIPPON DECIMAL SYSTEM?
2
THE BOOKS AND SHELVES ARE ASSIGNED NUMBERS.
IT'S SOMETHING LIKE A TABLE OF CONTENTS FOR THE LIBRARY ITSELF.
933
H
THIS IS CALLED A "CALL NUMBER."
THE BOOKS ARE SEPARATED BY SUBJECT AND ASSIGNED A NUMBER, ZERO THROUGH NINE.
FROM THERE, THEY'RE NARROWED DOWN INTO TEN MORE CATEGORIES, THEN TEN MORE...
IF YOU HAVE A GENERAL IDEA OF WHAT YOU WANT, YOU CAN START WITH JUST THE FIRST NUMBER!
9: LITERATURE
: GENERAL
7: AR
1: PHILO
ECHNOLOGY
4: NATURAL SCIENCES
LANGUAGES
"HALLO"!
"BONJOUR"!
I SEE...
I DIDN'T KNOW ABOUT THAT.
YOU'RE LIKE A LIBRARY EXPERT.
OH, NO, THIS ISN'T MUCH...
I JUST KNOW FROM SPENDING SO MUCH TIME IN THE LIBRARY AND NURSE'S OFFICE...
HIBARI-CHAN!
BOTAN-CHAAAN!

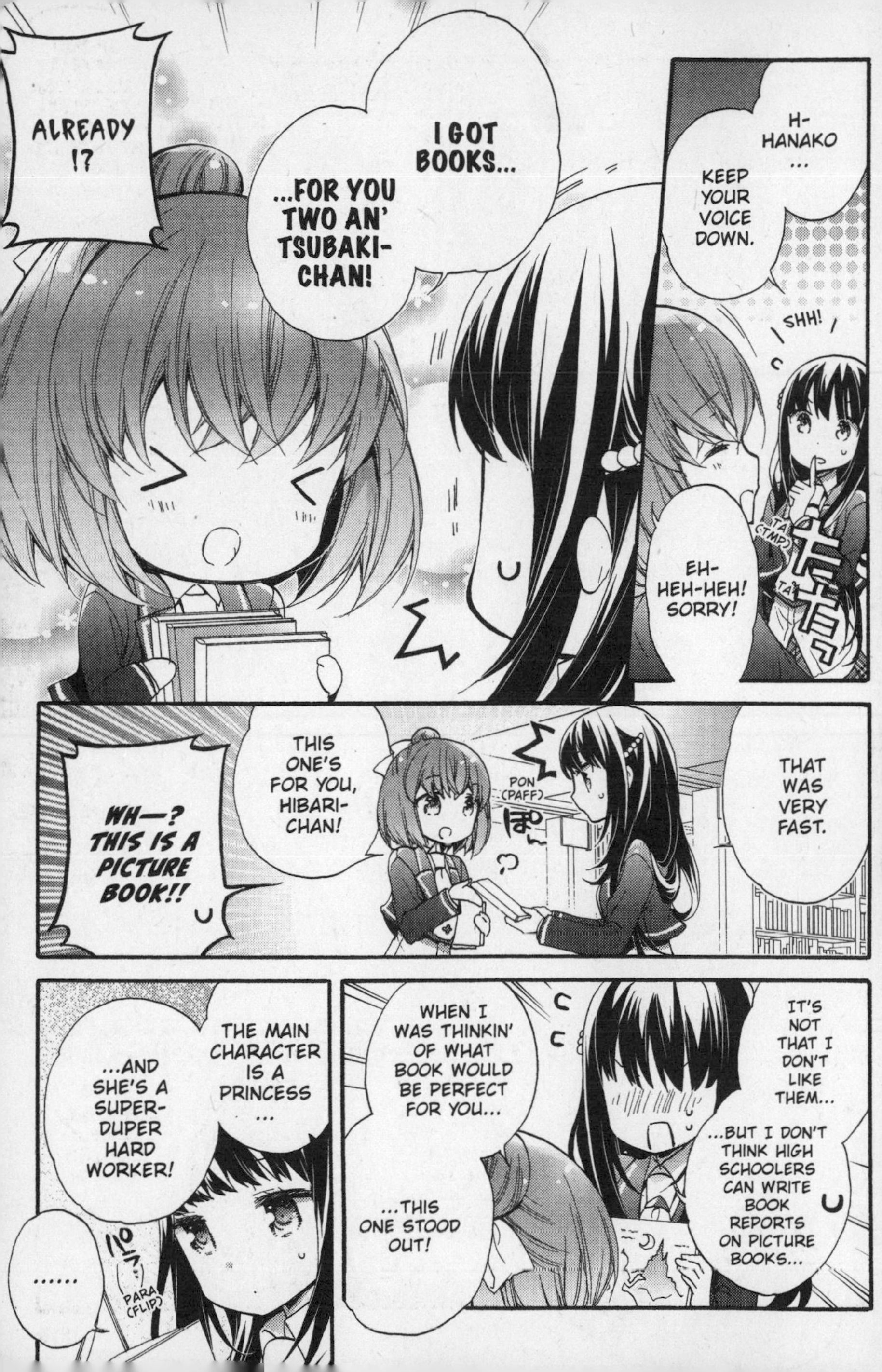
H-HANAKO …
KEEP YOUR VOICE DOWN.
SHH!
TA (TMP)
TA
EH-HEH-HEH! SORRY!
I GOT BOOKS…
…FOR YOU TWO AN' TSUBAKI-CHAN!
ALREADY !?
THAT WAS VERY FAST.
THIS ONE'S FOR YOU, HIBARI-CHAN!
PON (PAFF)
WH—? THIS IS A PICTURE BOOK!!
IT'S NOT THAT I DON'T LIKE THEM…
…BUT I DON'T THINK HIGH SCHOOLERS CAN WRITE BOOK REPORTS ON PICTURE BOOKS…
WHEN I WAS THINKIN' OF WHAT BOOK WOULD BE PERFECT FOR YOU…
…THIS ONE STOOD OUT!
THE MAIN CHARACTER IS A PRINCESS …
…AND SHE'S A SUPER-DUPER HARD WORKER!
PARA (FLIP)
……

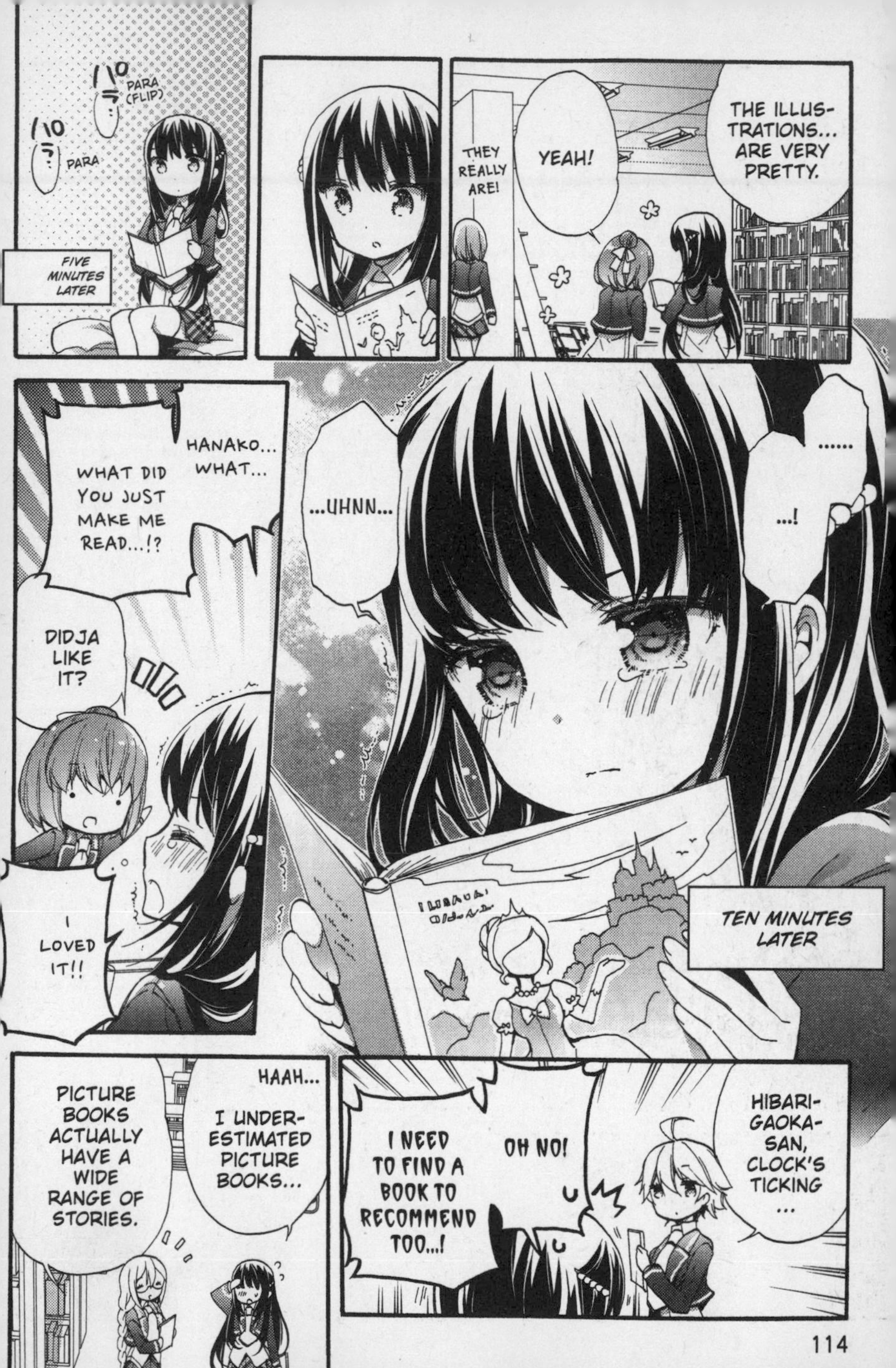
THE ILLUSTRATIONS... ARE VERY PRETTY.
YEAH!
THEY REALLY ARE!
PARA (FLIP)
PARA
FIVE MINUTES LATER
......
...!
...UHNN...
TEN MINUTES LATER
HANAKO... WHAT...
WHAT DID YOU JUST MAKE ME READ...!?
DIDJA LIKE IT?
I LOVED IT!!
HIBARIGAOKA-SAN, CLOCK'S TICKING...
OH NO!
I NEED TO FIND A BOOK TO RECOMMEND TOO...!
HAAH...
I UNDERESTIMATED PICTURE BOOKS...
PICTURE BOOKS ACTUALLY HAVE A WIDE RANGE OF STORIES.

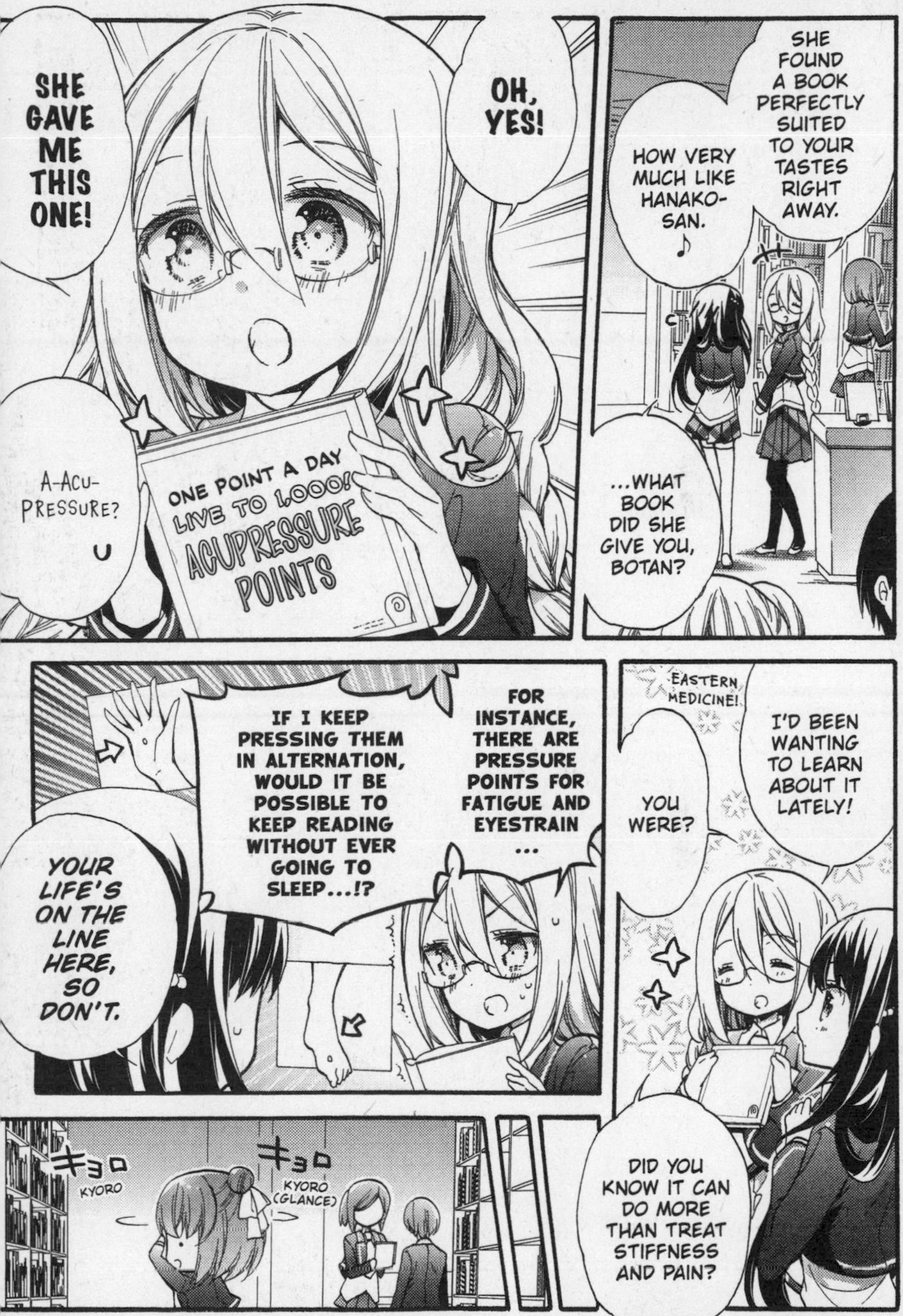
SHE FOUND A BOOK PERFECTLY SUITED TO YOUR TASTES RIGHT AWAY.
HOW VERY MUCH LIKE HANAKO-SAN. ♪
...WHAT BOOK DID SHE GIVE YOU, BOTAN?
OH, YES!
SHE GAVE ME THIS ONE!
ONE POINT A DAY LIVE TO 1,000! ACUPRESSURE POINTS
A-ACU-PRESSURE?
I'D BEEN WANTING TO LEARN ABOUT IT LATELY!
EASTERN MEDICINE!
YOU WERE?
DID YOU KNOW IT CAN DO MORE THAN TREAT STIFFNESS AND PAIN?
FOR INSTANCE, THERE ARE PRESSURE POINTS FOR FATIGUE AND EYESTRAIN ...
IF I KEEP PRESSING THEM IN ALTERNATION, WOULD IT BE POSSIBLE TO KEEP READING WITHOUT EVER GOING TO SLEEP...!?
YOUR LIFE'S ON THE LINE HERE, SO DON'T.
キョロ
KYORO (GLANCE)
キョロ
KYORO

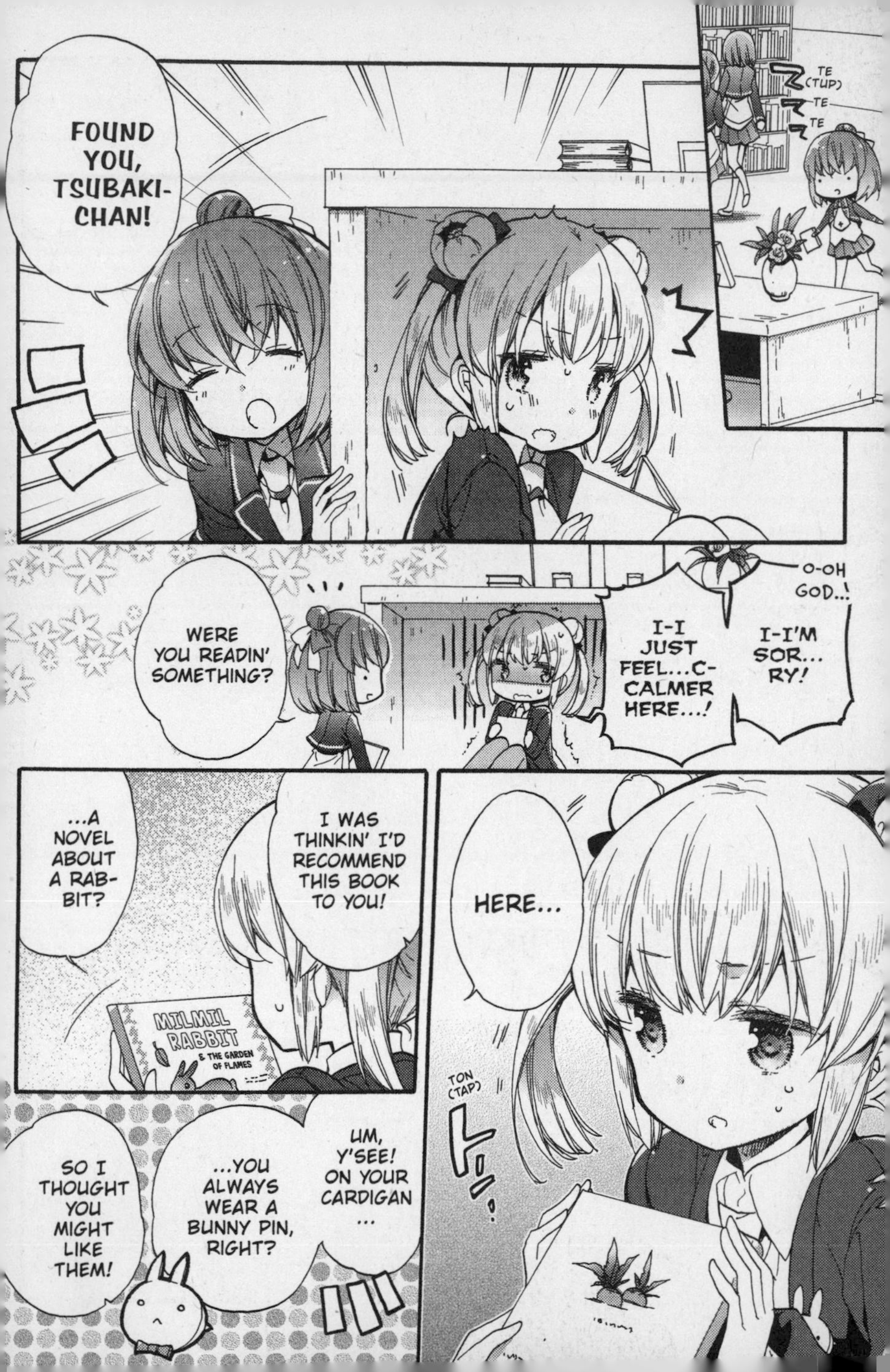

TE (TUP)
TE
TE
FOUND YOU, TSUBAKI-CHAN!
O-OH GOD..!
I-I'M SOR... RY!
I-I JUST FEEL...C-CALMER HERE...!
WERE YOU READIN' SOMETHING?
HERE...
TON (TAP)
I WAS THINKIN' I'D RECOMMEND THIS BOOK TO YOU!
...A NOVEL ABOUT A RAB-BIT?
MILMIL RABBIT & THE GARDEN OF FLAMES
UM, Y'SEE! ON YOUR CARDIGAN ...
...YOU ALWAYS WEAR A BUNNY PIN, RIGHT?
SO I THOUGHT YOU MIGHT LIKE THEM!

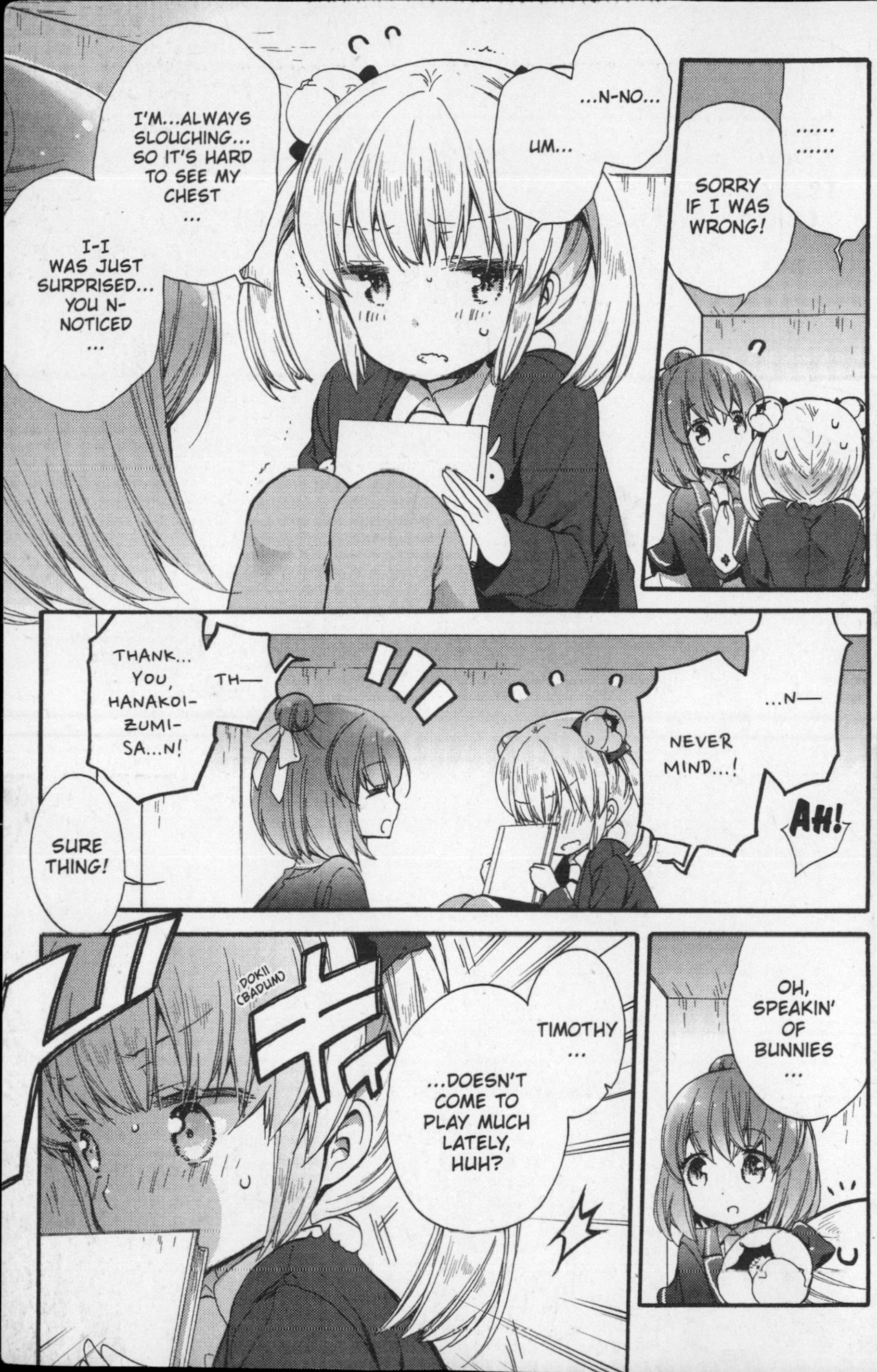
......
......
SORRY IF I WAS WRONG!
...N-NO...
UM...
I'M...ALWAYS SLOUCHING... SO IT'S HARD TO SEE MY CHEST ...
I-I WAS JUST SURPRISED... YOU N-NOTICED ...
...N—
NEVER MIND...!
AH!
TH—
THANK... YOU, HANAKOI-ZUMI-SA...N!
SURE THING!
OH, SPEAKIN' OF BUNNIES ...
TIMOTHY ...
...DOESN'T COME TO PLAY MUCH LATELY, HUH?
DOKI! (BADUM)

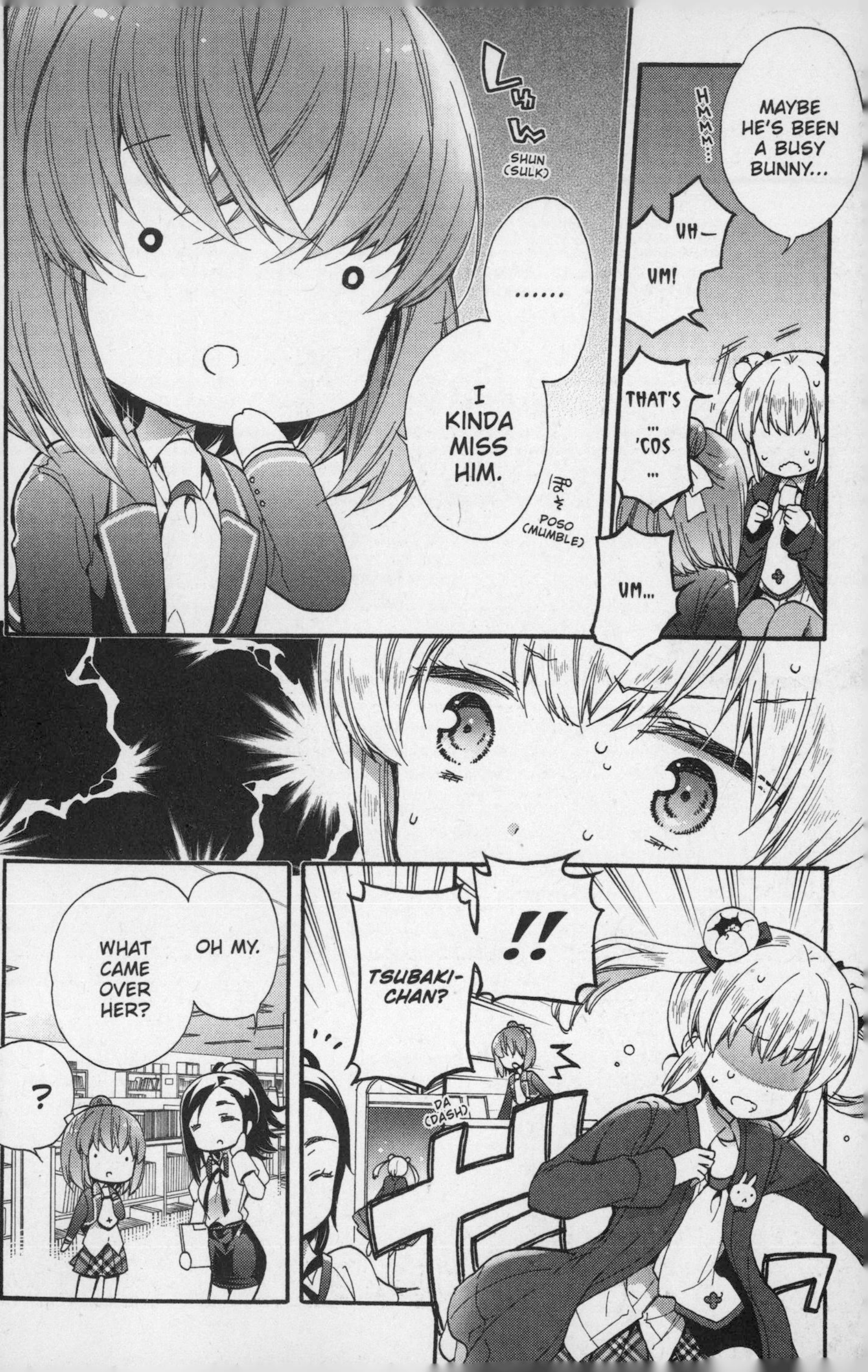
MAYBE HE'S BEEN A BUSY BUNNY...
HMMM...
UH— UM!
THAT'S ... 'COS ...
UM...
SHUN (SULK)
......
I KINDA MISS HIM.
POSO (MUMBLE)
!!
TSUBAKI-CHAN?
DA (DASH)
OH MY.
WHAT CAME OVER HER?
?

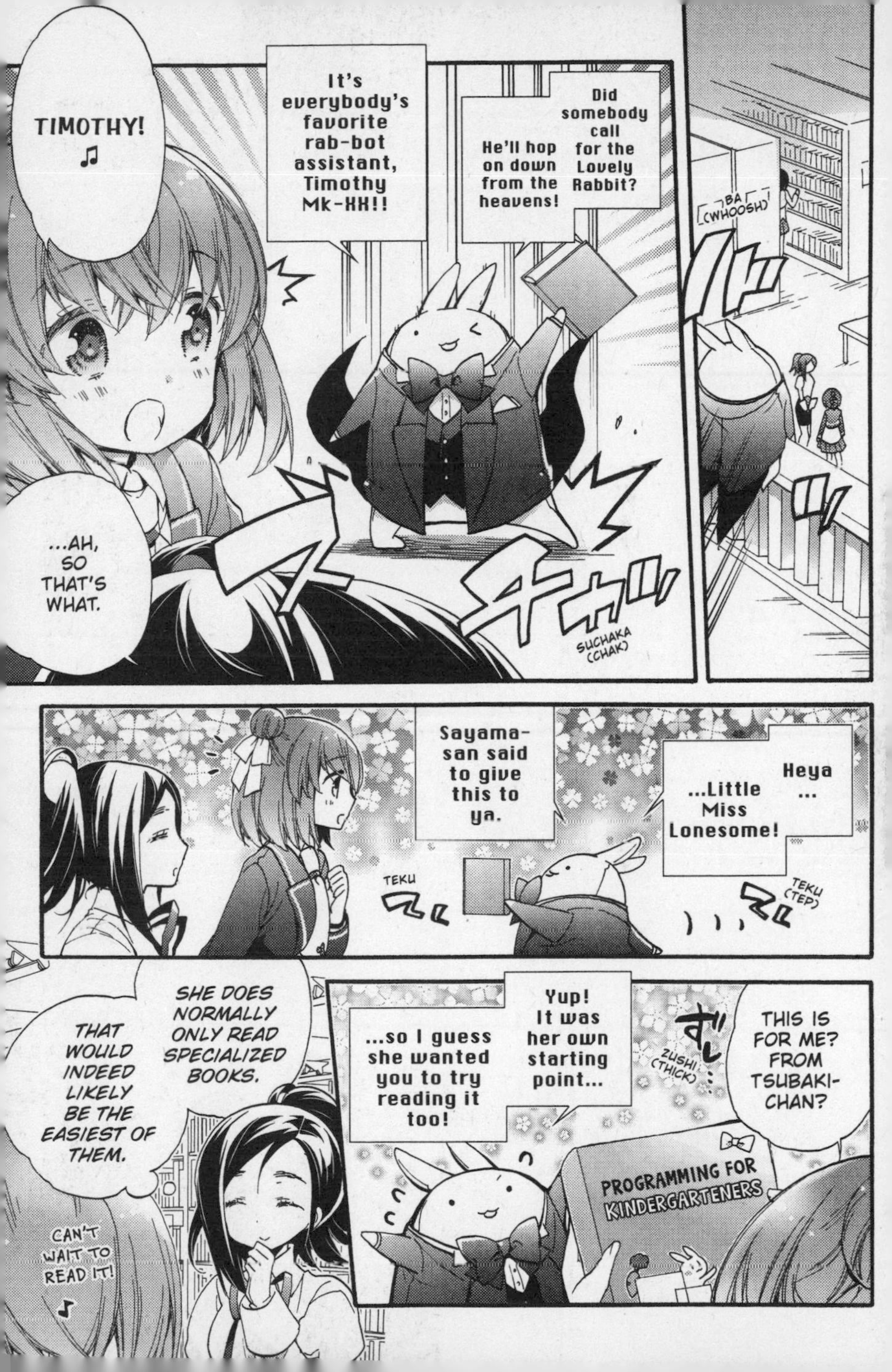
BA (WHOOSH)
Did somebody call for the Lovely Rabbit?
He'll hop on down from the heavens!
It's everybody's favorite rab-bot assistant, Timothy Mk-XX!!
TIMOTHY! ♫
SUCHAKA (CHAK)
...AH, SO THAT'S WHAT.
Heya... ...Little Miss Lonesome!
TEKU (TEP)
Sayama-san said to give this to ya.
TEKU
THIS IS FOR ME? FROM TSUBAKI-CHAN?
ZUSHI (THICK)
Yup! It was her own starting point...
...so I guess she wanted you to try reading it too!
PROGRAMMING FOR KINDERGARTENERS
SHE DOES NORMALLY ONLY READ SPECIALIZED BOOKS.
THAT WOULD INDEED LIKELY BE THE EASIEST OF THEM.
CAN'T WAIT TO READ IT! ♪

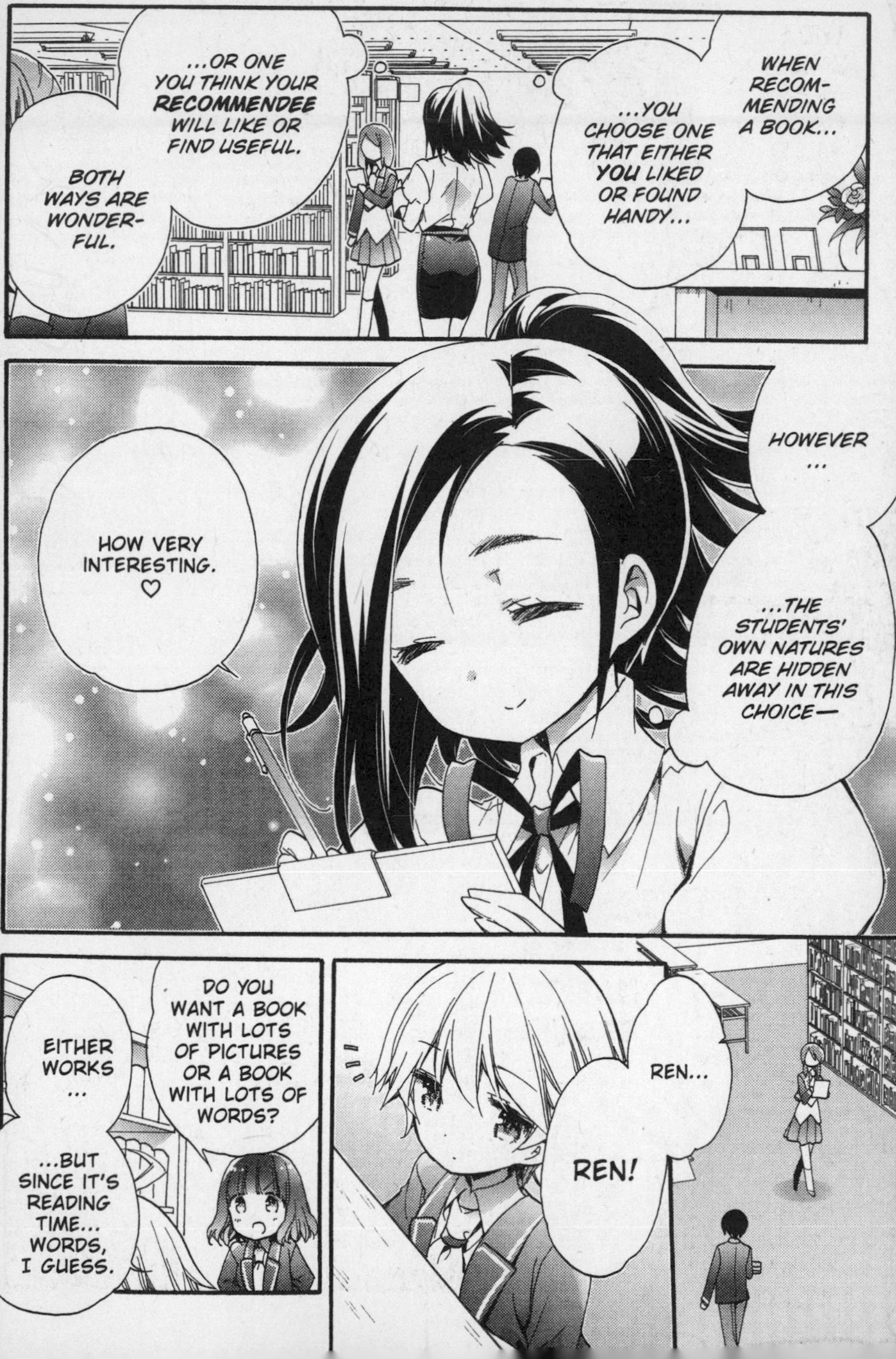

WHEN RECOMMENDING A BOOK...
...YOU CHOOSE ONE THAT EITHER YOU LIKED OR FOUND HANDY...
...OR ONE YOU THINK YOUR RECOMMENDEE WILL LIKE OR FIND USEFUL.
BOTH WAYS ARE WONDERFUL.
HOWEVER...
...THE STUDENTS' OWN NATURES ARE HIDDEN AWAY IN THIS CHOICE—
HOW VERY INTERESTING. ♡
REN...
REN!
DO YOU WANT A BOOK WITH LOTS OF PICTURES OR A BOOK WITH LOTS OF WORDS?
EITHER WORKS...
...BUT SINCE IT'S READING TIME... WORDS, I GUESS.

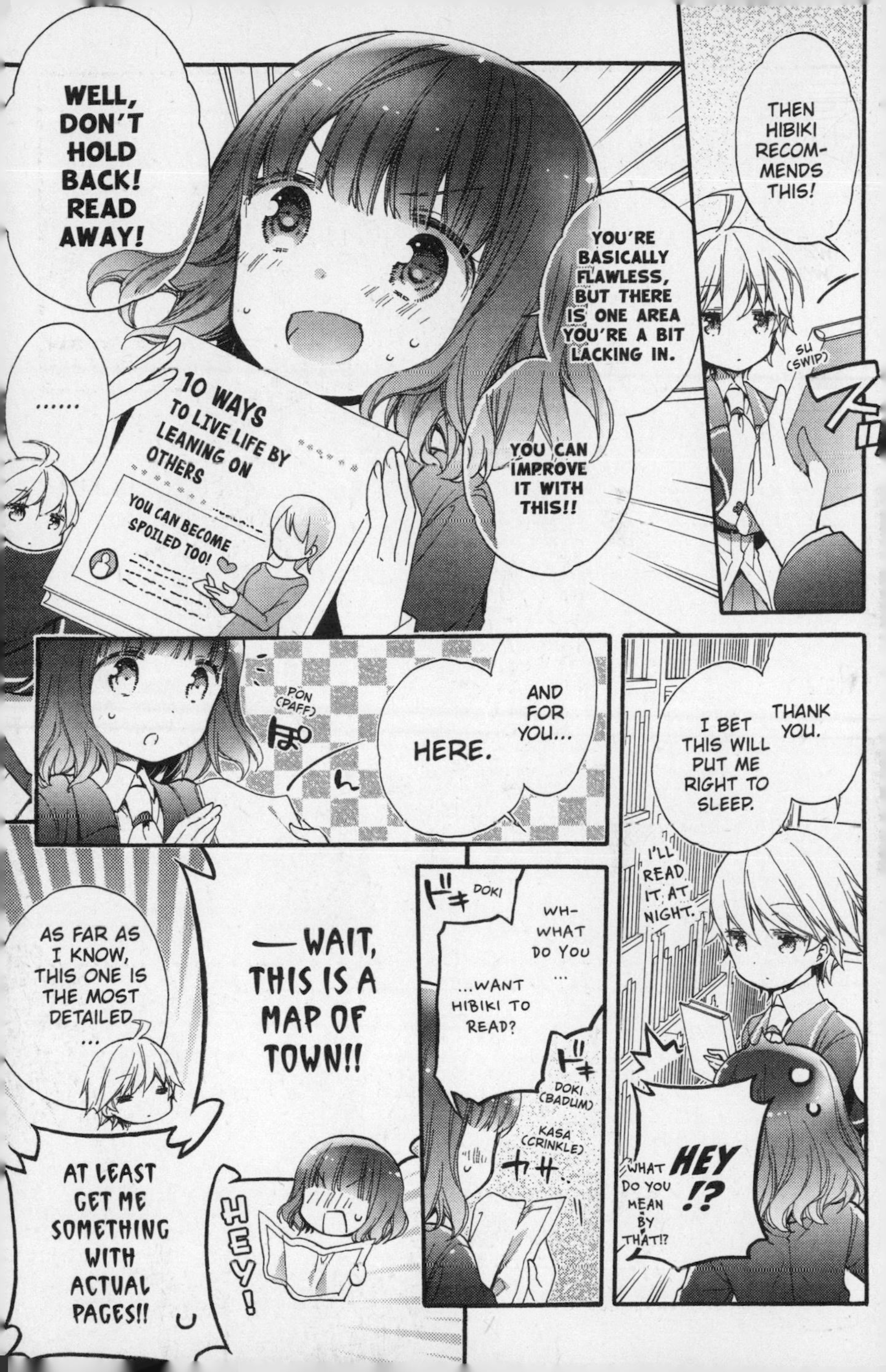
THEN HIBIKI RECOMMENDS THIS!
SU (SWIP)
YOU'RE BASICALLY FLAWLESS, BUT THERE IS ONE AREA YOU'RE A BIT LACKING IN.
YOU CAN IMPROVE IT WITH THIS!!
WELL, DON'T HOLD BACK! READ AWAY!
......
10 WAYS TO LIVE LIFE BY LEANING ON OTHERS
YOU CAN BECOME SPOILED TOO!
THANK YOU.
I BET THIS WILL PUT ME RIGHT TO SLEEP.
I'LL READ IT AT NIGHT.
HEY !?
WHAT DO YOU MEAN BY THAT!?
AND FOR YOU...
HERE.
PON (PAFF)
DOKI
WH-WHAT DO YOU ...
...WANT HIBIKI TO READ?
DOKI (BADUM)
KASA (CRINKLE)
—WAIT, THIS IS A MAP OF TOWN!!
AS FAR AS I KNOW, THIS ONE IS THE MOST DETAILED ...
AT LEAST GET ME SOMETHING WITH ACTUAL PAGES!!
HEY!

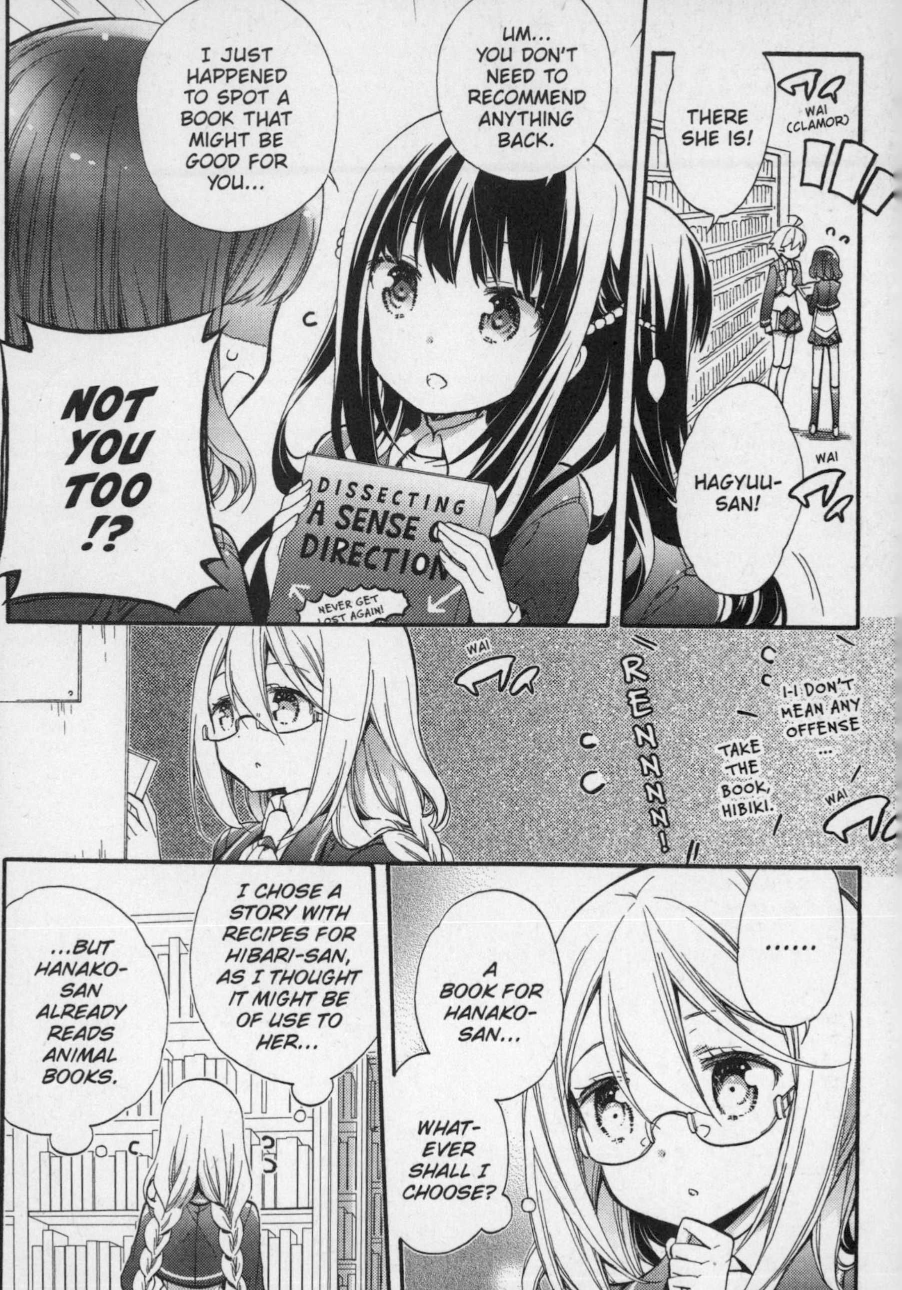
THERE SHE IS!
WAI (CLAMOR)
HAGYUU-SAN!
WAI
UM... YOU DON'T NEED TO RECOMMEND ANYTHING BACK.
I JUST HAPPENED TO SPOT A BOOK THAT MIGHT BE GOOD FOR YOU...
DISSECTING A SENSE
DIRECTIO
NEVER GET LOST AGAIN!
NOT YOU TOO!?
WAI
I-I DON'T MEAN ANY OFFENSE...
TAKE THE BOOK, HIBIKI.
RENNNN!
WAI
......
A BOOK FOR HANAKO-SAN...
WHAT-EVER SHALL I CHOOSE?
I CHOSE A STORY WITH RECIPES FOR HIBARI-SAN, AS I THOUGHT IT MIGHT BE OF USE TO HER...
...BUT HANAKO-SAN ALREADY READS ANIMAL BOOKS.

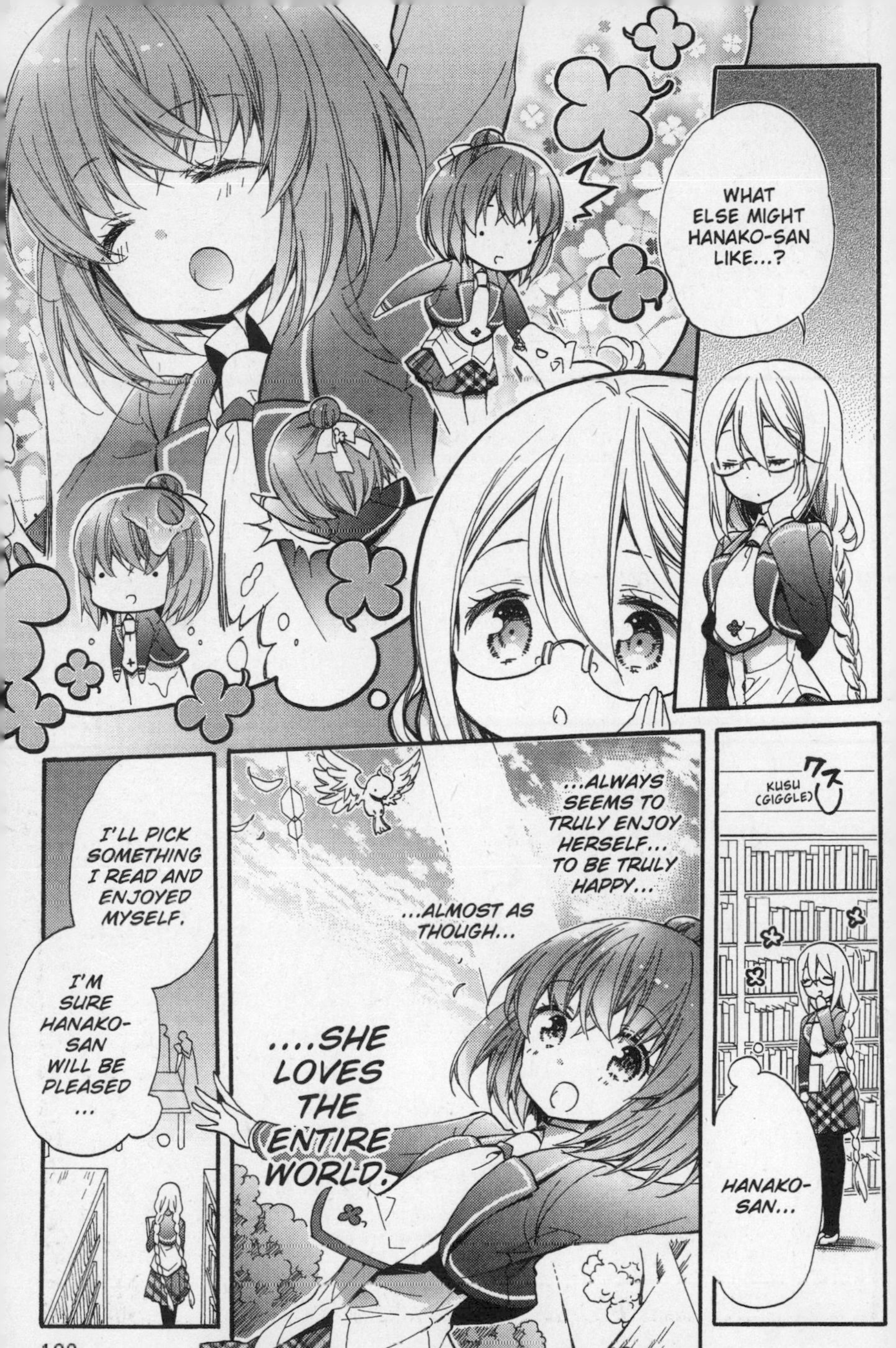

WHAT ELSE MIGHT HANAKO-SAN LIKE...?
KUSU (GIGGLE)
HANAKO-SAN...
...ALWAYS SEEMS TO TRULY ENJOY HERSELF... TO BE TRULY HAPPY...
...ALMOST AS THOUGH...
....SHE LOVES THE ENTIRE WORLD.
I'LL PICK SOMETHING I READ AND ENJOYED MYSELF.
I'M SURE HANAKO-SAN WILL BE PLEASED ...

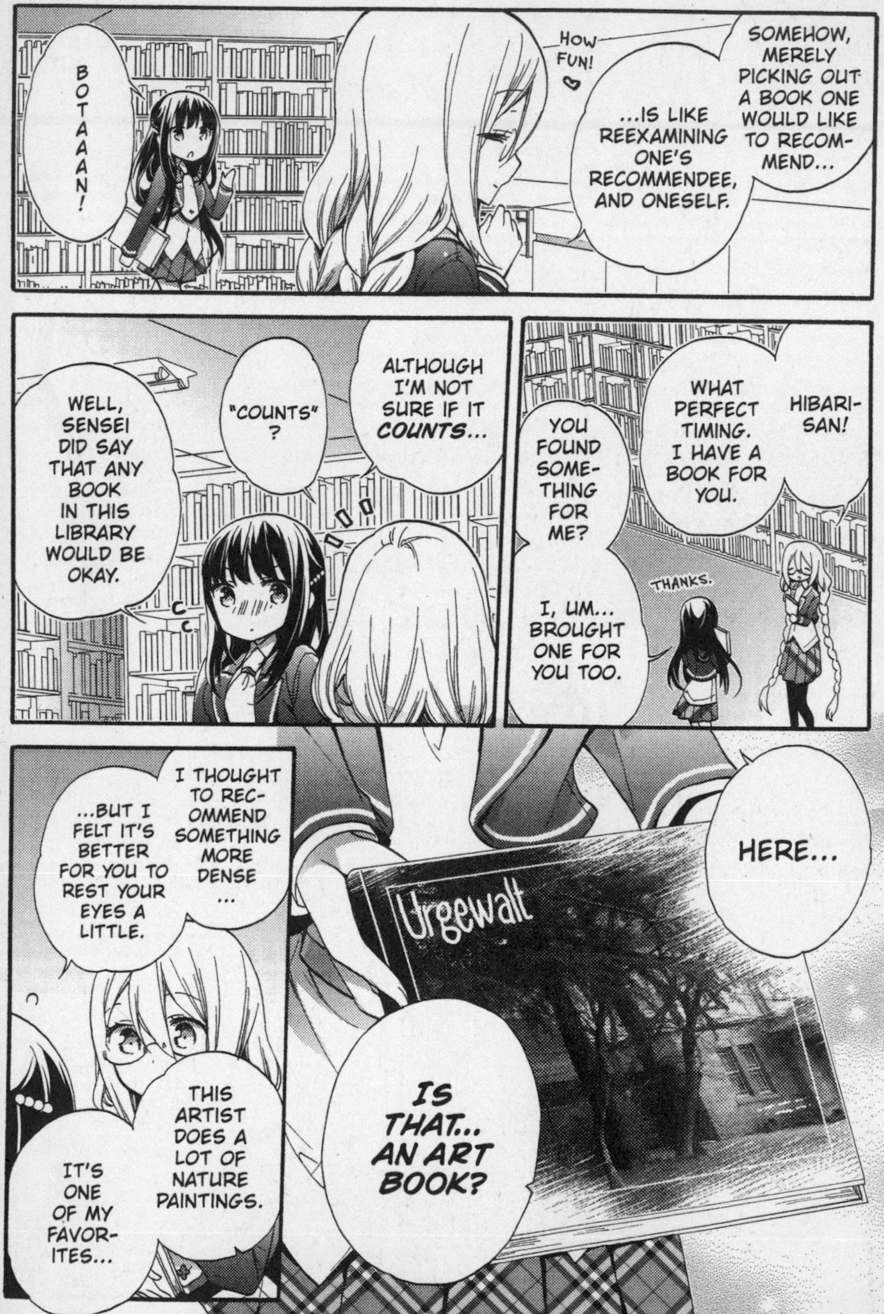
SOMEHOW, MERELY PICKING OUT A BOOK ONE WOULD LIKE TO RECOMMEND...
HOW FUN!
...IS LIKE REEXAMINING ONE'S RECOMMENDEE, AND ONESELF.
BOTAAAAN!
HIBARI-SAN!
WHAT PERFECT TIMING. I HAVE A BOOK FOR YOU.
YOU FOUND SOMETHING FOR ME?
THANKS.
I, UM... BROUGHT ONE FOR YOU TOO.
ALTHOUGH I'M NOT SURE IF IT *COUNTS*...
"COUNTS"?
WELL, SENSEI DID SAY THAT ANY BOOK IN THIS LIBRARY WOULD BE OKAY.
HERE...
Urgewalt
I THOUGHT TO RECOMMEND SOMETHING MORE DENSE...
...BUT I FELT IT'S BETTER FOR YOU TO REST YOUR EYES A LITTLE.
IS THAT... AN ART BOOK?
THIS ARTIST DOES A LOT OF NATURE PAINTINGS.
IT'S ONE OF MY FAVORITES...

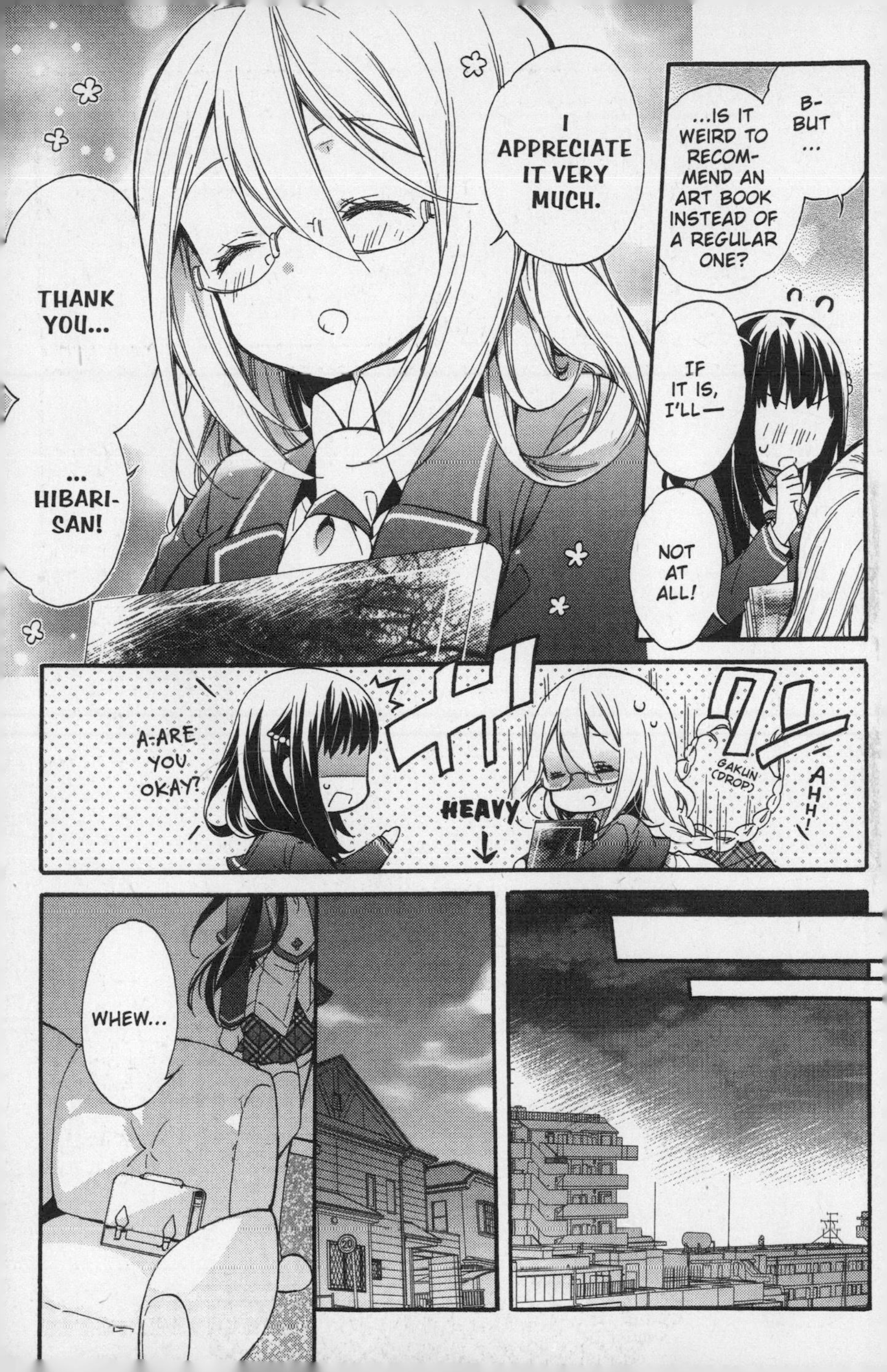
B-BUT ...
...IS IT WEIRD TO RECOMMEND AN ART BOOK INSTEAD OF A REGULAR ONE?
IF IT IS, I'LL—
NOT AT ALL!
I APPRECIATE IT VERY MUCH.
THANK YOU...
... HIBARI-SAN!
AHH!
GAKUN (DROP)
HEAVY
A-ARE YOU OKAY?
WHEW...

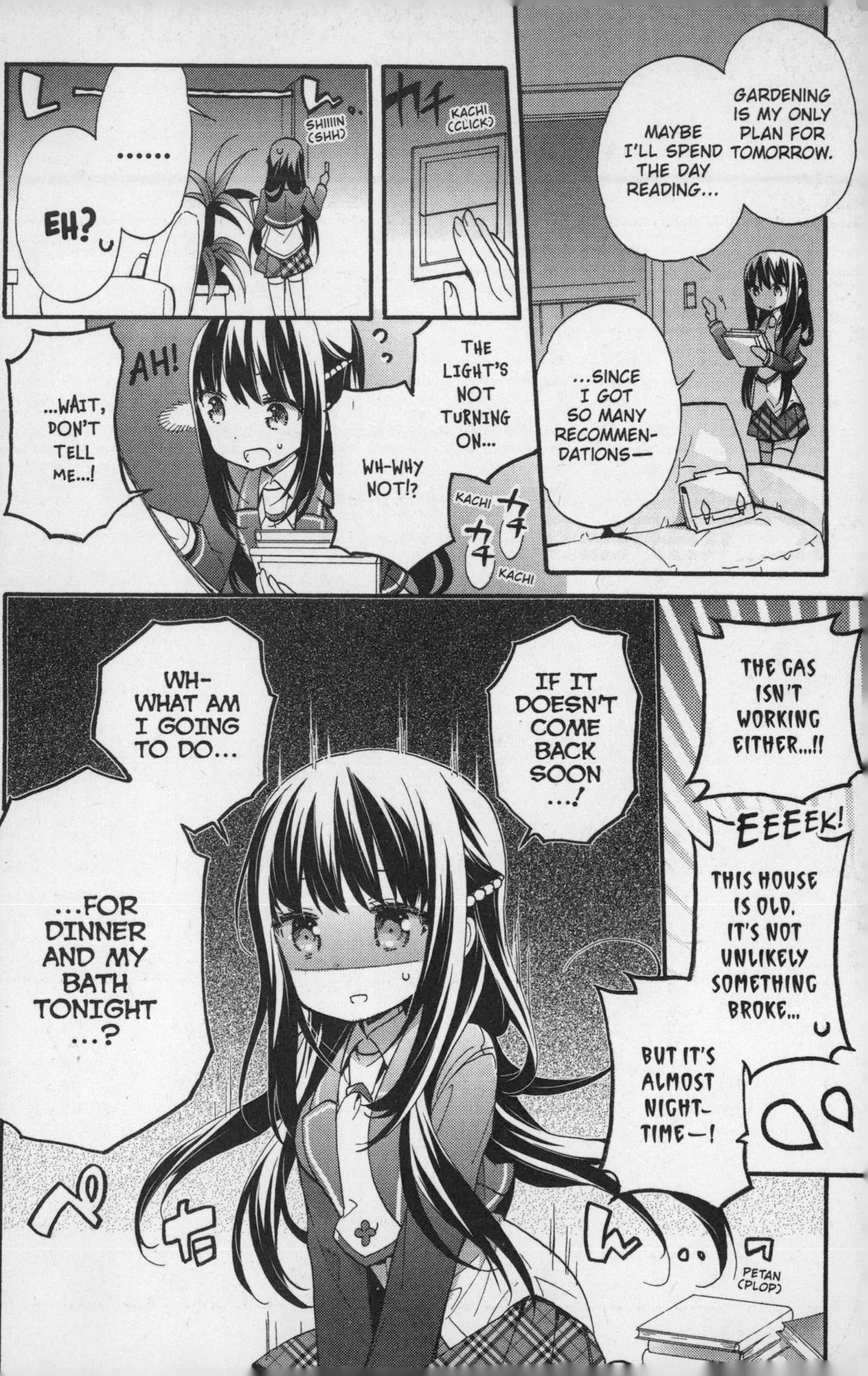
GARDENING IS MY ONLY PLAN FOR TOMORROW.
MAYBE I'LL SPEND THE DAY READING...
...SINCE I GOT SO MANY RECOMMEN-DATIONS—
KACHI (CLICK)
SHIIIIN (SHH)
......
EH?
THE LIGHT'S NOT TURNING ON...
WH-WHY NOT!?
KACHI
KACHI
AH!
...WAIT, DON'T TELL ME...!
THE GAS ISN'T WORKING EITHER...!!
EEEEK!
THIS HOUSE IS OLD. IT'S NOT UNLIKELY SOMETHING BROKE...
BUT IT'S ALMOST NIGHT-TIME—!
IF IT DOESN'T COME BACK SOON...!
WH-WHAT AM I GOING TO DO...
...FOR DINNER AND MY BATH TONIGHT...?
PETAN (PLOP)

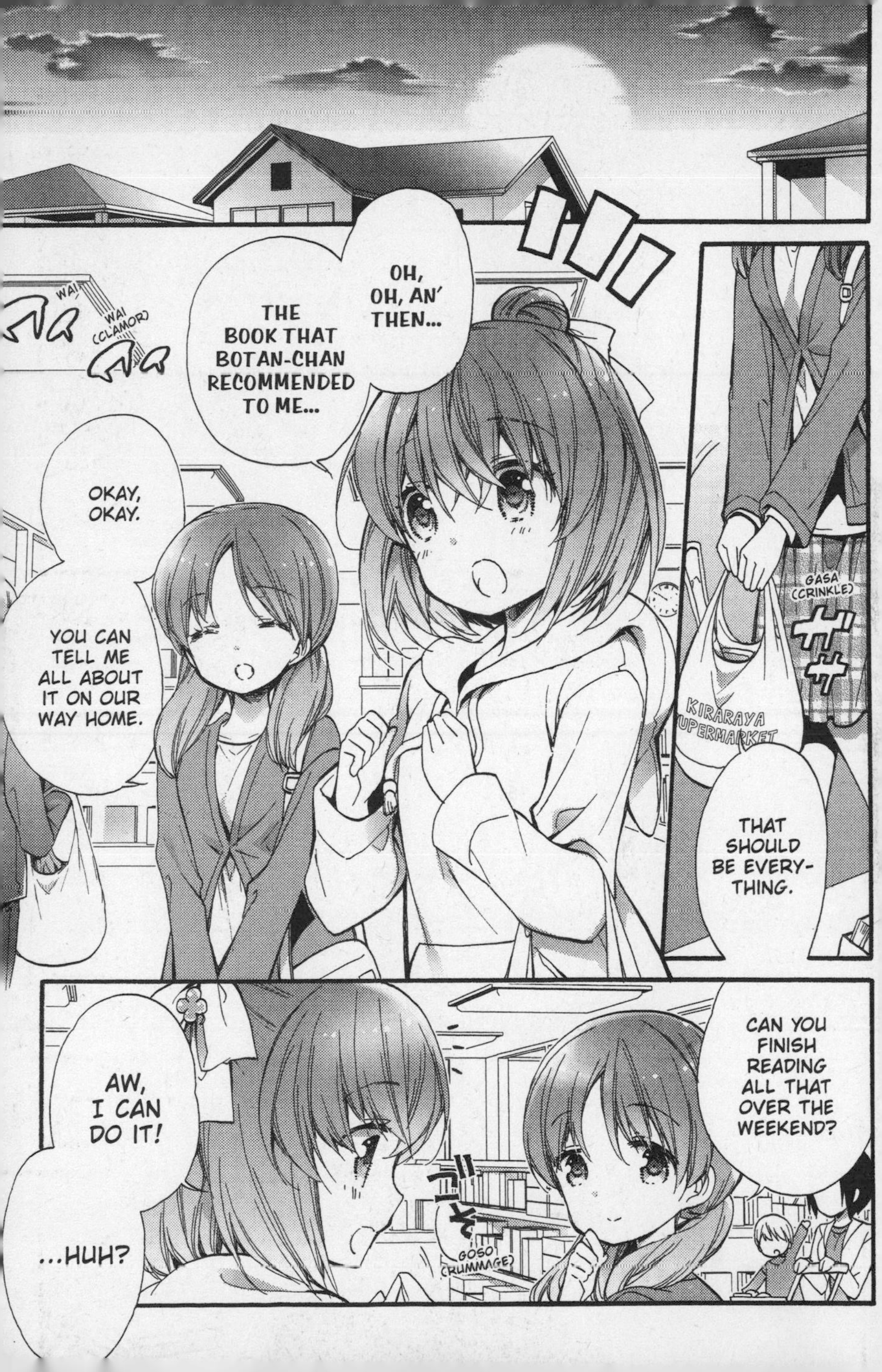
GASA (CRINKLE)
KIRARAYA SUPERMARKET
THAT SHOULD BE EVERY-THING.
OH, OH, AN' THEN...
THE BOOK THAT BOTAN-CHAN RECOMMENDED TO ME...
WAI WAI (CLAMOR)
OKAY, OKAY.
YOU CAN TELL ME ALL ABOUT IT ON OUR WAY HOME.
CAN YOU FINISH READING ALL THAT OVER THE WEEKEND?
GOSO (RUMMAGE)
AW, I CAN DO IT!
...HUH?

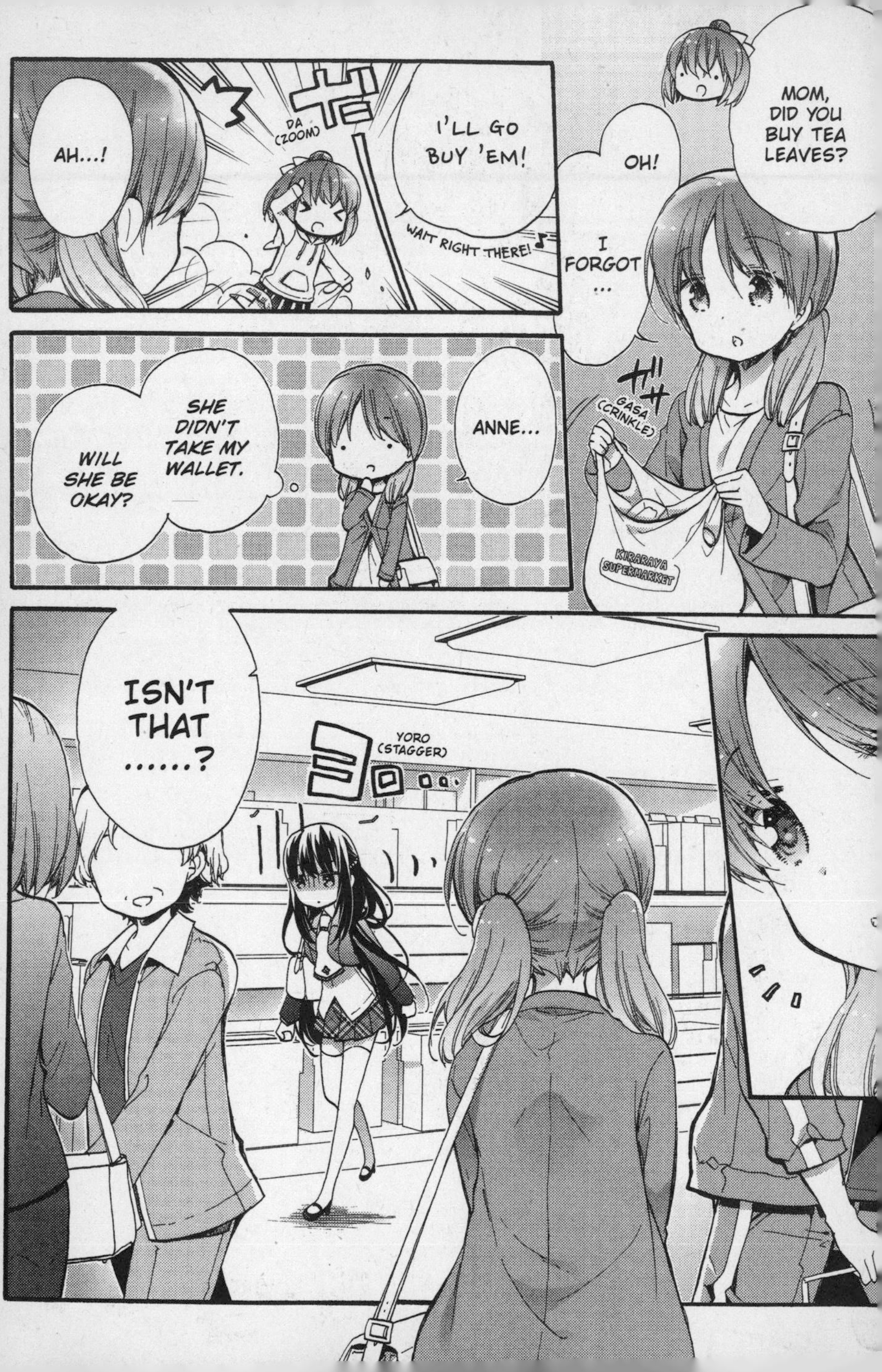
MOM, DID YOU BUY TEA LEAVES?
OH!
I FORGOT...
GASA (CRINKLE)
KIRARAYA SUPERMARKET
I'LL GO BUY 'EM!
DA (ZOOM)
WAIT RIGHT THERE!
AH...!
ANNE...
SHE DIDN'T TAKE MY WALLET.
WILL SHE BE OKAY?
ISN'T THAT ......?
YORO (STAGGER)

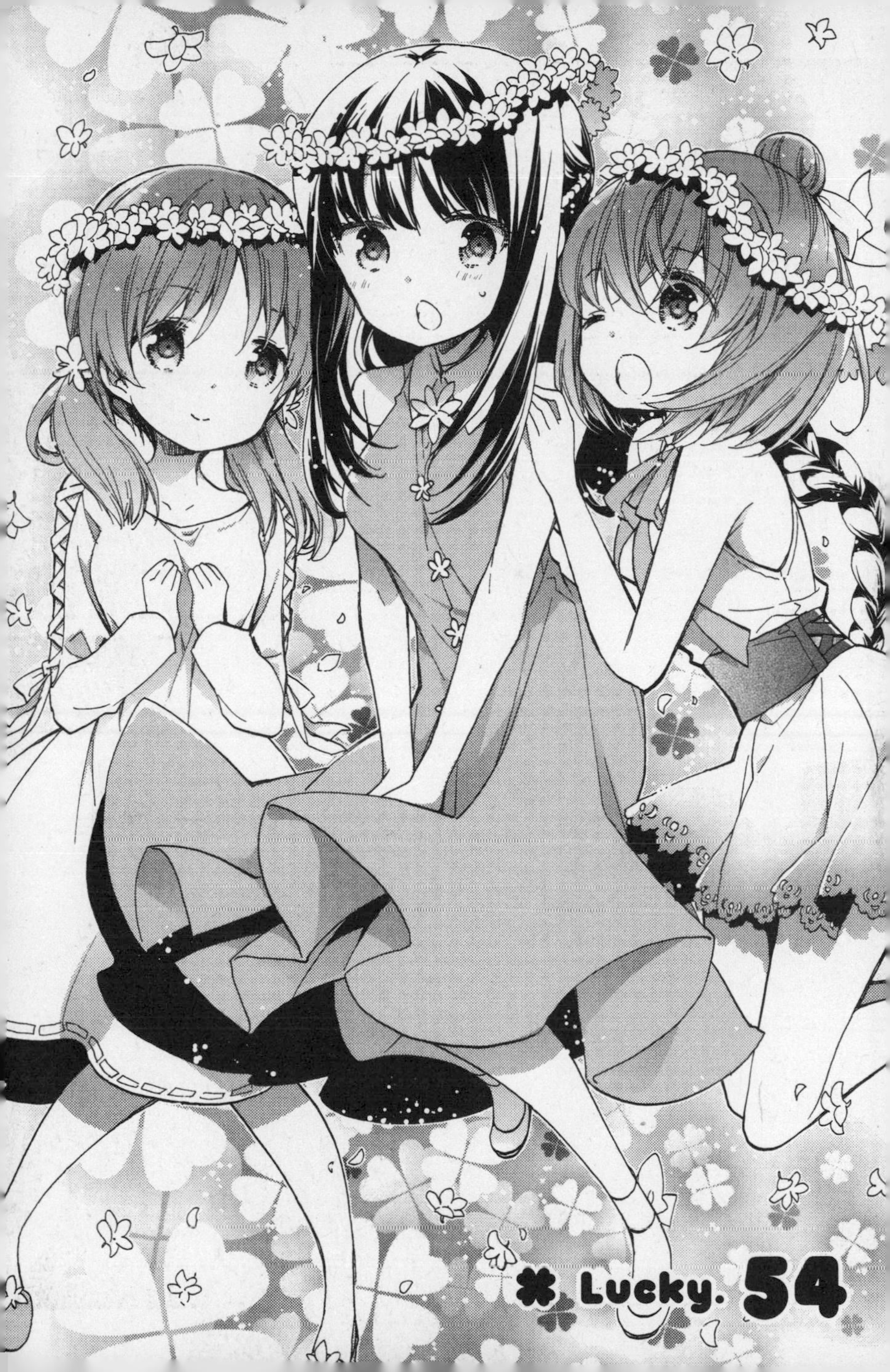
Lucky. 54

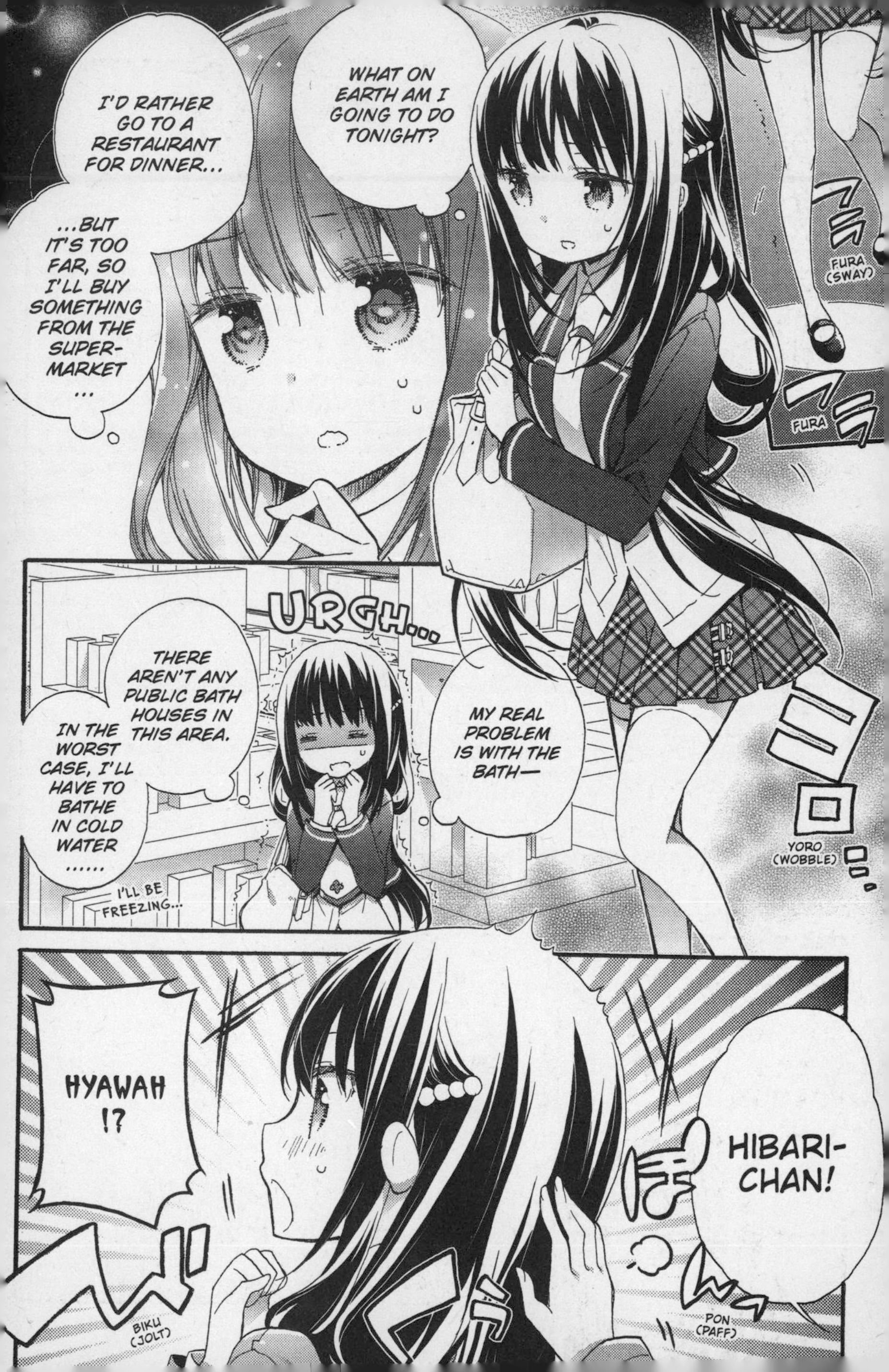
FURA (SWAY)
FURA
WHAT ON EARTH AM I GOING TO DO TONIGHT?
I'D RATHER GO TO A RESTAURANT FOR DINNER...
...BUT IT'S TOO FAR, SO I'LL BUY SOMETHING FROM THE SUPER-MARKET ...
YORO (WOBBLE)
MY REAL PROBLEM IS WITH THE BATH—
URGH...
THERE AREN'T ANY PUBLIC BATH HOUSES IN THIS AREA.
IN THE WORST CASE, I'LL HAVE TO BATHE IN COLD WATER ......
I'LL BE FREEZING...
HIBARI-CHAN!
PON (PAFF)
HYAWAH !?
BIKU (JOLT)

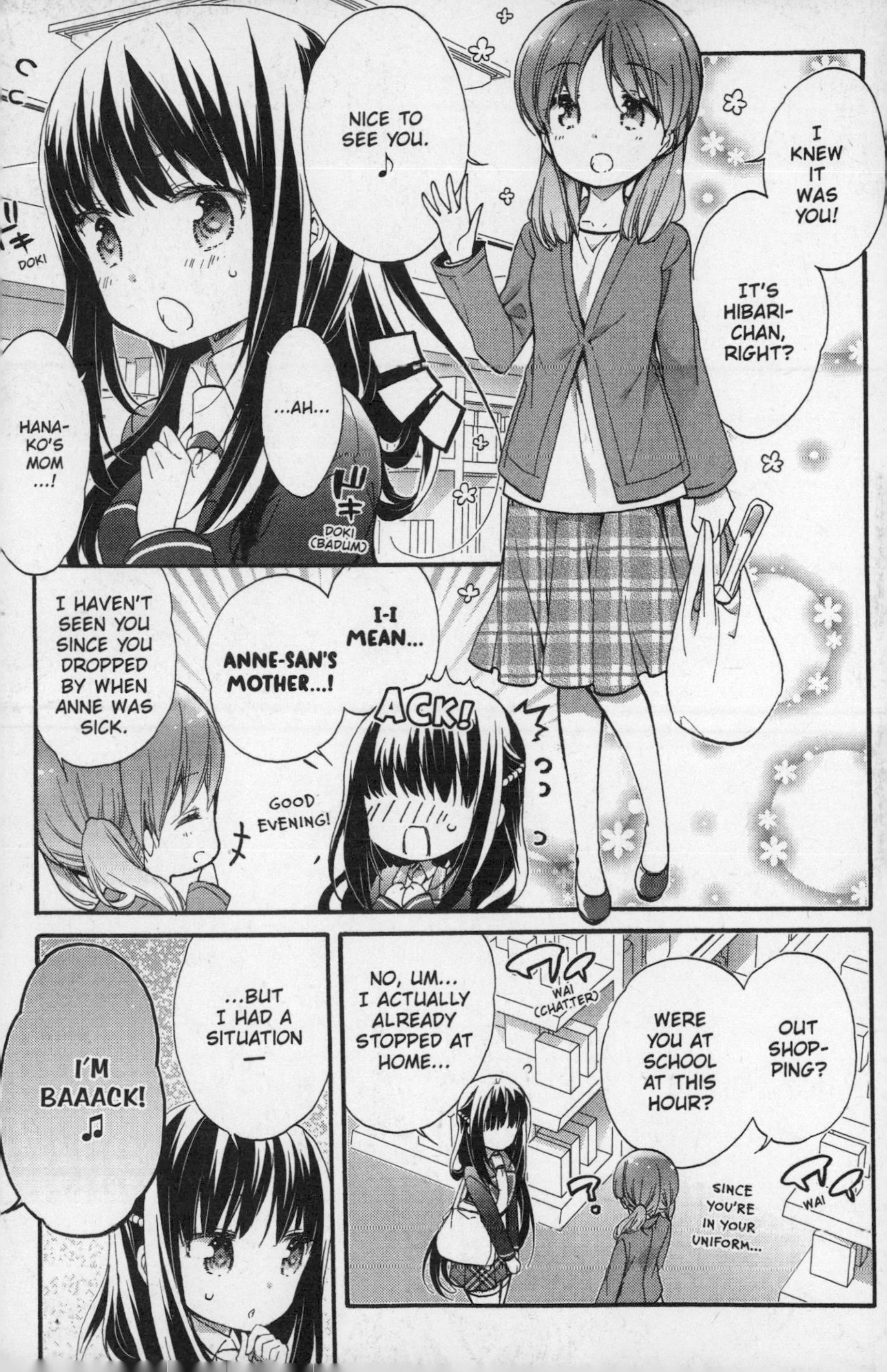
I KNEW IT WAS YOU!
IT'S HIBARI-CHAN, RIGHT?
NICE TO SEE YOU. ♪
DOKI
...AH...
DOKI (BADUM)
HANA-KO'S MOM ...!
I-I MEAN...
ANNE-SAN'S MOTHER...!
ACK!
GOOD EVENING!
I HAVEN'T SEEN YOU SINCE YOU DROPPED BY WHEN ANNE WAS SICK.
OUT SHOP-PING?
WERE YOU AT SCHOOL AT THIS HOUR?
WAI
SINCE YOU'RE IN YOUR UNIFORM...
WAI (CHATTER)
NO, UM... I ACTUALLY ALREADY STOPPED AT HOME...
...BUT I HAD A SITUATION —
I'M BAAACK! ♫

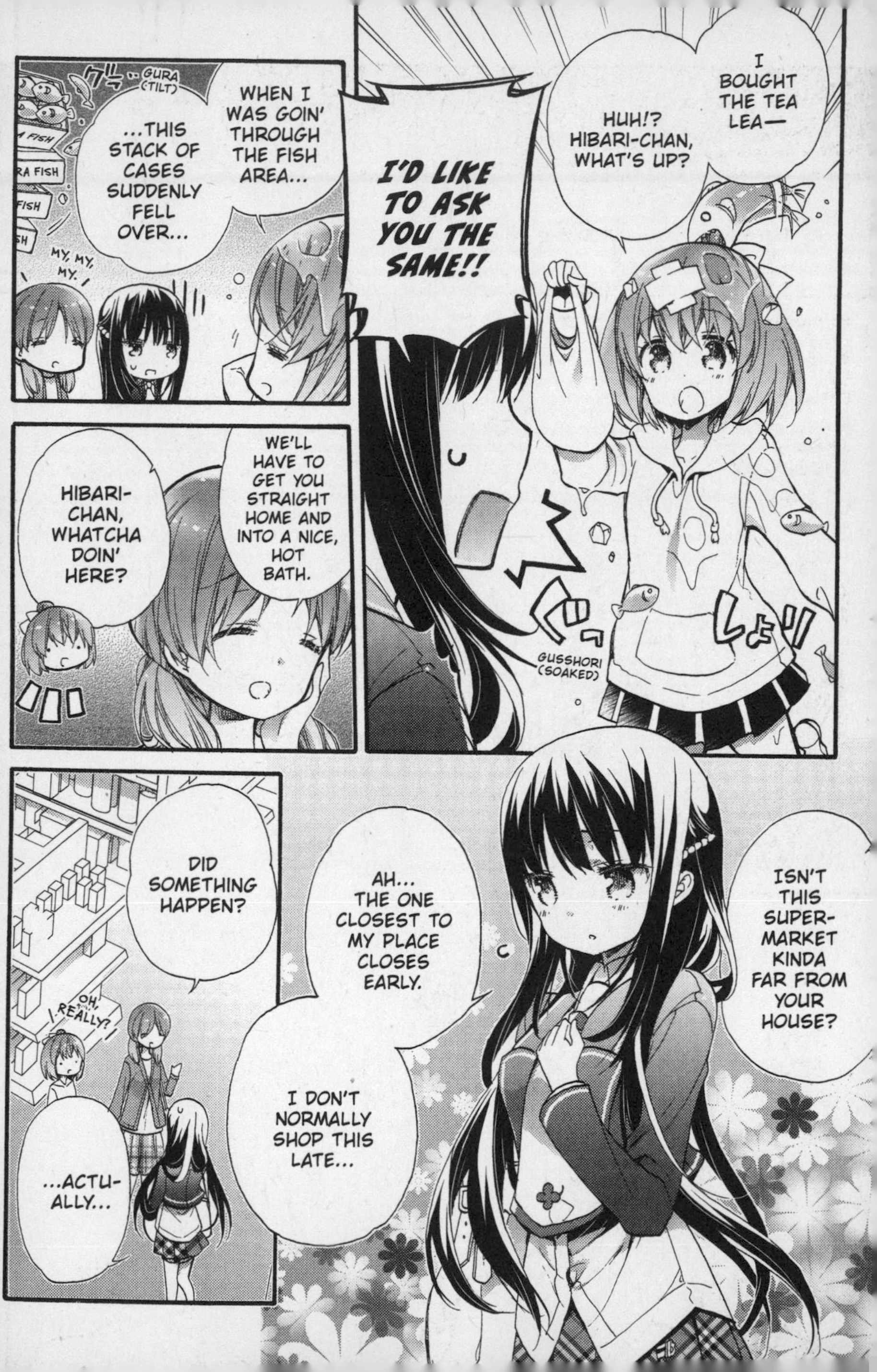
I BOUGHT THE TEA LEA—
HUH!? HIBARI-CHAN, WHAT'S UP?
I'D LIKE TO ASK YOU THE SAME!!
GUSSHORI (SOAKED)
GURA (TILT)
WHEN I WAS GOIN' THROUGH THE FISH AREA...
...THIS STACK OF CASES SUDDENLY FELL OVER...
MY, MY, MY.
WE'LL HAVE TO GET YOU STRAIGHT HOME AND INTO A NICE, HOT BATH.
HIBARI-CHAN, WHATCHA DOIN' HERE?
ISN'T THIS SUPER-MARKET KINDA FAR FROM YOUR HOUSE?
AH... THE ONE CLOSEST TO MY PLACE CLOSES EARLY.
I DON'T NORMALLY SHOP THIS LATE...
DID SOMETHING HAPPEN?
OH, REALLY?
...ACTU-ALLY...

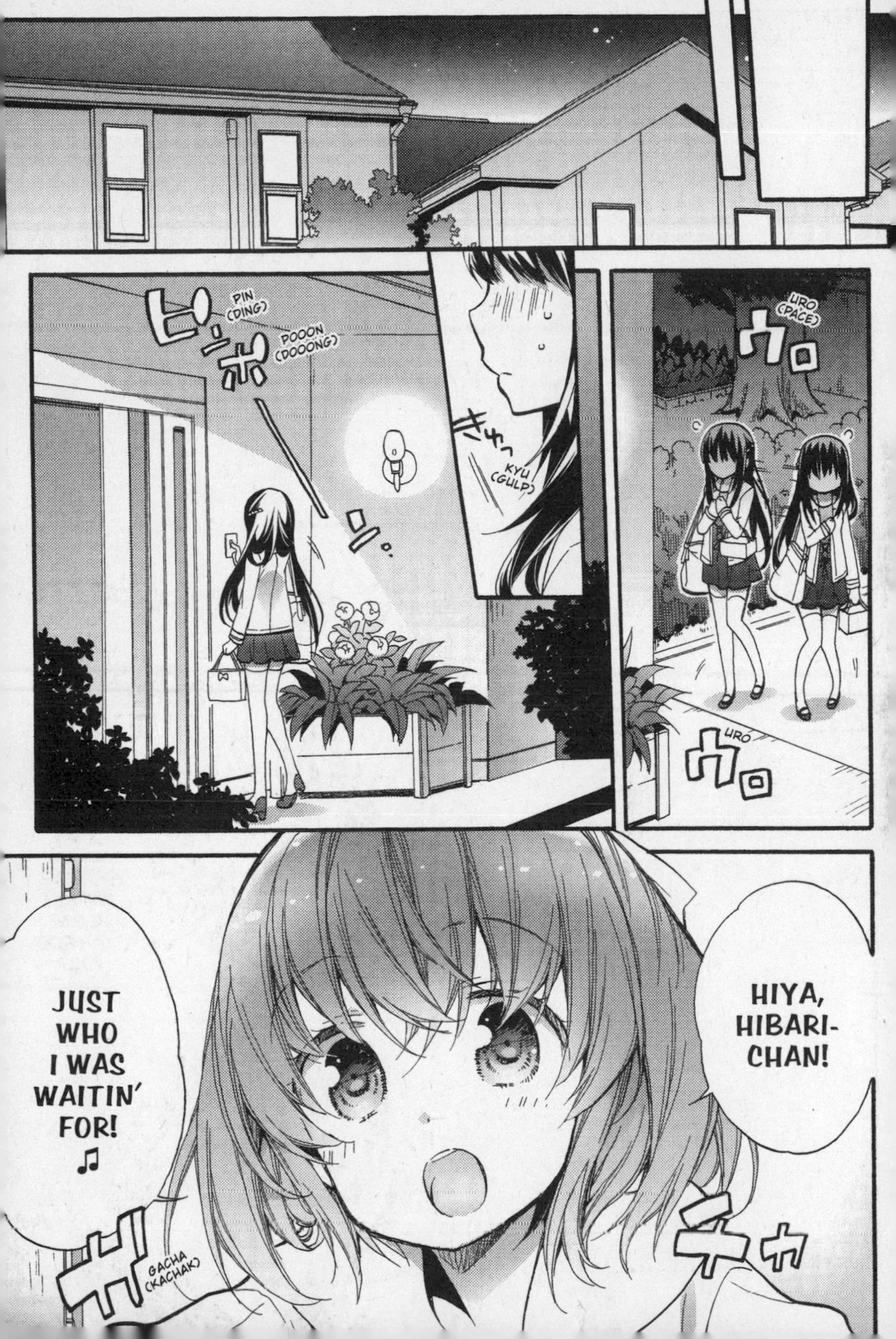
URO (PACE)
URO
KYU (GULP)
PIN (DING)
POOON (DOOONG)
HIYA, HIBARI-CHAN!
JUST WHO I WAS WAITIN' FOR! ♫
GACHA (KACHAK)

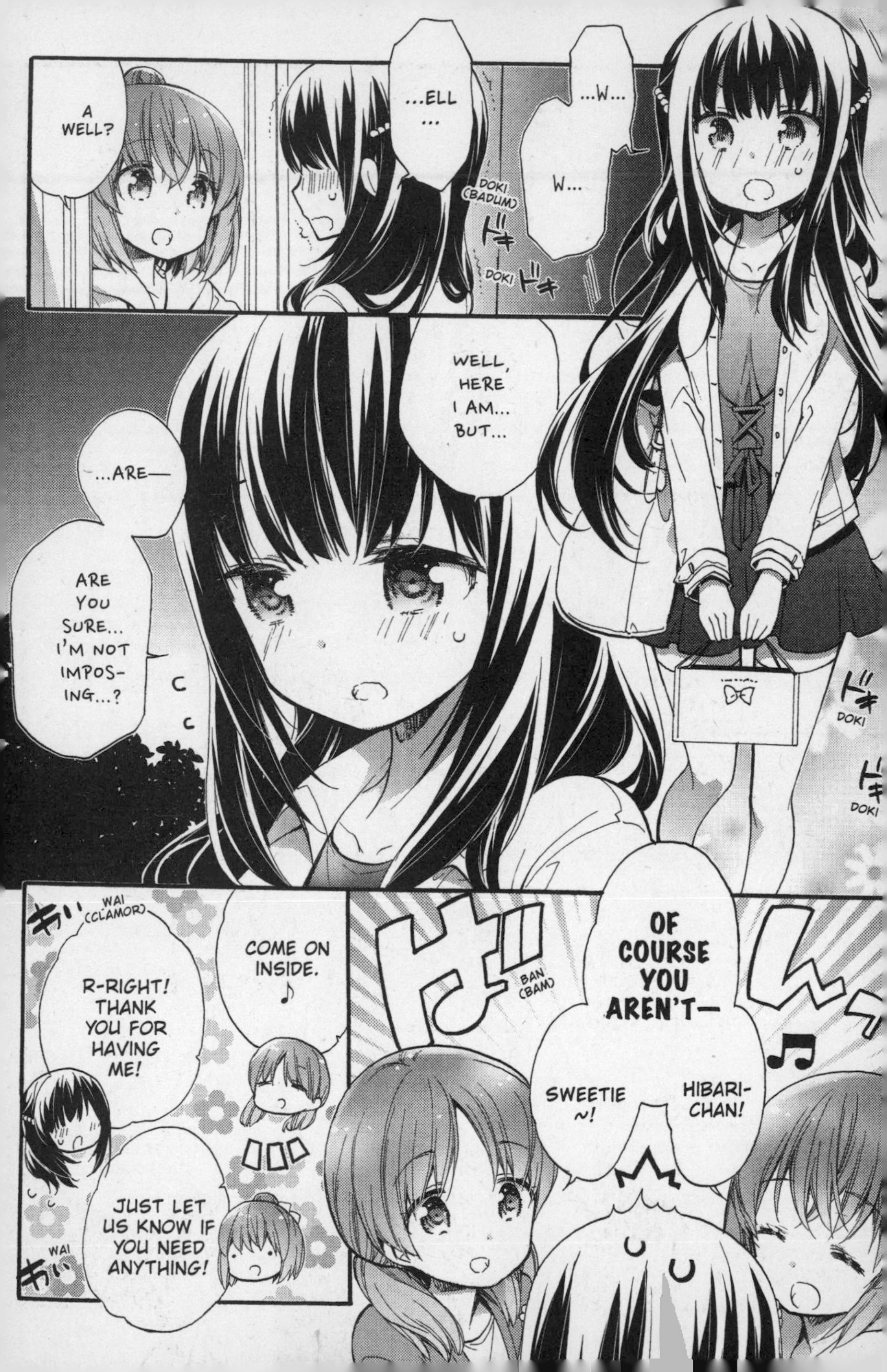
...W...
W...
DOKI
DOKI
DOKI
...ELL
...
DOKI (BADUM)
A WELL?
WELL, HERE I AM... BUT...
...ARE—
ARE YOU SURE... I'M NOT IMPOSING...?
OF COURSE YOU AREN'T—
HIBARI-CHAN!
SWEETIE ~!
BAN (BAM)
COME ON INSIDE. ♪
WAI (CLAMOR)
R-RIGHT! THANK YOU FOR HAVING ME!
JUST LET US KNOW IF YOU NEED ANYTHING!
WAI

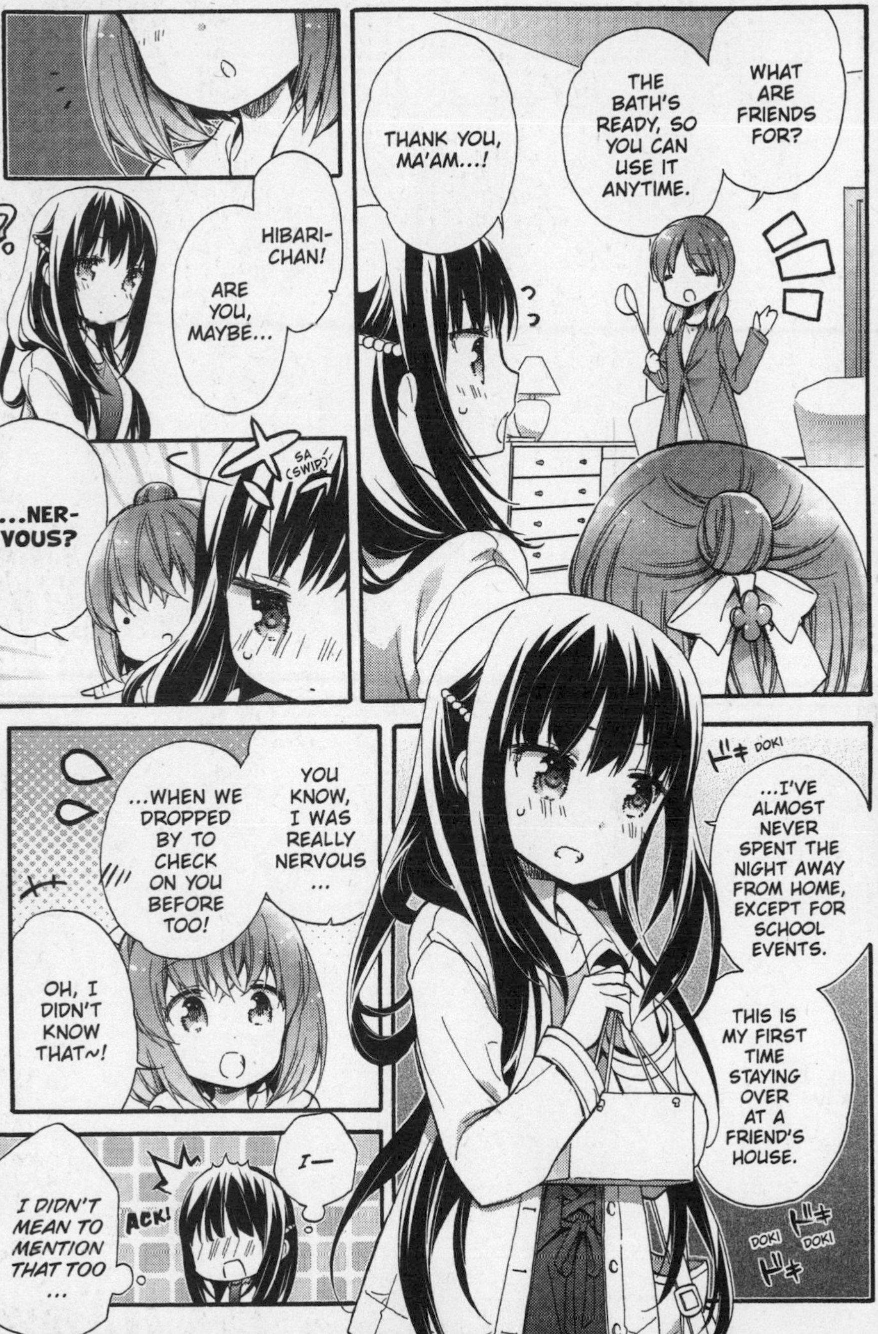
WHAT ARE FRIENDS FOR?
THE BATH'S READY, SO YOU CAN USE IT ANYTIME.
THANK YOU, MA'AM...!
HIBARI-CHAN!
ARE YOU, MAYBE...
SA (SWIP)
...NER-VOUS?
ドキ DOKI
...I'VE ALMOST NEVER SPENT THE NIGHT AWAY FROM HOME, EXCEPT FOR SCHOOL EVENTS.
THIS IS MY FIRST TIME STAYING OVER AT A FRIEND'S HOUSE.
ドキ DOKI
ドキ DOKI
YOU KNOW, I WAS REALLY NERVOUS...
...WHEN WE DROPPED BY TO CHECK ON YOU BEFORE TOO!
OH, I DIDN'T KNOW THAT~!
I—
ACK!
I DIDN'T MEAN TO MENTION THAT TOO...

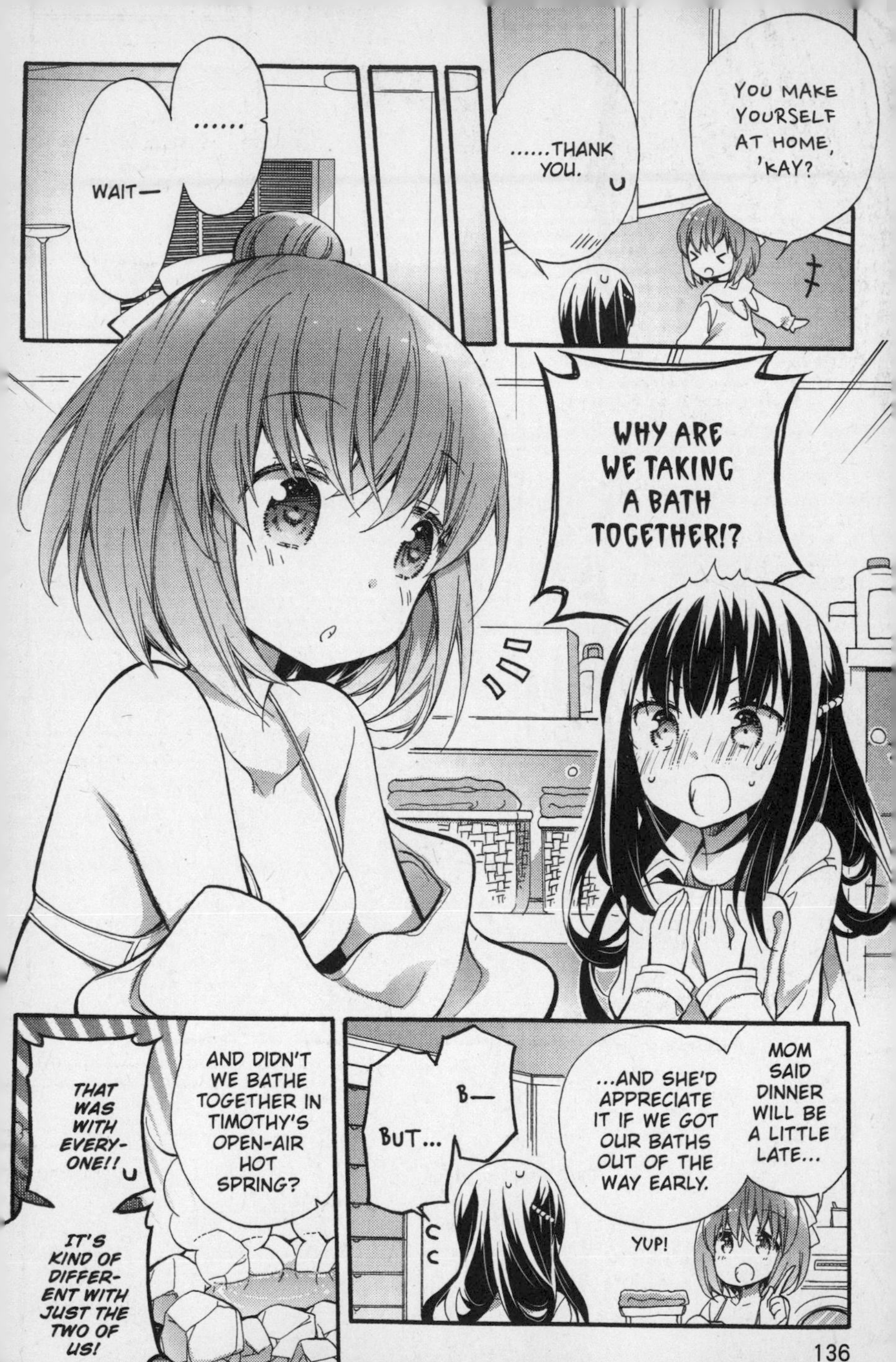
YOU MAKE YOURSELF AT HOME, 'KAY?
......THANK YOU.
......
WAIT—
WHY ARE WE TAKING A BATH TOGETHER!?
MOM SAID DINNER WILL BE A LITTLE LATE...
...AND SHE'D APPRECIATE IT IF WE GOT OUR BATHS OUT OF THE WAY EARLY.
YUP!
B—
BUT...
AND DIDN'T WE BATHE TOGETHER IN TIMOTHY'S OPEN-AIR HOT SPRING?
THAT WAS WITH EVERY-ONE!!
IT'S KIND OF DIFFER-ENT WITH JUST THE TWO OF US!

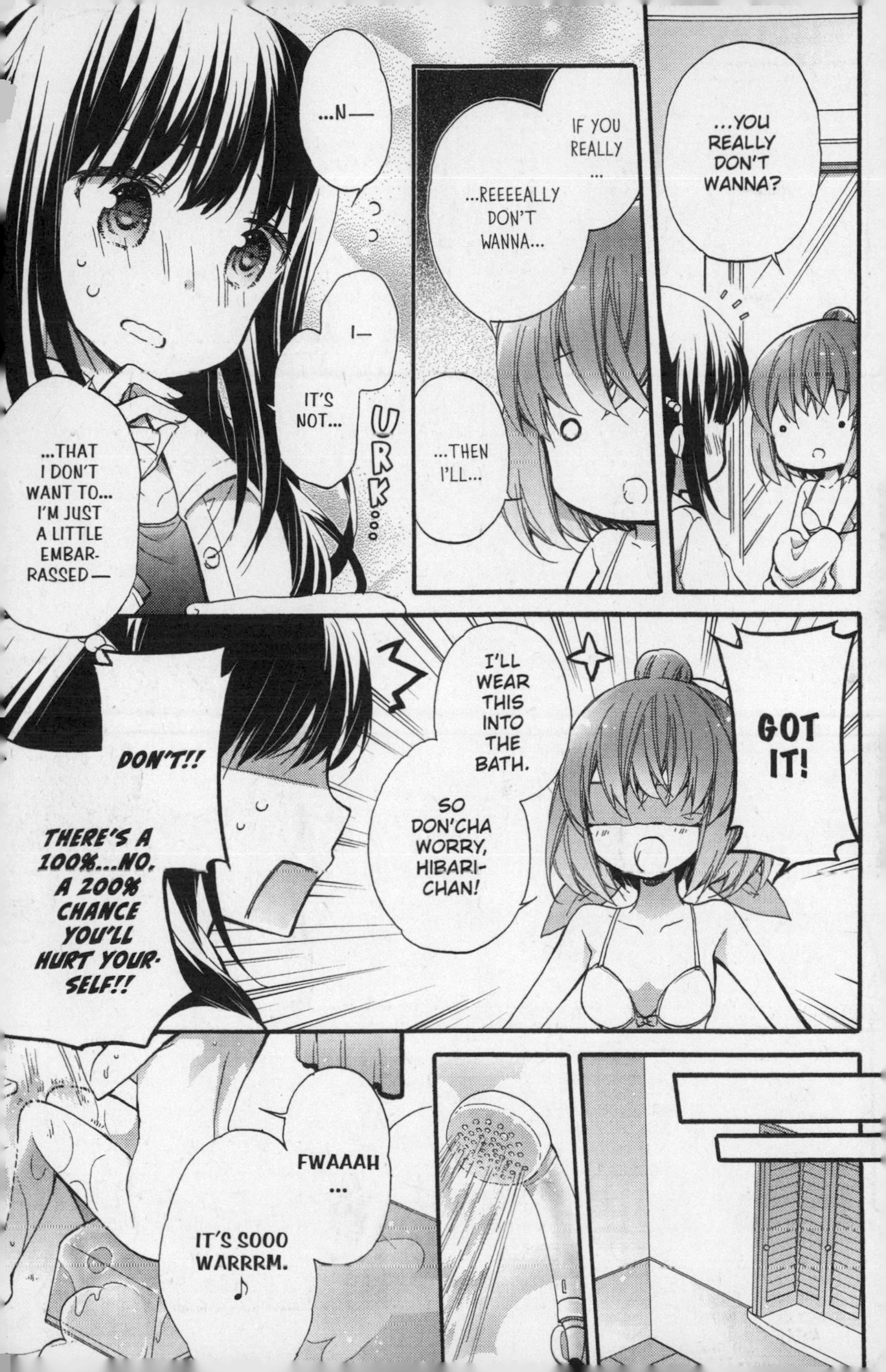
...YOU REALLY DON'T WANNA?
IF YOU REALLY...
...REEEEALLY DON'T WANNA...
...THEN I'LL...
...N—
I—
IT'S NOT...
URK...
...THAT I DON'T WANT TO... I'M JUST A LITTLE EMBARRASSED—
GOT IT!
I'LL WEAR THIS INTO THE BATH.
SO DON'CHA WORRY, HIBARI-CHAN!
DON'T!!
THERE'S A 100%...NO. A 200% CHANCE YOU'LL HURT YOURSELF!!
FWAAAH...
IT'S SOOO WARRRM. ♪

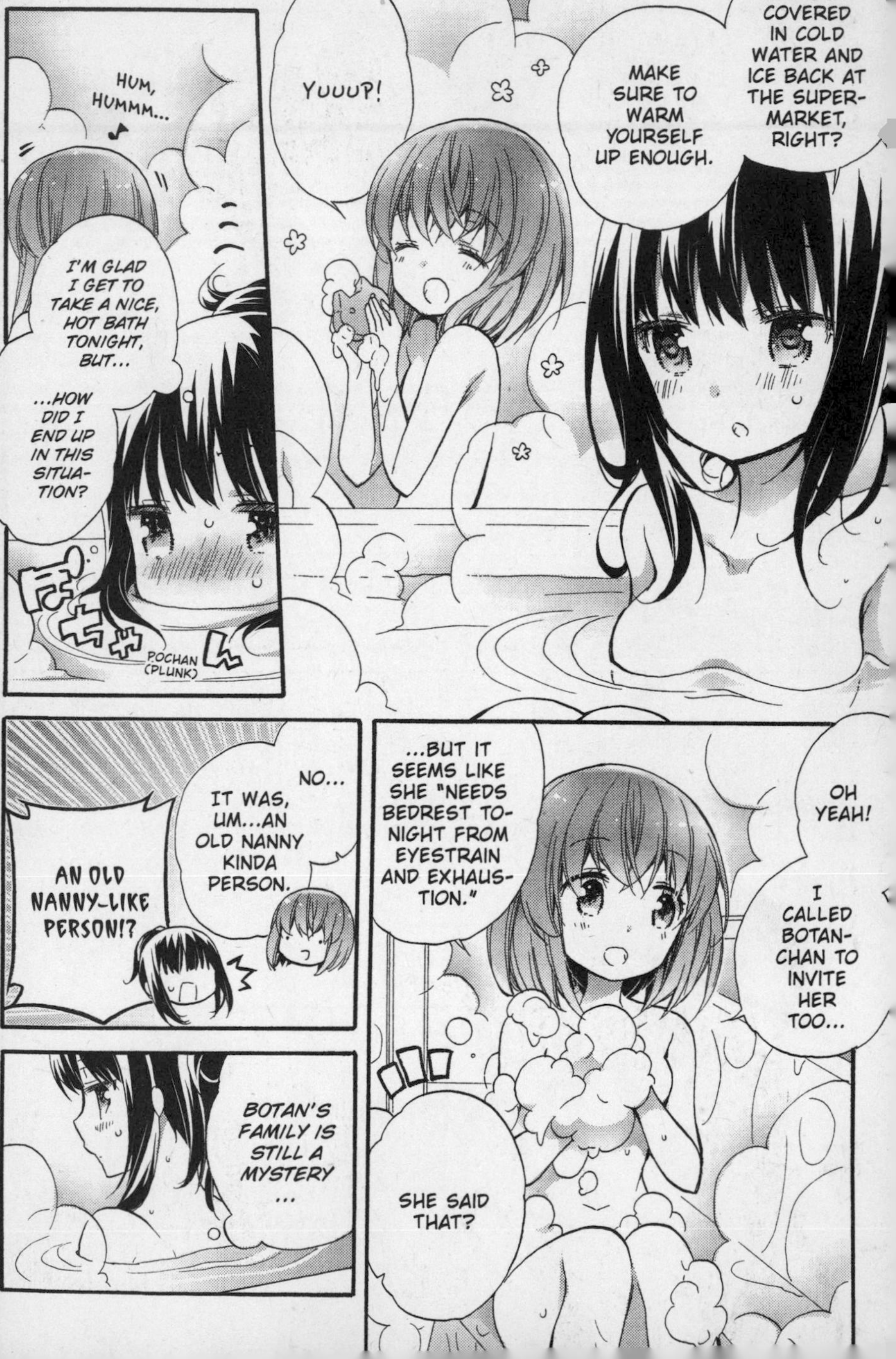
YOU GOT COVERED IN COLD WATER AND ICE BACK AT THE SUPER-MARKET, RIGHT?
MAKE SURE TO WARM YOURSELF UP ENOUGH.
YUUUP!
HUM, HUMMM... ♪
I'M GLAD I GET TO TAKE A NICE, HOT BATH TONIGHT, BUT...
...HOW DID I END UP IN THIS SITUA-TION?
POCHAN (PLUNK)
OH YEAH!
I CALLED BOTAN-CHAN TO INVITE HER TOO...
...BUT IT SEEMS LIKE SHE "NEEDS BEDREST TO-NIGHT FROM EYESTRAIN AND EXHAUS-TION."
SHE SAID THAT?
NO...
IT WAS, UM...AN OLD NANNY KINDA PERSON.
AN OLD NANNY-LIKE PERSON!?
BOTAN'S FAMILY IS STILL A MYSTERY ...

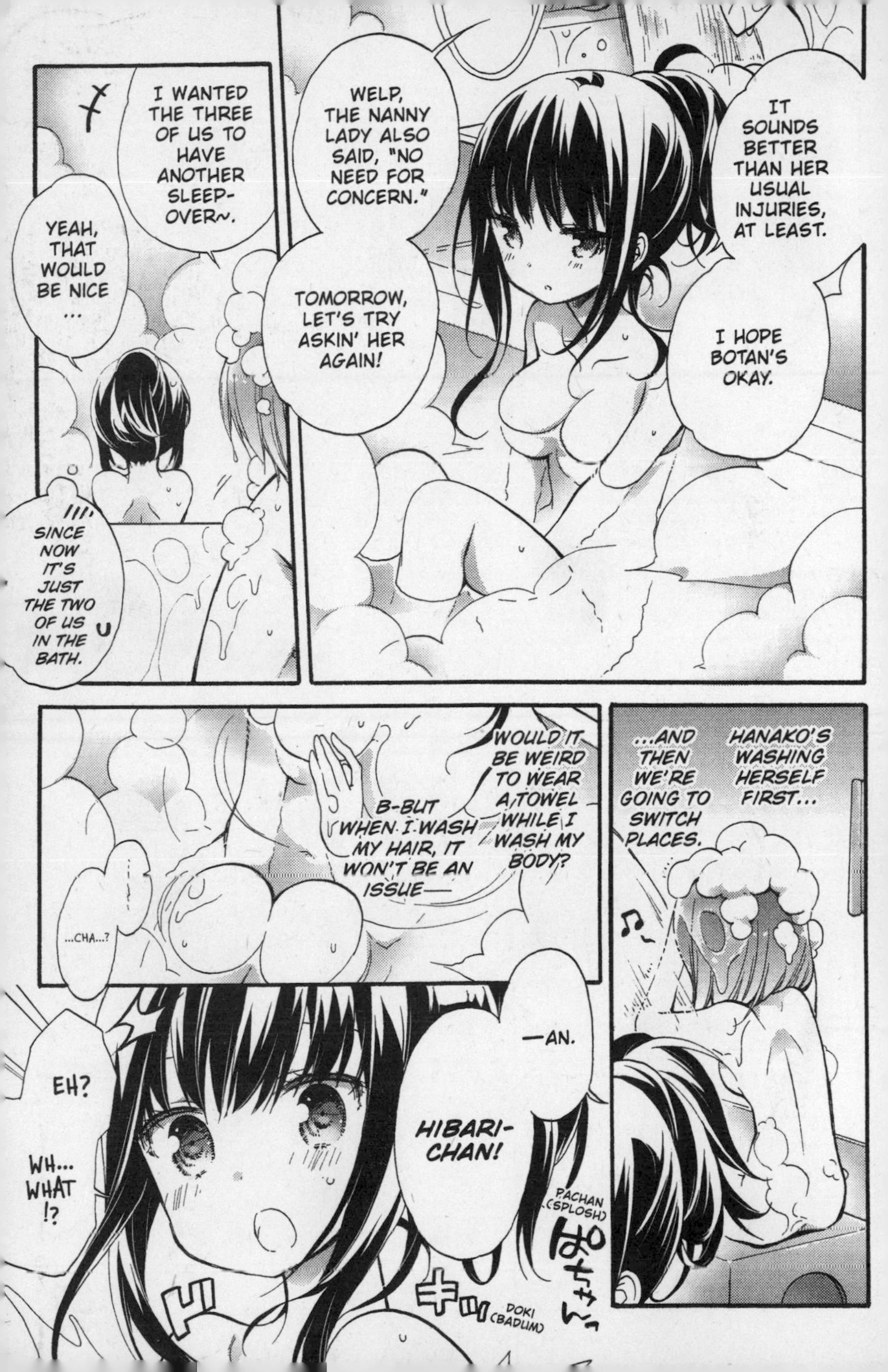
IT SOUNDS BETTER THAN HER USUAL INJURIES, AT LEAST.
WELP, THE NANNY LADY ALSO SAID, "NO NEED FOR CONCERN."
I HOPE BOTAN'S OKAY.
TOMORROW, LET'S TRY ASKIN' HER AGAIN!
I WANTED THE THREE OF US TO HAVE ANOTHER SLEEP-OVER~.
YEAH, THAT WOULD BE NICE ...
/// SINCE NOW IT'S JUST THE TWO OF US IN THE BATH.
HANAKO'S WASHING HERSELF FIRST...
...AND THEN WE'RE GOING TO SWITCH PLACES.
WOULD IT BE WEIRD TO WEAR A TOWEL WHILE I WASH MY BODY?
B-BUT WHEN I WASH MY HAIR, IT WON'T BE AN ISSUE—
...CHA...?
—AN.
HIBARI-CHAN!
PACHAN (SPLOSH)
DOKI (BADUM)
EH?
WH... WHAT!?

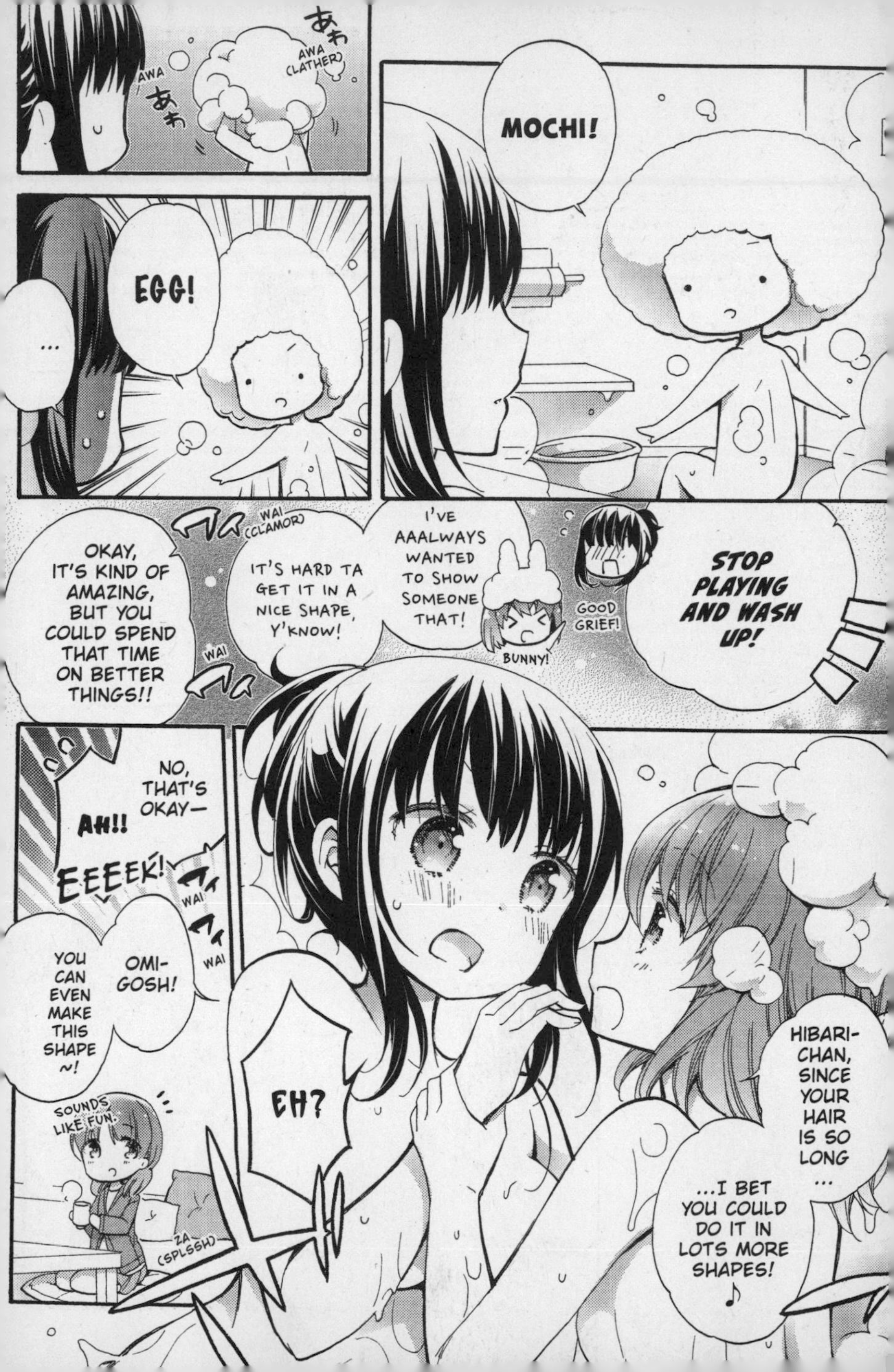
MOCHI!
あわ
AWA (LATHER)
AWA
あわ
EGG!
...
STOP PLAYING AND WASH UP!
GOOD GRIEF!
BUNNY!
I'VE AAALWAYS WANTED TO SHOW SOMEONE THAT!
IT'S HARD TA GET IT IN A NICE SHAPE, Y'KNOW!
WAI (CLAMOR)
OKAY, IT'S KIND OF AMAZING, BUT YOU COULD SPEND THAT TIME ON BETTER THINGS!!
WAI
HIBARI-CHAN, SINCE YOUR HAIR IS SO LONG...
...I BET YOU COULD DO IT IN LOTS MORE SHAPES! ♪
EH?
NO, THAT'S OKAY—
AH!!
EEEEK!
WAI
WAI
OMI-GOSH!
YOU CAN EVEN MAKE THIS SHAPE ~!
SOUNDS LIKE FUN.
ZA (SPLSSH)

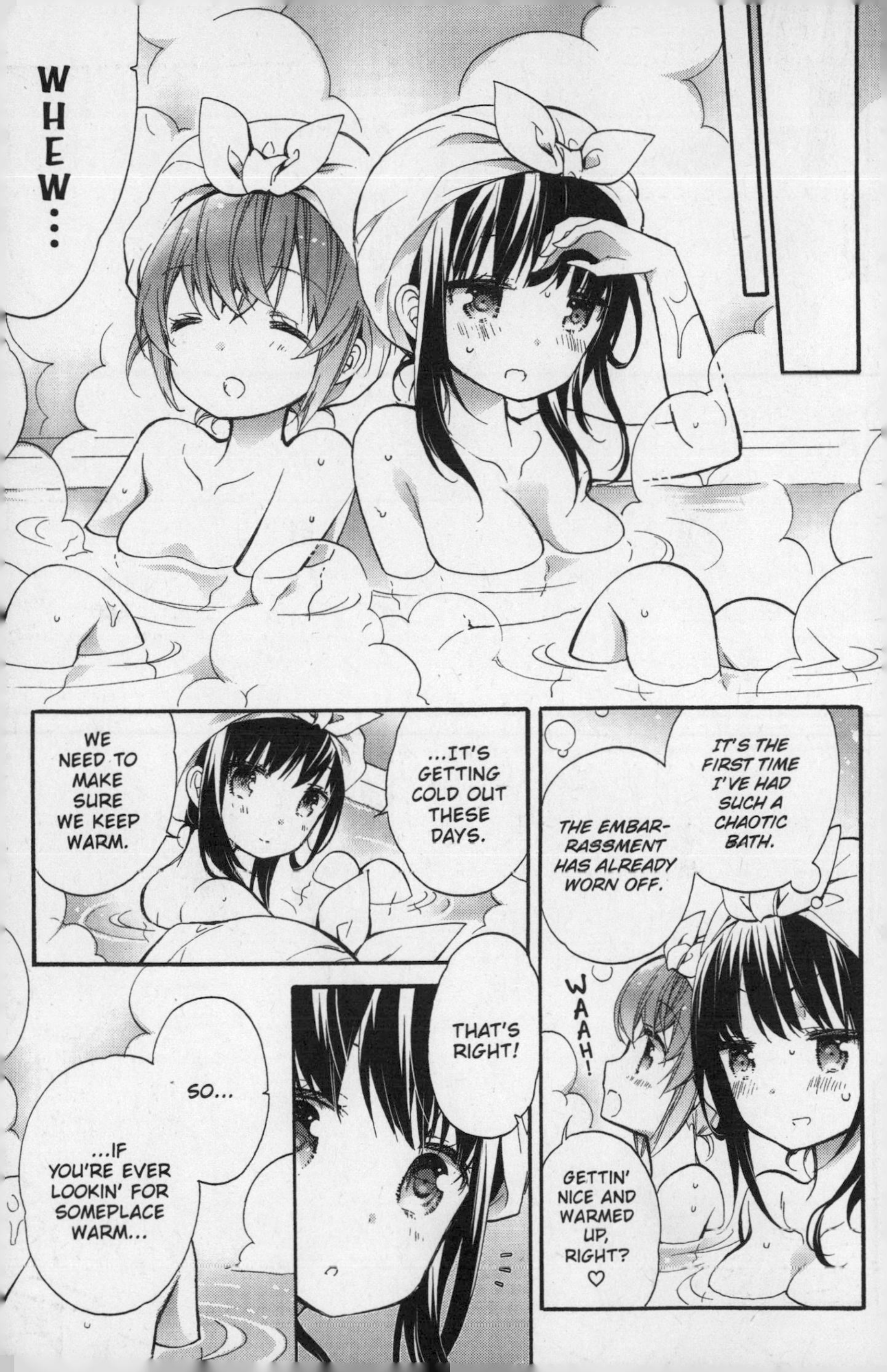
WHEW...
IT'S THE FIRST TIME I'VE HAD SUCH A CHAOTIC BATH.
THE EMBARRASSMENT HAS ALREADY WORN OFF.
WAAH!
GETTIN' NICE AND WARMED UP, RIGHT? ♡
...IT'S GETTING COLD OUT THESE DAYS.
WE NEED TO MAKE SURE WE KEEP WARM.
THAT'S RIGHT!
SO...
...IF YOU'RE EVER LOOKIN' FOR SOMEPLACE WARM...

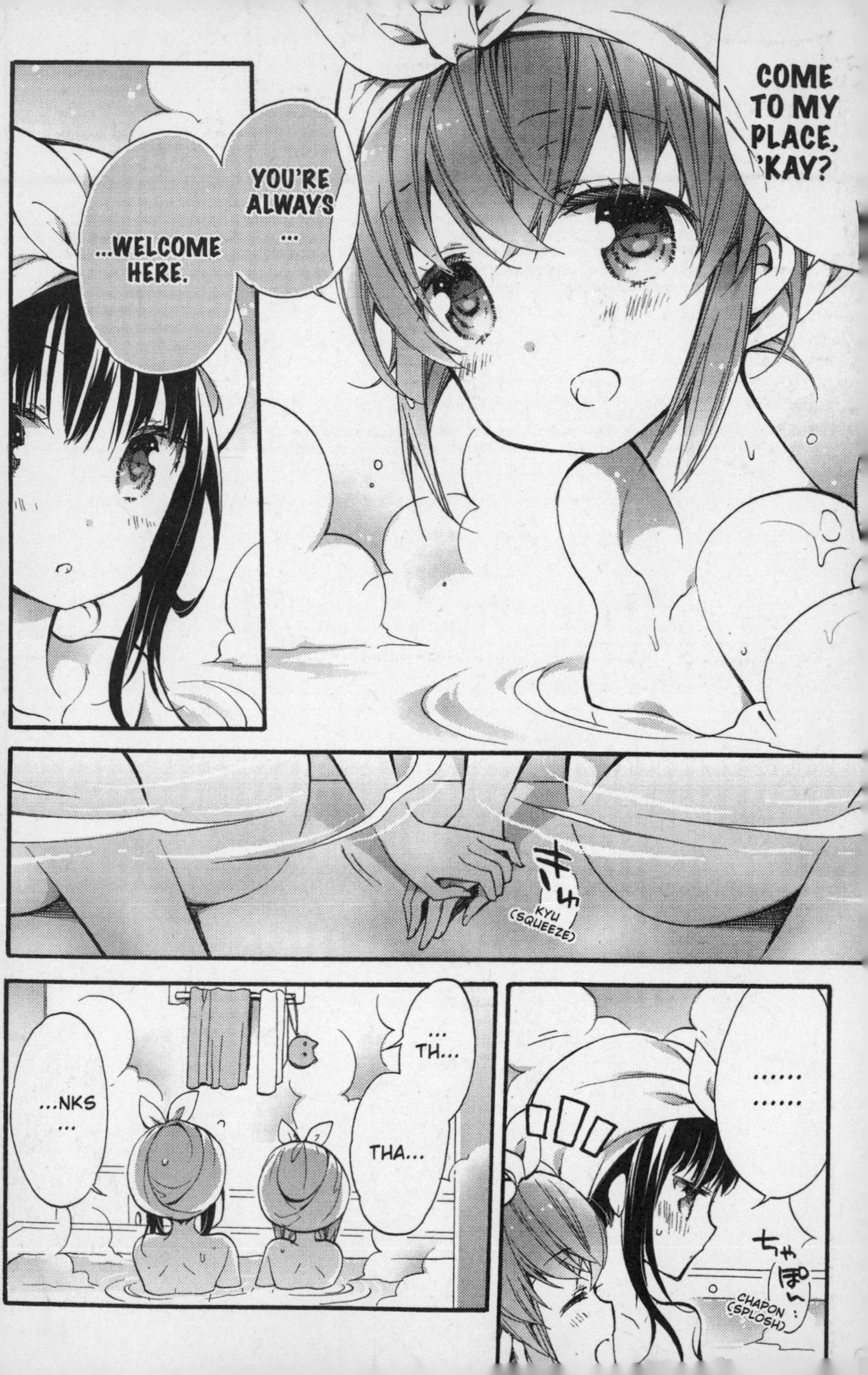
COME TO MY PLACE, 'KAY?
YOU'RE ALWAYS ...
...WELCOME HERE.
きゅ
KYU (SQUEEZE)
....
ちゃぽん
CHAPON (SPLOSH)
... TH...
THA...
...NKS ...

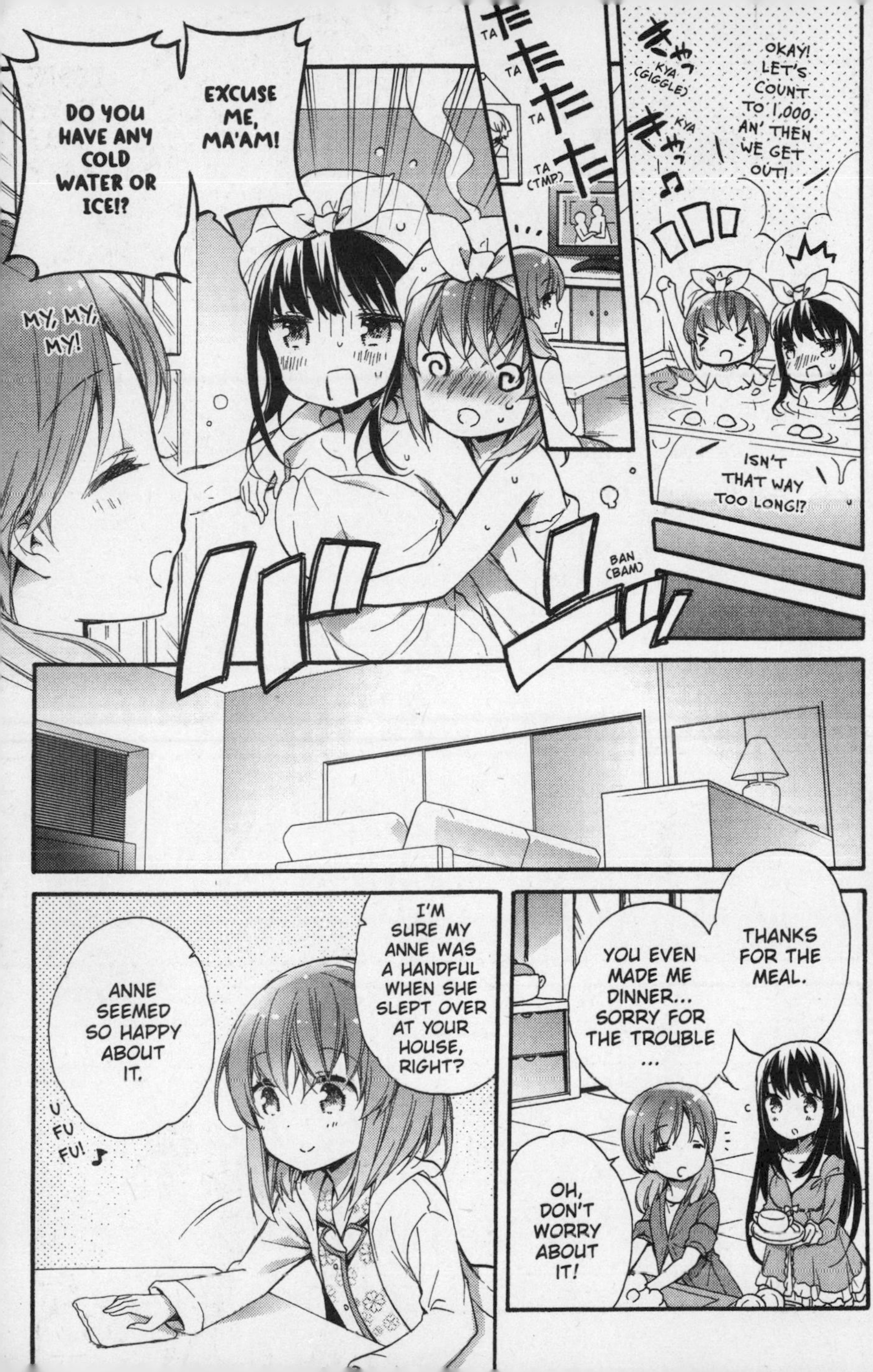

OKAY! LET'S COUNT TO 1,000, AN' THEN WE GET OUT!
きゃっ KYA (GIGGLE)
きゃっ KYA
ISN'T THAT WAY TOO LONG!?
たたたた TA TA TA TA (TMP)
BAN (BAM)
EXCUSE ME, MA'AM!
DO YOU HAVE ANY COLD WATER OR ICE!?
MY, MY, MY!
THANKS FOR THE MEAL.
YOU EVEN MADE ME DINNER... SORRY FOR THE TROUBLE ...
OH, DON'T WORRY ABOUT IT!
I'M SURE MY ANNE WAS A HANDFUL WHEN SHE SLEPT OVER AT YOUR HOUSE, RIGHT?
ANNE SEEMED SO HAPPY ABOUT IT.
U FU FU!

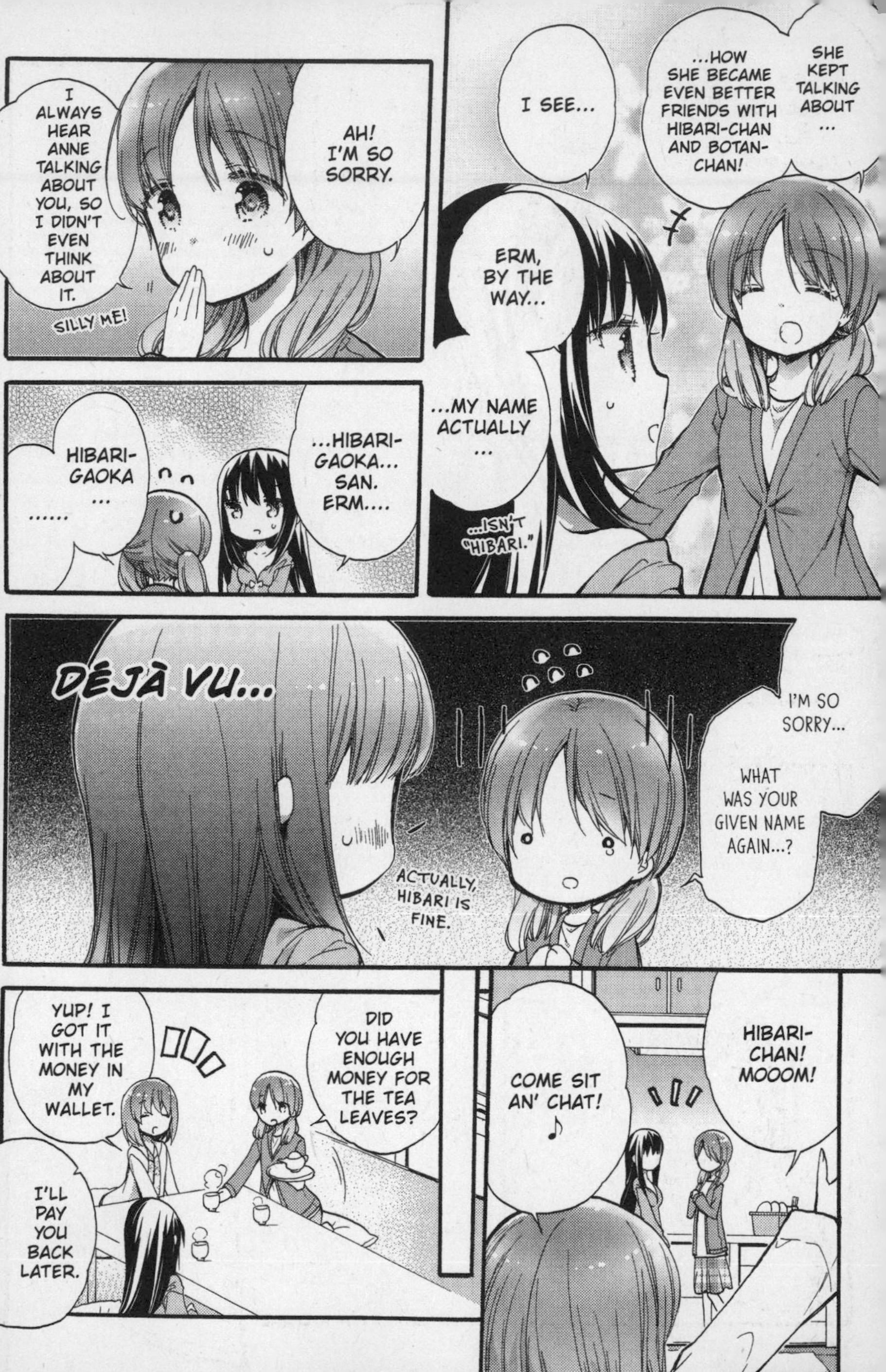
SHE KEPT TALKING ABOUT ...
...HOW SHE BECAME EVEN BETTER FRIENDS WITH HIBARI-CHAN AND BOTAN-CHAN!
I SEE...
ERM, BY THE WAY...
...MY NAME ACTUALLY ...
...ISN'T "HIBARI."
AH! I'M SO SORRY.
I ALWAYS HEAR ANNE TALKING ABOUT YOU, SO I DIDN'T EVEN THINK ABOUT IT.
SILLY ME!
...HIBARI-GAOKA... SAN. ERM....
HIBARI-GAOKA ... .
I'M SO SORRY...
WHAT WAS YOUR GIVEN NAME AGAIN...?
DÉJÀ VU...
ACTUALLY, HIBARI IS FINE.
HIBARI-CHAN! MOOOM!
COME SIT AN' CHAT! ♪
DID YOU HAVE ENOUGH MONEY FOR THE TEA LEAVES?
YUP! I GOT IT WITH THE MONEY IN MY WALLET.
I'LL PAY YOU BACK LATER.

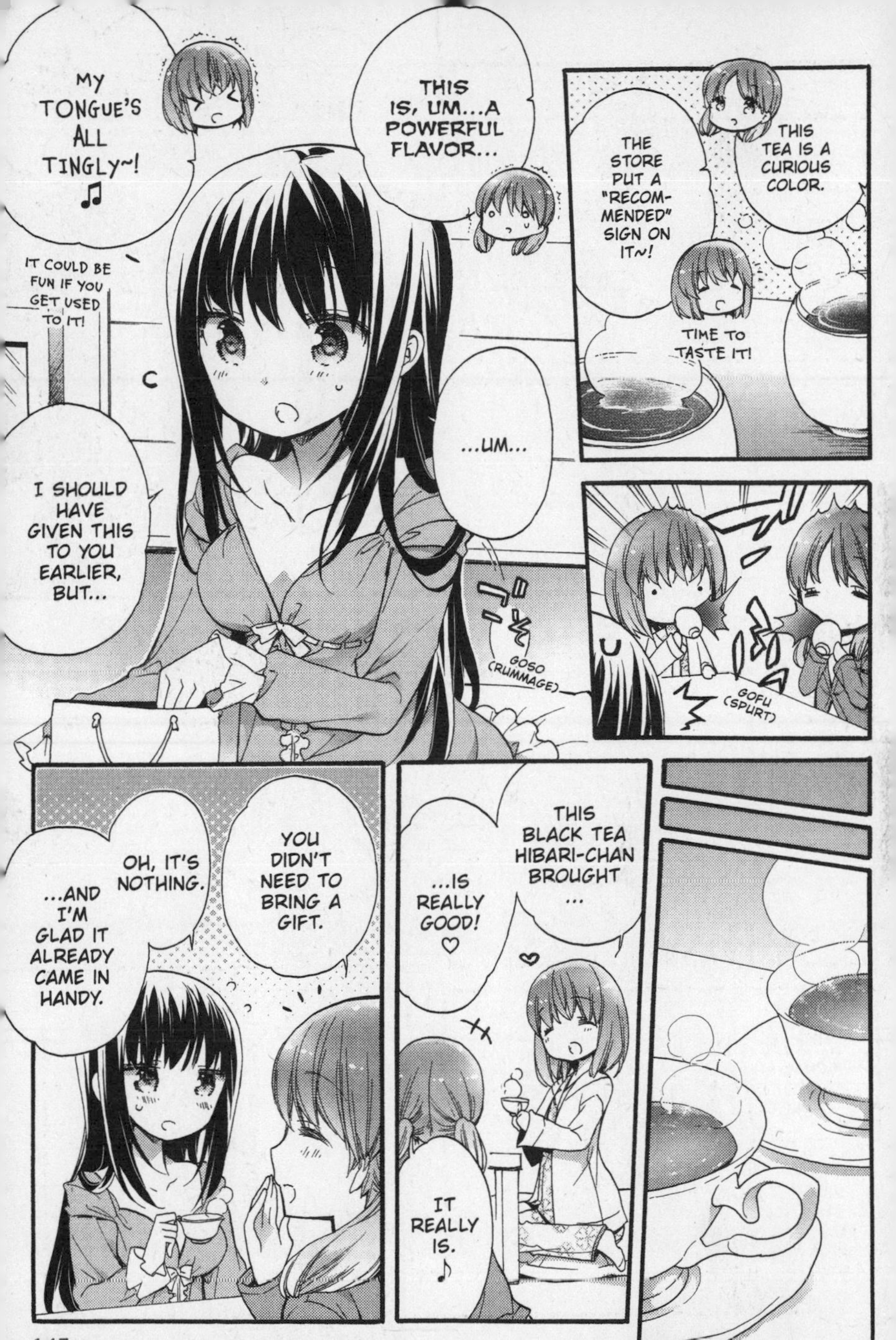
THIS TEA IS A CURIOUS COLOR.
THE STORE PUT A "RECOMMENDED" SIGN ON IT~!
TIME TO TASTE IT!
GOFU (SPURT)
THIS IS, UM...A POWERFUL FLAVOR...
MY TONGUE'S ALL TINGLY~! ♫
IT COULD BE FUN IF YOU GET USED TO IT!
...UM...
GOSO (RUMMAGE)
I SHOULD HAVE GIVEN THIS TO YOU EARLIER, BUT...
THIS BLACK TEA HIBARI-CHAN BROUGHT...
...IS REALLY GOOD! ♡
IT REALLY IS. ♪
YOU DIDN'T NEED TO BRING A GIFT.
OH, IT'S NOTHING.
...AND I'M GLAD IT ALREADY CAME IN HANDY.

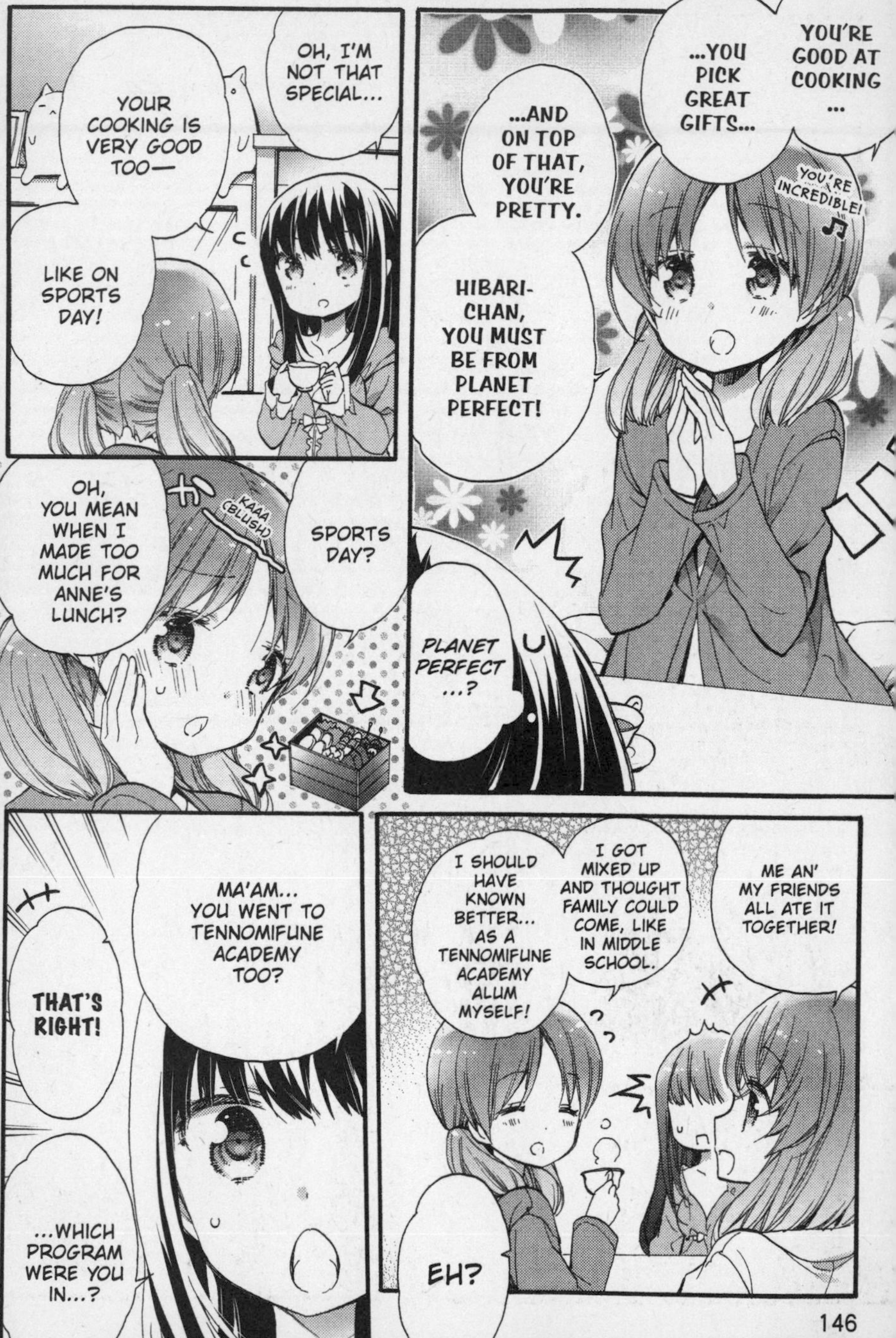
YOU'RE GOOD AT COOKING ...
...YOU PICK GREAT GIFTS...
...AND ON TOP OF THAT, YOU'RE PRETTY.
YOU'RE INCREDIBLE! ♫
HIBARI-CHAN, YOU MUST BE FROM PLANET PERFECT!
PLANET PERFECT ...?
OH, I'M NOT THAT SPECIAL...
YOUR COOKING IS VERY GOOD TOO—
LIKE ON SPORTS DAY!
SPORTS DAY?
KAAA (BLUSH)
OH, YOU MEAN WHEN I MADE TOO MUCH FOR ANNE'S LUNCH?
ME AN' MY FRIENDS ALL ATE IT TOGETHER!
I GOT MIXED UP AND THOUGHT FAMILY COULD COME, LIKE IN MIDDLE SCHOOL.
I SHOULD HAVE KNOWN BETTER... AS A TENNOMIFUNE ACADEMY ALUM MYSELF!
EH?
MA'AM... YOU WENT TO TENNOMIFUNE ACADEMY TOO?
THAT'S RIGHT!
...WHICH PROGRAM WERE YOU IN...?

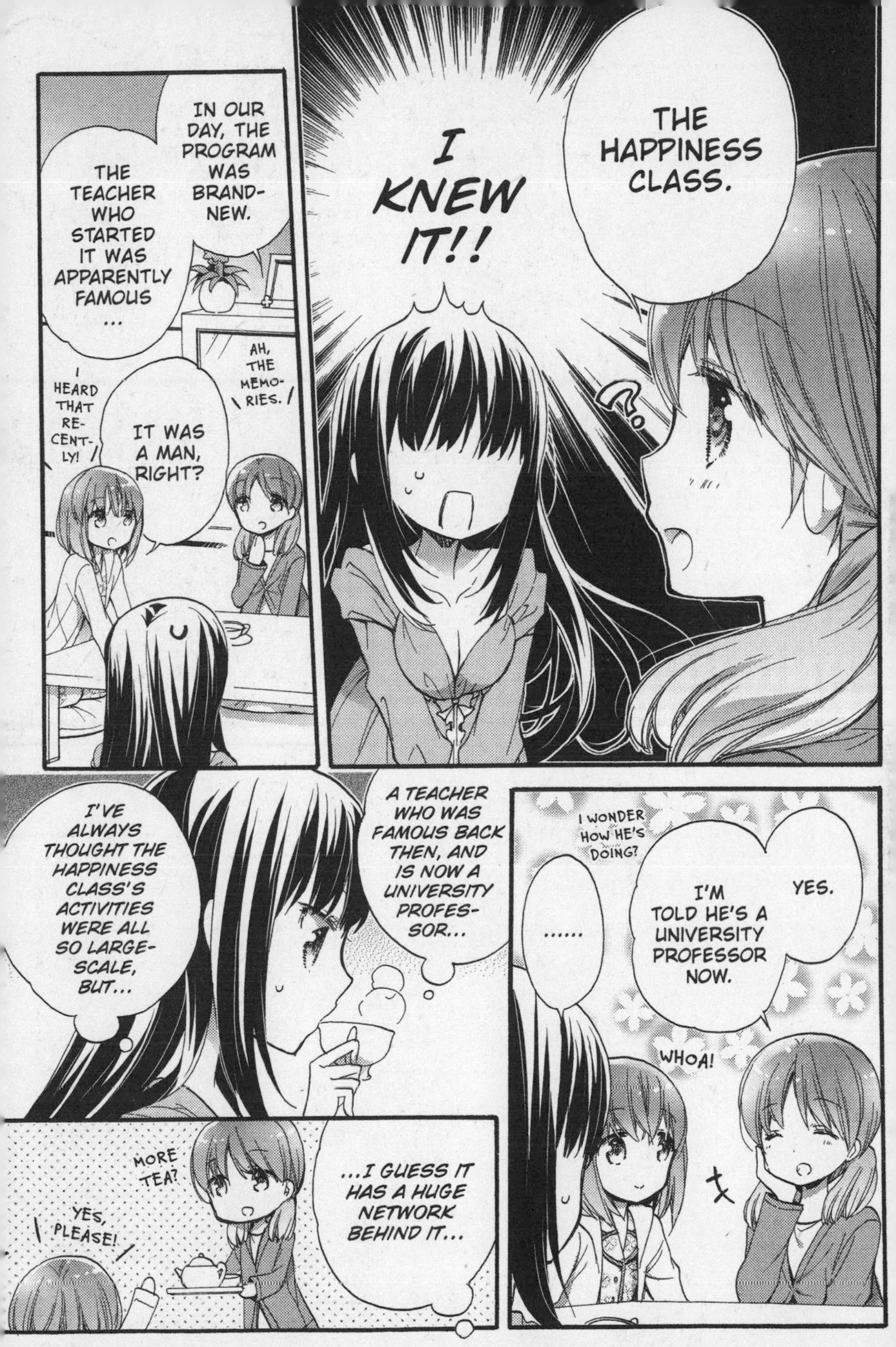
THE HAPPINESS CLASS.
I KNEW IT!!
IN OUR DAY, THE PROGRAM WAS BRAND-NEW.
THE TEACHER WHO STARTED IT WAS APPARENTLY FAMOUS ...
AH, THE MEMORIES.
IT WAS A MAN, RIGHT?
I HEARD THAT RE-CENT-LY!
YES.
I WONDER HOW HE'S DOING?
I'M TOLD HE'S A UNIVERSITY PROFESSOR NOW.
......
WHOA!
A TEACHER WHO WAS FAMOUS BACK THEN, AND IS NOW A UNIVERSITY PROFES-SOR...
I'VE ALWAYS THOUGHT THE HAPPINESS CLASS'S ACTIVITIES WERE ALL SO LARGE-SCALE, BUT...
...I GUESS IT HAS A HUGE NETWORK BEHIND IT...
MORE TEA?
YES, PLEASE!

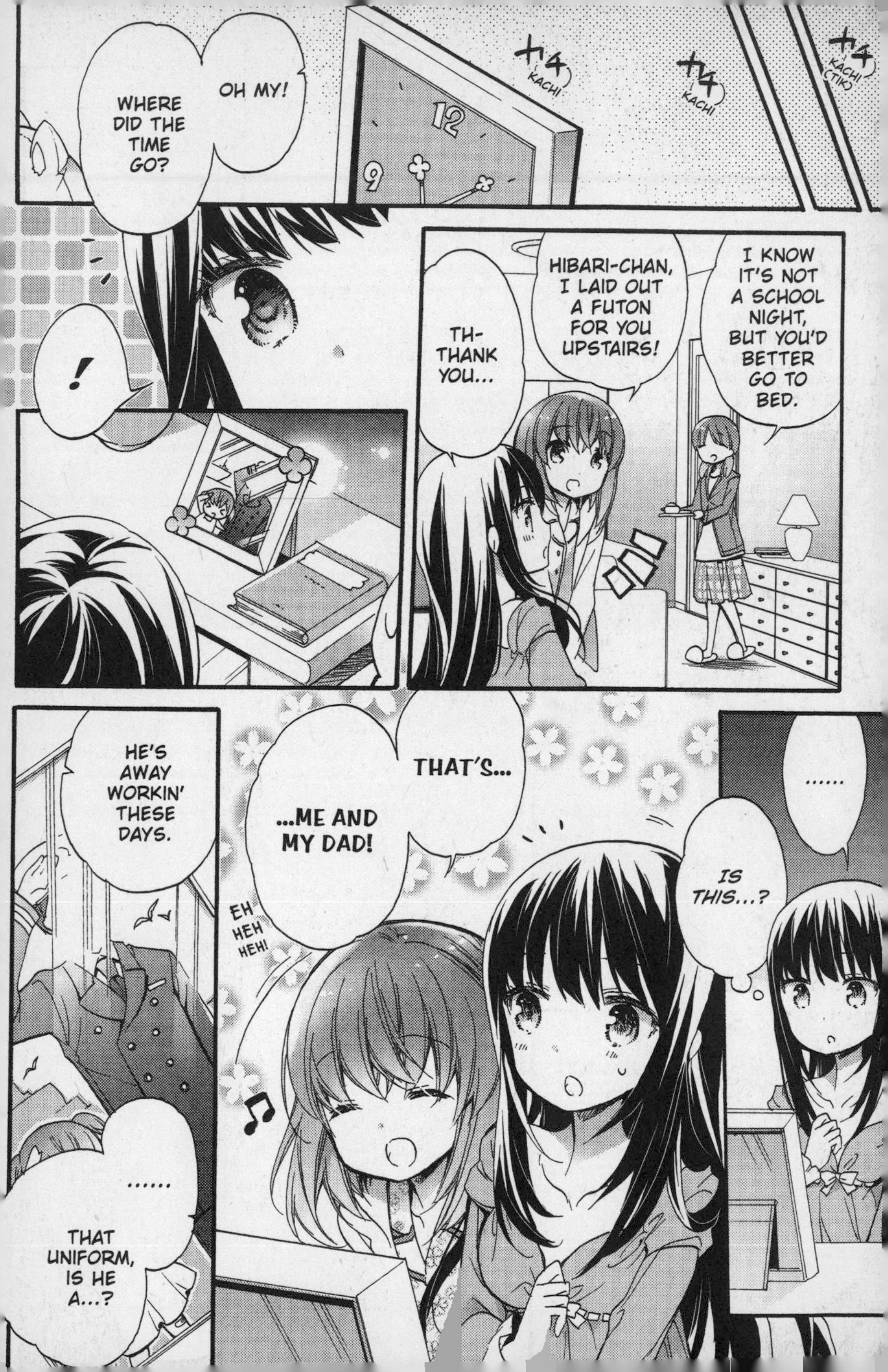
KACHI (TIK)
KACHI
KACHI
OH MY!
WHERE DID THE TIME GO?
I KNOW IT'S NOT A SCHOOL NIGHT, BUT YOU'D BETTER GO TO BED.
HIBARI-CHAN, I LAID OUT A FUTON FOR YOU UPSTAIRS!
TH- THANK YOU...
!
......
IS THIS...?
THAT'S...
...ME AND MY DAD!
EH HEH HEH!
HE'S AWAY WORKIN' THESE DAYS.
......
THAT UNIFORM, IS HE A...?

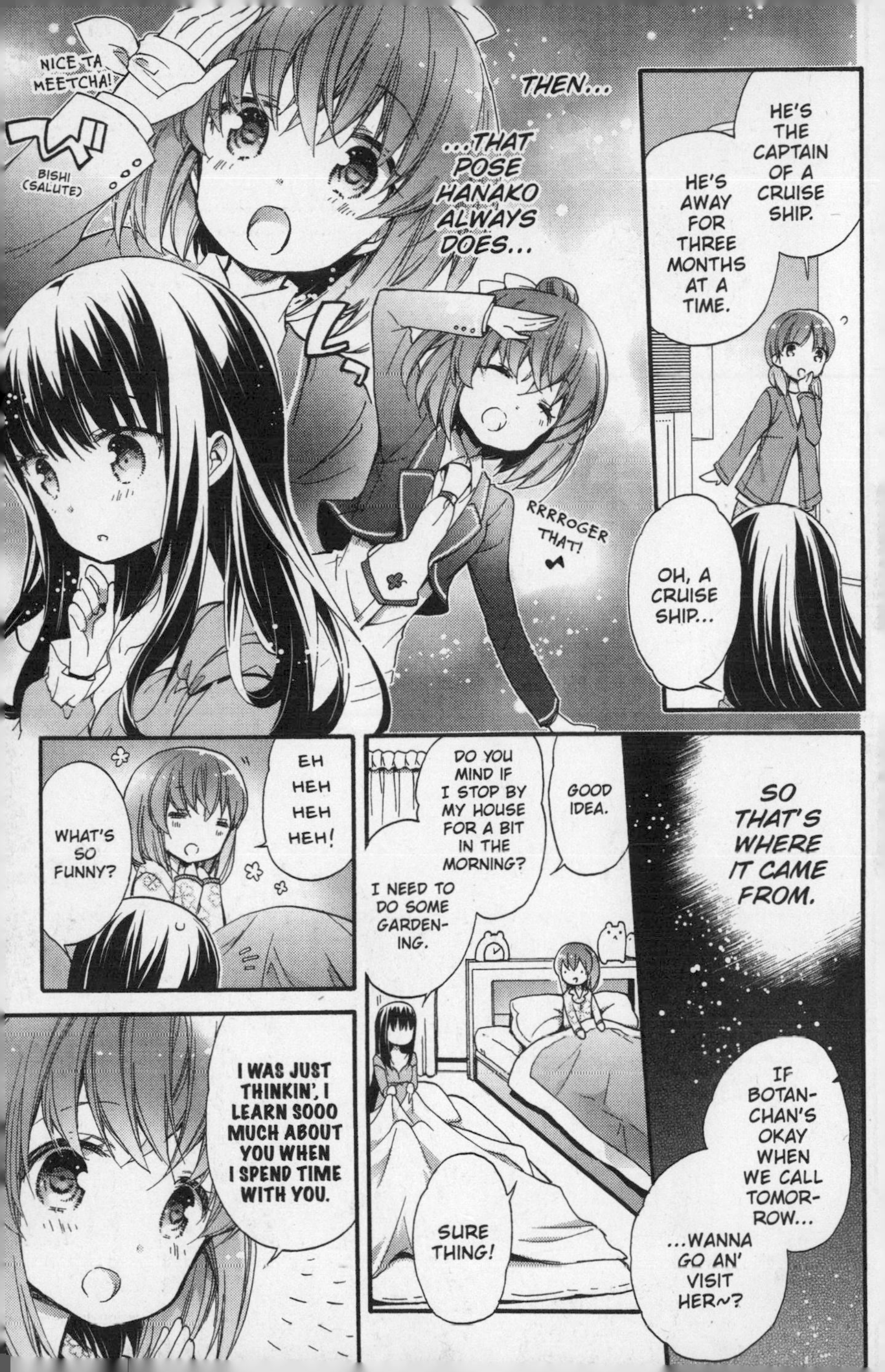
HE'S THE CAPTAIN OF A CRUISE SHIP.
HE'S AWAY FOR THREE MONTHS AT A TIME.
OH, A CRUISE SHIP...
THEN...
...THAT POSE HANAKO ALWAYS DOES...
NICE TA MEETCHA!
BISHI (SALUTE)
RRRROGER THAT!
SO THAT'S WHERE IT CAME FROM.
IF BOTAN-CHAN'S OKAY WHEN WE CALL TOMORROW...
...WANNA GO AN' VISIT HER~?
GOOD IDEA.
DO YOU MIND IF I STOP BY MY HOUSE FOR A BIT IN THE MORNING?
I NEED TO DO SOME GARDENING.
SURE THING!
EH HEH HEH HEH!
WHAT'S SO FUNNY?
I WAS JUST THINKIN', I LEARN SOOO MUCH ABOUT YOU WHEN I SPEND TIME WITH YOU.

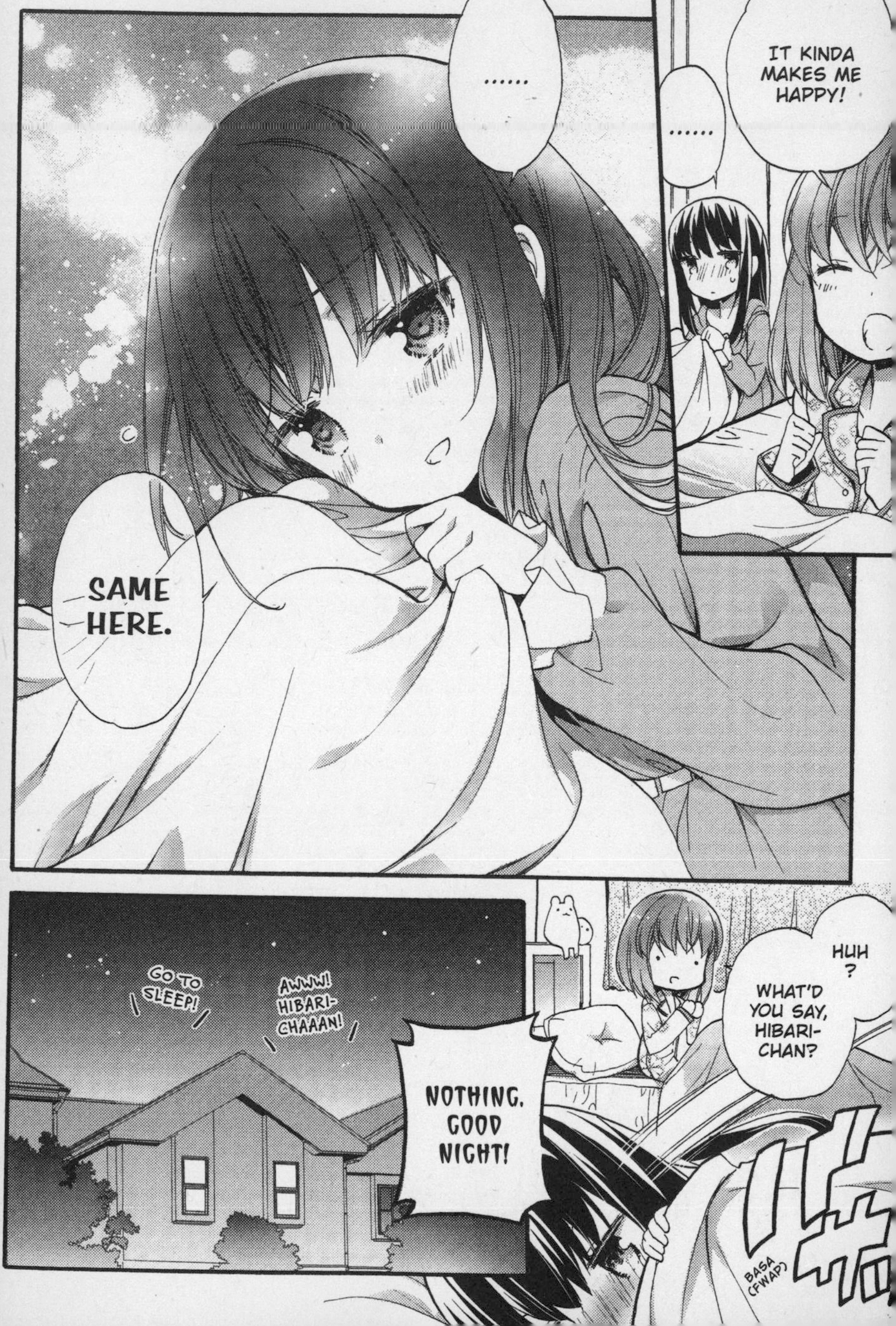
IT KINDA MAKES ME HAPPY!
......
......
SAME HERE.
HUH? WHAT'D YOU SAY, HIBARI-CHAN?
NOTHING. GOOD NIGHT!
BASA (FWAP)
AWWW! HIBARI-CHAAAN!
GO TO SLEEP!

Anne Happy

unhappy go lucky!

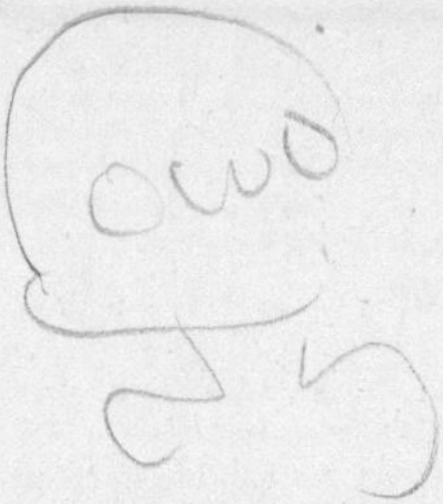

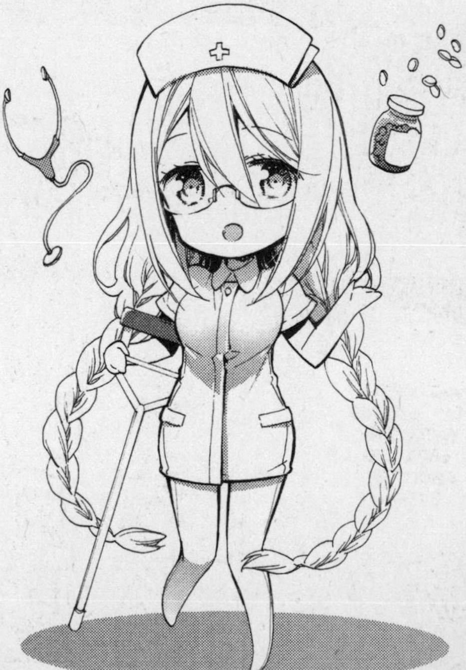

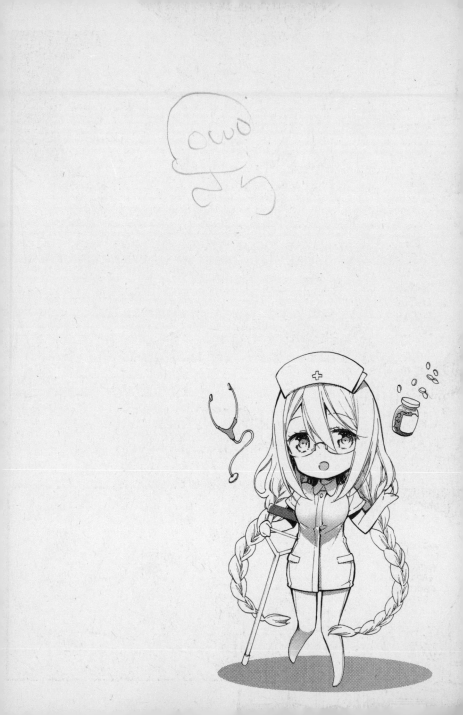

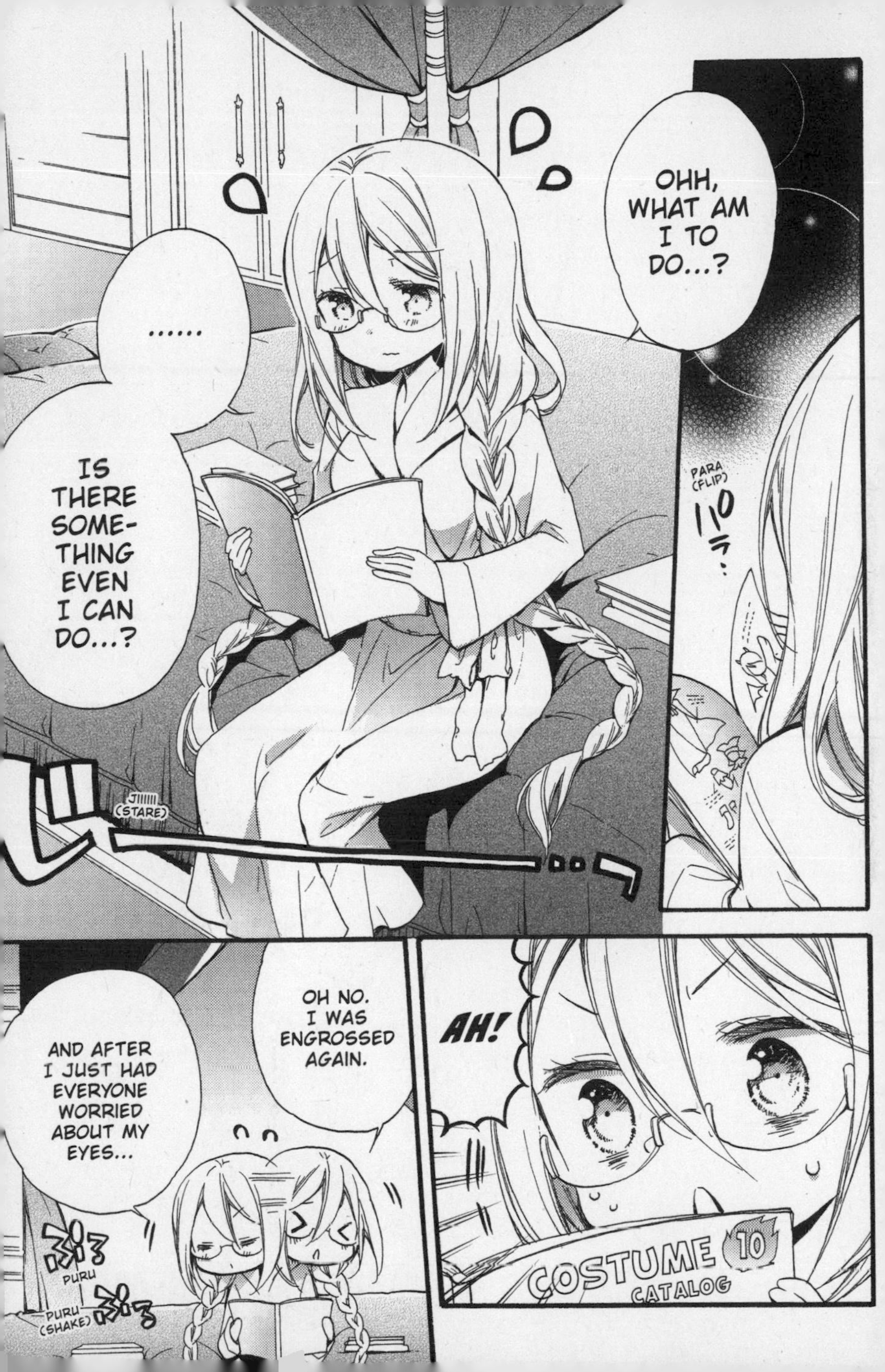
OHH, WHAT AM I TO DO...?
PARA (FLIP)
......
IS THERE SOME-THING EVEN I CAN DO...?
JIIIII (STARE)
AH!
COSTUME 10 CATALOG
OH NO. I WAS ENGROSSED AGAIN.
AND AFTER I JUST HAD EVERYONE WORRIED ABOUT MY EYES...
PURU
PURU (SHAKE)

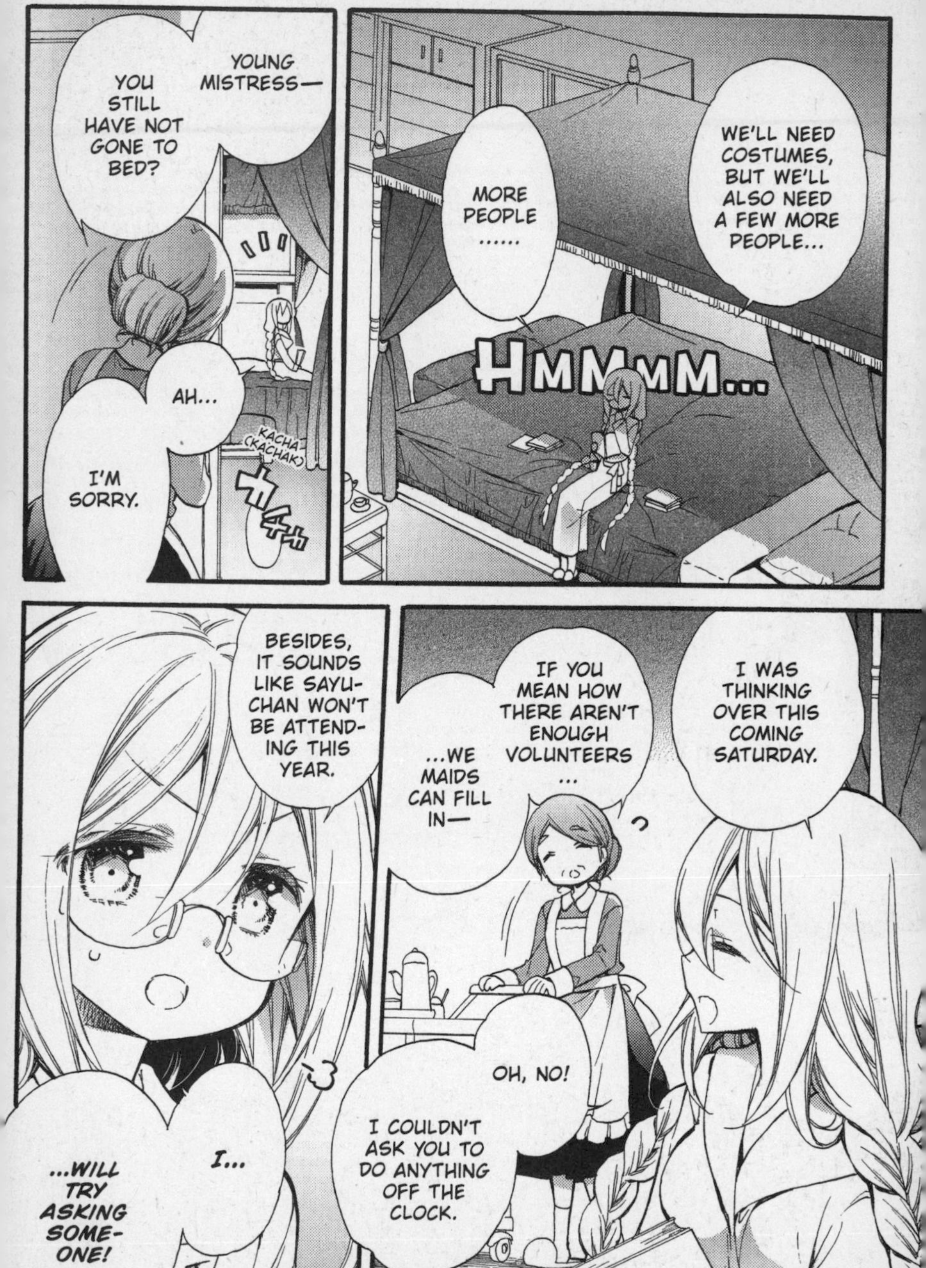
WE'LL NEED COSTUMES, BUT WE'LL ALSO NEED A FEW MORE PEOPLE...
MORE PEOPLE ......
HMMMMM...
YOUNG MISTRESS—
YOU STILL HAVE NOT GONE TO BED?
KACHA (KACHAK)
AH...
I'M SORRY.
I WAS THINKING OVER THIS COMING SATURDAY.
IF YOU MEAN HOW THERE AREN'T ENOUGH VOLUNTEERS ...
...WE MAIDS CAN FILL IN—
OH, NO!
I COULDN'T ASK YOU TO DO ANYTHING OFF THE CLOCK.
BESIDES, IT SOUNDS LIKE SAYU-CHAN WON'T BE ATTENDING THIS YEAR.
I...
...WILL TRY ASKING SOMEONE!

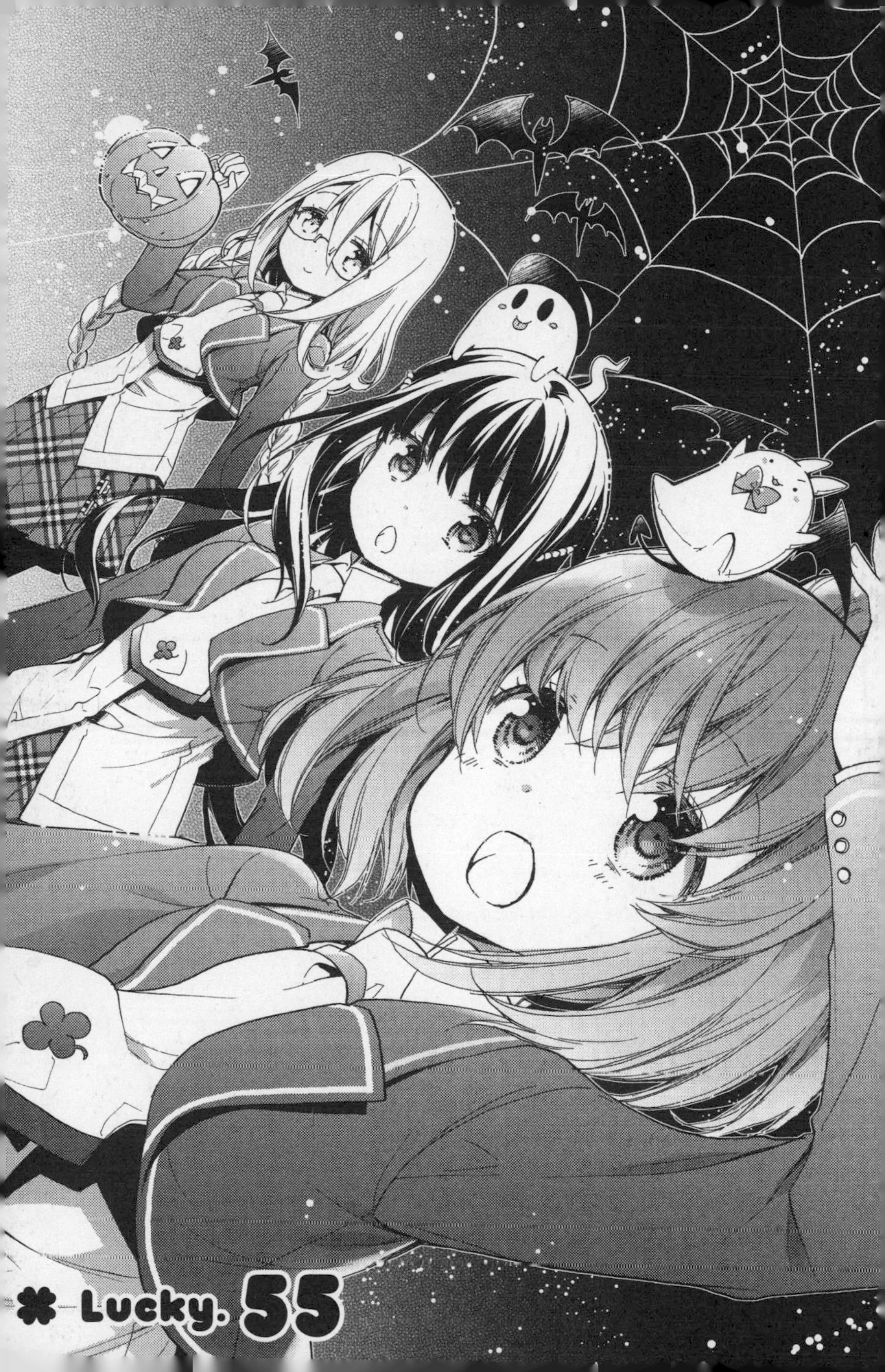
Lucky. 55

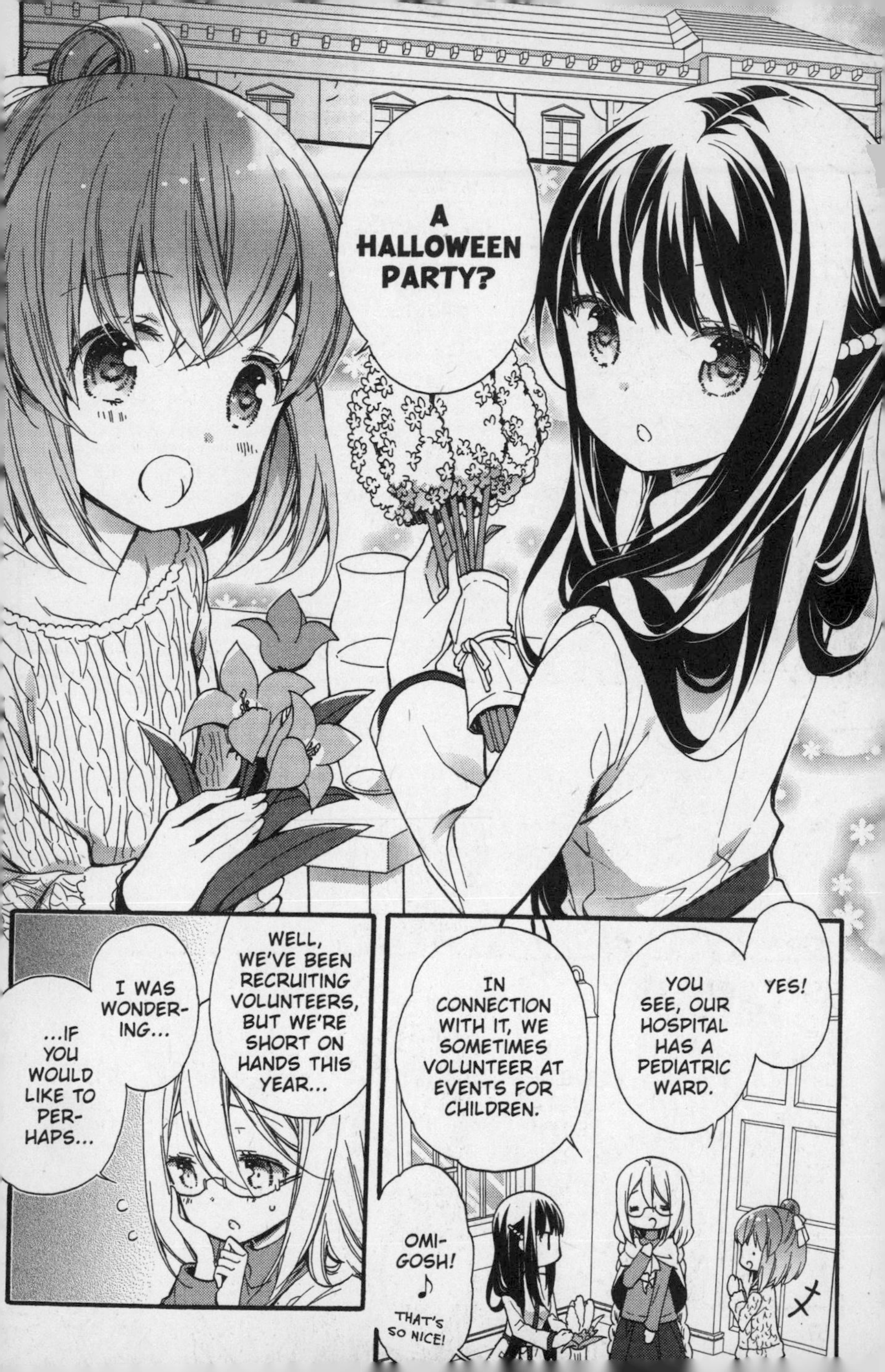
A HALLOWEEN PARTY?
YES!
YOU SEE, OUR HOSPITAL HAS A PEDIATRIC WARD.
IN CONNECTION WITH IT, WE SOMETIMES VOLUNTEER AT EVENTS FOR CHILDREN.
OMI-GOSH! ♪
THAT'S SO NICE!
WELL, WE'VE BEEN RECRUITING VOLUNTEERS, BUT WE'RE SHORT ON HANDS THIS YEAR...
I WAS WONDER-ING...
...IF YOU WOULD LIKE TO PER-HAPS...

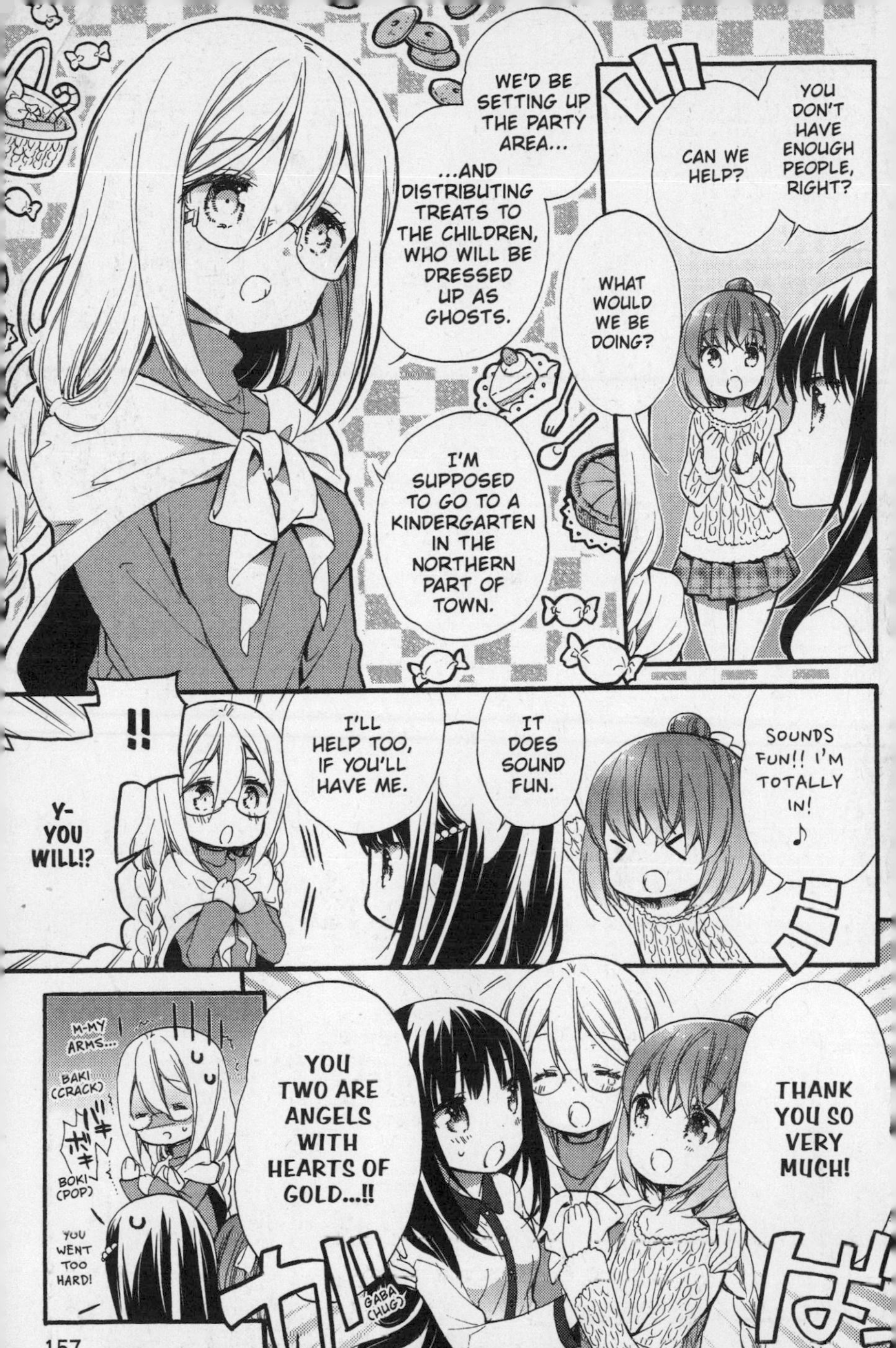
YOU DON'T HAVE ENOUGH PEOPLE, RIGHT?
CAN WE HELP?
WHAT WOULD WE BE DOING?
WE'D BE SETTING UP THE PARTY AREA...
...AND DISTRIBUTING TREATS TO THE CHILDREN, WHO WILL BE DRESSED UP AS GHOSTS.
I'M SUPPOSED TO GO TO A KINDERGARTEN IN THE NORTHERN PART OF TOWN.
SOUNDS FUN!! I'M TOTALLY IN! ♪
IT DOES SOUND FUN.
I'LL HELP TOO, IF YOU'LL HAVE ME.
!!
Y-YOU WILL!?
THANK YOU SO VERY MUCH!
YOU TWO ARE ANGELS WITH HEARTS OF GOLD...!!
GABA (HUG)
M-MY ARMS...
BAKI (CRACK)
バキ
ボキ
BOKI (POP)
YOU WENT TOO HARD!

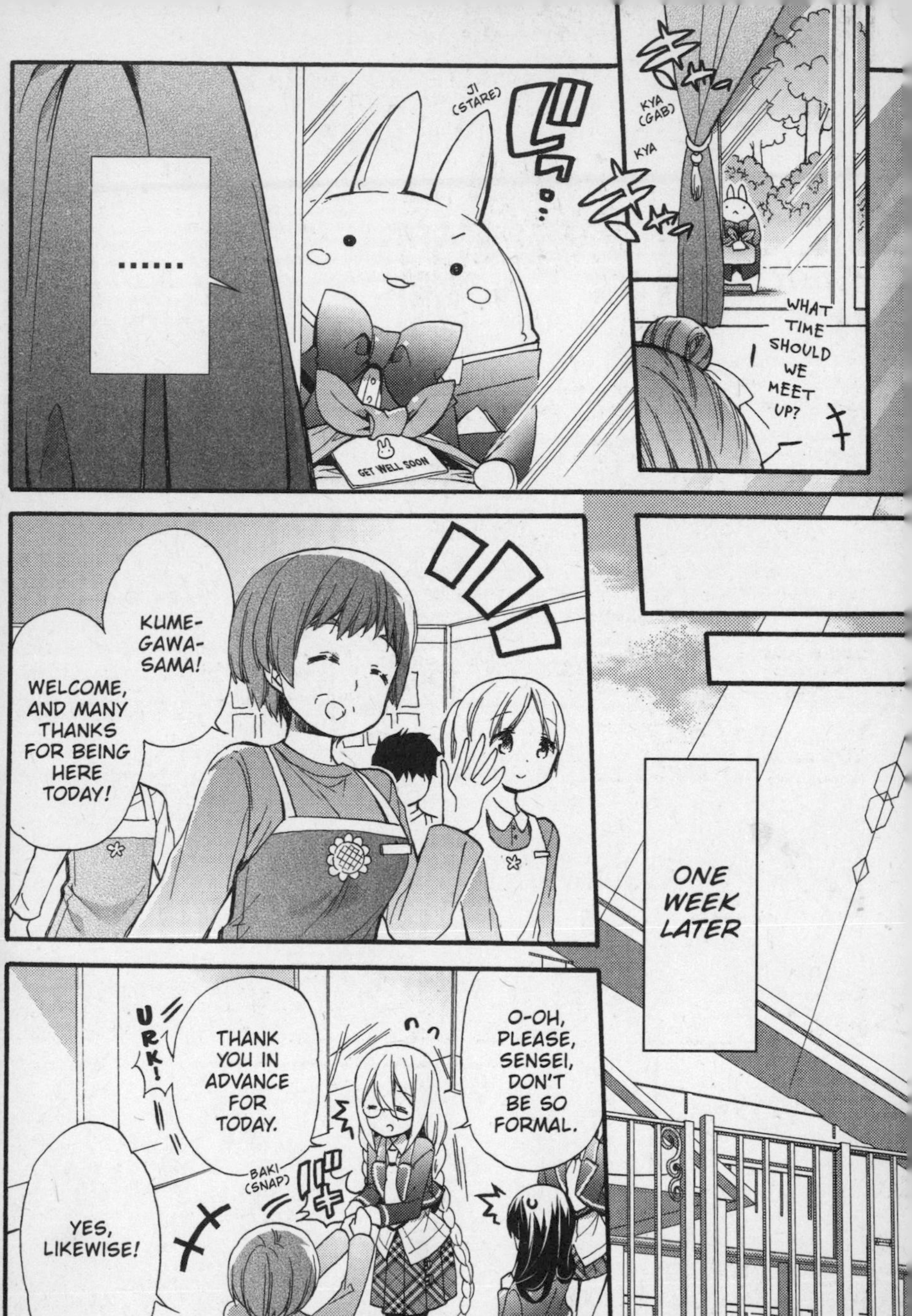
KYA (GAB)
KYA
WHAT TIME SHOULD WE MEET UP?
JI (STARE)
......
GET WELL SOON
ONE WEEK LATER
KUME-GAWA-SAMA!
WELCOME, AND MANY THANKS FOR BEING HERE TODAY!
O-OH, PLEASE, SENSEI, DON'T BE SO FORMAL.
THANK YOU IN ADVANCE FOR TODAY.
URK!
BAKI (SNAP)
YES, LIKEWISE!

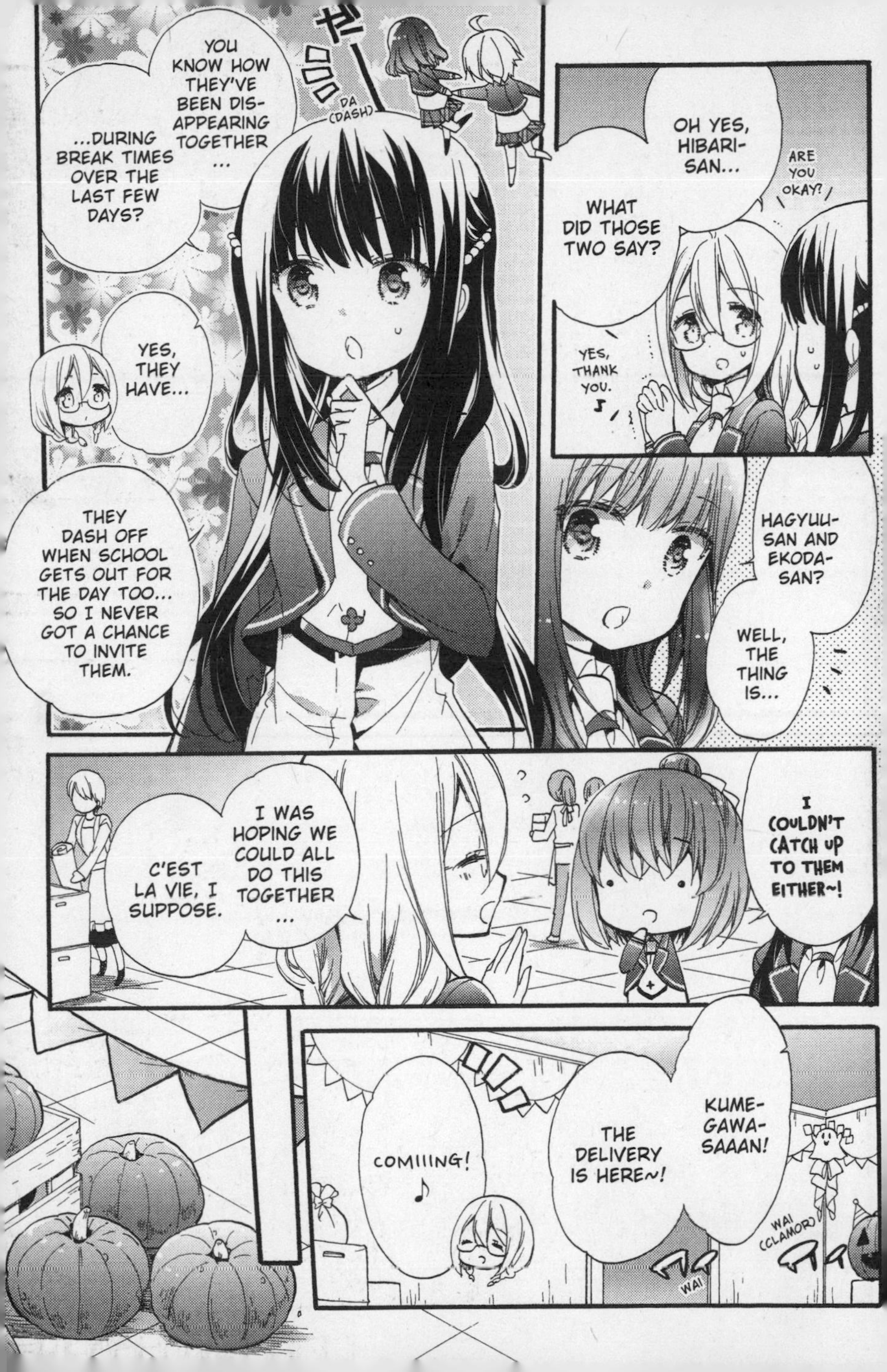
OH YES, HIBARI-SAN...
WHAT DID THOSE TWO SAY?
ARE YOU OKAY?
YES, THANK YOU.
HAGYUU-SAN AND EKODA-SAN?
WELL, THE THING IS...
DA (DASH)
YOU KNOW HOW THEY'VE BEEN DIS-APPEARING TOGETHER ...
...DURING BREAK TIMES OVER THE LAST FEW DAYS?
YES, THEY HAVE...
THEY DASH OFF WHEN SCHOOL GETS OUT FOR THE DAY TOO... SO I NEVER GOT A CHANCE TO INVITE THEM.
I COULDN'T CATCH UP TO THEM EITHER~!
I WAS HOPING WE COULD ALL DO THIS TOGETHER ...
C'EST LA VIE, I SUPPOSE.
KUME-GAWA-SAAAN!
THE DELIVERY IS HERE~!
COMIIING!
WAI (CLAMOR)
WAI

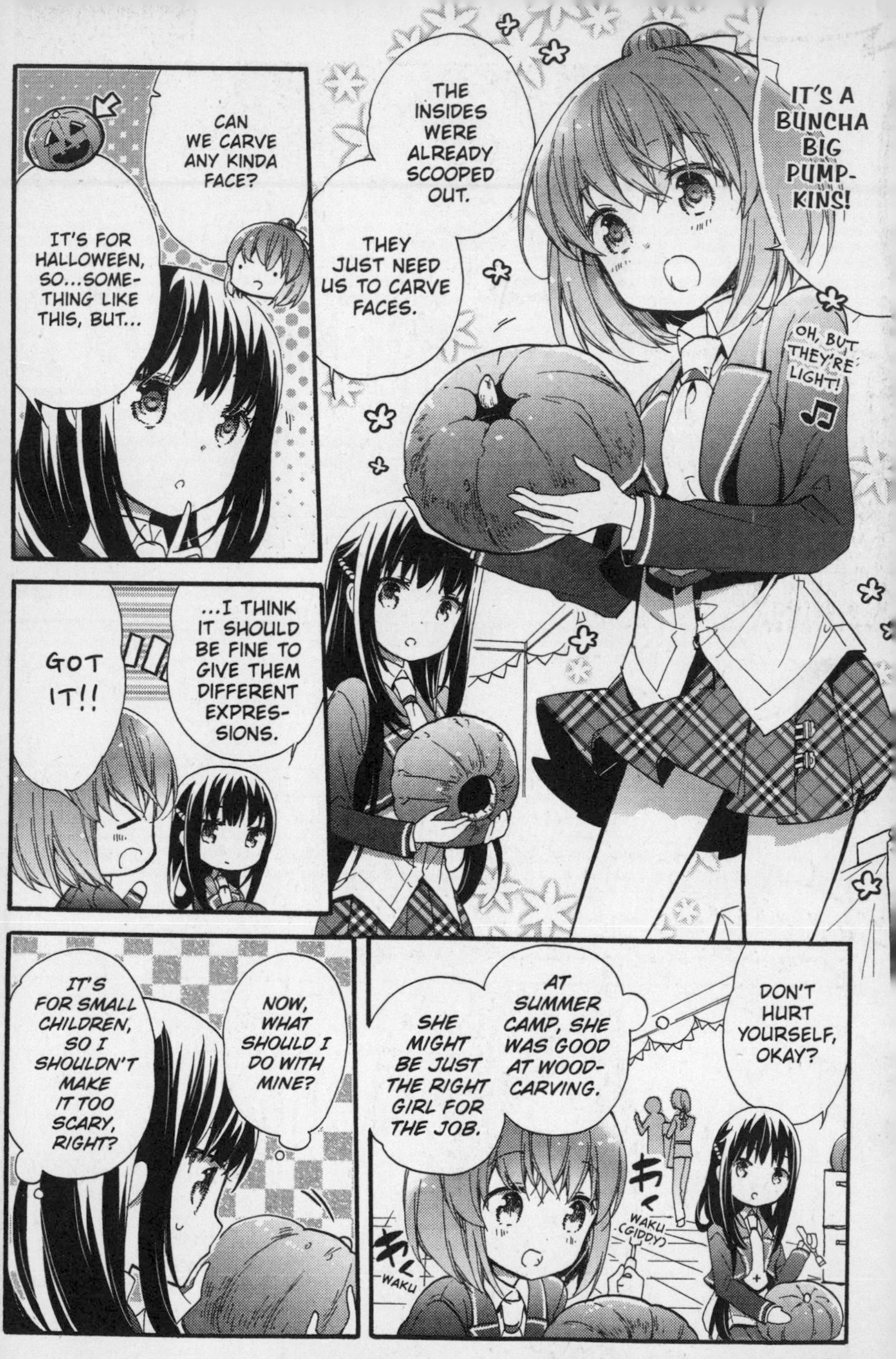
IT'S A BUNCHA BIG PUMPKINS!
OH, BUT THEY'RE LIGHT!
THE INSIDES WERE ALREADY SCOOPED OUT.
THEY JUST NEED US TO CARVE FACES.
CAN WE CARVE ANY KINDA FACE?
IT'S FOR HALLOWEEN, SO...SOMETHING LIKE THIS, BUT...
...I THINK IT SHOULD BE FINE TO GIVE THEM DIFFERENT EXPRESSIONS.
GOT IT!!
DON'T HURT YOURSELF, OKAY?
AT SUMMER CAMP, SHE WAS GOOD AT WOOD-CARVING.
SHE MIGHT BE JUST THE RIGHT GIRL FOR THE JOB.
WAKU (GIDDY)
WAKU
NOW, WHAT SHOULD I DO WITH MINE?
IT'S FOR SMALL CHILDREN, SO I SHOULDN'T MAKE IT TOO SCARY, RIGHT?

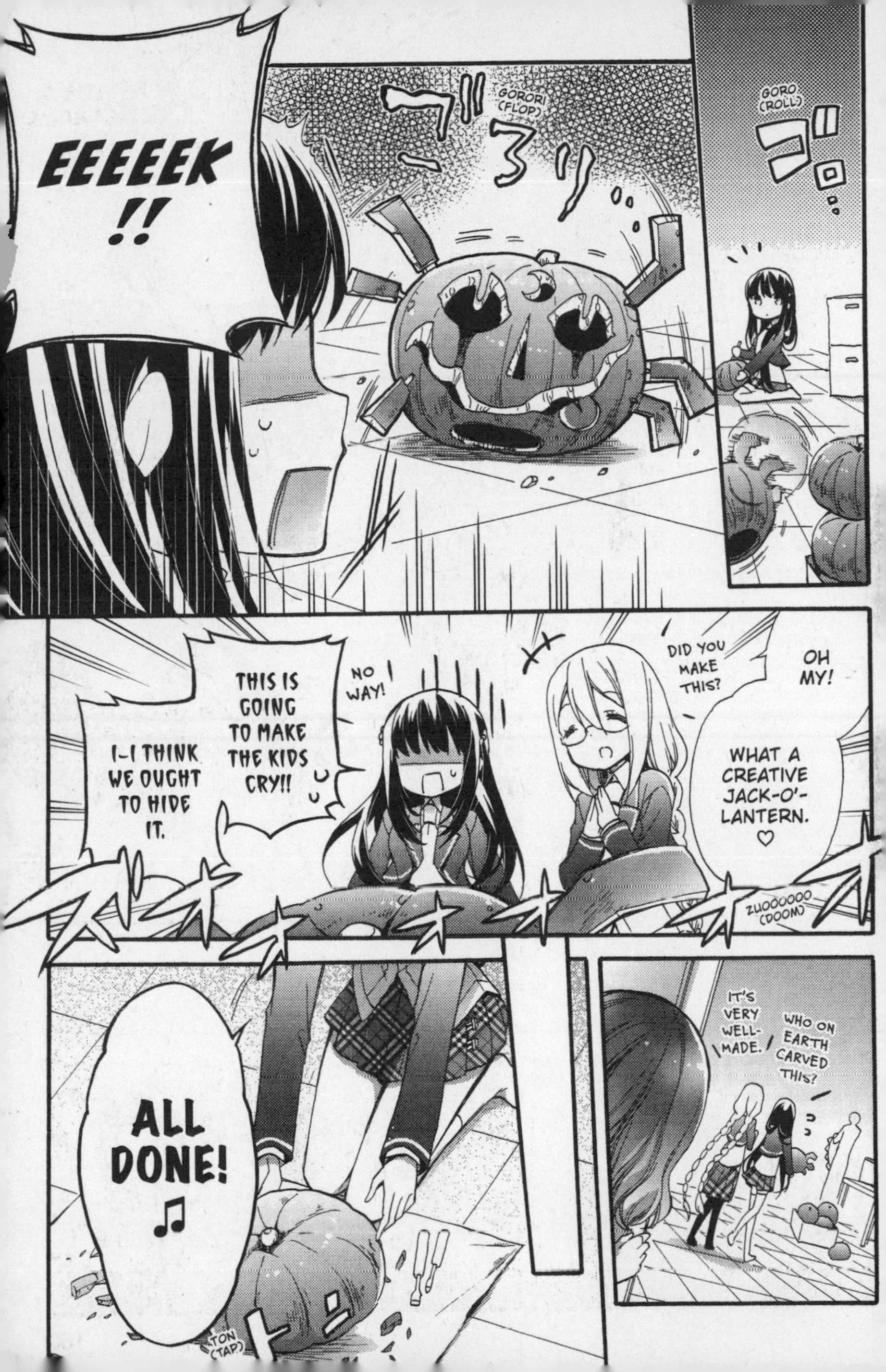
GORO (ROLL)
GORORI (FLOP)
EEEEEK!!
OH MY!
WHAT A CREATIVE JACK-O'-LANTERN. ♡
DID YOU MAKE THIS?
NO WAY!
THIS IS GOING TO MAKE THE KIDS CRY!!
I-I THINK WE OUGHT TO HIDE IT.
ZUOOOOOO (DOOM)
WHO ON EARTH CARVED THIS?
IT'S VERY WELL-MADE.
ALL DONE! ♫
TON (TAP)

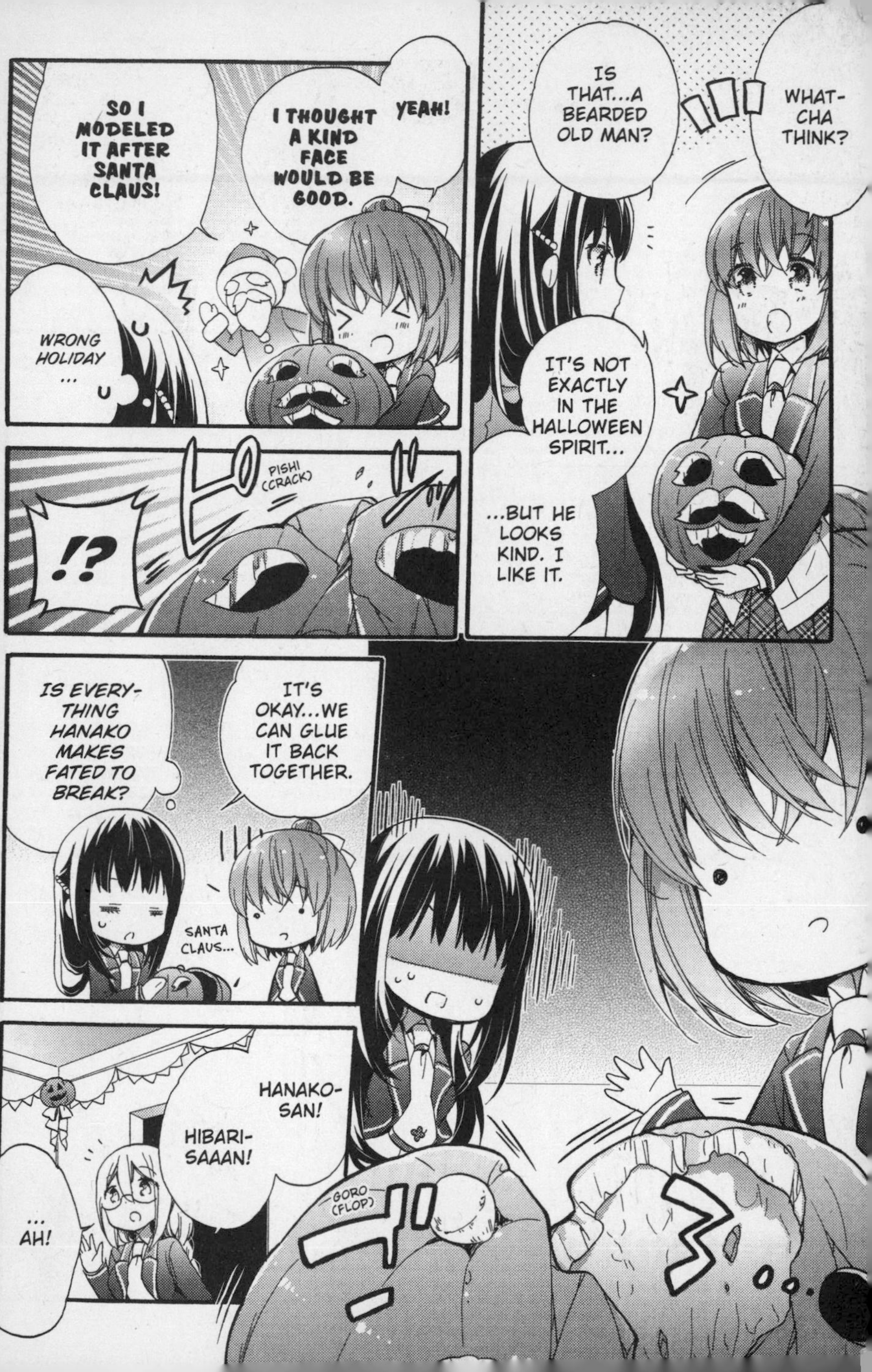
WHAT-CHA THINK?
IS THAT...A BEARDED OLD MAN?
IT'S NOT EXACTLY IN THE HALLOWEEN SPIRIT...
...BUT HE LOOKS KIND. I LIKE IT.
YEAH!
I THOUGHT A KIND FACE WOULD BE GOOD.
SO I MODELED IT AFTER SANTA CLAUS!
WRONG HOLIDAY...
PISHI (CRACK)
!?
GORO (FLOP)
IT'S OKAY...WE CAN GLUE IT BACK TOGETHER.
IS EVERYTHING HANAKO MAKES FATED TO BREAK?
SANTA CLAUS...
HANAKO-SAN!
HIBARI-SAAAN!
...AH!

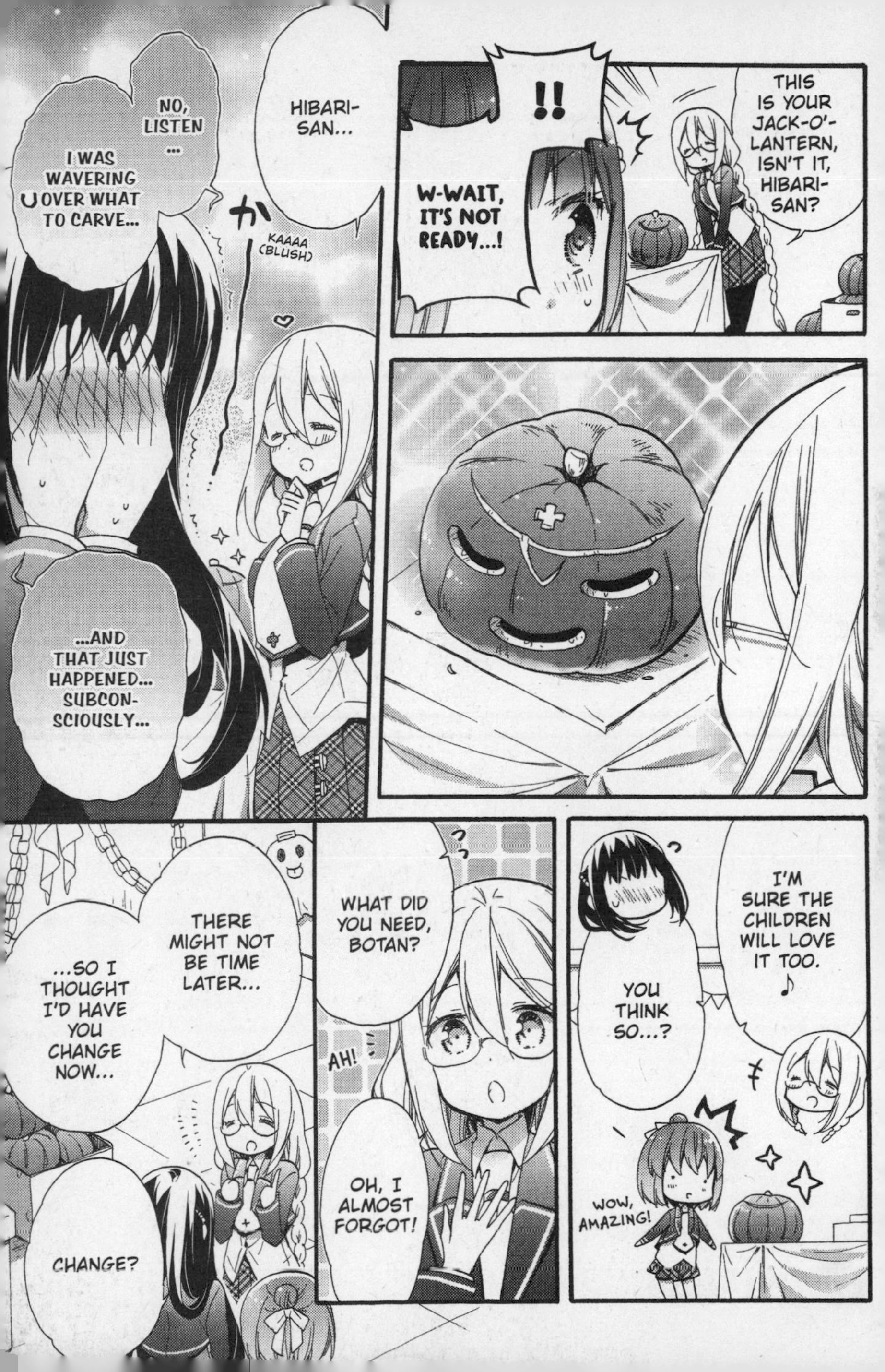
THIS IS YOUR JACK-O'-LANTERN, ISN'T IT, HIBARI-SAN?
!!
W-WAIT, IT'S NOT READY...!
HIBARI-SAN...
NO, LISTEN...
I WAS WAVERING OVER WHAT TO CARVE...
か
KAAAA (BLUSH)
...AND THAT JUST HAPPENED... SUBCONSCIOUSLY...
I'M SURE THE CHILDREN WILL LOVE IT TOO. ♪
YOU THINK SO...?
WOW, AMAZING!
WHAT DID YOU NEED, BOTAN?
AH!
OH, I ALMOST FORGOT!
THERE MIGHT NOT BE TIME LATER...
...SO I THOUGHT I'D HAVE YOU CHANGE NOW...
CHANGE?

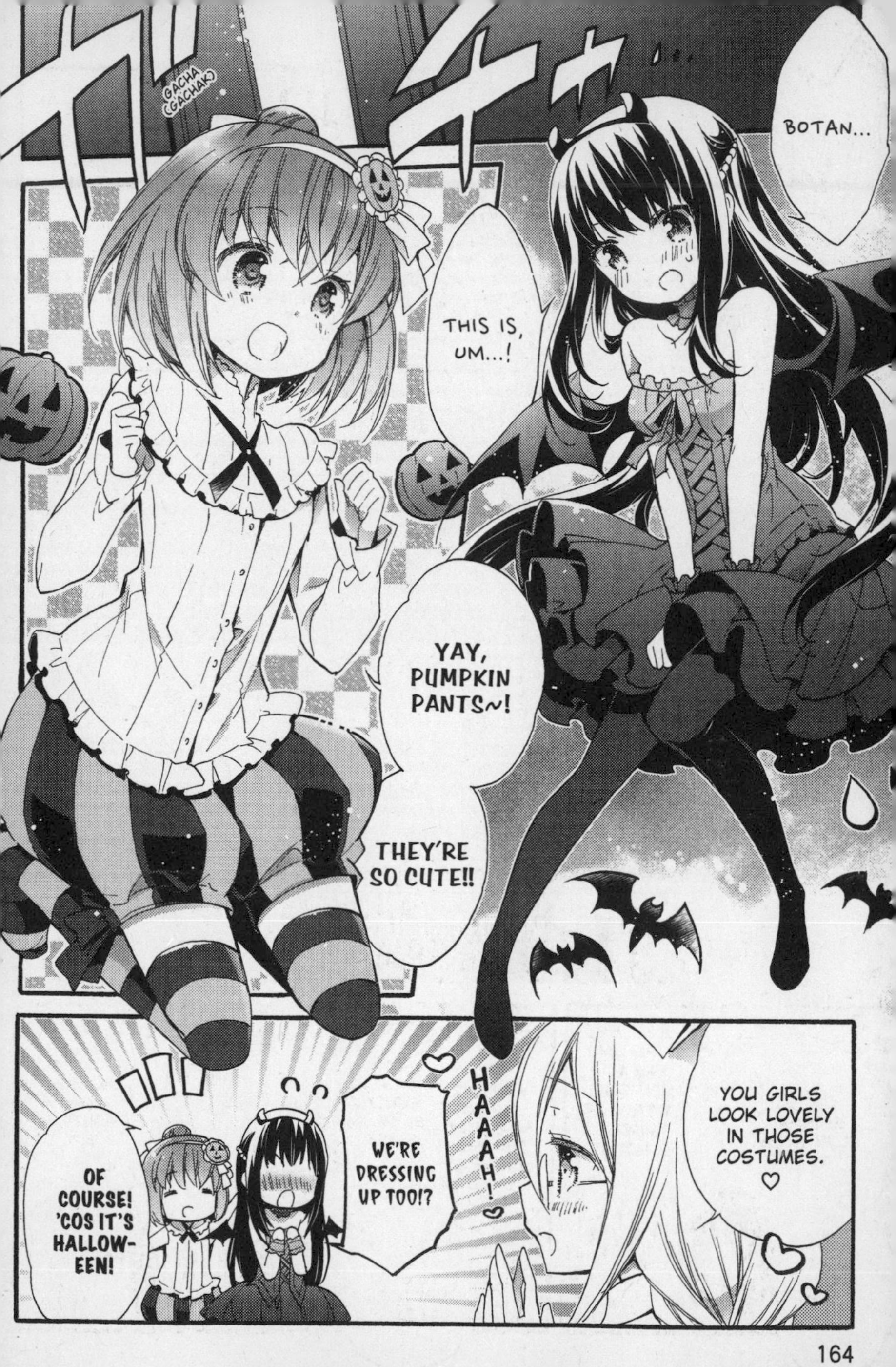
BOTAN...
GACHA (GACHAK)
THIS IS, UM...!
YAY, PUMPKIN PANTS~!
THEY'RE SO CUTE!!
YOU GIRLS LOOK LOVELY IN THOSE COSTUMES. ♡
HAAAAH! ♡
WE'RE DRESSING UP TOO!?
OF COURSE! 'COS IT'S HALLOW-EEN!

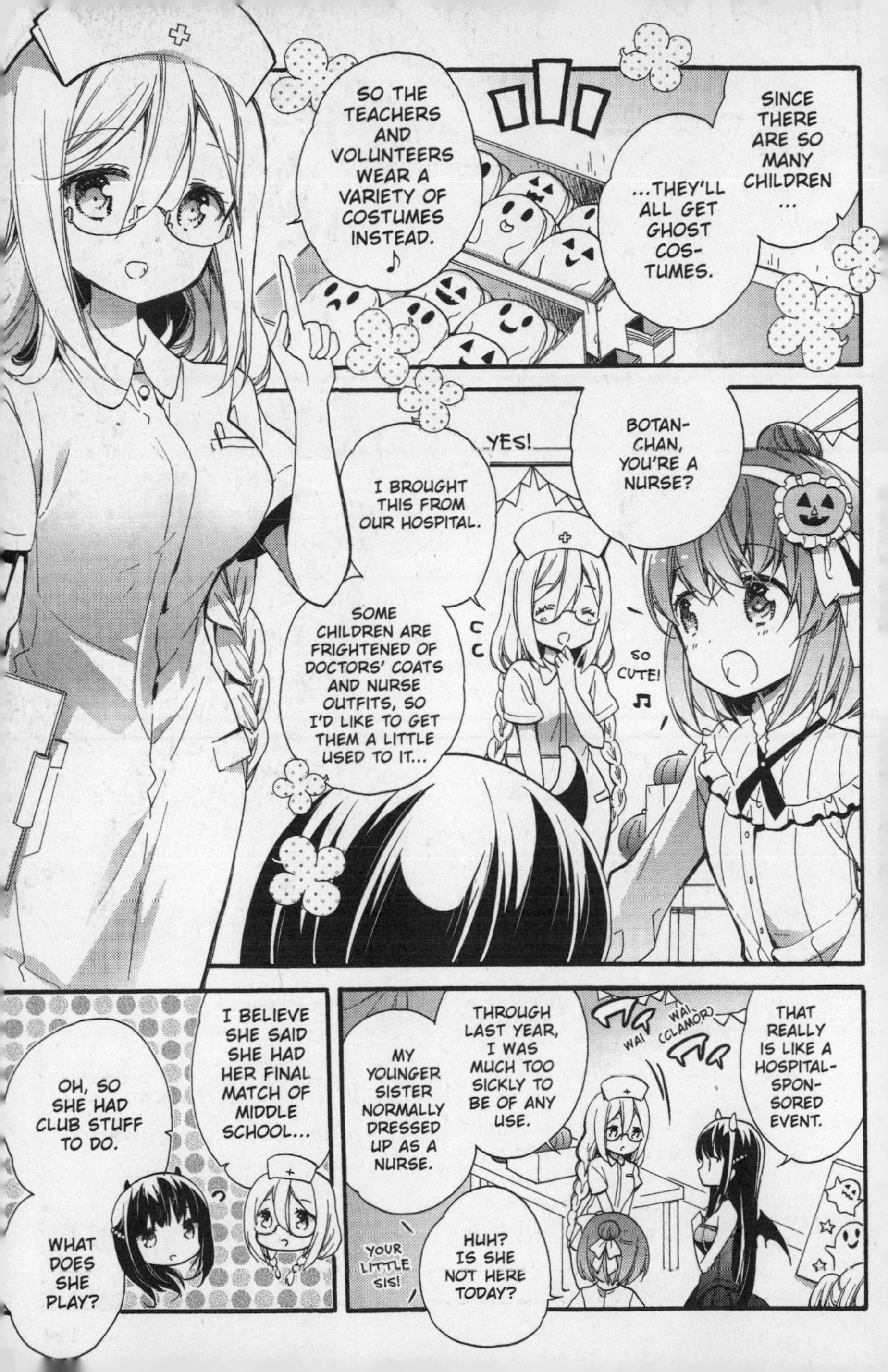
SINCE THERE ARE SO MANY CHILDREN ...
...THEY'LL ALL GET GHOST COS-TUMES.
SO THE TEACHERS AND VOLUNTEERS WEAR A VARIETY OF COSTUMES INSTEAD. ♪
BOTAN-CHAN, YOU'RE A NURSE?
YES!
SO CUTE! ♫
I BROUGHT THIS FROM OUR HOSPITAL.
SOME CHILDREN ARE FRIGHTENED OF DOCTORS' COATS AND NURSE OUTFITS, SO I'D LIKE TO GET THEM A LITTLE USED TO IT...
THAT REALLY IS LIKE A HOSPITAL-SPON-SORED EVENT.
WAI WAI (CLAMOR)
THROUGH LAST YEAR, I WAS MUCH TOO SICKLY TO BE OF ANY USE.
MY YOUNGER SISTER NORMALLY DRESSED UP AS A NURSE.
YOUR LITTLE SIS!
HUH? IS SHE NOT HERE TODAY?
I BELIEVE SHE SAID SHE HAD HER FINAL MATCH OF MIDDLE SCHOOL...
OH, SO SHE HAD CLUB STUFF TO DO.
WHAT DOES SHE PLAY?

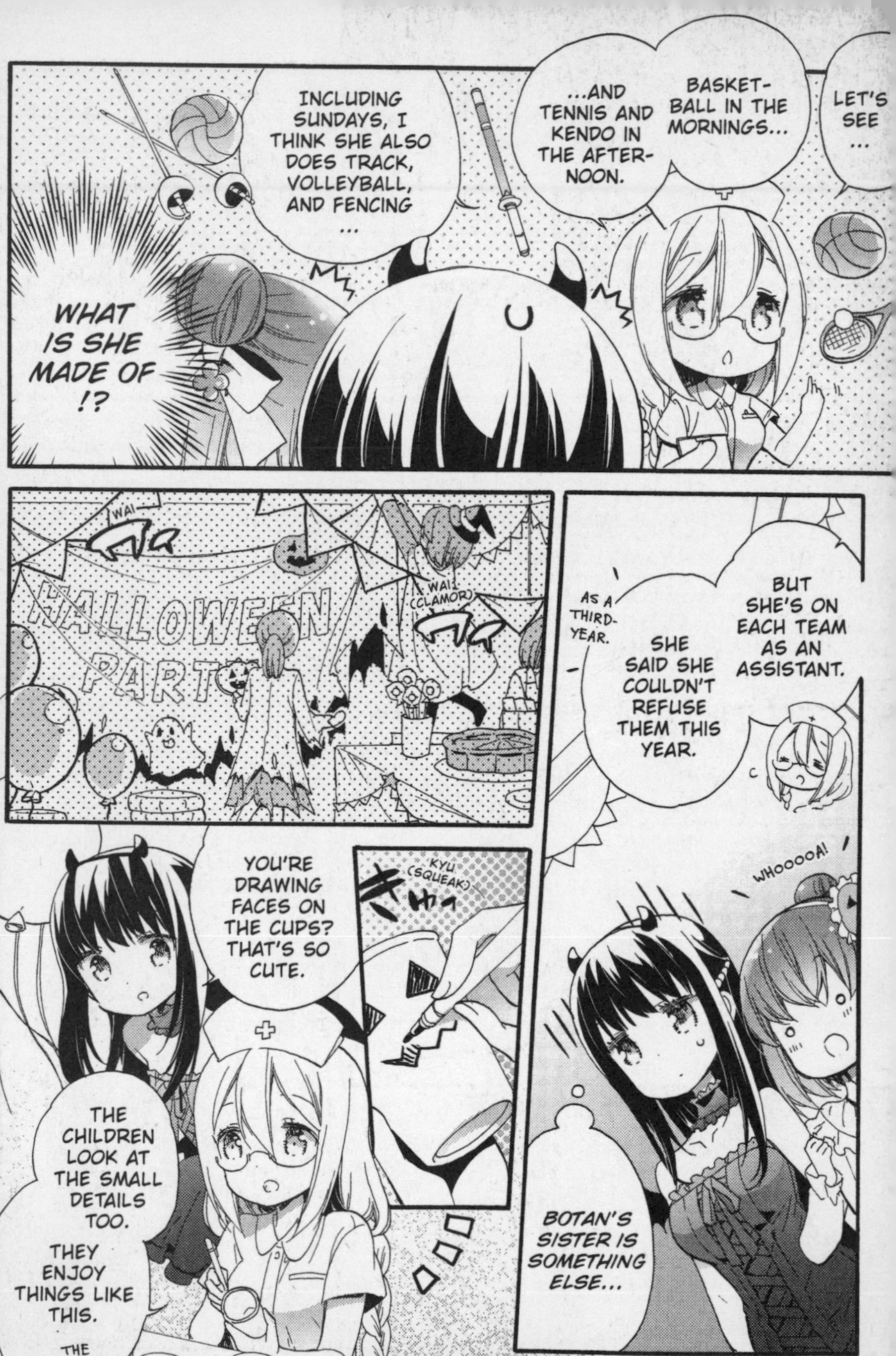
LET'S SEE ...
BASKET-BALL IN THE MORNINGS...
...AND TENNIS AND KENDO IN THE AFTER-NOON.
INCLUDING SUNDAYS, I THINK SHE ALSO DOES TRACK, VOLLEYBALL, AND FENCING ...
WHAT IS SHE MADE OF !?
BUT SHE'S ON EACH TEAM AS AN ASSISTANT.
SHE SAID SHE COULDN'T REFUSE THEM THIS YEAR.
AS A THIRD-YEAR.
WHOOOOA!
BOTAN'S SISTER IS SOMETHING ELSE...
WAI
WAI (CLAMOR)
KYU (SQUEAK)
YOU'RE DRAWING FACES ON THE CUPS? THAT'S SO CUTE.
THE CHILDREN LOOK AT THE SMALL DETAILS TOO.
THEY ENJOY THINGS LIKE THIS.
THE TEACHERS TOLD ME.

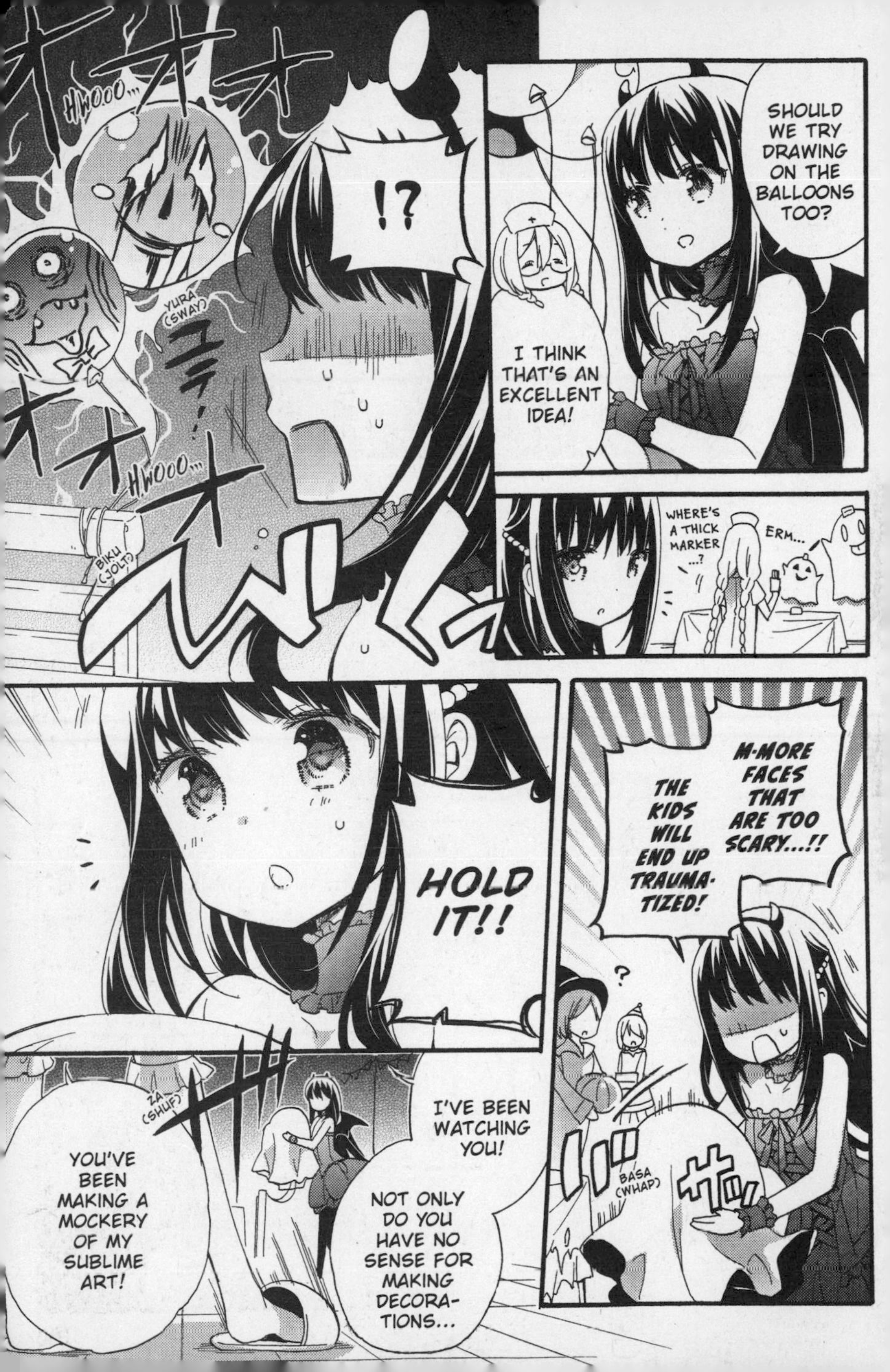
SHOULD WE TRY DRAWING ON THE BALLOONS TOO?
I THINK THAT'S AN EXCELLENT IDEA!
WHERE'S A THICK MARKER ...?
ERM...
!?
HWOOO...
YURA (SWAY)
HWOOO...
BIKU (JOLT)
M-MORE FACES THAT ARE TOO SCARY...!!
THE KIDS WILL END UP TRAUMA-TIZED!
?
BASA (WHAP)
HOLD IT!!
I'VE BEEN WATCHING YOU!
NOT ONLY DO YOU HAVE NO SENSE FOR MAKING DECORA-TIONS...
YOU'VE BEEN MAKING A MOCKERY OF MY SUBLIME ART!
ZA (SHUF)

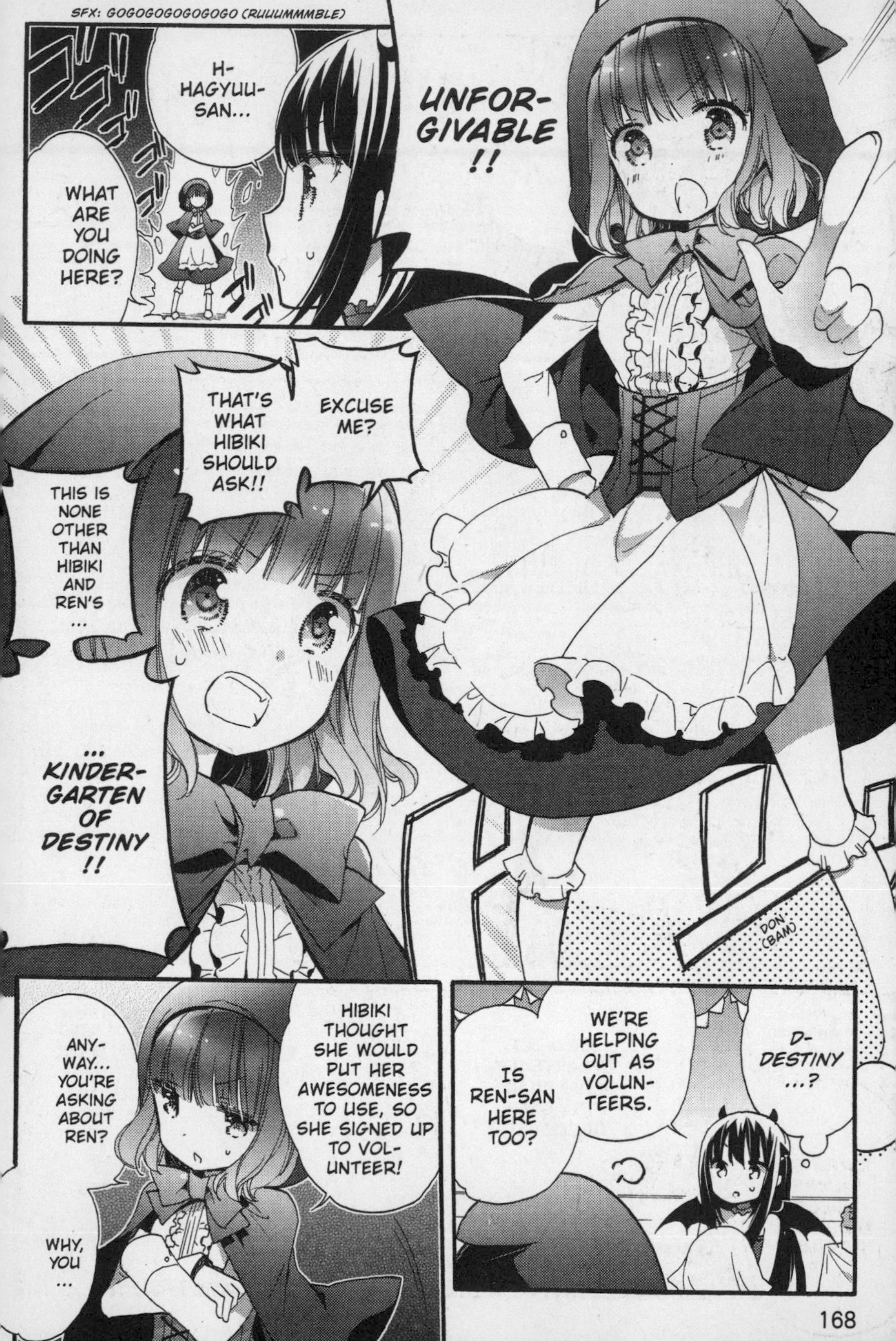
SFX: GOGOGOGOGOGOGO (RUUUMMMBLE)
UNFORGIVABLE!!
H-HAGYUU-SAN...
WHAT ARE YOU DOING HERE?
EXCUSE ME?
THAT'S WHAT HIBIKI SHOULD ASK!!
THIS IS NONE OTHER THAN HIBIKI AND REN'S ...
... KINDERGARTEN OF DESTINY!!
DON (BAM)
D-DESTINY ...?
WE'RE HELPING OUT AS VOLUNTEERS.
IS REN-SAN HERE TOO?
HIBIKI THOUGHT SHE WOULD PUT HER AWESOMENESS TO USE, SO SHE SIGNED UP TO VOLUNTEER!
ANYWAY... YOU'RE ASKING ABOUT REN?
WHY, YOU ...

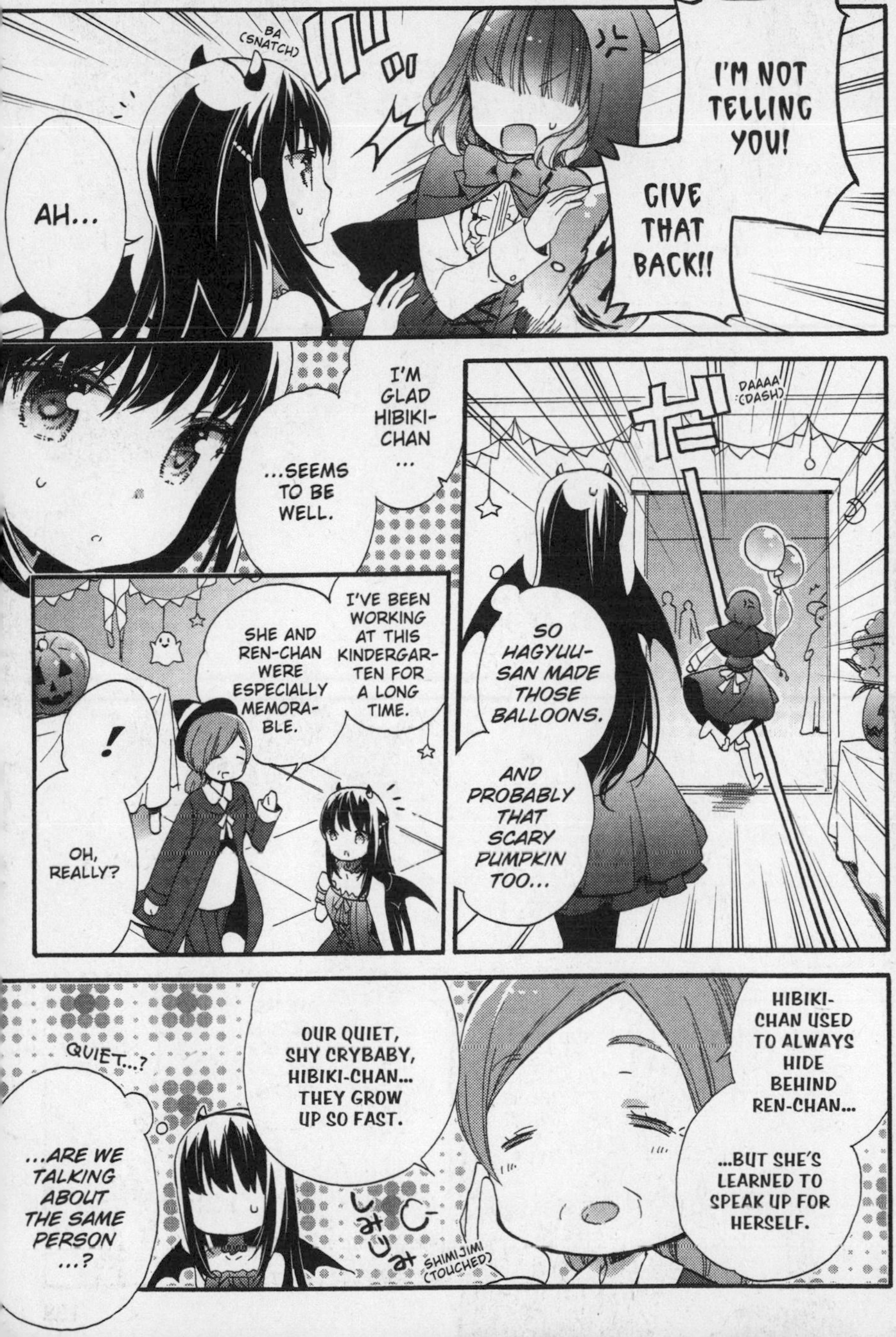
I'M NOT TELLING YOU!
GIVE THAT BACK!!
BA (SNATCH)
AH...
DAAAA (DASH)
SO HAGYUU-SAN MADE THOSE BALLOONS.
AND PROBABLY THAT SCARY PUMPKIN TOO...
I'M GLAD HIBIKI-CHAN...
...SEEMS TO BE WELL.
I'VE BEEN WORKING AT THIS KINDERGAR-TEN FOR A LONG TIME.
SHE AND REN-CHAN WERE ESPECIALLY MEMORA-BLE.
!
OH, REALLY?
HIBIKI-CHAN USED TO ALWAYS HIDE BEHIND REN-CHAN...
...BUT SHE'S LEARNED TO SPEAK UP FOR HERSELF.
SHIMIJIMI (TOUCHED)
OUR QUIET, SHY CRYBABY, HIBIKI-CHAN... THEY GROW UP SO FAST.
QUIET...?
...ARE WE TALKING ABOUT THE SAME PERSON...?

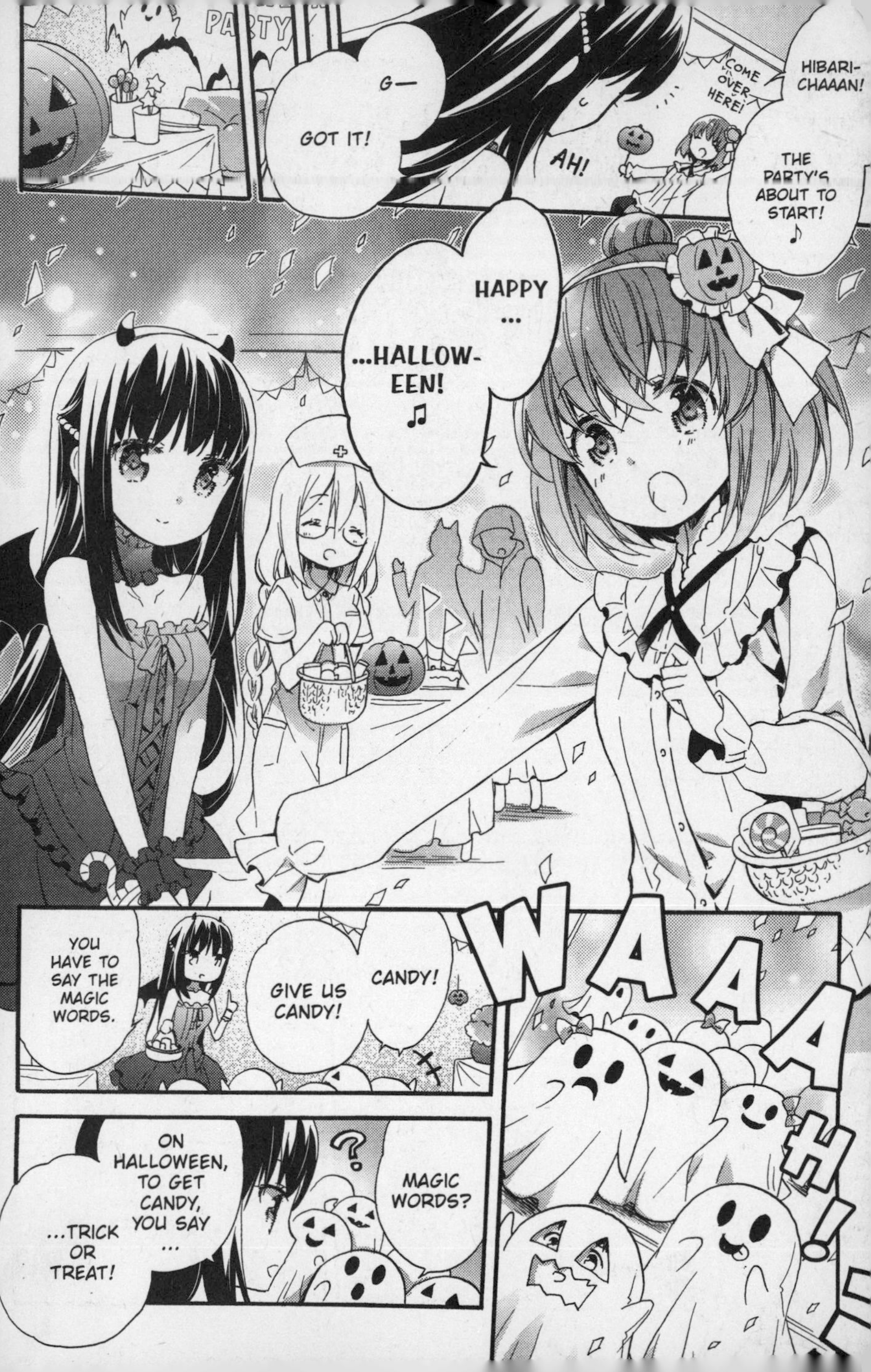
HIBARI-CHAAAN!
COME OVER HERE!
THE PARTY'S ABOUT TO START! ♪
AH!
PARTY
G—
GOT IT!
HAPPY ...
...HALLOW-EEN! ♫
WAAAAH!!
CANDY!
GIVE US CANDY!
YOU HAVE TO SAY THE MAGIC WORDS.
MAGIC WORDS?
?
ON HALLOWEEN, TO GET CANDY, YOU SAY ...
...TRICK OR TREAT!

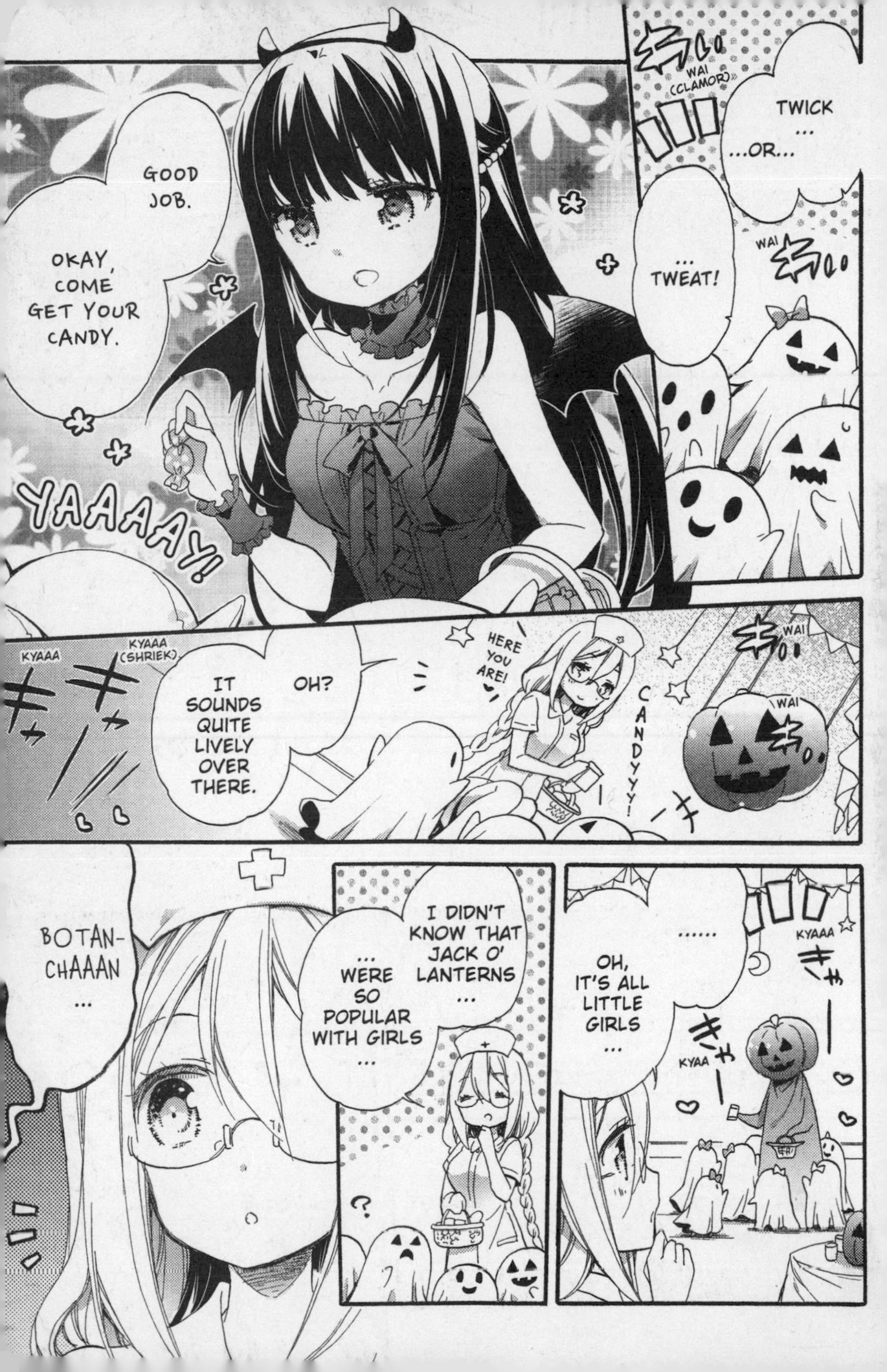
WAI (CLAMOR)
TWICK ... ...OR...
... TWEAT!
WAI
GOOD JOB.
OKAY, COME GET YOUR CANDY.
YAAAAAY!
WAI
WAI
CANDYYY!
HERE YOU ARE!
OH?
IT SOUNDS QUITE LIVELY OVER THERE.
KYAAA (SHRIEK)
KYAAA
......
OH, IT'S ALL LITTLE GIRLS ...
KYAAA
KYAA
I DIDN'T KNOW THAT JACK O' LANTERNS ...
... WERE SO POPULAR WITH GIRLS ...
BOTAN-CHAAAN ...

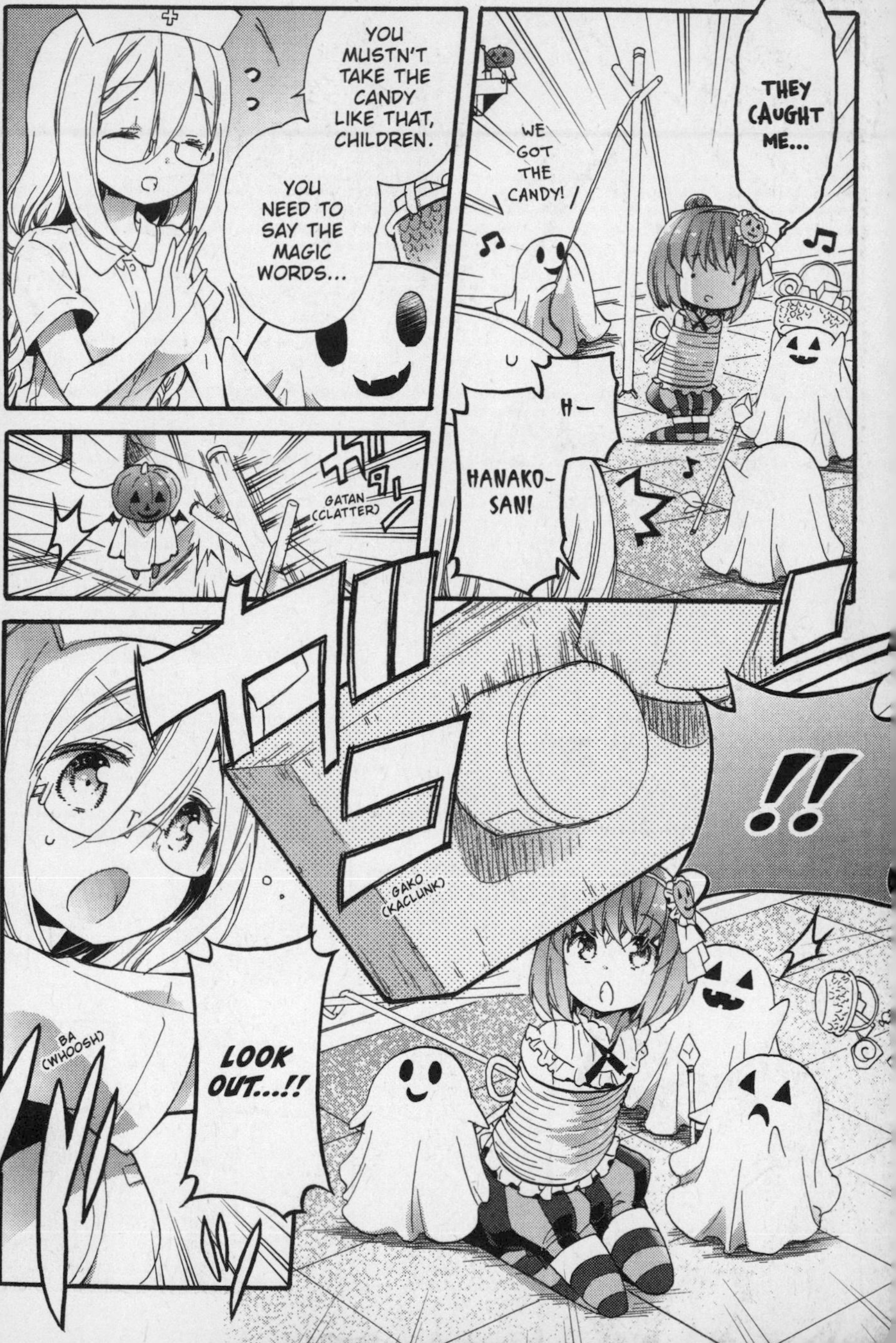

THEY CAUGHT ME...
WE GOT THE CANDY!
H—
HANAKO-SAN!
YOU MUSTN'T TAKE THE CANDY LIKE THAT, CHILDREN.
YOU NEED TO SAY THE MAGIC WORDS...
GATAN (CLATTER)
!!
GAKO (KACLUNK)
LOOK OUT...!!
BA (WHOOSH)

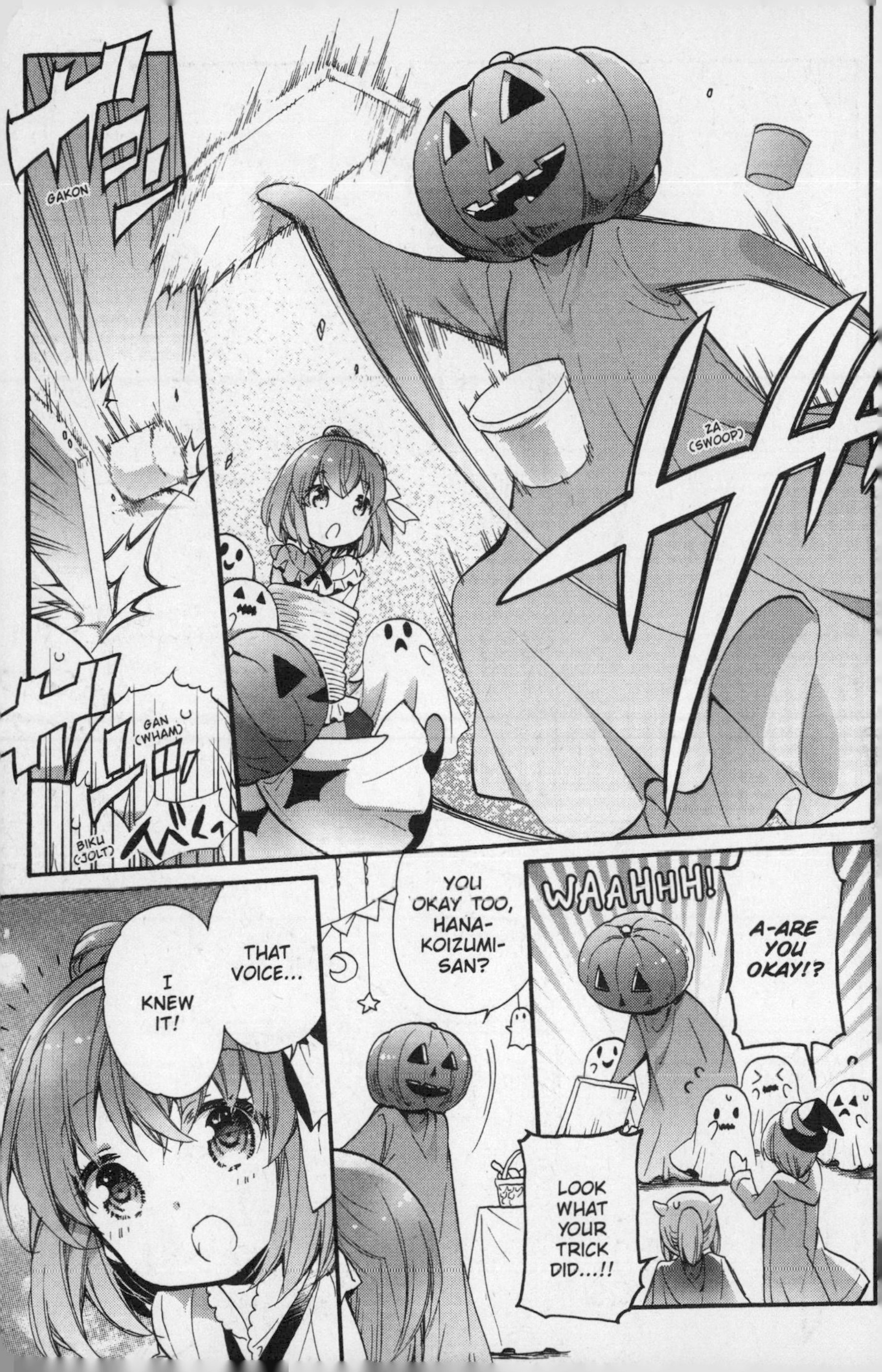
ZA (SWOOP)
GAKON
GAN (WHAM)
BIKU (-JOLT)
WAAHHH!
A-ARE YOU OKAY!?
LOOK WHAT YOUR TRICK DID...!!
YOU OKAY TOO, HANA-KOIZUMI-SAN?
THAT VOICE...
I KNEW IT!

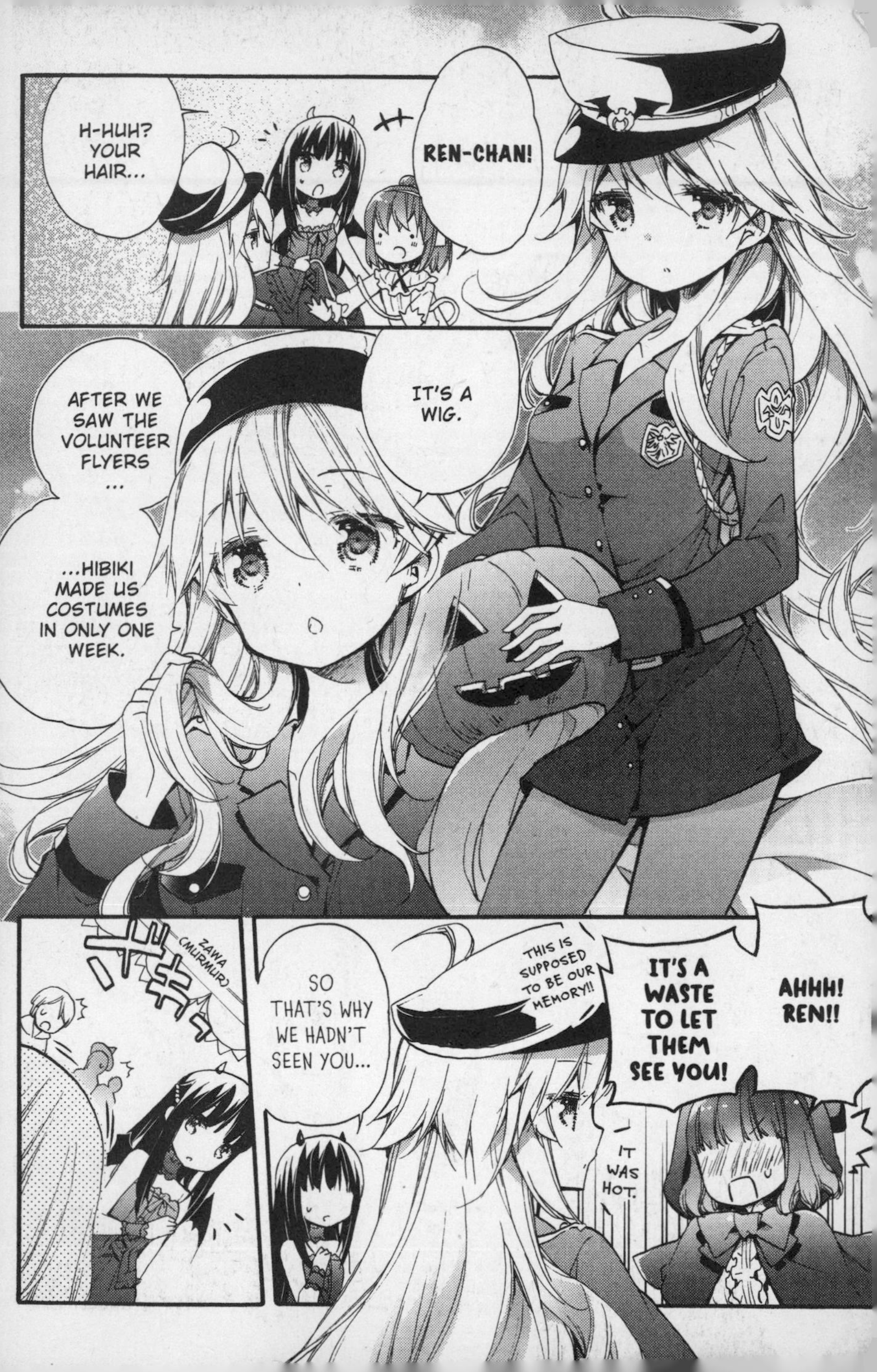

REN-CHAN!
H-HUH? YOUR HAIR...
IT'S A WIG.
AFTER WE SAW THE VOLUNTEER FLYERS ...
...HIBIKI MADE US COSTUMES IN ONLY ONE WEEK.
AHHH! REN!!
IT'S A WASTE TO LET THEM SEE YOU!
THIS IS SUPPOSED TO BE OUR MEMORY!!
SO THAT'S WHY WE HADN'T SEEN YOU...
IT WAS HOT.
ZAWA (MURMUR)

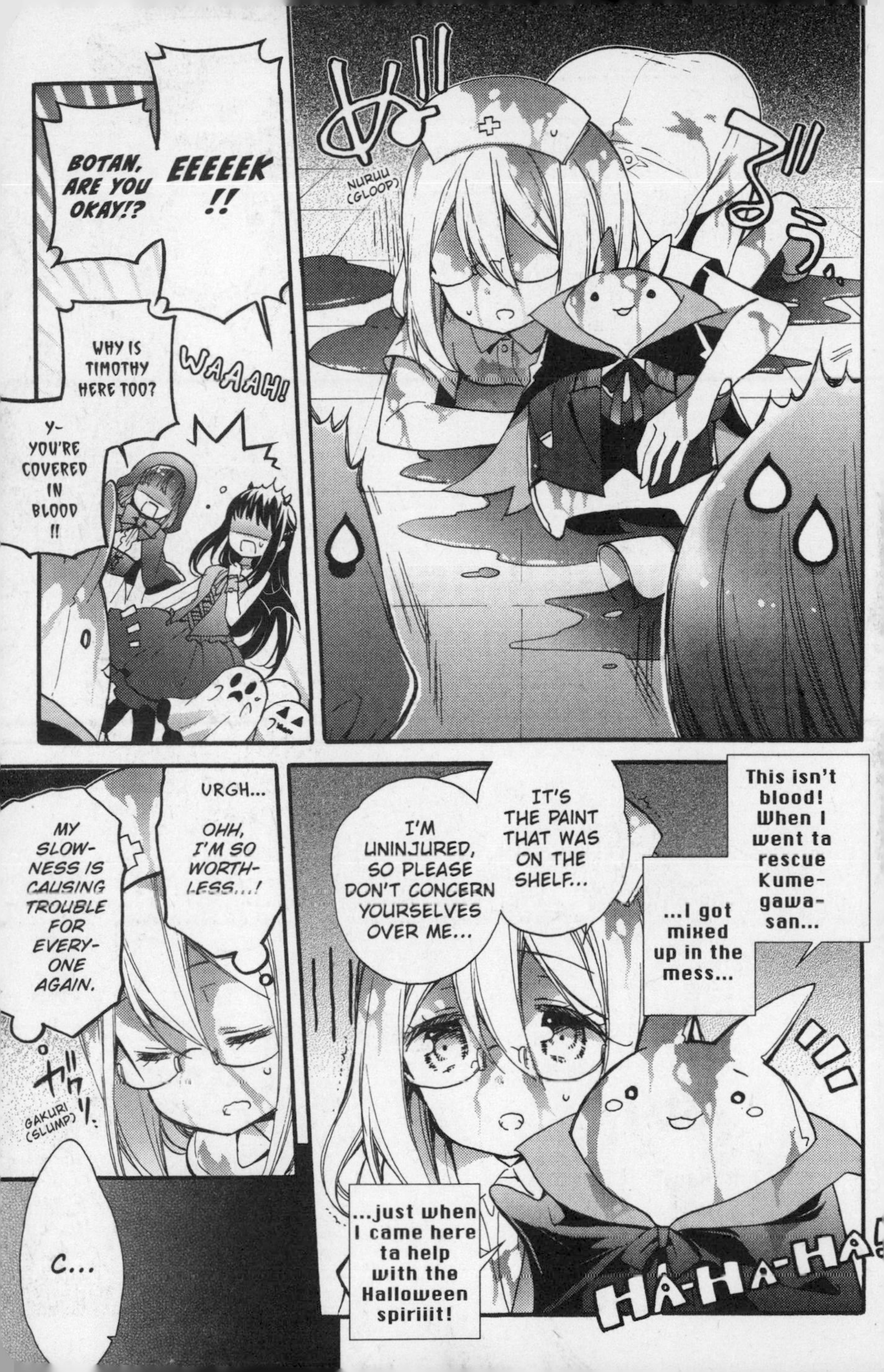
NURUU (GLOOP)
EEEEEK!!
BOTAN, ARE YOU OKAY!?
WAAAAH!
WHY IS TIMOTHY HERE TOO?
Y-YOU'RE COVERED IN BLOOD!!
This isn't blood! When I went ta rescue Kume-gawa-san...
IT'S THE PAINT THAT WAS ON THE SHELF...
...I got mixed up in the mess...
I'M UNINJURED, SO PLEASE DON'T CONCERN YOURSELVES OVER ME...
...just when I came here ta help with the Halloween spiriiit!
HA-HA-HA!
URGH...
OHH, I'M SO WORTH-LESS...!
MY SLOW-NESS IS CAUSING TROUBLE FOR EVERY-ONE AGAIN.
GAKURI (SLUMP)
C...

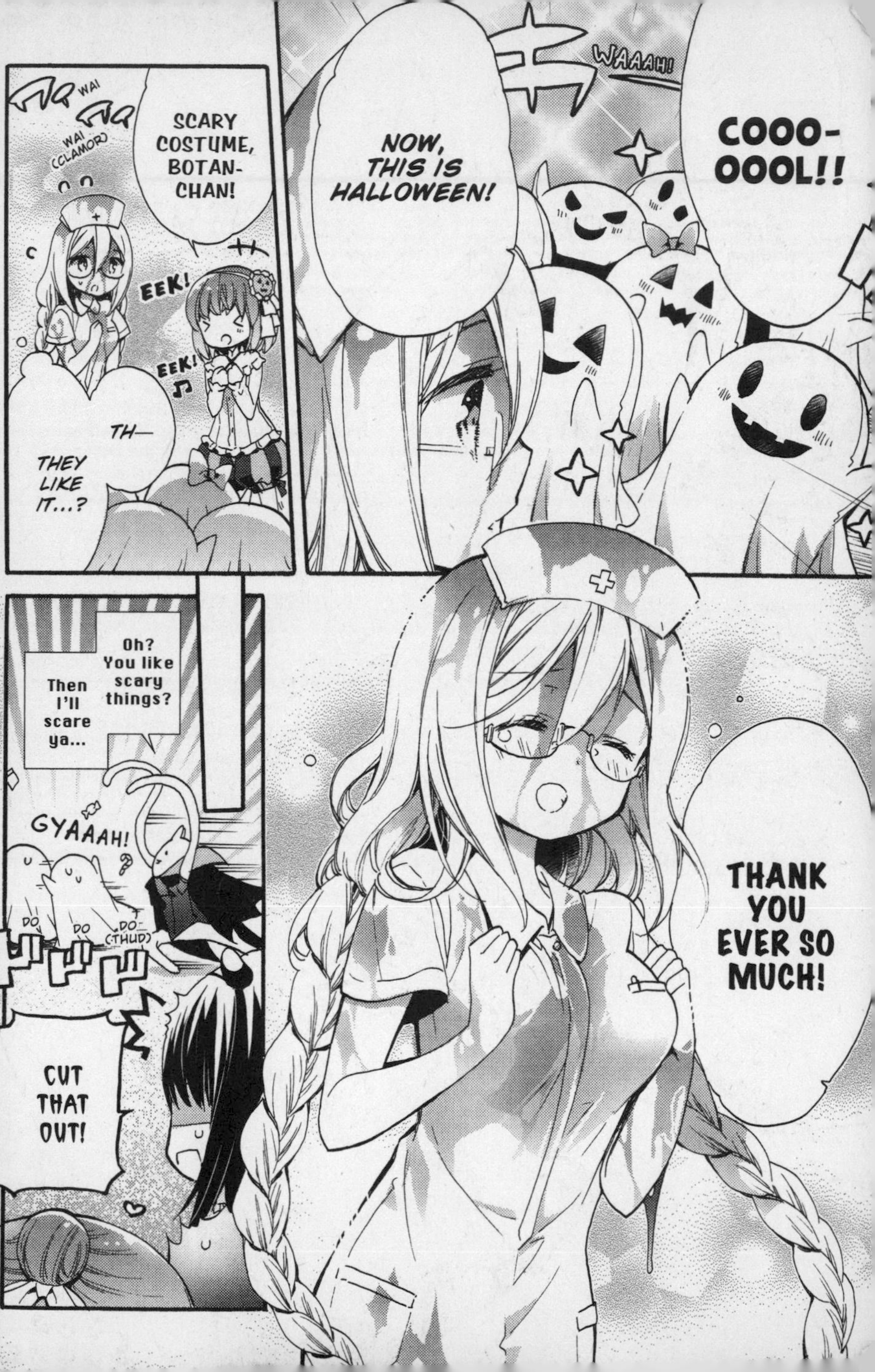
WAAAH!
COOO-OOOL!!
NOW, THIS IS HALLOWEEN!
SCARY COSTUME, BOTAN-CHAN!
WAI WAI (CLAMOR)
EEK!
EEK!
TH—
THEY LIKE IT...?
THANK YOU EVER SO MUCH!
Oh? You like scary things?
Then I'll scare ya...
GYAAAH!
DO DO DO (THUD)
CUT THAT OUT!

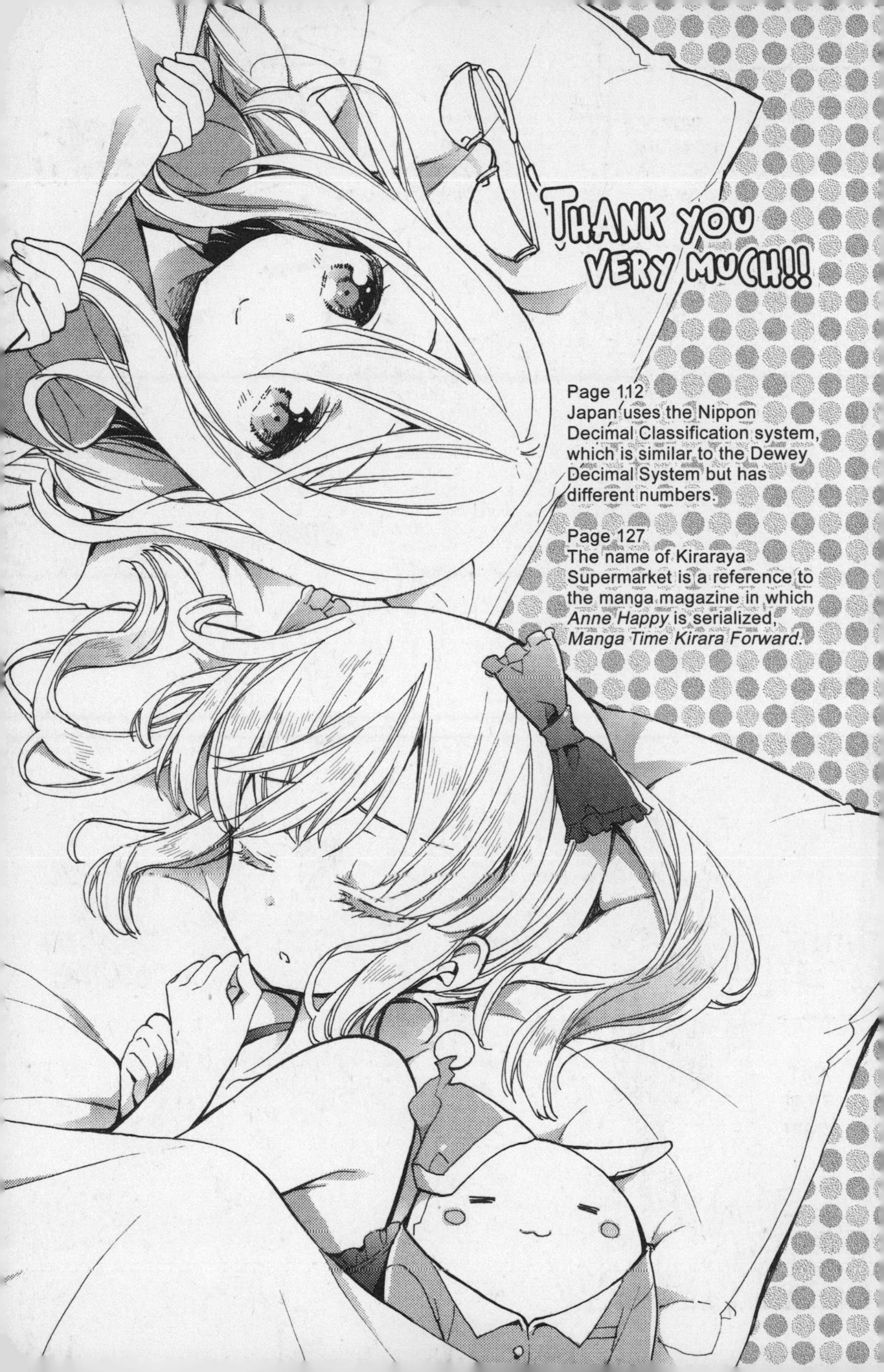
THANK YOU VERY MUCH!!

Page 112
Japan uses the Nippon Decimal Classification system, which is similar to the Dewey Decimal System but has different numbers.

Page 127
The name of Kiraraya Supermarket is a reference to the manga magazine in which *Anne Happy* is serialized, *Manga Time Kirara Forward*.

COTOJI

Translation: Amanda Haley
Lettering: Rochelle Gancio

ANNE HAPPY ♪ VOL. 8
© 2017 Cotoji. All rights reserved. First published in Japan in 2017 by HOUBUNSHA CO., LTD., TOKYO. English translation rights in United States, Canada, and United Kingdom arranged with HOUBUNSHA CO., LTD. through Tuttle-Mori Agency, Inc., Tokyo.

English translation © 2018 by Yen Press, LLC

Yen Press
1290 Avenue of the Americas
New York, NY 10104

Visit us at yenpress.com
facebook.com/yenpress
twitter.com/yenpress
yenpress.tumblr.com
instagram.com/yenpress

First Yen Press Edition: October 2018

Yen Press is an imprint of Yen Press, LLC.
The Yen Press name and logo are trademarks of Yen Press, LLC.

Library of Congress Control Number: 2016931012

ISBNs: 978-1-9753-0239-9 (paperback)
       978-1-9753-0240-5 (ebook)

10 9 8 7 6 5 4 3 2 1

WOR

Printed in the United States of America